THE BRITISH IN THE AMERICAS
1480–1815

STUDIES IN MODERN HISTORY

General editors: John Morrill and David Cannadine

This series, intended primarily for students, will tackle significant historical issues in concise volumes which are both stimulating and scholarly. The authors combine a broad approach, explaining the current state of our knowledge in the area, with their own research and judgements: and the topics chosen range widely in subject, period and place.

Titles already published

FRANCE IN THE AGE OF HENRY IV (*2nd Edn*) *Mark Greengrass*

VICTORIAN RADICALISM *Paul Adelman*

WHITE SOCIETY IN THE ANTEBELLUM SOUTH *Bruce Collins*

BLACK LEADERSHIP IN AMERICA: FROM BOOKER T. WASHINGTON TO JESSE JACKSON (*2nd Edn*) *John White*

THE TUDOR PARLIAMENTS *Michael A.R. Graves*

LIBERTY AND ORDER IN EARLY MODERN EUROPE *J.H. Shennan*

POPULAR RADICALISM *D.G. Wright*

'PAX BRITANNICA'? BRITISH FOREIGN POLICY 1789–1914 *Muriel E. Chamberlain*

IRELAND SINCE 1800 *K. Theodore Hoppen*

IMPERIAL MERIDIAN: THE BRITISH EMPIRE AND THE WORLD 1780–1830 *C.A. Bayly*

A SYSTEM OF AMBITION? BRITISH FOREIGN POLICY 1660–1793 *Jeremy Black*

BRITANNIA OVERRULED: BRITISH POLICY AND WORLD POWER IN THE 20TH CENTURY *David Reynolds*

POOR CITIZENS: THE STATE AND THE POOR IN TWENTIETH-CENTURY BRITAIN *David Vincent*

THE HOUSE OF LORDS IN BRITISH POLITICS AND SOCIETY 1815–1911 *E.A. Smith*

POLITICS UNDER THE LATER STUARTS: PARTY CONFLICT IN A DIVIDED SOCIETY 1660–1715 *Tim Harris*

BRITAIN AND LATIN AMERICA IN THE NINETEENTH AND TWENTIETH CENTURIES *Rory Miller*

THE BRITISH IN THE AMERICAS 1480–1815 *Anthony McFarlane*

THE BRITISH IN THE AMERICAS 1480–1815

Anthony McFarlane

Longman
London and New York

LONGMAN GROUP LIMITED,
Longman House, Burnt Mill,
Harlow, Essex CM20 2JE, England
and Associated Companies throughout the world.

*Published in the United States of America
by Longman Publishing, New York*

First published 1994

ISBN 0 582 20950 1 CSD
ISBN 0 582 20949 8 PPR

British Library Cataloguing-in-Publication Data

A catalogue record for this book is available from the British Library

Library of Congress Cataloguing-in-Publication Data

McFarlane, Anthony, 1946–
    The British in the Americas, 1480–1815 / Anthony McFarlane.
    p.   cm. -- (Studies in modern history)
    Includes bibliographical references and index.
    ISBN 0–582–20950–1 (CSD). -- ISBN 0–582–20949–8 (PPR)
    1. United States--History--Colonial period, ca. 1600–1775.
    2. Great Britain--Colonies--America--History.   3. Caribbean Area-
    -History--To 1810.   4. West Indies, British--History.   I. Title.
    II. Series: Studies in modern history (Longman (Firm))
    E188.M15   1994
    970.02—dc20   94–6450
                                                                       CIP

Set by 7.00 in 10/12 Bembo
Produced by Longman Singapore Publishers (Pty) Ltd
Printed in Singapore

For my parents,
Alice and Victor McFarlane

Contents

List of Tables

List of Maps

Preface

The purpose of this book is to provide a brief, integrated account of British involvement in the Americas over the three centuries in which Europeans built land and maritime empires in the New World. Based on secondary sources, it owes a great debt to the many historians who have contributed to constructing the histories of colonial empires in the Americas, especially to those who have written on the British possessions in North America and the Caribbean. The notes and bibliography reflect my reliance on their work, albeit in an abbreviated and imperfect form: references to sources are generally restricted to books rather than articles in scholarly journals, and have been chosen to show both major sources and works which provide pathways into the larger historiography of colonial British America.

My intention in this book is, however, different from that of most of the works from which information and analysis are drawn. I seek neither to provide new information based on archival research nor to revise interpretations in specialist fields, but aim instead at a synthesis which embraces the development of colonies in the whole of Anglo-America, over the arc of British territories that eventually stretched from the Caribbean to Canada. This synthesis is structured chronologically, in order to provide a narrative framework for understanding the origins and evolution of British colonialism in the Americas from the antecedents of empire in the Tudor period to the realignments of empire following the American Revolution. Taking advantage of the rich and growing historiography on the social and economic history of the Anglo-American world, I have tried to blend a narration of significant moments and movements in its evolution with an analysis of the salient structures of colonial economy and society in both North America and the Caribbean. In so doing, I concur with the recent tendency (notably exemplified in the works of Jack P. Greene) against treating the American mainland colonies, particularly New England, as though they constituted the core of the Anglo-American empire and the epicentre of its culture.

I have in addition sought to set the Anglo-American world against the broader background of Euro-American colonialism, by pointing to similarities and differences between the colonies of Britain and its major European rivals, particularly Spain, and by drawing attention to the part that rivalries between European powers played in the expansion of Britain's empire. In a short book which focuses on the British in the Americas, these comparisons can be only episodic and illustrative rather than continuous and systematic; nevertheless, they do at least indicate how British colonization enmeshed with and related to the larger process of European expansion, and provide a perspective on the peculiarities of British America. In such a broadly conceived study, I am unable to do justice to issues which scholars have investigated in depth and detail, particularly the histories of subordinate or marginalized groups in society; I have however used the notes and bibliography to indicate works which the reader might use to pursue these themes.

If the bibliography must serve to acknowledge my debt to the large number of historians whose works I have used in writing this book, I would like personally to thank colleagues who encouraged me to write it. First, my thanks to Professor John Fisher for his suggestion that I might profitably turn my attention from Spain's colonial empire to Britain's, and to Professor John Lynch who, as consulting editor for the Fundación Mapfre América of Madrid, provided me with the initial opportunity to do so. I am also grateful to my colleagues in the School of Comparative American Studies at Warwick University, established by Professor Alistair Hennessy, for the agreeable working environment they have provided over the years, and to an ex-colleague, Professor Edward Countryman of Southern Methodist University, who, in our jointly-taught course on revolutions and independence in the Americas, helped to arouse an interest in the American Revolution. Thanks, too, to the editors of this series, Dr John Morrill and Professor David Cannadine, for their very encouraging comments on this work, and to Longman for its efforts in bringing it to press. Responsibility for any errors or omissions, whether of fact or interpretation, is of course mine alone.

Last but certainly not least, I am glad, as always, to thank Angela O'Boyle for her usual support and good-humoured tolerance of the interruptions to normal life which prolonged bouts of writing invariably entail.

Concerning the chronology and terms employed in this book, the following observations should be borne in mind. First, the dates given in the title are not intended as precise markers of a clearly defined period: the British presence in the Americas neither began in 1480 nor ended in 1815. These dates have been given simply to indicate the scope of a study designed to trace the origins and emergence of the Anglo-American world from the very earliest English essays in Atlantic exploration until the moment, more than three centuries later, when the age of the Euro-American empires was coming to an end. A second point concerns the terms used to describe indigenous American peoples, and the Africans and their descendants who were enslaved in the Americas. When speaking of the former, I have generally referred to 'Indians' when not describing specific groups, as this is a generic term that is still more widely used outside the United States than the term 'Native Americans'. When discussing slavery in the Euro-American world, I refer to Africans and blacks, rather than using the term 'African Americans', for though the latter is now often used to describe the descendants of slaves in the United States, it is not a description commonly applied to the peoples who were forced into slavery in the Caribbean or other regions of the Americas.

The publishers would like to thank Cambridge University Press for granting permission to reproduce Table 8.5 from Gary M. Walton and James F. Shepherd, *The Economic Rise of Early America*.

Introduction

Of all the North European countries, the British had the greatest impact on American life. In the early nineteenth century, Alexis de Tocqueville already discerned the makings of a great future power in the British ex-colonies of North America, 'marked out by the will of Heaven to sway the destinies of half the globe'.[1] Within a century of their independence, his prediction was fulfilled. At the close of the nineteenth century, the United States had emerged as a great industrial economy whose economic might was increasingly matched by the weight of its political power and the global reach of its cultural influence. The history of the British in the Americas is not, however, simply the story of the creation and development of the colonies which later became the United States. While the North American colonies inevitably loom large (partly because of the sheer volume of historical work devoted to them), their history does not embrace the entire experience of the British in the Americas, nor does it set the boundaries of British influence in the development of the Americas.

In fact, England first became involved with the Americas a century before establishing permanent colonies on the Atlantic seaboard of North America, and the British presence long outlived the loss of those colonies. For, at the outset of the nineteenth century, Britain not only possessed colonies in the Caribbean Basin which outlasted those of North America, but had also acquired French territories in Canada which were long to remain under British sovereignty. Furthermore, British political and economic influence had a powerful impact on Latin America. This began during the period of Iberian colonial rule, especially during the eighteenth century, when Britain began seriously to penetrate Iberian American markets; it became still more acute after the collapse of the Spanish and Portuguese empires when,

1

during the nineteenth century, Britain established a species of 'informal empire' in Latin America, based on commercial supremacy and the migration of capital.

This book does not, then, confine itself simply to the colonial history of North America during the seventeenth and eighteenth centuries, but has a wider scope. It is concerned with the part played by the British in the Americas throughout the whole period in which Europeans established and developed empires in the west, from the first explorations of the late fifteenth century until the disintegration of European colonialism in the late eighteenth and early nineteenth centuries. It also examines the experience of all the main British colonies, in the Caribbean as well as on the American mainlands, sets their history in the broad comparative context of the general movement of Europeans into the New World, and seeks, in passing, to identify some of the characteristics which distinguished British colonization from its Iberian, French and Dutch counterparts.

As this book is about the origins, development and character of British colonies in the Americas, I concentrate on the colonial periphery rather than the metropolitan centre. However, where necessary I draw attention to those developments in the metropole that underpinned expansion in the Atlantic, and indicate the major points of interaction between the political and economic history of the mother country and its colonies. Each of the three parts of the book therefore includes brief references to those developments in metropolitan political and economic life which are essential for understanding the general process of growth in English (after 1707, British) America.

Part One deals with English activities in the Americas during the long period of the Tudor and early Stuart monarchies from 1485 to 1642, when the Spaniards and Portuguese were the great leaders of American colonization and the English merely aspired to empire. Chapter 1 traces the movements of English maritime enterprise into the Atlantic from the first hesitant probes of the late fifteenth and early sixteenth centuries to the more confident thrusts of the Elizabethan period. It shows why English activity in the Americas became more aggressive during the latter half of the sixteenth century, how colonizing plans arose from commercial and political energies in England, how they connected with the emergence of an English state supported by an increasingly assertive Protestant nationalism, and why, despite the vitality of Elizabethan maritime endeavours, England's first colonial projects were stillborn. Chapter 2 then turns to the early Stuart period, to examine the foundation of the first permanent

Introduction

English colonies when, in an extension of Elizabethan expansionary thrusts, embryos of empire were formed from the interaction of mercantile capital and Puritan politics. It also examines the character of the colonies established in Virginia, New England and the West Indies during the first quarter of the seventeenth century, and traces the problems caused by inadequate support from the corporate merchants and landed classes of England. Starting with the 'great migration' of the 1630s, Chapter 3 depicts the first mass immigrations into Anglo-America, and sketches subsequent patterns of continuity and change in English migration during the century that followed; it also takes up themes in the domestic history of early Anglo-America, with brief portraits of the main colonial societies which emerged during the 1630s, and a short account of English settlers' attitudes towards, and relations with native Americans.

Part Two takes the Civil War as a point of departure, and focuses on the colonies during the phase of colonial expansion and consolidation that was inaugurated by Protestant republicans in the 1650s and continued after the Restoration in the struggle against Dutch economic power. Chapter 4 outlines the expansion of empire after the English Civil War, showing how, from being a relative latecomer to the Americas, England promoted the growth of its territorial empire and, through struggle with competing European powers for control of the most profitable and productive trades and territories, became a more formidable colonial power by the end of the seventeenth century. The focus then shifts to the internal economic and social development of the major colonies during the late seventeenth century. Chapter 5 traces the economic and social transformation of the Anglo-Caribbean, where colonies of settlement became colonies of exploitation, as dynamic export economies and deeply divided societies were built on sugar and slavery. Chapter 6 defines the major regions of British North America, mapping them according to the patterns of social and economic life found in New England, the American South, the Middle Atlantic and on the internal frontier. Having charted the transformation of the southern American colonies from slaveowning into slave societies, akin to those of the West Indies, this chapter also includes a brief sketch of mainland slavery and its distinguishing characteristics, before concluding with a general analysis of the character of North American colonial societies as they developed from the mid-seventeenth century. Chapter 7 traces the characteristics of the political order and the major facets of the colonial political culture which emerged under English rule from the earliest establishment of colonies until the early eighteenth century.

3

Despite the fact that the overthrow of James II and his replacement by William of Orange is generally (and deservedly) regarded as a major turning point in British political history, I have extended the period covered in Part Two beyond the Glorious Revolution of 1688 into the opening years of the eighteenth century; this has been done in order to embrace the entrenchment of the new regime in Britain, the unification of the British Isles in 1707, and the beginnings of the long struggle with France which was to dominate British foreign policy throughout the eighteenth century. Part Three therefore opens in 1713, the year of the Treaty of Utrecht. Although a much less significant moment in British history than the 1688 revolution, this is a useful starting point for considering a century that brought major adjustments in the Anglo-American empire, and in Britain's position in the Americas. First, the treaty was the culmination of the War of the Spanish Succession (1702–1713), and thus reflected the commitment of Britain's emerging 'fiscal-military state' to war against the Franco-Spanish alliance that was to be its great rival during the ensuing century; second, the territorial and trading concessions which Britain demanded at Utrecht started a series of such advances during the eighteenth century, and signalled the inauguration of a policy of colonial and commercial expansion that was to transform Britain's empire and presence in the Americas.

The chapters in Part Three trace the processes of growth, conflict and realignment which affected the Anglo-American empire during the eighteenth and early nineteenth centuries. Chapter 8 shows how the Anglo-American colonies developed in the context of international war, and how their development interacted with the twin forces of British commercial expansion and colonial demographic growth during the decades before the American Revolution. Chapter 9 enquires into why, having reached its fullest extent in 1763, the Anglo-American empire then suffered partial disintegration during the American Revolution of Independence in 1776-1783; it also shows how the constitutional conflict stirred by changes in British policy interacted with internal changes in American societies to arouse colonial protest and separatist rebellion, and examines the political foundations of the first independent state to emerge from British colonial rule. Finally, Chapter 10 maps out developments in British America after the American Revolution, when Britain adjusted to the loss of its principal North American colonies and then, between 1796 and 1815, entered into prolonged international warfare with France and Spain. Here several major issues are discussed: first, the emergence of a new configuration of British colonial society in the Americas, as Canada became Britain's leading North American colony and the West Indies adapted to the destruction of economic links with the newly-independent United States; second, the abolition of the slave trade and its implications for the West Indies; third, the spread of British influence through commercial contacts with the United States and Latin America, where Britain found space for economic expansion in regions where it had no formal empire. Here it becomes clear that although the independence of the United States hurt British pride and prestige, it neither concluded British colonialism in the Americas nor impaired Britain's economic connections with the Atlantic world. Indeed, the struggle against Revolutionary and Napoleonic France strengthened landed and commercial interests in Britain in ways that underpinned a revitalized, conservative imperialism. Thus, while Britain extended its commercial influence in the newly-independent states of the Americas, it also sought to tighten political control over an emerging second empire that incorporated the American territories, new colonies of white settlement in Australia and southern Africa, and areas of imperial dominion in India. Chapter 10 therefore concludes with a brief examination of the repercussions in the Americas of this shift from the first empire, built in the west, to a second, greater empire which, during the later nineteenth century, was to develop its major bases in Asia, Australasia and Africa.

NOTES

1. Alexis de Tocqueville, *Democracy in America*, (ed. H.S. Commager, Oxford, 1946) p. 287.

PART ONE

Emergence of Empire, 1480–1642

CHAPTER ONE

English Explorations in the Atlantic

In the late Middle Ages, England was an economic and political backwater, distant from Europe's largest concentrations of wealth and power. These lay far to the south, in the Mediterranean, where the Italian city-states had grown rich as intermediaries in the luxury trades between the east and northern Europe, and to the north, in the German towns, where the Hanseatic League controlled the richest flows of commerce in the products of northern seas, mines, forests and farms. During the sixteenth century, however, Europe's economic centre of gravity shifted away from these traditional foundations. After 1500, medieval patterns of trade were increasingly supplemented by new maritime routes for commerce, opened by voyages of discovery made from Portugal and Spain during the late fifteenth century. Reaching into the Atlantic Ocean from Lisbon and Seville, these routes reached towards Africa, Asia and the Americas, bringing into Europe resources that were to transform its economy in the centuries that followed.

The first consequence of this shift was to enrich the countries that controlled the new circuits of commerce. Both Spain and Portugal saw an unprecedented increase in their economic and political weight within Europe, as their discoveries led to the formation of great empires overseas. By the end of the sixteenth century, the economic balance which had swung from Italy to Iberia began again to move on, towards north-western Europe, where France, Holland and England gradually emerged as the heartland of the world economy that had taken shape around the maritime routes to Asia and the Americas. In the long term, then, the development of England and its rise to power within Europe was inseparably linked to the broader process of European economic transformation that had been set in motion by the

Iberian voyages of exploration. England was, in this sense, merely the recipient of an economic and political legacy created by Spain and Portugal. It would be unjust, however, to see England as a mere parasite, for like the French and Italians, Englishmen played their own part in widening the horizons of the European world through oceanic exploration. To understand their role, we must recall the context in which such exploration originated and developed during the late Middle Ages.

THE EUROPEAN DISCOVERIES

In the closing decades of the fifteenth century, England was one of several fronts for voyaging and exploration in the Atlantic, though by no means the most important. Much more significant were the activities of the Iberian kingdoms of Portugal and Castile, of which the Portuguese were the true pioneers of Atlantic maritime exploration.[1] Following Portugal's capture of Ceuta from the Moors in 1415, Portuguese mariners began to range along the shores of west Africa, with two objectives in mind. One was economic, and centred upon a concern to find the sources of gold and spices which were carried to north African ports by overland caravans that traversed territories dominated by Islam. Reinforcing the desire for gain were political and religious motives, derived from the traditions of crusade against Islam and encapsulated in the myth of a lost Christian kingdom, known as the land of Prester John. Believed to be somewhere to the rear of the great Islamic sphere of influence that extended from Morocco to the Black Sea, the kingdom of Prester John added to the lure of contacts with new lands and new sources of wealth in Africa, for contact with this lost Christian realm offered the possibility of opening a second front in the struggle with the Moors.

Inspired by these goals, Portuguese exploration moved in two related directions. One led to the Atlantic islands: Portuguese colonists established themselves at Madeira in *c.*1419, at the Azores around 1439 and in the Cape Verde Islands in 1456–60, giving Portugal a vantage point in the Atlantic where it might experiment with overseas colonization and from which it might conduct further voyages of exploration. The other main direction lay directly southwards along the west African coast, where the Portuguese searched for gold, tropical commodities and, after the taking of the Atlantic islands, slaves to cultivate the sugar produced there. In 1434, the first great breakthrough came with the rounding of Cape Bojador, which mariners had long seen as a limit to the navigable world. By 1482, the trade in gold and slaves with the Guinea coast and Senegambia had become so established that Portugal's King João II ordered the construction of a fort at El Mina to act as its centre and stronghold; the resources derived from this trade also encouraged the Portuguese to push still farther south in a more systematic search for the mythical kingdom of Prester John and, increasingly, for a route that would lead them to the fabled trade of Asia. In 1488, the second great advance was made, when Bartolomé Dias rounded the Cape of Good Hope, showing a way to the Orient that was triumphantly extended by Vasco da Gama's famous voyage to India in 1497–9.[2]

While unquestionably the pioneers of oceanic exploration, the Portuguese were not alone in their quest into the Atlantic. Their neighbours in Spain were also active during the later fifteenth century, if only because they wished to share in the spoils taken by the Portuguese. In 1475, Spain successfully fought Portugal for possession of the Canary Islands and, by conquering the larger islands in 1478–96, secured both an interest in overseas expansion and a stepping stone from which it might advance further into the 'Ocean Sea'. In Spain, too, interest in finding a route to the east intensified during the closing years of the fifteenth century, so that when Columbus prevailed upon the Spanish crown to support a westward voyage to reach the shores of Asia, he received a sympathetic hearing. After his plans had been rejected by Portugal, France and possibly England, Columbus received from Ferdinand and Isabella the sanction and support he needed to undertake his first voyage. His subsequent landfall in the Caribbean in 1492 then turned Spain into a major force in transoceanic exploration, on a par with Portugal.

So, by the end of the fifteenth century the centres of Atlantic exploration in southern Europe had yielded rich rewards. The eastern sea route to Asia around Africa laid the foundations for the emergence of an expansive Portuguese seaborne empire, while the westward route, though it would ultimately also lead to contact with Asia, allowed Spain to establish bases from which it was, within a few decades, to build a vast territorial empire in the Americas. Compared to these achievements, England played only a secondary role in expanding the horizons of the European world. But, if the English contribution was a minor one when placed in the broader context of European transoceanic expansion during the late fifteenth and early sixteenth centuries, it is nonetheless an important element in the history of the British in the Americas, since early voyages gave

11

Englishmen their first direct contacts with the New World and helped to nurture an interest in American lands which was later to issue in schemes for colonization.

EARLY ENGLISH VOYAGES TO THE WEST

When discussing the origins of the English presence in the Americas, the first issue that arises concerns the part which Englishmen played in the discovery of the New World. Was America discovered by Columbus in 1492, or was Columbus's voyage preceded, as some historians suggest, by unknown Englishmen who sailed across the Atlantic a decade earlier, in 1481? This is, perhaps, a problem of purely academic interest, since in the long term the identity of the first Europeans to arrive in the Americas matters less than the impact that their settlement had on native peoples and on the subsequent development of European economic life. It is, nevertheless, a question which merits a brief mention, as it throws light on early English connections with the New World and helps us to understand how the English were drawn into transatlantic exploration and settlement.

The first recorded voyages of discovery from Bristol took place in 1480 and 1481, when ships from the port sailed beyond the west coast of Ireland in search of the legendary 'island of Brasil'. Years later, when an English correspondent wrote to Columbus to tell him of John Cabot's successful voyage from Bristol to America in 1497, he mentioned that Cabot had revisited a land which Bristol men had found 'en otros tiempos'. This has convinced some historians that the voyage from Bristol to 'Brasil', made in 1481, was the first European contact with the north-eastern coast of North America, nearly two decades before Cabot's arrival in 1497 and more than a decade before Columbus's southerly landfall of 1492.[3] However, intriguing though it is, the argument for an English discovery of America remains inconclusive, for it rests upon a series of suppositions and inferences which, however logical, lack the support of direct, written evidence. In the end, it is not certain that the island of Brasil which had allegedly been found in 1481 was a cape on the North American shoreline, nor is it absolutely clear that the reference to a voyage 'en otros tiempos' alluded to the voyage of 1481. It is therefore safer to assume that Englishmen participated in the exploration of America after Columbus, when they were able to take advantage of knowledge gleaned from Iberian and Italian mariners. Englishmen with connections in Lisbon and Andalusia must have been aware of the oceanic voyages undertaken from Portuguese and Spanish ports, and were possibly interested in mounting similar ventures in northerly latitudes. What is certain, however, is that when the first fully verified transatlantic voyage from England took place, revealing the existence of North America to the European world, it was under the command of an Italian, licensed by the English crown.

In 1496, John Cabot, a Venetian citizen of possible Genoese birth, was living in Bristol and spreading the notion, common to the geographers and educated mariners of his time, that Asia was accessible to ships sailing westwards from Europe. This was of course the same idea that had inspired Columbus, but because Columbus had not found the land of the 'Great Khan' or the rich spice islands, there was still room for further voyages which might accomplish this goal. Cabot therefore sought and obtained from Henry VII (1485–1509) a patent that empowered him to sail into the Atlantic in search of lands which had not been visited by Christians and to establish trade with, or dominion over them. After an unsuccessful first attempt, Cabot took a tiny craft with a crew of eighteen men across the Atlantic in 1497, and landed either at Newfoundland or perhaps further west, in the region of Cape Breton, now in Canada. Although the expedition met with no natives and did not attempt to penetrate inland, Cabot was convinced that this was a land unknown to Europe and he left tokens of English possession and Christian overlordship. Flushed with success, he persuaded the King that he had been on the northern extension of the coast of Asia and that, by coasting southwards and westwards with a better-equipped expedition, he would find China and Japan. The King duly provided Cabot with financial support for another voyage in 1498, but without the anticipated results. John Cabot never returned to England, having presumably perished at sea.[4]

After this setback, Henry VII never again gave any substantial help to overseas exploration from his realm. After this rather paltry attempt by the English monarchy to emulate the feats of its Spanish and Portuguese peers, the initiative was now left to private individuals and resources. However, if the King was insufficiently optimistic to support any continuation of Cabot's endeavours, some of his subjects still retained the hope that westward voyages might yield some gains. Again, the port of Bristol played a leading role, with a series of voyages conducted each year between 1501 and 1505, some of them in conjunction with Portuguese colonists from the Azores, sent in search of the 'new found land'. These ventures brought the return of some native artefacts, some American fauna and even apparently some indigenous people, brought to satisfy English curiosity, and it is possible that they culminated in 1508 in a long journey southwards along the North American coastline, made by John Cabot's son Sebastian.[5] However, though Sebastian Cabot always encouraged the story of this voyage, it is not certain that it actually took place.[6] What is clear is that the results of all the voyages made since the 1480s were insufficient to fire the imagination of the monarch or his merchants. The explorers had failed to create any trade or to divert the attention of London merchants from their commerce with Europe, and, though English interest in finding new lands and passages to the east did not disappear completely, the failure to make any spectacular gains of the kind made by the Iberian monarchies definitely dampened the exploring spirit. It was perhaps for this reason that Sebastian Cabot left the employ of Henry VIII to enter the service of Spain, as a pilot in the Casa de Contratación in Seville.[7]

English interest in finding a transatlantic route to the east was not rekindled until well into the reign of Henry VIII (1509–47). In 1527, John Rut made what was probably the first full north–south reconnaissance of the eastern seaboard of North America, and this was followed in 1536 by a curious venture led by Richard Hore, a gentleman of London. Hore gathered a group of friends, apparently simply to see something of the New World, and took them on a journey to North America that ended in a tragic fiasco. After encountering difficulties at sea, the starving survivors took to eating each other, and were saved only by capturing a French ship which provided them with sufficient supplies to limp back to England.

Following these voyages, English exploration of North America's coastlines lapsed. The cod fisheries of Newfoundland were increasingly frequented by English fishing vessels, together with growing numbers of Portuguese and French fishermen, but larger visions of either a trade with the east or new lands to conquer had been temporarily erased. In 1553, the dream of a direct route to the east was briefly revived, with the voyage undertaken by Willoughby and Chancellor in search of a north-east passage to the Orient, by way of Norway and Russia. Their search failed, but the voyage did have some long-term significance. It not only revived interest in oceanic navigation, but also opened a trade with Russia that was to give English merchants some experience of organizing a long-distance commerce through a joint-stock company. Furthermore, the Muscovy Company (1553–5), which was granted a monopoly to exploit this trade, became a patron of geographical study and a sponsor of maritime enterprise during the ensuing decades.[8]

These were, of course, very slight achievements compared to the expansion of overseas settlement and commerce made by Spain and Portugal during the first half of the sixteenth century. In 1519, Spaniards had advanced from their colonies in the Caribbean into Mexico, where Cortés conquered a great Amerindian civilization; then, twenty years after Balboa had crossed the Isthmus of Panama to discover the Pacific in 1513, Francisco Pizarro thrust southwards to take the Andean heartlands of South America. Meanwhile, Portugal had won the race to the east. In 1513, Portuguese ships sailing around Africa and through the Indian Ocean reached the spice islands of the Moluccas, and in 1519 Magellan embarked on the transatlantic and trans-Pacific voyage that was finally to reveal the enormous distance of the western route from Europe to Asia. Although preoccupied with the rich trades that they had found in Asia, the Portuguese had also begun to establish an effective colonial presence in Brazil, which Cabral had claimed for Portugal in 1500. Even France, which had a late start in Atlantic exploration, had attempted to establish a colony on the St Lawrence River in 1541–2, following Jacques Cartier's first two exploratory voyages of 1534–6, and in Brazil, where, between 1555 and 1559, Villegagnon sought to create a *France Antarctique* as a refuge for French Protestants. England had been left far behind in the race for new trade and territory. When Elizabeth I began her reign in 1558, England had found neither a commerce to promote, nor lands considered worthy of settlement in the regions of North America where its mariners had been pioneers; any ambitions that Englishmen might once have entertained for expanding commerce and settlement overseas had been entirely overshadowed by the achievement of the Iberian monarchies.

Why had England made so little progress in following the example of Spain and Portugal in the Americas? The reasons are not difficult to find. English voyages had always lacked consistent support from government and, although its monarchy became stronger and more stable in the late fifteenth century, England remained a poor country whose merchants were more interested in trade with Europe than the exploration and development of new commercial routes or colonies in the west. This does not mean that the English economy was stagnating. On the contrary, the old trading links with Europe were changing during the reigns of the first Tudor kings; as the export of cloth increasingly replaced the raw wool trade that had once been the staple of English overseas trade, English merchants sought to widen their markets. But this reorientation of English commerce initially diverted attention from the far Atlantic. The new trade led towards

15

profitable outlets in France, the Low Countries and the Iberian peninsula, and the merchants of the English east coast ports, especially the increasingly powerful London merchants, were too occupied in taking advantage of these markets to concern themselves with the pursuit of uncertain goals in the west.[9] Furthermore, during the reign of Henry VIII, attention to projects for overseas expansion received little attention from a monarchy that was deeply entangled in the political machinations needed to sustain its foreign policy in Europe, to support its challenge to the Papacy, and to resolve the political problems involved in its Reformation of the church in England.

Although it achieved little overseas during the first half of the sixteenth century, England was nonetheless being drawn into a European world in which both political and economic life were being transformed by the release of new ideological and commercial energies. In these changing conditions, English activity in the Americas gradually moved on to a new plane during the latter half of the sixteenth century. First, English merchants sought to take advantage of the burgeoning colonial trades of the Iberian powers, as parasites on the commerce of Spain and Portugal. Then, as England was drawn into conflict with Spain, English adventurers turned into predators on Spain's American empire, plundering colonial shipping and settlements. Finally, as experience of the New World widened, influential Englishmen sought to persuade their government of the need for England to create its own colonial empire. What lay behind this expansive impulse, and what were to be its consequences?

ELIZABETHAN ADVENTURES IN THE AMERICAS

To explain why the English were increasingly drawn to the Americas in the latter half of the sixteenth century, we must first appreciate the changes in international conditions that affected England during the reign of Elizabeth I (1558–1603). The great stimulus to English maritime activity on the other side of the Atlantic came from alterations in England's relations with the continental powers which led to increasingly sharp conflict with Spain.

Traditionally, France had been England's major enemy in Europe. While Elizabeth's predecessors inherited territory in France and asserted claims to the French throne, the French retaliated by making alliances with Scotland that threatened the English monarchy on its own side of the Channel. To counter the challenge from France, English kings treated Spain as an ally, a tendency that culminated in the marriage of Queen Mary (1553–8) to Philip II of Spain. However, as both national and international politics became increasingly polarized around the conflicts of Protestants and Catholics, England's relations with Spain changed from cautious friendship to outright enmity. The change did not take place immediately. French intervention on the side of Elizabeth's enemies in Scotland meant that, in the opening years of her reign, France continued to be the main external threat; Elizabeth therefore tried to remain on friendly relations with Spain because the Habsburg monarchy offered a counterweight to France. But as France was weakened by its internal wars of religion, English foreign policy became increasingly focused on combating Habsburg Spain, the new hegemonic force on the continent. When Philip II decided to suppress the revolt of the Netherlands by force in 1566–7, thereby beginning the Eighty Years War between Spain and the Dutch Protestants, the Anglo-Spanish relationship turned from uneasy coexistence into growing hostility, culminating in open war during the 1580s and 1590s.[10]

In the same period, English commercial interests became more attuned to extra-European expansion. Most of the country's trade was still with the Low Countries but, after the slump in the English cloth trade in the 1550s and early 1560s, merchants sought new markets in the Baltic, Russia, the eastern Mediterranean and Africa. This did not lead to the formation of a coherent imperialist strategy, in which the crown coordinated commercial and colonizing interests with its foreign policy in Europe. Throughout her reign, Elizabeth recognized that England's principal interest lay in preventing the rise of a single great power in Europe, and she refused to divert resources from military operations on the continent into a more outward-looking maritime strategy. Nonetheless, as England was drawn into ever sharper political and religious rivalry with Spain and trade with Europe was disrupted, English merchants began to seek out new areas of overseas trade, beyond traditional European circuits, and their enterprises led to the formation of important groups of merchants dedicated to expanding long-distance trades. One important frontier for new commercial ventures lay in the Near and Far East, where merchants sought to secure direct access to spices, silks and other commodities which had previously been channelled through intermediaries in Portugal and the Low Countries. With the foundation of the Levant or Turkey Company in 1581, a powerful new mercantile interest emerged in the City of London, dedicated to importing these luxury products. These merchants became important advocates for commercial expansion; members of the Levant Company later played a leading part in setting up the East India Company (chartered in 1600), a joint-stock venture designed to forge direct maritime links to the rich spice trade of the Far East. During the same years, English adventurers were also increasingly drawn towards American waters and aroused by the prospect of creating settlements in the New World to rival Spain's empire.[11]

Against this background of changing political conditions and the emergence of merchant groupings seeking opportunities in new areas of overseas commerce, we can distinguish several overlapping phases in the development of English activity in the Americas. The first was associated with English efforts to break into Iberian colonial trade during the 1560s and centred on attempts to profit from the slave trade between Africa and the Americas. A second phase of activity involved the search for a north-west passage through or around America to Asia, together with more forceful trading and raiding in the Spanish Caribbean during the 1570s and 1580s, and England's first, abortive experiments in colonization in the Americas. The third and final phase of English action in the Americas during the Elizabethan period extended into the years of open and continuous warfare between England and Spain between 1585 and 1603, when English merchants and seamen from London and provincial ports (mainly in the West country) engaged as privateers in the widespread plunder of Spanish transatlantic shipping.

The first breakthrough into Spanish American trade came in the 1560s, and developed out of English efforts to profit from the west African trades which had been created by the Portuguese at the end of the fifteenth century. Between about 1480 and 1530, the Portuguese had established a virtually undisputed command over a great maritime triangle between Lisbon, the Azores and Guinea, enclosing valuable trades in gold, pepper, slaves, ivory, sugar, wax and fish. In the 1530s, the French and, to a lesser extent, the English began to break into the region's trade. Some, indeed, became involved in another triangle of colonial trade, which led from Europe to west Africa and thence to Brazil, prefiguring a commerce that was to become much more important in later years. Among the English, William Hawkins of Plymouth was the pioneer, but after he had made some profitable voyages in the 1530s, the English turned away from this risky trade towards the more assured profits of legal commerce with Lisbon and Seville. In the 1550s and 1560s, however, English interest in trade with Guinea revived, as both London merchants and the crown backed trading ventures designed to obtain African gold. Out of this arose a trade in slaves with the Caribbean, led by John Hawkins, son of the William Hawkins who had dabbled in the Guinea trade in the 1530s. In 1562, John Hawkins made a series of expeditions carrying slaves from west Africa to sell to Spanish colonists in the islands and mainlands of the Caribbean. Here, for the first time, Englishmen intervened directly in a direct commerce with Spanish America, initiating an activity that was to become more determined and aggressive in the 1570s and 1580s.[12]

At first, Hawkins's intention was to trade peacefully, taking advantage of shortages of slaves and other supplies among Spanish colonists and testing Spain's capacity to defend its monopoly of trade with the Indies. After three voyages to the Caribbean, however, Hawkins's probes into the trade of the Spanish Indies came to an abrupt halt in 1568, when he was attacked off the port of Veracruz by a fleet under the command of the Viceroy of Mexico. This defeat had greater political than economic significance. Hawkins had already found that the Spanish Caribbean was not such a promising field for contraband as he had supposed, and the future of such interloping was doubtful. But, as Anglo-Spanish relations deteriorated in Europe, the attack on Hawkins reinforced growing English hostility towards Spain and helped to justify a rising tide of attacks on Spanish shipping in European waters. Indeed, after the Duke of Alba's assault on the Netherlands in 1568 and amidst the turmoil caused by the wars of religion in France, the English began to imitate the French Protestant corsairs, turning away from trade to plunder Spanish shipping in the Caribbean. Thus the decade of the 1570s saw the start of a new and violent phase of English action in the Americas, bound up with the wars of the Protestant nations against Spain.

English exploration in the north Atlantic did not entirely cease, despite the new interest in trading and raiding in the Caribbean. In 1576-8, Martin Frobisher made three voyages in search of a north-west passage to Asia; a decade later, in 1585-7, John Davis made three further voyages into the Arctic regions north of Labrador with the same objective.[13] Neither achieved their goal, however, and, though their voyages had extended geographical knowledge of the northern shores of North America, the English quest for a direct route to Asia through these icy seas was discontinued for several decades, until Hudson's voyage of 1610. The most striking aspect of English activity in the Americas during these years was the aggression of English seamen in the Caribbean. Between 1571 and 1573, Francis Drake conducted swift, damaging raids in Spanish territory on the Isthmus of Panama, captured Spanish treasure shipments on sea and land, and, by making alliances with escaped slaves, threatened Spanish power in a strategic area. Indeed, for a few years it seemed that English and French corsairs might use their black allies to mount a guerrilla war on the Isthmus, where they could sever communications with Peru and sustain a stronghold that linked directly with the ports of Protestant Europe.[14]

In the event, the English failed to pursue this campaign and temporarily abandoned their aspirations to penetrate Spain's colonial heartlands. This was partly because they did not fully understand the importance of commanding the Isthmus, but mainly because their government lacked the resources to sustain such a conquest at the heart of Spanish America. Instead of cutting the artery of Spanish colonial commerce at Panama, Drake and his compatriots deflected their attacks to other areas of Spain's empire. In 1577, Drake sailed south of the Tropic of Capricorn and entered the Pacific. There he raided the harbour at Callao, the port of Lima, attacked Spanish shipping and seized a valuable treasure cargo before sailing northwards of California. In California he claimed territory for England, calling it Nova Albion, but made no attempt to occupy the land. Instead he sailed across the Pacific to the spice islands of the Moluccas, where he took on a cargo of cloves before going on to complete his circumnavigation of the world by returning to Plymouth late in 1580.[15] This extraordinary feat made Drake a popular hero in England and weakened Spain's prestige in Europe, but its tangible results were few. The threat to Panama had been lifted and England had shown that it was incapable of inflicting any lasting defeats on Spain in the Indies. If the English had exposed weaknesses in Spanish American defences, they were still very far from mounting any serious challenge to Spain's possessions in the Indies.[16]

From the 1580s until the end of the century, English probes into the Americas became increasingly aggressive. In Europe, Spain's repression of the Dutch rebels continued to poison Anglo-Spanish relations, until in 1585 the two countries embarked on a prolonged war. The main theatre for this struggle was on land in Europe, where Elizabeth provided her allies with armies and subsidies, and along the north–south Atlantic route between Gibraltar and the North Sea. But the contest in Europe also spread into the far Atlantic, with far-reaching consequences for England's future in the Americas. Francis Drake again played a prominent part in attacking Spanish possessions. In his expedition of 1585–8, he sacked Cartagena de Indias and Santo Domingo, taking plunder and ransom, before attacking the Spanish colony of St Augustine in Florida on his return into the Atlantic.[17]

The Anglo-Spanish struggle did not come to a definitive conclusion; in the end, both sides were exhausted by their efforts. The war in the Atlantic, which reached its highest intensity in the 1590s, was nevertheless a significant stage in England's entry into the Americas. On the one hand, Spain's resources were drained by constant harassment of its shipping and by the demands of defence over a huge area, both of which gradually sapped its will and ability to defend all the territories which it claimed in the Americas. On the other hand, the war strengthened English ambitions and maritime capacity. Privateering greatly increased the number of ships and seamen available to England, while also enhancing confidence in the future of oceanic enterprise. Furthermore, though England had still not established any colonies in the New World when its war with Spain ended in 1604, an imperialist vision had undoubtedly taken firm shape in the English political imagination, hardened both by the struggle with Spain and by the practical experience of colonial experimentation in the Americas.

COLONIAL EXPERIMENTS

English interest in creating colonies in the New World is first found in the early English voyages at the end of the fifteenth century. In the patent that the King granted to John Cabot in 1496, it was stated that Cabot and his heirs or deputies

> may conquer, occupy and possess whatsoever such towns, castles, cities and islands by them thus discovered that they may be able to conquer, occupy and possess, as our vassals and governors, lieutenants and deputies therein, acquiring for us the dominion, title and jurisdiction of the same.[18]

Other grants of these years contained similar provisions, but, as nothing came of these voyages, the notion of colonization lay dormant. It was revived in the 1560s and 1570s when the deepening conflict with Spain sharpened interest in planting English settlements in the Americas, if only to provide bases from which to harass Spanish shipping.

The first positive effort to plan and undertake English colonization was made by Sir Humphrey Gilbert, a soldier–courtier from the Devonshire landed gentry. Gilbert seems to have become interested in the Americas during the 1560s, through his contact with French Huguenot corsairs who were planning a colony in Florida. At this stage, he seems to have been primarily interested in finding a passage to Asia, either by a north-westerly route via the St Lawrence (a route previously explored by the Frenchman, Cartier) or by a south-western route via the mid-latitude lands (where Spanish explorers, followed by Verrazano, believed there was an isthmus that gave access to the Pacific).[19] In 1566, he wrote a tract advocating the *Discovery of a New Passage to Cataia* (printed a decade later, in 1576), but during the late 1560s, Gilbert was diverted from schemes for voyaging to America and Asia by his involvement in planting English settlements in Ireland.

In Ireland, Gilbert behaved with extreme brutality and, like several of his contemporaries, he seems to have regarded the colonization of Ireland as an enterprise for subjugating a barbarian peasantry to the rule of English landlords in the same manner that the Spanish conquistadors had subordinated American Indians. It is not surprising, then, that when his Irish ventures proved fruitless, Gilbert looked to America as an area for pursuing his ambitions. In 1577, he proposed an expedition to conquer Santo Domingo and Cuba, so that they might provide bases from which to launch an invasion of Mexico. When presented to the crown, this plan was rejected, but Gilbert also entertained ideas about planting English settlements outside the orbit of Spanish control and, in 1578, he obtained permission from Queen Elizabeth to organize a colonizing expedition to North America. His objective was to set up colonies on the coast north of Florida, especially in the region then known as 'Norumbega' (later New England). Although not immediately activated, Elizabeth's concession to Gilbert marked the beginning of English colonizing efforts on the North American continent.

Gilbert was slow to start his colonizing venture. Despite support from among friends and relatives among the landed gentry, he was beset by financial difficulties, and sold off rights to huge tracts of still unexplored land in North America to different individuals and groups, including a very large grant to a group of Catholic gentlemen who proposed to settle English Catholics in America. Gilbert retained a role for himself, however, as explorer, future landlord and governor; after several setbacks, he finally set out with a small fleet for North America in 1583, with rather vague plans for establishing colonies somewhere on the eastern seaboard, probably in 'Norumbega'. In the event, Gilbert landed at Newfoundland and there, in the vicinity of St John's harbour (an area already much frequented by fishing vessels from Europe), he formally annexed the island to the English monarchy. After a fruitless search for precious metals and a reconnaissance along the coast, Gilbert decided to return to England to seek support for two fresh expeditions, one to the north and another to the south, but he was lost at sea on the homeward journey.[20]

Gilbert's efforts were not entirely fruitless, however; from them, there emerged another colonizing expedition to North America, organized by his half-brother, Walter Raleigh. In 1584, Queen Elizabeth granted Raleigh a patent for discovering and colonizing new lands, thereby extending to him the patent given to Gilbert which was due to expire, though without the fishery rights in Newfoundland enjoyed by Gilbert. Shortly afterwards, Raleigh dispatched two vessels to reconnoitre the eastern shore of North America. This voyage on the Carolina Outer Banks and its offshore islands yielded very positive reports from its captains, Arthur Barlow and Philip Amadas; they commended the fertility of the soil and tractability of its native peoples, took possession of the country in the name of the English crown, and thus focused Raleigh's attention on the region as a place for planting England's first continental American settlement. In 1585, Raleigh dubbed this territory 'Virginia', as a tribute to the Virgin Queen; after receiving the title of Lord and Governor of Virginia, in April 1585 he sent his associate Richard Grenville to establish a colony there.

From this venture, English colonization began. In 1585 a small colony, of some 108 men, was put down on the island of Roanoke, on the coast south of Chesapeake Bay. There, settlers tried to construct a fort and village, and traded with the local Indians, while Grenville returned to England for reinforcements and fresh supplies. However, in his absence the colonists ran desperately short of food; when Drake's fleet called at Roanoke on its return from the West Indies in 1586, it found the settlers eager to return home. So, when Grenville arrived back at Roanoke, the colony had been deserted, and he decided simply to leave a small holding party, while he again returned to England to seek fresh recruits. This band of 15 men came to a sad end. After an attack by Indians, the survivors took to the sea, aiming either to encamp elsewhere on the coast or to link up with English privateers in the Caribbean, possibly even trying to return to England; whatever happened, nothing was ever heard from them again.

In 1587, another effort was made to colonize the area. It was organized by John White who, after returning from the first voyage in 1585, had contracted with Raleigh to act as governor of the colony and now went back with a party of some 117 men, women and children. Shortly after arriving, White himself was then forced to return to England to organize support for the colony, leaving his daughter, her husband and their child (who, having been the first child born in the colony, was named Virginia). In England, he found a nation mobilizing against the attack of the Spanish Armada, and the war with Spain prevented him from returning to Roanoke until 1590. When he finally arrived, the colony had mysteriously disappeared. White tried to conduct a search, but was dragged away by his ship's crew; in spite of later searches, the lost colonists were never found. White returned to England, a disappointed and grieving man, and, amidst the continuing urgency of war, Raleigh abandoned the Roanoke venture.[21]

With the end of Roanoke, English schemes for colonization in North America were displaced in favour of privateering, as maritime war with Spain reached its peak in the last years of the century. As for Raleigh, he transferred his attention to South America where, in his first voyage to Guiana in 1595, he became mesmerized by the prospect of finding 'that great and golden city, which the Spaniards call El Dorado'.[22] Convinced that the English could combat Spain on its own colonial territory by founding an empire with comparable sources of precious metal, Raleigh went in search of a legendary lost Indian civilization, believed to lie somewhere in the region of the River Orinoco. On his return, he wrote an extraordinary account of his voyage; by describing the fabulous potential of Guiana, he hoped to drum up financial support for a further expedition.

Raleigh's vision was more than just a catalogue of riches to attract the greedy and gullible. It offered a dream of empire in a virgin land, where soldiers might find wealth and glory, and the crown a vantage point from which it might attack Spain in its colonial heartlands, perhaps even conquer Peru. Unlike the previous ventures in North America, Raleigh envisaged an English tropical colony founded on native communities rather than English settlers. His 1595 voyage had no immediate sequel, however, and many years passed before Raleigh was able to return. Finally, after enduring political disgrace and periods of imprisonment, Raleigh sailed again for Guiana in 1617, in a last gamble to restore his fortunes. The expedition turned out to be another tragic failure, in which Raleigh lost his son, his fortune and his hope of political rehabilitation. Discredited by his enemies, Raleigh was executed by James I in 1618. With Raleigh dead, the era of the Elizabethan maritime adventurers and privateers was definitively over.[23]

ENGLISH COLONIZING EXPERIMENTS: CONDITIONS AND CONSEQUENCES

Looking back over the colonial experiments undertaken by Englishmen during the Elizabethan period, it is obvious that, for all their ambitions, they did not constitute a colonizing movement of any substance. Together, the ventures of Gilbert and Raleigh had involved no more than a few hundred people; very few of them remained in America for more than short periods of time, or many did not survive the experience. This does not mean that these ventures were entirely without significance. On the contrary. Gilbert's enterprise of 1583 had aroused strong interest in English intellectual and political circles, and both reflected and encouraged English aspirations to found a colonial empire in the New World. In particular, it prompted the compilation and publication of works that were considerably to advance the cause of colonization, both by gathering information on western voyages and other extra-European travels, and by arguing systematically for settlement in the Americas as a means of furthering English prosperity and power.

The most important of such writings were those of Richard Hakluyt. A member of the circle of Elizabethan expansionists which included Gilbert and Raleigh, Hakluyt became the leading propagandist for overseas expansion, by writing, translating and compiling material to persuade the Queen to support colonizing ventures. Convinced that England's best means of increasing its wealth and influence lay in overseas trade and in settlement in America, Hakluyt did much to make the notion of colonization respectable and viable. In 1582, Hakluyt published his first book, the *Divers Voyages touching the discoverie of America*, in support of Gilbert's plans for colonizing 'Norumbega'. In 1584, he took this a stage further. At Raleigh's instigation, he wrote a *Discourse on Western Planting* in order to persuade the Queen and her ministers to support Raleigh's plans for a colony in North America; he followed this, in 1589, with his most famous work, the *Principal Navigations, Voyages and Discoveries of the English Nation*.[24] In these works, Hakluyt not only amassed contemporary information on overseas travel to show the potential for overseas enterprise, but also advanced a powerful and systematically organized range of arguments and justifications in favour of American colonization, thereby providing powerful intellectual reinforcement both for the first colonial projects of the late sixteenth century and for those that followed in the early seventeenth century. What, then, lay behind this growing concern with colonies, and what were the ideas and methods of the men who attempted to put them into practice?

The writings of Gilbert, Hakluyt and Raleigh all show the powerful influence of Spain on English thinking and action in the field of colonization, both as an example and an enemy. These propagandists for colonization, together with a number of lesser-known contemporaries, argued the need for settlement on several grounds. In the first place, they saw it as a means to find riches like those upon which Spain had built its power, or, at the very least, a place that might provide an alternative source of commodities usually drawn from the Mediterranean and act as a base to reconnoitre for a route to Asia. A second reason was to provide bases in the New World from which England might attack the ships and colonies of its Spanish enemy; third, they connected colonial 'planting' with the good of England's society and economy, arguing that it would relieve domestic social problems by providing an outlet for the unemployed poor, while stimulating the national economy by creating a new market for English goods, especially woollen cloth. By selling land to English Catholics who wanted to escape religious persecution at home, Sir Humphrey Gilbert also anticipated an idea that was later to play an important role in Anglo-American colonization: the notion, borrowed from the French Huguenots, of America as a refuge for dissenting religious minorities. Last but not least, Englishmen legitimized their colonizing ambitions by presenting England as the nation chosen by Providence to bring Christianity to the benighted natives in North America, in lands where God had allowed neither the Spaniards nor the French to prosper.[25]

All these ideas arose, directly or indirectly, from England's political interaction and struggle with Spain. The dream of finding precious metals was evidently inspired by the Spanish example, and was reinforced by the growing recognition that Spain's formidable military power in Europe derived much of its strength from the influx of American treasure. The plan to create fortified military settlements in the New World also stemmed directly from the struggle against Spain, since such settlements were conceived as bases from which to attack Spanish shipping. Equally, the preoccupation with creating colonies to stimulate the English economy derived indirectly from interaction with Spain. Not only did Spanish colonialism demonstrate the huge economic potential of New World colonies, but colonies also seemed to provide an answer to economic difficulties in England which had been exacerbated by the disruption of English trade caused by conflict in Europe. Even the search for settlements as a home for religious dissidents was connected to Anglo-Spanish relations, insofar as the conflict between Protestant England and Catholic Spain had made the position of English Catholics increasingly problematical. Spain also influenced the choice of geographical area for English colonization. Its proponents focused on the North American coastline because, apart from Florida, this was a region which the Spaniards had failed to people and could not easily defend. When defending their right to invade regions claimed by Spain, such spokesmen for colonization as Hakluyt and Raleigh argued that, by taking new lands, England would liberate Indian peoples from the cruel oppression of the Spaniards, so vividly described in Las Casas's *Brief narration of the destruction of the Indies by the Spaniards* (first translated into English in 1583), and evangelize them into the purer form of Christianity offered by English Protestantism.

Throughout the latter half of the sixteenth century, the search for a route to Asia continued to interest Englishmen, and reflected a growing determination among English merchants to share in the Asian spice trade that was dominated by Portugal. Pursuit of the Iberian example was also apparent in the diligence with which Englishmen searched for precious metals when they set foot on American soil. For many Elizabethan merchants and adventurers, the best means of acquiring treasure was by stealing it from Spaniards; some took their passion for gold a step further, however, and aspired to emulate the Spaniards by finding Indian treasure and mines in unknown lands. Thus, when searching for a north-west passage, Martin Frobisher was alert for signs of gold and, after deluding himself into believing that he had found a rich source of gold, he shipped tons of iron pyrite (fool's gold) to England in 1577–8. In 1583, Gilbert had immediately sought out gold on landing in Newfoundland, in a search that proved as fruitless as the rest of his expedition. Obsession with gold had also gripped the first colonists at Roanoke in 1585, to such an extent that they neglected their own subsistence and would have starved without Indian assistance. But Raleigh's projected 'empire' of Guiana was the most striking example of this fixation on precious metal. Indeed, his scheme descended directly from the dreams that had inspired Spanish conquistadors in South America, drawing on legends told by Spanish chroniclers and perpetuated by Spanish adventurers.

Though often quixotic, the quest for gold was entirely understandable. Precious metals were, after all, as great a prize as spices and as yet Englishmen saw no reason why they should not have the same good fortune as the followers of Cortés and Pizarro. Gold and silver were, after all, a basic element in the contemporary European view of America, together with its strange pagan peoples. But gold was not simply an end in itself. Promoters of colonization also saw it an essential means to encourage overseas settlement, since the discovery of precious metals would attract colonists and provide a means for supporting a colony in its early stages. The English advocates of colonization did not, then, simply want to copy the Spanish model, in

27

which Europeans ruled a native countryside from urban centres. Instead, their idea of 'plantation' in America was to create cells of English society overseas, modelled on the social and political order of the mother country.

A picture of the kind of New World colony envisaged by Elizabethan Englishmen is found in a document drafted by Sir Humphrey Gilbert prior to his voyage of colonization to Newfoundland in 1583. Basically, Gilbert saw himself and his heirs as the lords of a new land, ruling an hierarchical agrarian society akin to that of England itself. Gilbert thought that gentlemen should receive large land grants which they would people with their own tenants, brought with them to create a yeomanry. Poor people would also be sent at the government's expense, presumably to provide smallholders, artisans and agricultural labourers. According to his plan, settlers would provide military equipment and pay taxes for maintaining military and naval forces, and all would pay seigneurial dues to Gilbert and his heirs. To complete this microcosm of English agrarian society, estates were to be apportioned to the Anglican church, to support an ecclesiastical establishment of parish priests, bishops and an archbishop, with the land divided into parishes whose members would pay tithes. His plans for government were vague: Gilbert and his heirs were to maintain order, while the settlers were to choose councillors for war and maritime affairs. Gilbert failed to give much consideration to the native inhabitants of the lands he intended to acquire. Perhaps he was confident that there would be sufficient land for both whites and Indians to coexist; more probably, his Irish experience suggested that 'barbarian' natives could simply be pushed aside. Nor did he have any specific recommendations for developing an export commerce from the colony: he wanted simply to turn over a monopoly of trade to a group of merchants in return for money and a share of customs duties and other imposts. In this scheme, profit from trade was to come from supplying the colonists with European goods, rather than sending American exports to England. Thus, the 'plantation' was seen as an agrarian community in which trade played a secondary role; it was not a 'plantation' in the later sense of a colony engaged in large-scale commercial production for an overseas market.[26]

After Gilbert's project had been stillborn, Raleigh's Virginia colony at Roanoke Island was less elaborately designed, and reflected the emergence of a different model. Raleigh initially believed that the survival of the colony depended on a connection with privateering, since this was the only means of enticing seamen to participate in the voyages that linked the colony with England. Thus the first colony at

Roanoke, under the leadership of Ralph Lane, was organized on a military basis, and Lane was more concerned to explore the region for undiscovered treasure than to establish a firm and durable economic base for the community. The settlers simply became parasites on local Indian villagers and eventually used terror tactics to force the Indians to supply them with food. When he left Roanoke, Lane was pessimistic about the colony's prospects, stating that 'the discovery of a good mine . . . or a passage to the South Sea, or someway to it, and nothing else can bring this country to be inhabited by our nation'.[27] Informed by this advice, Raleigh sent the expedition under John White with instructions to make a fresh start by moving to the Chesapeake Bay, where it was thought that conditions might be better. Plans for settlement now went beyond the military base previously established by Lane, and beyond the quasi-feudal agrarian community conceived by Gilbert. A seigneurial element was retained, in that Raleigh remained the overlord of the project, with the right to choose his governor and laid down the terms on which the colony was to be established. But the colony was to be strictly civilian, without the aristocratic bias that had infused Gilbert's thinking. Land was to be apportioned to settlers with families recruited not from the landed gentry and its tenants but from among farmers, some educated middle-class people and some London tradesmen, with neither military nor privateering connections. Here, then, we can see a different style of colonization, one which was in some ways to prefigure the future.

This was, however, a style that was ahead of its time; investors were not yet ready to support such ventures without the promise of immediate returns. Raleigh himself reverted to the idea of simply imitating the Spanish conquistadors. When he returned from his voyage to South America of 1595, the plan which he put before the Queen was for territorial conquest by military means, to create a tributary dominion of a kind familiar in Spanish America. Raleigh proposed that the Queen support an expedition that would build forts, establish sovereignty over the tribes bordering Guiana, and, having found the realm of the lost Inca, convert this land into a subordinate state which would pay tribute to the English crown and serve as a base for fresh conquests. To secure support for his scheme, Raleigh conjured up a vision of Guiana as a virgin land in which Englishmen might emulate the feats of the conquistadors, and find equal rewards:

> Guiana is a country that hath yet her maidenhead, never sacked, turned, nor wrought, the face of the earth hath not been torn, nor the virtue and salt of the soil spent by manurance, the graves not opened for gold, the mines not broken with sledges, nor with their images pulled down out of their temples. . . .

29

The common soldier shall here fight for gold, and pay himself instead of pence, with plates of half a foot broad. . . . Those commanders and chieftains, that shoot at honour, and abundance, shall find here more rich and beautiful cities, more temples adorned with golden images, more sepulchres filled with treasure, than either Cortez found in Mexico, or Pizarro in Peru.[28]

Raleigh's imperial project was, however, treated with the scepticism which, with hindsight, we can now see that it deserved, and Raleigh himself was left to fall back on his colonial enterprise in Ireland, ransacking Irish forests for timber to export. Indeed, passing from Raleigh's fabulous vision of golden cities and conquered native kingdoms to the more mundane realities of contemporary English experience, it is interesting to note the interaction of American colonization projects with English experience in Ireland.

The effort to bring Ireland under effective English control and to people it with Protestant settlers had started in the 1570s and was still very much in progress at the time when Englishmen began to con-template colonization schemes for the Americas. Of course, the situation encountered in Ireland differed in many ways from that found in America. Ireland was a populated region within easy reach of England, to which it was connected by a long history of cultural and political contacts, and there was a framework of English military and civil administration already in place. Nevertheless, there were ways in which English colonization in Ireland was related to the emergence of ideas and methods for settlement in America.

First, there was an overlap between promoters of colonization in both regions: the circle of West Country gentry (focused on Gilbert, Raleigh and Grenville) that was closely connected with Irish planting also played a leading role in proposing and activating plans for colonies in America. Indeed, contemporary Englishmen came to regard the 'wild Irish' and the 'wild Indians' as similar in the sense that both were barbarian peoples awaiting the civilizing touch of a superior nation.[29] Second, in both regions private economic ambitions interacted with reasons of state in motivating colonization; Ireland and America were seen as theatres in the wider struggle against Spain, in which Ireland had to be defended against possible Spanish subversion and invasion, while the American coast had potential as a military base for attacking Spanish ships and colonies in the Indies. (The crucial difference was that Irish colonization received strong support from the Elizabethan state, while American projects received virtually none.) Another influence of Ireland on Anglo-American colonization was to become apparent only in the longer term. This was the fact that the flow of English migrants to Ireland before 1630 made the idea and practice of overseas settlement part of the experience of common people in English society, preparing the way for the 'great migration' of the English to North America after about 1630. Equally, the idea of colonies as a safety-valve for English society, which appeared after 1585 in schemes to send both radical Protestants and English Catholics to the Munster Plantation in Ireland, was to resurface in later migrations to America in the 1620s and after. Thus, while concern with Ireland may have diverted men and money which might otherwise have been devoted to schemes for 'plantation' in North America during the Elizabethan era, the colonization of Ireland in some respects foreshadowed that which was later to take root in the Americas.[30]

How, eventually, were these disparate strands of English experience and activity during the later sixteenth century to be drawn together in a movement that was to produce tangible results in America? First, there was a change in political conditions at the beginning of the seventeenth century, when Elizabeth was succeeded by James I, and England came to terms with Spain. When peace between England and Spain was formally resumed at the Treaty of London in 1604, the English had not yet established settlements in the Americas, and Spain still insisted on its exclusive sovereignty over the whole of the western hemisphere except Brazil. But by this time Spain was too enfeebled to enforce this claim, while the English had become more capable of challenging it. Under James I's government privateering was curtailed, making it much less profitable, and the English mercantile community, particularly that of London, now began to take a more active and aggressive interest in American colonization. This brought an increasing emphasis on the mercantile function of colonies, as markets and sources of trade which might strengthen the English economy, and the 'plantation' idea of the sixteenth century gave way to the notion of market-oriented overseas settlements. When this fused with the search of religious dissidents for a refuge where they might preserve their principles and build a new life, it was to realize the dreams of Elizabethan colonial propagandists, giving birth to the first enduring English colonies in the Americas.

NOTES

1. On fifteenth-century European exploration in the Atlantic, see Felipe Fernández-Armesto, *Before Columbus: Exploration and Colonisation from the Mediterranean to the Atlantic, 1229–1492* (London, 1987), especially Part

Two. For a general review of European exploration, see J.H. Parry, *The Age of Reconnaissance: Discovery, Exploration and Settlement, 1450–1650* (London, 1963); for American voyages, a classic work is Samuel Eliot Morison, *The European Discovery of America: The Northern Voyages, A.D. 500–1600* (New York, 1971) and *The European Discovery of America: The Southern Voyages, A.D. 1492–1616* (New York, 1974).

2. C.R. Boxer, *The Portuguese Seaborne Empire* (Harmondsworth, 1969) pp. 15–38.

3. The fullest discussion of the thesis of an 'English discovery' is found in David B. Quinn, *England and the Discovery of America, 1481–1620* (London, 1974) pp. 5–87.

4. The standard work on Cabot is James A. Williamson, *The Cabot Voyages and Bristol Discovery under Henry VII*, Hakluyt Society, 2nd series, vol. 120 (Cambridge, 1962). Morison, *The European Discovery of America: The Northern Voyages*, pp. 147–209, argues that Cabot landed at Newfoundland; Quinn, *England and the Discovery of America*, pp. 117–18, suggests a Cape Breton landing.

5. On these voyages, see Quinn, *England and the Discovery of America*, pp. 93–130.

6. A positive interpretation of the evidence for Sebastian Cabot's voyage of 1508 is found in Quinn, *England and the Discovery of America*, pp. 139–44. A sceptical view is taken by Kenneth R. Andrews, *Trade, Plunder and Settlement: Maritime Enterprise and the Genesis of the British Empire, 1480–1630* (Cambridge, 1984) pp. 50–2; this book makes a major contribution to understanding Elizabethan and Jacobean expansion, and is a basic source for this chapter.

7. On Sebastian Cabot's voyages for Spain, see Morison, *The European Discovery of America: The Southern Voyages*, pp. 537–61.

8. Andrews, *Trade, Plunder and Settlement*, pp. 65–75.

9. On changes in English foreign trade in this period, see Laurence Stone, 'Elizabethan overseas trade', *Economic History Review*, 2nd series (1949) **II**: 30–58.

10. For a general account of the development of English dynastic and foreign policy against the background of national politics, see John Guy, *Tudor England* (Oxford, 1990) *passim*. For an account of Anglo–Spanish relations seen from the Spanish side, see John Lynch, *Spain under the Hapsburgs*, 2 vols (Oxford, 1965) vol. 1, especially pp. 96–100, 271–331.

11. On the development of interests in trade with the east, see Robert Brenner, 'The social basis of English commercial expansion, 1550–1660', *Journal of Economic History* (1972) **32**: 362–71. For a recent statement on the causes and consequences of English expansion in the later sixteenth and early seventeenth centuries, see Robert Brenner, *Merchants and Revolution: Commercial Change, Political Conflict, and London's Overseas Traders, 1550–1653,* (Cambridge, 1993), pp 4–23.

12. Andrews, *Trade Plunder and Settlement,* pp. 101–34. James A. Williamson, *Sir John Hawkins: The Times and the Man* (Oxford, 1927) pp. 78–204, recounts the slaving voyages; Irene Wright, *Spanish Documents concerning English Voyages to the Caribbean, 1527–1568*, Hakluyt Society, 2nd series, vol. 62 (London, 1929) provides evidence on these English voyages from Spanish archives.

13. Andrews, *Trade, Plunder and Settlement*, pp. 167–82; Morison, *The European Discovery of America: The Northern Voyages*, pp. 500–54; 583–616. Detailed accounts are found in V. Stefansson (ed) *The Three Voyages of Martin Frobisher* (London, 1938); Albert Markham, *Voyages and Works of John Davis the Navigator* (London, 1880).

14. Spanish accounts of English raids on the Isthmus are compiled in Irene Wright, *Spanish Documents concerning English Voyages to the Spanish Main*, Hakluyt Society, 2nd series, vol. 71 (London, 1932)

15. On Drake's voyage, see K.R. Andrews, *Drake's Voyages. A Reassessment of their Place in Elizabethan Maritime Expansion* (London, 1967).

16. For a general account of English activity in the Americas in the 1560s and 1570s, see Andrews, *Trade, Plunder and Settlement*, pp. 116–66; on Spanish responses, see Paul E. Hoffman, *The Spanish Crown and the Defence of the Caribbean, 1535–1585* (Baton Rouge, La, and London, 1980), pp. 63–236.

17. For a brief account of English (and French) privateering in the Caribbean in this period, see Kenneth R. Andrews, *The Spanish Caribbean: Trade and Plunder, 1530–1630* (London, 1978) pp. 135–70.

18. Williamson, *The Cabot Voyages*, pp. 204–5.

19. The first full, documented account of the explorations that gave rise to the belief in a southern route is given by Paul E. Hoffman, *A New Andalucia and a Way to the Orient: The American Southeast during the Sixteenth Century* (Baton Rouge, LA and London, 1990); for the influence of this belief on English exploration and colonizing projects, see pp. 274–307.

20. The principal source of information and documentation relating to Gilbert's life and activities is David B. Quinn, *The Voyages and Colonising Enterprises of Sir Humphrey Gilbert*, 2 vols, Hakluyt Society, 2nd series, vols 83–4 (London, 1940); this includes Edward Hayes's eyewitness account of the Newfoundland expedition in vol. 2, pp. 385–423. An abbreviated version of Hayes's chronicle, in modernized English, is found in Richard Hakluyt, *Voyages to the Virginia Colonies* (compiled by A.L. Rowse, London, 1986) pp. 21–48. For a narrative of Gilbert's colonizing venture, see D.B. Quinn and Neil M. Cheshire, *The New Found Land of Stephen Parmenius* (Toronto, 1970) especially pp. 50–8.

21. For a summary of the Roanoke venture and a discussion of the 'lost colony', see Quinn, *England and the Discovery of America*, pp. 282–306, 432–81. The definitive collection of source material is D.B. Quinn, *The Roanoke Voyages, 1584–1590: Documents to Illustrate the English Voyages to North America under the Patent granted to Sir Walter Raleigh in 1584*, 2 vols, Hakluyt Society, 2nd series, vols 104–5 (London, 1955).

22. V.T. Harlow (ed), *The Discoverie of the large and bewtiful Empire of Guiana, by Sir Walter Ralegh*, (London, 1928) p. 4.

23. For an account of Raleigh's life and career, see Norman Lloyd Williams, *Sir Walter Raleigh* (Harmondsworth, 1965).

24. On Hakluyt, see George B. Parks, *Richard Hakluyt and the English Voyages* (New York, 1961); for a sample of his writings, see Richard Hakluyt, *Voyages and Discoveries* (Harmondsworth, 1972); for the *Discourse on Western Planting*, see E.G.R Taylor (ed) *Original Writings and Correspondence of the two Richard Hakluyts*, 2 vols, Hakluyt Society, 2nd series, vols 76–7 (London, 1935) vol. 2, pp. 313–19.

25. See, for example, the comments of Edward Hayes and George Peckham, in H.C. Porter, *The Inconstant Savage: England and the North American Indian, 1500–1600* (London, 1979) p. 218.
26. For Gilbert's plan, see Quinn, *Gilbert*, pp. 266–77.
27. Quinn, *Roanoke Voyages*, vol. I, p. 273.
28. Quoted by Williams, *Sir Walter Raleigh*, p. 149.
29. In 1617, Francis Bacon referred to Ireland as a country 'reclaimed from desolation . . . and from savage and barbarous customs, to humanity and civility'. Similar terms were used in talking of the Indians of North America who were also supposed to live in a wilderness, steeped in 'savagery'. Quoted in Porter, *Inconstant Savage*, p. 203.
30. For perspectives on the relation between Ireland and America in this period, see David B. Quinn, 'Ireland and sixteenth-century expansion', in T.D. Williams (ed) *Historical Studies I* (London, 1958); Karl S. Bottigheimer, 'Kingdom and colony: Ireland in the westward enterprise, 1536–1660', in K.R. Andrews, N.P. Canny and P.E.H. Hair (eds) *Westward Enterprise: English Activities in Ireland, the Atlantic and America, 1480–1650* (Liverpool, 1978) pp. 45–64; Nicholas Canny, *Kingdom and Colony: Ireland in the Atlantic World, 1560–1800* (Baltimore, Md, and London, 1988). On Raleigh's activities in Ireland, see David B. Quinn, *Raleigh and the British Empire* (London, 1947) pp. 129–61. For a view that places English American colonization in a very broad perspective, starting with expansion of the western margins of Britain, see A.L. Rowse, *The Expansion of Elizabethan England* (London, 1955).

CHAPTER TWO

First Colonies

By the beginning of the seventeenth century, the English, like their Dutch Protestant allies, had proved to be very effective mariners, adept at overseas trading and in pillaging on the margins of the Spanish empire. But they had not yet found a formula for conquering and settling new territories in the manner of the Spanish and Portuguese. Thus, when James VI of Scotland inherited Elizabeth's throne in 1603, to become James I of England (1603–25), Elizabethan ambitions for creating a 'New England' in the Americas remained unfulfilled. Roanoke had vanished, Drake was dead, while Raleigh, the great promoter of colonial projects, was imprisoned in the Tower of London. Moreover, the new King wanted peace with Spain, a prospect which dismayed those who thought that an English empire could be attained only by continuing aggression against the Catholic enemy.

When peaceful relations with Spain were formalized by the Treaty of London in 1604, the prospects for creating such an empire seem to have been no farther forward than they had been half a century earlier. Spain still claimed its right to an exclusive sovereignty over the territory and seas of the Americas, and the London treaty appeared simply to restore the status quo that had prevailed before the Anglo-Spanish struggle of the late sixteenth century. However, when James I died in 1625, permanent English colonies had taken root in the Americas for the first time; under his successor, Charles I (1625–42), they were consolidated and strengthened by English migration on a scale which the Elizabethans could only have imagined. What made this possible, after the false starts and delays of the Elizabethan years? Why did English interest in American colonization revive, and how were schemes for 'plantation' in the New World, so frequently canvassed in the past, suddenly and successfully translated into reality?

ENGLISH EXPANSION IN THE EARLY SEVENTEENTH CENTURY: CONTEXT

One factor that facilitated progress towards the creation of English colonies was the shift in the European balance of power that had taken place during the late sixteenth century. Even if prominent Spaniards detected signs of decadence in their society, Spain remained a dominating force in European politics, of colossal strength and immense resources. However, its strength was continuously sapped by the enormous effort of fighting its enemies in northern Europe.[1] The English and Dutch, on the other hand, had made substantial commercial and economic gains from their offensives against Spain. The Dutch rebels not only had survived the onslaught of Philip II's armies, but also continued to fight with Spain until 1648, carrying the war ever deeper into the heart of the Iberian colonial empires. Dutch shipping dominated the main sea-routes of the European world, from the Baltic to the Mediterranean; Amsterdam became the continent's greatest commercial emporium, and, during the first half of the seventeenth century, Dutch seamen and merchants created an overseas seaborne empire by overrunning the possessions of Portugal in Asia and America. In 1603, the Dutch East India Company took the principal Indonesian spice islands; in 1628, an admiral of the Dutch West India Company captured the Mexican silver fleet, together with its enormous cargo of treasure; in 1630, the Dutch tightened their grip on the Portuguese sugar trade by seizing control of north-east Brazil, converting it into a Dutch territory until local rebellion returned the region to Portuguese rule in 1654.[2]

English achievements were more modest, but England too was becoming a vigorous and expansive society, ready to take advantage of the enfeeblement of Spain. At the beginning of the seventeenth century, the English economy was less dependent on the old trades with northern and central Europe, and looked outward on to a wider world. Moreover, under James I its political position was unusually stable. The accession of the Scottish House of Stuart to the throne of England meant that the mainland of the British Isles was brought under one ruler; though this certainly did not eliminate internal frictions, it helped to provide a brief respite from the regional strife that had plagued English politics in the past. More important, perhaps, was the fact that both James and Parliament were anxious to avoid heavy military expenditures, so that when the Thirty Years War began in 1618, England did not immediately become involved in the conflicts that absorbed the energies of other European powers. Foreign entanglements could not be avoided indefinitely, of course, and in 1624–30, England went to war with Spain and then with France, severely disrupting its export trade and leading to a resurgence of privateering. But from 1604, after nearly two decades of war, England had enjoyed twenty years of peace, providing a breathing space in which its people were able to concentrate on peaceful commerce, colonization abroad, and the pursuit of religious and political differences at home.

With the return of peace in 1604, merchants, landowners and courtiers who had made fortunes from preying on enemy shipping in time of war looked for speculative commercial ventures in which to invest their accumulated capital. The trades with Russia and Turkey, started in the later sixteenth century by the Muscovy and Levant companies, had been a beginning; now that the windfall profits culled from privat- eering had dried up, merchants and investors turned with renewed interest to the Mediterranean, the Far East and the Americas as areas for commercial advance. James I's desire to avoid conflict with Spain did not exclude possibilities for overseas commercial and terri- torial expansion. Despite strong Spanish pressure on England to abjure any colonial ambitions in the Americas, the Treaty of London had carefully preserved England's right to colonize in areas that were not effectively occupied by Spain. Indeed, James's concern to maintain peace with Spain, by stamping out privateering, probably improved the prospects for overseas settlement, since it reduced the profits of an activity which had diverted capital and enterprise from colonization over the previous half century.

The reign of James I was not one of uninterrupted prosperity. England was periodically afflicted by famines and pestilence and, after a ten year boom in the cloth trade from 1604, the country entered a profound economic crisis after 1614.[3] Nevertheless, in the opening years of Stuart government, the atmosphere was very different from that of the final, war-torn years of the Elizabethan period. In the first surge of peacetime prosperity before 1614, there was a rush of investment into overseas ventures which laid the foundations for a fresh advance of the Elizabethan expansionary thrust under the early Stuarts.[4] A new and powerful mercantile political elite emerged in London, a new kind of policy began to take shape, in which the pursuit of national power was linked to commercial aggrandizement, and the state began to take a more active role in promoting trade at the expense of its European neighbours. Under Elizabeth, patriotism and profit had become close companions; during the reigns of the first two Stuart kings, the 'good of England' became increasingly associated with expanding English commerce and nurturing an incipient seaborne empire.

RECONNAISSANCE

After the failure of Roanoke in the 1580s, English attempts at colonization in the New World turned from North to South America. There, in an area of the north-eastern coast of South America that was not settled by Spaniards, English colonizing projects developed as offshoots from trading links formed with Spanish colonies during the closing years of Elizabeth's reign. In the 1590s, English traders had engaged in an illegal traffic in tobacco with the Spanish colonies at Trinidad and on the Venezuelan coast; when Spanish attacks on contraband made this trade more difficult, English adventurers tried to create their own independent tobacco-producing colonies on the nearby mainland.

The first such effort was made in 1604, when Charles Leigh sought to plant an English colony on the banks of the River Wiapoco in the Amazon delta region; though it did not survive Leigh's death in 1606, the project marked the beginning of a prolonged effort to create a niche for English settlement in the Lower Amazon area. It led in turn to the establishment of English colonies in the Caribbean islands where, after being forced away from the South American mainland by the Spanish and Portuguese, English promoters founded settlements in the Leeward Islands. The development of Anglo-Caribbean colonies (to which we shall return shortly) was, however, temporarily over-shadowed during the second decade of the seventeenth century by the revival of colonizing projects in North America. It was there, on the Atlantic coasts where Englishmen had explored, fished and made their first experiments in colonization in the sixteenth century, that the first foundations of an English colonial empire were laid.

After the collapse of the Roanoke colony of 1585–6, English interest in settling North America had diminished, but, while they neglected the land, Englishmen continued to sail the waters off the American coast where they exploited the fishing banks off

Newfoundland, the St Lawrence River, and the shores of what was later Nova Scotia and the northern part of New England. Long famed for its abundant fish stocks, this region was increasingly frequented by the fishermen of various nations; as the demand for fish grew from the 1580s, there was fierce competition between the French, Basques and English for cod and for the oil taken from whale and walrus. The furs traded by the Indians of the region were also a magnet to traders, who came in search of the beaver pelts which fetched high prices among the fashionable rich in Europe. By the end of the sixteenth century, the French had developed a regular fur trade which, together with their interests in finding a north-west passage to Asia, encouraged them to restart colonizing ventures in this northern area during the early seventeenth century. In 1604–7, Frenchmen established a small agricultural colony at Port Royal in Acadia (modern Nova Scotia); after it had been abandoned in 1607, Samuel Champlain sailed up the St Lawrence to establish the tiny colony of Quebec in 1608, thereby laying the foundations for a 'New France' in America.[5] During the same years the English also became increasingly interested in penetrating the lands that lay inshore from the fishing banks and, though somewhat slower than France to try permanent settlement on the North American mainland, eventually implanted an important and enduring presence south of the French settlements, in New England.

At first, this land of ferocious winters could not attract settlers, though a small expedition that took place in 1597 did point to the future. In that year, a group of religious dissidents petitioned the English government for the right to emigrate to the 'province of Canada', and attempted to land on an island near Nova Scotia. Their design failed, and these first Puritan 'pilgrims' returned to London, from whence they moved to Amsterdam, and later to Leiden.[6] Though it came to nothing, this expedition showed that earlier ideas about America as a refuge for religious dissenters were still alive, ready to be activated in the right circumstances. Indeed, the idea remained dormant within this very community: two decades later it was to provide recruits for a successful Puritan colonization in New England.

English voyaging on this northern oceanic circuit, where England had formed its first contacts with the New World a century before, rekindled interest in North American colonization in the opening years of the seventeenth century. In 1602, a small expedition led by Bartholomew Gosnold sailed from Falmouth to the coast of Maine and after exploring the Massachusetts Bay area, fuelled interest by making very favourable reports on the region and its people.[7] This was followed in 1603 by a two-vessel voyage from Bristol, commanded by

Martin Pring, which also sailed to the New England coast and reported very positively on the country and its resources. Pring imported a cargo of sassafras, a plant considered a panacea for syphilis, plague and other diseases; as London was suffering a plague in 1603, this was presumably useful publicity for the promoters of American colonies. It was, however, another voyage, made in 1605, that led directly into a serious colonizing project.[8] Directed by Captain George Waymouth, this expedition visited Penobscat Bay and its surrounding region; on his return to Plymouth, Waymouth aroused considerable interest in the region's potential among merchants and gentry in the west of England, and began to plan a scheme for exploiting this potential. Those who backed his project were then drawn into a larger venture, through an alliance with influential merchants in London that led to the foundation of the Virginia Company in 1606.[9] Mercantile enterprise and capital in the City of London, built up during the Elizabethan expansion, now sought new opportunities in the west and gave crucial support to renewed efforts to establish colonies in North America.

COMPANIES AND COLONIES

Founding colonies required capital, and the contribution made by English mercantile capital in initiating colonization is clearly reflected in the venture which established England's first permanent colony in America, at Jamestown in Virginia. For this colony was created by the Virginia Company, a chartered company in the tradition of commercial organization which had provided the vehicles for overseas trading ventures throughout the Elizabethan period. Two distinct groups of promoters came together to establish the company, forming a joint venture which, while it had rival wings, could claim to be a national project.

One group was mainly from the West Country, where links with American fishing, fur trading and trade in the drug sassafras encouraged merchants and gentry to look to the north-eastern coast of America as a place for colonization. This group included the Devonshire relatives and friends of Sir Humphrey Gilbert's family, and two influential political figures: Sir John Popham, the Lord Chief Justice in Somerset and Sir Ferdinando Gorges, the Governor of Plymouth. The other group, led by Richard Hakluyt and Sir Thomas Smythe, was from London, and drew on Raleigh's past plans for a colony in Virginia, in the area of Chesapeake Bay. Though they were rivals, the two groups united to appeal for a royal grant of land in America; having won this charter in April 1606, they proceeded to organize and dispatch separate expeditions across the Atlantic. The London branch of the Virginia Company was authorized to settle in an area to the south of modern New York, the Plymouth group to its north; both were to be under a Council of Virginia, based in England, and the intention was to commission subordinate councils to organize colonies as they should arise.

When the London group sent its first ships, with 144 men and boys, they went to the region which Raleigh had named 'Virginia'. In April 1607, 105 survivors of the voyage landed in the area of Chesapeake Bay and founded Jamestown. The Plymouth company meanwhile sent an expedition of some 120 men to the Sagadahoc River (in modern Maine), founding a settlement under the leadership of Raleigh Gilbert, youngest son of Sir Humphrey Gilbert. In both cases, the people sent were company employees rather than settlers, and included no women; this reflected the promoters' concern to establish trading posts rather than to plant miniature English societies. Of the two settlements, only one survived. The northern group soon fell to quarrelling among themselves, and by 1609 all had returned to England. The Jamestown group also had a very difficult time, as its members were very ill prepared for their task. Only 38 of the first colonists were still alive at the end of 1607, and the arrival of new batches of recruits in 1608 and 1609 barely managed to keep the settlement going. On these slender foundations, the first English colony was built and took root.

An essential feature of this colonizing project was its character as a trading venture which drew on the experience of overseas commercial expansion during the Elizabethan period. Then, joint-stock companies had become important vehicles for long-distance trades which required relatively large amounts of capital, and these companies had played an important role in developing trade with Russia, the Mediterranean, Turkey and the Far East. They had also been used to finance privateering voyages and, by coupling the pursuit of profit with the nation's war effort, had provided a technique for combining private gain with the aims of royal policy. Thus, when merchants and investors became interested in colonizing ventures, they had at their disposal an institution that was a proven means for promoting long-distance commerce of the kind that colonies were supposed to provide.[10] The Virginia Company also represented a link with earlier English commercial expansion in another respect. It not only employed the same institutional structure developed by English merchants for distant overseas trades, but also drew backing from powerful London merchants involved in the Levant and East India Companies, from whom it drew both capital and leadership. This linkage between English commercial expansion in the east and English colonization in the west was however soon broken. The great London merchants lost interest in the venture when they discovered that it demanded investment in commodity production, rather than offering quick profits from precious metals or trade in furs, and involved competition with merchants outside their control. So, from the mid-1620s, the great mercantile magnates of London retreated from engagement in colonial commerce and left it to other, smaller merchants. It seems that 'the entrepreneurs behind the vital expansionary thrust which put the American trades on a firm foundation were . . . men of the "middling sort" . . . almost always from outside London and by and large the sons of smaller gentry or prosperous yeoman.'[11] Nevertheless, commercial enterprise and capital played a key role in England's renewed drive to colonize in the Americas and conditioned the development of the colonies founded with mercantile support. The joint-stock companies that organized and financed the colony in Virginia (and colonies subsequently founded in the Caribbean) were interested more in trade than land; their desire for a rapid return on their investment meant that the early colonies were quickly pushed towards production of exportable crops. Colonizing companies were not generally a financial success and their survival rate was low. Nonetheless, as a successful tobacco trade blossomed during the 1620s, a new group of merchants without monopoly privileges began to appear, and they played a vital part in providing the capital and organization which were to sustain the colonies in the early years. Indeed, these new men challenged the dominant position of the rich mercantile elite of the City and, amid the political turbulence of the 1640s, were to gain an influence in government which underpinned a more aggressive commercial expansion following the English Civil War.[12]

VIRGINIA: THE FIRST YEARS

The colony established at Jamestown by the Virginia Company was publicly presented as more than just a commercial venture designed solely for private advantage. Organized by a trading company, the colony established at Jamestown in 1607 was launched on a wave of high hopes and pious rhetoric. Its founders drew their ideas from the Elizabethan proponents of English expansion and were accordingly influenced by their models for colonization (models which, in turn, had been strongly influenced by observation of the Spanish experience in the New World). Thus, imitating the Spaniards, they hoped to combine private profit with the purposes of the monarchy, and to merge both with the task of evangelizing native peoples, a mission for which England had allegedly been chosen by Providence. Indeed, such ideas about America in general and Virginia in particular had so penetrated English thinking that they surface in the works of the early seventeenth-century English theatre. The most famous literary reflection of America is found in Shakespeare's *The Tempest* (first performed in 1611), but lesser works made direct allusions to Virginia, which was portrayed as an exotic cornucopia, rich in gold and peopled by Indians who, bedecked in precious ornaments, were ripe for conquest, or at least ready for commerce.[13]

If gold was one powerful magnet for adventurers and investors, the prospect of creating an export agriculture was also an important plank in the company's propaganda, in the tradition of Elizabethan reports which had stressed the region's fertility and its capacity to produce vines, sugar cane, flax and a whole range of Mediterranean crops.[14] This emphasis on immediate returns very nearly destroyed the colony in its first years. Little attention was given to finding food, many colonists died from starvation and, under the leadership of Captain John Smith, the colony survived largely because the local Indian tribes, the very people whom it considered enemies, provided food supplies.[15]

Despite this unpromising start, the Virginia colony endured. In May 1609, the company was reorganized as a joint-stock company owned by some 50 firms and more than 600 individuals; after an intensive publicity campaign, it raised sufficient capital to send another 800 colonists to Jamestown. This fresh infusion of men and money did not immediately solve the colony's problems, however. About half of the new recruits had been shipwrecked en route, and those who arrived were unwilling to work on the company's lands. Without sufficient food supplies and unable to support themselves from agriculture, the people of Jamestown were afflicted by a famine so severe that corpses were allegedly dug up from their graves and eaten. By 1610 the situation was so desperate that an evacuation, organized by Governor Thomas Dale, was prevented only by the arrival of reinforcements under Lord de la Warr. Further reorganization of the company then kept the colony going through years of heavy mortality and continuing failure to find a profitable export crop.[16]

For the first decade of its life, the future of Virginia was delicately balanced, and the venture continually verged on extinction. While the company's capital deteriorated and the local Indians put up unexpected resistance to efforts to expand beyond Jamestown, only the imposition of strict military discipline kept the colony going. By 1618, the English population of Virginia was only about 600 people, and as a business venture the Virginia Company had failed to fulfil the hopes of its promoters and investors. The promise of quick profits had not been realized and the joint-stock company had not shown itself to be as efficient an instrument for colonizing a new land as its proponents had supposed. For, though the colony was rescued from chaos by the imposition of martial law, it was neither profitable to its investors nor attractive to settlers. If it was to become a permanent colony, the Virginia 'plantation' had to attract more investment and settlers; to achieve this, a faction led by Sir Edwin Sandys seized control of the company from within, and set about altering its operations.

Sandys's efforts to raise more capital for company investment in Virginia tobacco production had poor results. His supporters among the English nobility and gentry were as unwilling to provide substantial funds for long-term investment as City merchants had been, for, like the latter, they had better economic opportunities elsewhere. Nevertheless, Sandys implemented two reforms which, together with the introduction of Trinidad tobacco, played an essential part in converting Virginia into a viable colony. After 1614, the company had begun to allow settlers to work their own land; Sandys extended this policy of land grants to groups of investors who were given large tracts (called 'hundreds') to exploit for their own purposes. Individuals could also acquire fifty-acre parcels of land in return for each immigrant carried to the colony (the headright system), and indentured servants were to have land if they survived the four to seven years of service they owed the company. The political regime was altered, too. Martial law was superseded by a charter which brought colonists under English law and allowed them to participate in their own government through the institution of a representative assembly.

These measures did not revive the Virginia Company's flagging fortunes, but they did help to consolidate the colony. Now that private landownership was possible, opportunities to exploit a European market for tobacco attracted fresh investors and immigrants; moreover, since men could now hold land, engage in trade independently of the Virginia Company and govern themselves *in situ*, they became potentially permanent settlers rather than mere employees. Thus settlement spread along the banks of the James and York rivers, away from its narrow base in Jamestown.[17] The authorization of private plantations, effectively managed by their own subsidiary companies, nurtured the development of a series of autonomous settlements or micro-colonies (the 'hundreds') which dispersed the colonizing population over a widening area. The beginnings of a tobacco boom led to a scramble for land and profit, scattering settlers into Indian territories and producing a fragmented society composed of hardened individuals who pursued private profit in preference to community life. Formally, Jamestown remained the political centre of the colony and was the sole legal port, but it did not become a fully fledged commercial city. The trade in tobacco tended to be conducted directly with the riverside plantations; despite official efforts to found towns, there was little semblance of real urbanization in early Virginia.[18]

Under these conditions, the settlers continued to suffer chronic insecurity. Their appropriation of land without regard for the local Indians provoked a native revolt in 1622, in which nearly 350 settlers were killed, but even this tragedy did not convince the settlers of the need to cooperate either with the Indians or among themselves. The scramble for land continued, and in the anxiety to profit from the tobacco trade, basic food supplies were still neglected. Mortality, caused mainly by disease, was extremely high. In 1620, the settler population was close to 900; by 1624, it was still only about 1,275, despite an immigration of more than 3,500 people in the intervening years. Some of the migrants had returned home, but the great majority died in Virginia, mainly from diseases such as typhoid and dysentery, carried by bad water.[19]

The Virginia Company clearly had not succeeded in founding an 'English nation', much less an American utopia. On the contrary, its labours had spawned a deformed society, dedicated to producing what James I called 'that stinking weed' amidst conditions in which most settlers went to an early grave. By the mid-1620s, few of the original leaders of the community remained and, as power increasingly passed to the toughest and most ruthless of the planters, the Virginia Company directors in London found it increasingly difficult to assert their authority. Unable to agree on a coherent policy, they fell out among themselves; after a royal investigation into its affairs, the Virginia Company was dissolved in 1624, and government of the colony was taken over by the crown. For the first time, an English government was forced to accept direct responsibility for governing an

American colony, in circumstances which it would have preferred to have avoided.[20]

By the time that the Virginia Company was dissolved in 1624, Virginia was no longer the only English colony in the Americas. In 1610, a company was established to make permanent English settlement in Newfoundland, for many years simply a haven for fishermen, and the first formal colony on the island was created at Cupid's Cove.[21] More unexpected was the colonization of Bermuda. After the wreck of Sir George Somers's ship carrying supplies to Virginia in 1609 on the shores of this Atlantic island, Bermuda became another focus for English colonization in the Americas. In 1612, 150 members of the Virginia Company formed a subsidiary known as the Somers Island or Bermuda Company; between 1612 and 1616 it sent several hundred settlers to establish and work tobacco plantations on the island. The island colony quickly became a separate enterprise, independent of the Virginia Company but with little more immediate success. Its early years were also plagued by disaffection and contention among the settlers, requiring a reform of government in 1619 similar to that carried out in Virginia. Tobacco cultivation was successfully intro- duced, however, and although this nascent export economy was devastated by a hurricane in 1620, a population of some 1,500 people provided a solid foundation for the survival of a modest colony in Bermuda.[22]

In the long term, this offshoot of the Virginia colony in Bermuda was to be much less important than another settlement that sprang up on the coast of New England some years later. Although the Virginia Company's first attempt to implant a colony on the northern shores of America's Atlantic coast had failed in 1609, the rich fisheries and fur trade of the New England coast continued to attract English traders, and the company did not lose interest in the area. It not only used the coast as a source of food supplies for Jamestown in its lean years, but also sought to preserve its claim to the territory by attacking French settlement in the area. Still employed by the company on his release from responsibilities at Jamestown, Captain John Smith had surveyed the coast in 1614–15, and, impressed by what he saw, both recommended it as a site for future colonization and gave it the name 'New England'. Smith himself never returned to New England, but in 1620 a group of Puritans established a colony in the area, seeking a place where they could practise their religion unmolested by the English church and state.

SETTLEMENT IN NEW ENGLAND

The venture originated in 1617, when a small congregation of English Puritans living in exile in Leiden decided to seek a refuge in America. Known as 'separatists' because they refused any connection with the Church of England and practised an austere form of worship based on a self-chosen and self-disciplining congregation, these Puritans were anxious to find a permanent refuge where they could build a new society. After reaching an agreement with a group of London merchants, they received a 'patent' from the Virginia Company to settle in the Jamestown area. These 'Pilgrims' then joined with others of a similar religious persuasion from London, and in 1620 sailed to Cape Cod, where their ship, the *Mayflower*, landed 101 men, women and children. Later that year, these people founded the colony of New Plymouth, the first permanent settlement in the region which subsequently became known as 'New England'.

Like Jamestown in Virginia, the settlement at Plymouth had a precarious early life. Although it was helped by local Indians, who provided the Pilgrims with food and helped them to plant their first food crops, the tiny community lost half of its number in the first winter. Plymouth weathered this grim experience, however, and, free from any further serious food shortages, its settlers built a self-sufficient community based on farming and fishing, supplemented by some petty trading with the local Indian peoples.

From its first years, Plymouth was a very different colonial society than that established in Virginia. The most striking dissimilarity lay in its settlers' commitment to community and religious goals, rather than the pursuit of individual enrichment. Although differences of religious opinion caused internal frictions and heterodoxy tended to disperse the community away from its original base, unlike the indentured servants and settlers who went to Virginia, Plymouth people sought to create a self-sustaining community based on the family and religious congregation rather than immediate wealth for the individual. For all their early troubles, the Pilgrims were also fortunate in both their location and their leadership. The local Indians was more cooperative than those of Virginia, and as their population had already been depleted by European diseases prior to the Pilgrims' arrival, there was plenty of land for the settlers to cultivate without arousing native antagonism. Furthermore, in William Bradford the Pilgrims had a leader who was firm but fair, and who proved capable of drawing on his people's religious beliefs to hold them together amidst the hardships of the colony's early years.[23] The environment which the

47

Plymouth colonists entered was more benign than that of Virginia in another sense, too. Not only was the challenge from native peoples weaker in New England, but the threat of disease was also less dangerous to the health of immigrant peoples; with low mortality rates, Plymouth's population was more settled and better able to reproduce itself. Plymouth's population nevertheless remained very small. By 1630, it was fewer than about 400 people, because, despite much lower death rates, Plymouth had no exportable commodity which offered quick profits or required workers and thus failed to attract a flow of migrants comparable to that which went to Virginia to work in tobacco cultivation. So, although Plymouth was a more stable transplant of English society in America than was early Virginia, it too fell short of the goals envisaged by English imperialists, at least until this first Puritan colony was reinforced by another, more powerful wave of migration from the mother country.

While the village of Plymouth was growing slowly but steadily during the 1620s, there were a number of other attempts to establish permanent settlements in neighbouring areas of America's North Atlantic coast, on Newfoundland, in Nova Scotia and on the shores of Maine. But it was not until the 1630s that any substantial addition was made to the fragile foundation laid at Plymouth. This growth stemmed from the decision of a number of Puritans from London, East Anglia and the West Country to promote emigration to America, with support from Puritan aristocrats and London merchants. A small settlement had already been established by Puritans at Salem in 1628, and in 1629, the New England Company (initially created to support Salem as a place of religious refuge) was replaced by the Massachusetts Bay Company, a joint-stock company which received a royal charter and obtained rights to land and self-government in New England. In the same year, John Winthrop, a lawyer and lord of the manor at Groton in Suffolk, met with a number of other East Anglian Puritans to discuss emigration to the Americas. They decided that if they were conceded the right to take over the Massachusetts Bay Company's charter and government, they would take their families and belongings to the company's settlement at Salem in New England, re-rooting the company in America. Once this was agreed, Winthrop was duly elected Governor of the company, and in 1630 he sailed to America, followed by nearly 1,000 men, women and children.[24]

This venture was a great departure from precedent. Although organized through a joint-stock company, from the start it provided for self-government in America, rather than from a company base in England. The social and cultural character of the Puritan's project was also markedly different from that organized by the Virginia Company. It was based on family groups, travelling under their own leaders and inspired by religious ideals. Most of the heads of families had paid their own passage and owed no financial obligations to promoters in England. They were, instead, bound together under the leadership of Winthrop who, as Governor of the Massachusetts Bay Company, was to adapt the form of a government of this autonomous company into a basis for a civil order in the colony. This was not to be a democratic form of government. Puritan leaders felt that they had been called by God to establish a new kind of society and they believed in strong government by a chosen few. They were ready to allow political rights to those settlers who subscribed to a religious covenant, but envisaged an essentially theocratic government, led by pastors who guarded the consciences and guided the lives of their congregations.

This highly organized migration launched an extraordinary transplantation of English society to the North American continent. Over the next decade the company encouraged whole congregations to emigrate, and this set in motion a great Puritan exodus, organized by influential church leaders intent on founding a new Jerusalem on the other side of the Atlantic. In little more than a decade (between 1630 and 1642) 20,000 to 25,000 English people moved to New England to settle under the auspices of the Massachusetts Bay Company; as the great majority were farmers, artisans and members of families, they carried with them a social order that was more akin to that of England than was Virginia's unbalanced society, made up from young and unmarried male servants.

So, following the foundation of the Massachusetts Bay Company, the small, rather ill-prepared migration by a tiny community in 1620 turned into a major migratory movement to the Americas. This 'great migration' left its deepest cultural imprint in New England, but it strengthened incipient colonies in other regions too. Puritans and others went in force to the Caribbean islands during the decade after 1630, where between 20,000 and 30,000 English immigrants consolidated the occupation of the Lesser Antilles, begun on a small scale in the 1620s, and thereby laid the foundations of a commercial economy which, like Virginia, produced agricultural commodities for export to Europe.

THE WEST INDIES

The Caribbean had first become a focus for English colonizing activity in the first years of the seventeenth century, when attempts were made to establish permanent agricultural settlements on the northern coasts of South America. Started by Leigh on the banks of the Lower Amazon River in 1604–6, this process continued after Leigh's death when, in 1609, Robert Harcourt made another attempt to colonize the same place. Indeed, Harcourt had even greater ambitions; when at Wiapoco, he formally annexed the vast tract of territory between the Amazon and the Orinoco in the King's name, and was conceded a proprietary grant to this region of 'Guiana'. Like its predecessor, this venture quickly faded for want of financial support. However, when the Spaniards made a determined assault on illegal tobacco trading at Trinidad and Venezuela in 1611–12, English concern to create tobacco-producing colonies in the Amazon region swiftly revived.[25]

Driven by their interest in the tobacco trade, English and Irish projectors set up several small colonies in the Lower Amazon during the next decade, and in 1616 Raleigh made his last, abortive attempt to find the riches that he had long supposed to be somewhere in Guiana. Raleigh's failure cost him his life and El Dorado remained out of reach, but the prospect of colonizing this region continued to tempt speculators. In 1619, Roger North, who had accompanied Raleigh on his last voyage to Guiana, obtained consent to incorporate a company for trading and settling in the Amazon delta and rallied a group of nobles and gentlemen at court to support this 'Amazon Company'. Though it emphasized the planting of crops rather than the search for gold or native kingdoms, the company was suppressed in 1620, for fear that its pretensions would upset negotiations for an Anglo-Spanish dynastic marriage. Nonetheless, English and Irish colonists continued to settle on the banks of the Amazon, as did Dutchmen, much to Spain's annoyance. Such were their numbers that the Spanish government ordered military measures to expel foreigners in 1623, forcing many to leave. Some remained, however, and when Anglo-Spanish relations broke down again after the death of James I, another attempt was made to colonize Guiana. In 1627, Robert Harcourt and Roger North were granted a royal patent of incorporation for a 'Company for the Plantation of Guiana', under the governorship of the Duke of Buckingham, and hopes of creating an English colony in South America briefly revived. Merchants were sceptical, however, and the company withered away for lack of funds, leaving the few remaining English settlers in the Lower Amazon to be finally forced out of the region by the Portuguese in 1632.[26]

In spite of these repeated failures, the Amazon settlements were a significant element in the history of English colonization in the Americas. In them we see the main driving force behind the revival of English colonizing ventures during the early seventeenth century: namely, the interest of English merchants in commercial settlements which would provide a profitable trade in commodities that were not readily available to England. The same motive lay behind the formation of the various companies that obtained royal charters permitting them to colonize the areas of mainland North America and the Caribbean. There, outside the Spanish zone of influence, English merchants and investors tried to create colonies whose products would complement those of the mother country, and provide England with at least some of the riches of the Indies, such as tobacco, dyes and cotton, perhaps even gold or silver. The Amazon settlements were, moreover, to connect directly with another important facet of English colonization in the Americas. From the mouth of the River Amazon, Englishmen found their way to the Lesser Antilles, starting a process of occupation which was eventually to create a chain of English settlements in the islands of the Caribbean.

This process began in 1622, when Sir Thomas Warner, sailing home from the dwindling English tobacco-growing colonies in the Lower Amazon, touched at St Christopher in the Leeward Islands. Convinced that its fertile soils were suitable for tobacco cultivation, Warner raised financial support from a London merchant and returned to St Christopher with a tiny group of colonists in 1624. In 1625, a vessel owned by the Anglo–Dutch Courteen brothers and commanded by John Powell landed on Barbados while on a return journey from Brazil; before returning to England, Powell annexed the island in the name of James I. Two years later, a colonizing expedition arrived in Barbados, organized and financed by Sir William Courteen and backed by the Earl of Pembroke. Under Courteen, colonists were given wages rather than land, in return for producing tobacco which they had to sell to the merchant syndicate. Thus, like early Virginia, Barbados was a colony created by a commercial company, and its first white settlers were company employees rather than pioneering farmers.[27] From these enterprises, there followed a series of island annexations. St Croix in the Virgin Islands was jointly occupied by the English and Dutch in 1625, and between 1628 and 1632 English colonists spread away from their base in St Christopher (more commonly known as St Kitts) to annex the neighbouring islands of Nevis, Antigua and Montserrat. The

French, meanwhile, shared St Kitts with English colonists before beginning their colonization of the Windward Islands during the 1630s, when both English and French settlers 'poured like flies upon the rotting carcase of Spain's empire in the Caribbean', changing it forever.[28]

By 1630, small English colonies were in place at several points on the Atlantic fringes of the North American landmass and, far to the south, in the outer ring of the Caribbean islands. For those who had sought to emulate the Spaniards by finding lands rich in gold and Indians, these nascent colonies were a disappointment. The native populations of the regions occupied by the English were much smaller than those encountered by the Spanish in their principal zones of conquest and colonization, and offered neither gold nor silver with which to finance trade and attract immigrants. Captain John Smith, the pioneering explorer and colonizer, called attention to this vital difference in 1612. In his history of the Virginia Company, Smith doefully compared the Spaniards' good luck to arrive in 'those parts where were infinite numbers of people' who had a plentiful and varied agriculture, as well as gold and silver, with the English colonists' fate in Virginia, where they 'chanced in a land, even as God made it', and had to plant 'such colonies of our own that must first make provision how to live of themselves ere they can bring to perfection the commodities of the country'[29] Thus, however much they wished to do so, English settlers found it impossible to imitate the models created by the Spanish in Peru and Mexico, where bands of conquerors had found highly developed agricultural economies and tributary systems of native states which could be subjugated to sustain settler communities built on the values and practices of the seigneurial society they had known at home. English colonies were founded instead upon the labours of settlers who had to produce their own crops in order to survive, and, outside New England, had to satisfy companies and proprietors eager to profit from their investment.

The basis of the colonies that were established during the first quarter of the seventeenth century was fragile and unstable. At the end of the 1620s, at a time when Iberian America was passing into a stage of economic and political maturity, English America was simply a collection of tiny agrarian communities, numbering only a few thousand inhabitants who scraped a poor living from the soil and contributed little of value to the mother country's commerce. The chartered companies set up to exploit Virginia, Guiana and Newfoundland were all failures, due to the reluctance of the City's corporate merchants and the landed classes to commit sufficient capital to colonizing ventures. This was not because they lacked capital or were economically unsophisticated; it was rather that company merchants preferred to put money into the more profitable southern and eastern trades, while the nobility and gentry concentrated on managing their estates at a time when rising rents brought buoyant returns.

During the late 1620s and the 1630s, the English colonizing movement did become more vigorous, however, for two main reasons. First, merchants from outside the City companies and from relatively obscure backgrounds took up the task of developing plantation production, promoting emigration to the colonies, and organizing colonial commerce in both Virginia and the West Indies. A second stimulus to colonization came from Puritan religious–political dissidents who, faced with increasing difficulties in England, began to see American settlements as outposts for opposition and exile.[30] This combination of forces infused the nascent English empire with a new energy when, during the 1630s, the movement of migrants from England to the Americas suddenly swelled to unprecedented proportions. During this decade, English colonists were drawn to the New World in growing numbers, some lured by the promise of quick wealth, some by a vision of life in congenial Christian communities, and others by the prospect of life in a world where land was plentiful and the hand of government light. From this great migration of English men and women, England's colonies derived substance and permanence, as settlers acquired permanent dominion over American lands and confronted their native inhabitants.

NOTES

1. On Spain's wars, see John Lynch, *Spain under the Hapsburgs*, 2 vols (Oxford, 1965) vol. 2, Chapters 3–4. On Spanish perceptions of decline in the 1620s, and the roots of decay in Castile, see John H. Elliott, *Spain and its World, 1500–1700* (New Haven, Conn., and London, 1989) Part IV

2. On Dutch economic expansion in the seventeenth century, see Jonathan Israel, *Dutch Primacy in World Trade, 1585–1740* (Oxford, 1989) pp. 12–197; Dutch occupation of Brazil is recounted in detail in C.R. Boxer, *The Dutch in Brazil, 1624–1654* (Oxford, 1957).

3. For a detailed exposition of economic conditions in England during these years, see Barry Supple, *Commercial Crisis and Change in England, 1600–1642* (Cambridge, 1959) pp. 23–72.

4. T.K. Rabb, *Enterprise and Empire: Merchant and Gentry Investment in the Expansion of England, 1575–1630* (Cambridge, Mass., 1967) pp. 70–92.

For further analysis of commercial development in the early Stuart period, which links it to the internal transformation of England's agrarian social and property structures, see Robert Brenner, *Merchants and Revolution: Commercial Change, Political Conflict, and London's Overseas Traders, 1550–1653* (Cambridge, 1993) pp. 23–92.

5. W.J. Eccles, *The Canadian Frontier, 1534–1760* (Albuquerque, 1974 edition) especially Chapters 2–3; Marcel Trudel, *The Beginnings of New France, 1524–1663* (Toronto, 1973) Chapters 6–7.

6. David B. Quinn, *England and the Discovery of America, 1481–1620* (London, 1974) Chapter 12.

7. For a summary of these reports, see H.C. Porter, *The Inconstant Savage: England and the North American Indian, 1500–1600* (London, 1979) pp. 265–8.

8. These and other early voyages are recounted in D.B. Quinn and A.M. Quinn (eds) *The English New England Voyages, 1602–1608*, Hakluyt Society, 2nd series, vol.161 (London, 1983) pp. 1–90.

9. Kenneth R. Andrews, *Trade, Plunder and Settlement: Maritime Enterprise and the Genesis of the British Empire, 1480–1630* (Cambridge, 1984) pp. 304–11.

10. Rabb, *Enterprise and Empire*, pp. 26–35.

11. Robert Brenner, 'The social basis of English commercial expansion, 1550–1660', *Journal of Economic History* (1972) **32**: 374–84; quotation from pp. 378–9. For further comment on the sources of capital behind English colonization and early colonial development, see Richard Pares, 'Merchants and planters', *Economic History Review Supplements* (Cambridge, 1960) **4**: 1–12.

12. Brenner, *Merchants and Revolution*, pp. 92–112.

13. Porter, *Inconstant Savage*, pp. 272–5, for a description of *Eastward Ho*, performed in 1604, and the *Masque of the Indian Princess*, performed at Whitehall in 1614. On *The Tempest*, see Leo Marx, *The Machine in the Garden: Technology and the Pastoral Ideal in America* (New York, 1964), Chapter 2.

14. D.W. Meinig, *The Shaping of America: A Geographical Perspective on Five Hundred Years of History; Volume I: Atlantic America, 1492–1800* (New Haven, Conn., London, 1986) p. 145.

15. For a fully documented account of the early years of Jamestown, see Philip L. Barbour (ed) *The Jamestown Voyages under the First Charter, 1606–1609*, 2 vols, Hakluyt Society, 2nd series, vols 136–7 (Cambridge, 1969).

16. On Virginia's first decade, see Edmund S. Morgan, *American Slavery, American Freedom: The Ordeal of Colonial Virginia* (New York, 1975) pp. 71–91; also Wesley Frank Craven, *The Southern Colonies in the Seventeenth Century* (1949, Baton Rouge, La, 1970 edition), pp. 60–138.

17. James R. Perry, *The Formation of Society on Virginia's Eastern Shore, 1615–1655* (Chapel Hill, NC, and London, 1990) pp. 17–19.

18. This remained true of Virginia throughout the seventeenth century: see John W. Reps, *Tidewater Towns: City Planning in Colonial Virginia and Maryland* (Charlottesville, Va, 1972).

19. Carville V. Earle, 'Environment, disease and mortality in early Virginia', in Thad W. Tate and David L. Ammermann (eds) *The Chesapeake in the*

Seventeenth Century: Essays in Anglo-American Society (Chapel Hill, NC, 1979) pp. 96–125. For population figures, see Table 4, p. 119.

20. Morgan, *American Slavery, American Freedom*, pp. 92–138; Craven, *The Southern Colonies*, pp. 138–49. For a useful brief introduction to early Virginia, see T.H. Breen, *Puritans and Adventurers: Change and Persistence in Early America* (New York and Oxford, 1980) pp. 106–26. On the weakness of the church in early Virginia, see John Parke, 'Religion and the Virginia colony, 1609–10', in K.R. Andrews, N.P. Canny and P.E.H. Hair (eds), *Westward Enterprise: English Activities in Ireland, the Atlantic and America, 1480–1650* (Liverpool, 1978) pp. 245–70.

21. For a detailed review of early English colonies in Newfoundland, see Gillian T. Cell, *Newfoundland Discovered: English Attempts at Colonisation, 1610–1630*, Hakluyt Society, 2nd series, vol. 160 (London, 1982) pp. 1–10.

22. On early Bermuda, see Charles M. Andrews, *The Colonial Period of American History*, 4 vols (New Haven, Conn., and London, 1964 edition) vol. 1, pp. 214–35. The island's population grew quickly, but was always small: in 1628, it was 2,000, in 1656, 3,000, and in 1679, about 6,000. Also see Virginia Bernhard, 'Bermuda and Virginia in the seventeenth century: a comparative view', *Journal of Social History* (1985) **19**: 57–70.

23. On the Puritans who went to Plymouth and the early years of the settlement, see George D. Langdon, *Pilgrim Colony: A History of New Plymouth, 1620–1691* (New Haven, Conn., 1966) pp. 1–68. For a contemporary account and major historical source, see William T. Davis (ed) *Bradford's History of the Plymouth Plantation, 1606–1648* (repr. New York, 1964) Book 2.

24. Edmund S. Morgan, *The Puritan Dilemma: The Story of John Winthrop* (Boston, Mass., and Toronto, 1958) pp. 3–68.

25. Joyce Lorimer, 'The English contraband tobacco trade in Trinidad and Guiana, 1560–1617', in Andrews, Canny and Hair (eds) *Westward Enterprise*, pp. 124–50.

26. The best account of Amazon settlement is given in Joyce Lorimer (ed) *English and Irish Settlement on the River Amazon, 1550–1646*, Hakluyt Society, 2nd series, vol. 171 (London, 1989) pp. 1–125.

27. Vincent T. Harlow, *A History of Barbados, 1625–1685* (repr. New York, 1969) pp. 1–13.

28. A.P. Newton, *The European Nations in the West Indies, 1493–1688* (repr. London, 1966) p. 149.

29. John Smith, 'Description of Virginia and proceedings of the colonie', in Lyon G. Tyler (ed) *Narratives of Early Virginia* (New York, 1907) p. 178.

30. Brenner, *Merchants and Revolution*, pp. 113–59.

CHAPTER THREE

Migrants and Settlers

By 1630, the English had created several small niches of settlement in the Americas: Virginia in the Chesapeake Bay region, the Plymouth colony in New England, a few tiny fishing villages in Newfoundland, and some very small colonies in Bermuda and the islands of the eastern Caribbean. Of these, Virginia had attracted the largest number of English migrants, mostly servants taken there to provide labour for planters in the tobacco boom of the 1620s. But even this, England's largest colony in the Americas at this time, had only a tiny population, due to the high mortality of newcomers and the tendency of survivors to return to England. Thus, although about 8,500 immigrants moved to Virginia in the 1620s, to add to the 700 settlers already there, by 1630 the population was still only around 3,000 people. In the north, New England had around 1,800 inhabitants, and Newfoundland no more than a couple of hundred. The island colonies of the Caribbean, in Barbados and the Leeward Islands had about 3,000 English settlers between them, while the Atlantic island of Bermuda had another 2,000. So, two decades after the foundation of England's first settlement at Jamestown, there were fewer than 10,000 surviving English colonists in the whole of the Americas.[1]

THE 'GREAT MIGRATION'

In the decade after 1630, this exiguous pattern of settlement was transformed by a 'great migration' from England. Between 1630 and 1642 (before the outbreak of Civil War in England disrupted transatlantic migration), tens of thousands of English men, women and children left their homes to move overseas. It is impossible to measure precisely the scale of this migration, but it is likely that about 50,000 people went to the Americas, with possibly another 20,000 going to Ireland. Of migrants to the Americas, around 30,000 went to North America, to the two small but established colonies in Virginia and New England. Of these, about 21,000 went to the new Puritan colony of Massachusetts, founded in 1630, and to its adjoining areas. A lesser but nonetheless substantial flow of about 10,000 people went to the Chesapeake during the same period. Some were Puritans, who formed small but strong local enclaves of free farmers; most were male indentured servants taken to work on Virginian tobacco plantations. This migration increased the Chesapeake population, though on a lesser scale than in New England, since the adverse disease environment of the tidewater areas continued to cause high mortality among settlers. By 1640, the Chesapeake population was no more than 8,000 to 9,000 people, while that of New England was as high as 25,000. Thus the earlier demographic balance of the colonies was reversed, with New England suddenly becoming England's most populous colony in North America. This shift to the north was, however, counter-balanced by impressive growth in the English Caribbean islands, which, from their colonization in the late 1620s, swiftly became a major destination for migrants. More than 20,000 migrants went to the Caribbean islands during the 'great migration' and by 1640 Barbados and the Leeward Islands had over 31,000 inhabitants. If we add to these figures the smaller populations of lesser centres of colonization (in Bermuda, Providence Island and Newfoundland), we find that the English settler population in the Americas had expanded sevenfold between 1630 and 1640, from around 10,000 to nearly 70,000 people. What, then, were the reasons for this sudden mass migration, this 'swarming of the English'? Where did the emigrants come from, how was their migration organized, and how did it develop its extraordinary momentum?

A major force propelling the first great wave of migration in the 1630s was economic and social dislocation in England. Many emigrants came from areas where large sectors of the population were suffering distress due to the decline of the cloth industry, unemployment on the land, rising prices, and, in some areas, epidemic disease. But economic depression in England is only a partial explanation for the exodus to the Americas. Religious and political divisions within English society also played their part. During the reign of Charles I (1625–42), Puritans were harassed by the official church in England and by governments that tended to identify Puritanism with opposition to the crown; this, combined with despair over Catholic military successes against continental Protestants, undoubtedly helped to persuade some Puritans to emigrate, especially to Massachusetts. Indeed, some Puritans were convinced that human history had entered the last days before the second coming of Christ; they saw America as a place provided by Providence to save the 'saints' from the imminent cataclysm. Thus the Puritan migration responded to a changing and disordered society in England, and the search for social stability which it embodied not only encouraged its adherents to emigrate during the 1630s, but also was to fuel political conflict in England during the 1640s.[2]

Once in motion, the outflow from seventeenth-century England was promoted and facilitated by systematic organization of emigration. As colonies took firm roots, companies and other entrepreneurs increased their efforts to encourage emigration, both to meet demands for labour and to strengthen existing settler communities. The strong flow of migration towards Massachusetts was advanced by the organizational skill of Winthrop and his associates, by their ability to use their contacts among the Puritan gentry and clergy to recruit new settlers in Britain, and by colonists who encouraged kinsfolk to follow them from England. Virginia and the Caribbean islands, meanwhile, relied less on such family migration and more on recruiting servants, providing free passage in return for labour service over periods of between four and seven years. This movement acquired added momentum when successful settlers invested their own funds in order to acquire workers for their tobacco plantations. Indeed, migration became a trade in itself, in which merchants, shipowners and colonial entrepreneurs collaborated to persuade people from different sectors of English society that they might find a better living, even make their fortunes, in the New World.

BRITISH MIGRATION TO THE AMERICAS: GENERAL CHARACTERISTICS

Two basic types of migration developed during the 'great migration', setting a pattern that was to persist throughout the remainder of the colonial period.[3] The largest group of migrants were unfree labourers or indentured servants, bound by a contract or 'indenture' to work for a certain number of years. Broadly speaking, the poorer kind of emigrant, both male and female, went to the Americas under this arrangement. Contracts were drawn up in England or arranged on arrival, and then sold for money or land to established merchants or planters in the colonies, who thereby acquired the right to the servant's labour for the number of years specified in the indenture. This was not an entirely novel form of labour contract, but an adaption of the English system of apprenticeship and customary annual hirings of servants. It did, however, have one special feature. In most cases, indentured servants were promised land and sometimes money and equipment at the end of their term, so that they might become permanent settlers.[4]

The movement of indentured servants started early, to meet Virginia's need for labour when tobacco cultivation was established in the 1620s. It then assumed larger dimensions during the 1630s, when the growth of the tobacco economy drew large numbers of servants to Virginia and the English Caribbean islands. This pattern persisted in the Chesapeake region, where more than 75 per cent of all migrants during the seventeenth century were contracted workers, mostly young, single males. Indentured servants of a similar kind also formed a very high proportion of migrants to the British Caribbean, especially before about 1660, when the planters of the West Indies began increasingly to buy black slaves for labour to work their burgeoning sugar plantations. During the seventeenth century as a whole, 'unfree' migrants probably constituted about 60 per cent of all British emigrants to the Anglo-American colonies.[5]

The second, smaller category of migrants was composed of free people, sometimes known as 'planters', who were unencumbered by contracts to labour for others, paid their own passage, took families and sometimes servants and retainers with them, and either bought or were granted land in the place of their settlement. During the 'great migration' such people usually went to New England, with whole households, even groups from parishes in the same town or village, arriving and settling together.[6] Some Puritan 'free' migrants of this kind also arrived in the Chesapeake region in the 1630s, where they established small but strong communities. There, however, they were a small minority, greatly outnumbered by indentured servants, who continued to form the overwhelming majority of immigrants to this region throughout the seventeenth century.

Nonetheless, we should not overlook the Chesapeake's free settlers, because, while indentured servants provided most of the labour force, they brought capital which helped develop the region's economy and infrastructure.[7] 'Free' migration became more common later in the seventeenth century, when new colonies were founded in the mid-latitudes of North America at New York, Pennsylvania and New Jersey, and when the proprietors of these colonies sought to attract settlers by offering them lands to farm.

Aside from the distinction between 'unfree' and 'free' migration, some other broad characteristics of seventeenth-century migration to the Anglo-American colonies deserve attention. The first was the large scale of migration from metropolis to colonies. Approximately 400,000 people left England for the American colonies during the seventeenth century, more than half of whom went to the Caribbean. This was one of the largest migrations from Europe to newly formed colonies, comparable to that from Spain in 1500–1650, when between 395,000 and 438,000 Spaniards migrated to the Americas, and far larger than migration from France to the Americas. It also involved a higher ratio of emigrants to domestic population, almost twice as high as that of Spain in 1500–1650. Thus, in the first century of forming its colonies, Britain contributed a larger proportion of its native population to peopling the Americas than did other nations. During the eighteenth century, Britain continued to make a much larger contribution than did Spain, though then it was Portugal that sent the highest proportion of domestic population to the Americas, with the extraordinary exodus of about a fifth of its 2 million people to Brazil.[8]

The regional origins of migrants from Britain altered over the course of the seventeenth century. Among the 400,000 or so emigrants from the British Isles who went to the Americas, the majority were from England, rather than Scotland or Wales. During the 'great migration' of the 1630s, they came mostly from East Anglia, the West Country and the south of England. The Puritan migration to Massachusetts was in great part from East Anglia; before mid-century, between 80 and 90 per cent of indentured servants who went to the Chesapeake left from London and were probably mostly drawn from London and the Home Counties.[9] Of the origins of migrants to the West Indies, less is known, but most were probably from the west and south of England. Later, during the latter half of the seventeenth century and in the early eighteenth century, migration changed in both its destinations and sources. Then, most migrants went to North America rather than to the Caribbean, and other British regions made larger contributions. In the second major wave of migration to the Americas, between c.1642 and 1675, emigrants came largely from the English south and west. Between c.1675 and 1725, there was a strong movement from the north Midlands and Wales to the Delaware Valley, while in the sixty or so years after c.1718, most of the people who left the British Isles for America went from north Britain and northern Ireland, in another major phase of migration of more than 300,000 people. These shifts were to have a profound influence on the kinds of society that developed in the American colonies. In North America, they produced a pattern of regional cultures which, according to David H. Fischer, affected society and politics long after British rule had ended.[10] We shall return to these later streams of migration and the colonial societies later, when discussing the development of North America after the English Civil War.

Because migration occurred over such a protracted period and involved people from different areas in the British Isles (as well as from other parts of Europe), it is difficult to generalize about its social character. If, however, we compare British and Iberian colonization in the New World, certain general features stand out. First, few migrants were drawn from the highest ranks of society. Although several colonial schemes were patronized by members of the aristocracy, the number of noblemen who went to America was slight. Like the Spanish and Portuguese nobility, English aristocrats were very under-represented among the groups migrating to the Americas, for reasons which are easy to understand. The lesser nobility and the gentry, on the other hand, played an active and important part in early colonization. 'Gentlemen' financed and organized the companies that were instrumental in mounting colonial ventures; some, particularly the less well-off, went personally to the New World, where they provided leadership and set up their own 'plantations'. The Puritan clergymen who were prominent among such community leaders in New England were often themselves from this class of lesser gentry, with an ingrained belief in the hierarchical nature of society. Rather like the *hidalgos* (Castilian gentlemen) who were so important in the formation of early Spanish American colonial society, the English gentry seem to have played a part in shaping early Anglo-American society that was out of proportion to their numbers. As for the mass of migrants who left no records of their lives and activities, we know relatively little. It seems that they were drawn from the whole spectrum of English society, with a tendency (similar to that found among migrants to early Spanish America) for people from the top and bottom of the social hierarchy to make proportionately small contributions, compared to the 'middle classes' of farmers, artisans and skilled workers.

There were, on the other hand, some notable differences between migrations to the Hispanic and Anglo-American colonies. In the first place, although most Europeans who emigrated to the Americas were driven by economic aspirations or needs, migrants to the British

61

colonies entered into a social setting which was very different from that encountered by Spaniards. In Spanish America, Indians provided a plentiful supply of labour, supplemented or substituted when necessary by African slaves. There was consequently no need to organize a flow of dependent 'unfree' labour from the mother country, and immigrants in Spanish America were free of the kinds of obligations that bound the majority of English migrants. A second difference arose from the inclusion of relatively large numbers of women and children in the total flow of migrants to the Anglo-American colonies. While indentured servants tended to be young, single and male, migrants to British America included a higher proportion of women, usually as wives in established families. During the early phases of conquest and colonization, women and families were rare among Spanish migrants; although the proportion of female emigrants increased during the second half of the sixteenth century (about 28 per cent of all migrants were women in 1560–79), it seems to have fallen off during the seventeenth century.[11] Indeed, the dynamics of population growth in the Spanish colonies were quite different from those of Anglo-America. For, when the English were establishing their settler societies in the Americas, Spanish America already had substantial groups of *mestizos*, born of Spanish males and Indian women; these people of mixed race were to become substantial, sometimes preponderant, elements in the Spanish American societies of the eighteenth century. French and Dutch migrants to the Americas also tended to be mainly young, single males.[12] Anglo-American migration, by contrast, included larger numbers of women, particularly to New England during the 'great migration' and to the Middle Atlantic colonies during the late seventeenth and eighteenth centuries. Some were wives, emigrating with their husbands and children; many were single women who went to work as servants or travelled with the expectation of marriage in the colonies.

Migrants from Britain to the Americas were, then, a heterogeneous assortment. People emigrated from several regions, were impelled by distinctive motives, and left England in different circumstances, depending on age, gender, marital status, material position and religious beliefs. These factors not only influenced their destination in the New World, but also affected their behaviour when they arrived. Furthermore, when they arrived at their destinations, they encountered radically different physical environments which, interacting with variations in the character and culture of the immigrants, were to contribute to considerable diversity among Anglo-American colonial societies. Beneath their variations, however, two distinct patterns of

English colonization took consolidated form during the 'great migration' of the 1630s: one was in New England, the other in the Chesapeake Bay region and in the Caribbean islands. The latter regions both took large numbers of indentured servants, mainly young, unmarried males drawn from the lower ranks of society. Those who went to New England, on the other hand, were more likely to be inspired by religious zeal, and to be leaving England permanently in protest against the character of its church and state. Their migrations were usually carefully planned and organized, included a much higher proportion of married men accompanied by their women and children, and were more likely to be drawn from the ranks of small, independent farmers and artisans.[13] We shall now look more closely at English–American migration before the mid-seventeenth century, and identify the salient features of the societies that it engendered.

NEW ENGLAND

The most striking development of the period before mid-century was undoubtedly the emergence of New England as a major region for settlement, due largely to the foundation and growth of the Massachusetts Bay colony. In 1629, the region's English population was less than 1,000, focused on Plymouth and Salem. By 1640, it had grown to at least 13,500 and was possibly as high as 25,000, having received the majority of English people who went to North America during the 'great migration'.[14]

Historians have long debated whether this migration was primarily the result of economic hardship or religious dissent; in practice, however, it is difficult to separate these causes clearly and we must remember that individual decisions were strongly influenced by local factors, such as the quality of Puritan leadership, kinship and social ties, and the physical location of migrants.[15] On the one hand, the Puritan migration to Massachusetts was undoubtedly of an extraordinary kind, stamped with the character of a Christian exodus and conceived in the biblical terms of creating a new Zion in America. For most of the emigrants, religion was a powerful motive for emigration; though the religious impulse took different forms, it was the cradle of New England culture, marking it off from other major colonial regions of the English American world. Leaders of the Massachusetts Bay colony, notably John Winthrop, were inspired by the notion of creating an entirely new society, a 'Bible Commonwealth' that would be a model to the rest of the world. This vision is clearly communicated in Winthrop's famous injunction to his followers, that

> We must consider that we shall be as a City upon a Hill, so that if we deal falsely with our god in this work we have undertaken and so cause him to withdraw his present help from us, we shall be made a story and a byword throughout the world.[16]

Religion was not the sole impulse behind migration, however, nor was it necessarily the strongest influence on the formation of social institutions in the nascent New England colony. The emigrants to Massachusetts Bay were undoubtedly concerned with their own spiritual welfare, rather than with ambitions for converting heathens or acting as an example to a corrupted Europe, and were moved by a characteristically Puritan sense of personal spiritual aspiration. The majority belonged to community churches which, by demanding strict adherence to severe Calvinist doctrines and modes of behaviour, deeply influenced the life of the nascent colony. Furthermore, the colonists were not thrown together as a group of random migrants. The General Court of Massachusetts chose its colonists carefully, sometimes demanding proof of good character, and expelling those who did not conform to its rigorous standards.[17] But, Timothy Breen has argued, the colonists' ideas about social order were also shaped by their experience of political life in England and by the customs of the localities which they left behind. Under Charles I, the innovations of a government bent on strengthening central power, both civil and ecclesiastical, made new inroads into the life of civil communities and dissenting congregations, and thereby threatened the long-established autonomy of local communities in England. The response of the New England migrants to such changes was 'essentially defensive, con-servative, even reactionary' and, determined to recreate a traditional way of life, they exalted the independent community when they arrived in America and enlarged the scope of political participation within it. This, it has been suggested, owed more to their concern with 'averting absolutism' than to any desire to create an ideal 'Puritan commonwealth'.[18]

For all these caveats, the Puritan migration to Massachusetts undoubtedly carried a very specific kind of community from England to the New World. It was, in the first place, drawn largely from East Anglia and composed largely of entire family groups.[19] It was also unusual in other respects. While most migrants to seventeenth-century Anglo-America were young people, those to Massachusetts were generally either mature people of over 25, or children of less than 16 years of age. Indeed, although they included few people over 60, the age structure of the migrants was very similar to that of the English society which they had left. Women also formed a much larger contingent than in other migrations to the Americas. About two-thirds of emigrants to the Massachusetts Bay colony were women, a gender ratio that contrasts strongly with that of other regions of Euro-America. We have no exact figures for the numbers of women who took part in migration to the Americas from Spain and Portugal, but we can be sure that the proportions were much lower. So, too, were the numbers of women who went to Virginia, which received about six men for every woman in the mid-1630s, and to the Caribbean islands, where the ratio was about fourteen to one in the same years.[20] Unlike most of the English migrants to Virginia and the West Indies, the New England cohorts were not poor people, but in the main were farmers, traders and artisans from the middle ranks of society, mostly skilled and literate people from urban backgrounds. They were, in short, 'a people of substance, character and deep personal piety'.[21]

The first influx of migrants in 1630 created Boston and a network of small towns in its vicinity; continuing immigration and successful farming subsequently spread settlement along the coast and into the valleys and lowlands of its internal hinterland. Expansion was driven by the sheer numbers of immigrants seeking land, and by the tendency of congregations of new settlers to seek separate sites rather than joining existing settlements. It was later reinforced by the high rate of reproduction among settlers who had a very high rate of marriage, tended to produce large numbers of surviving children, and, untroubled by epidemics, often had relatively long lives. From this rapidly growing demographic base, the spatial extension of settlement was facilitated by three factors. The first was the low density of the Indian population, which, having already been much reduced by high mortality from epidemic diseases introduced by Europeans, gave room for largely unopposed territorial expansion. Another factor behind the spread of settlement arose from the ideological divisiveness of Puritans. Dissensions over religious and political issues tended to split communities, spawning breakaway sects which struck out into new areas to establish their own settlements. Finally, when pressure for land later became more intense, Puritan populations had few scruples about using force against the surviving natives, in order to open new space for settlement.[22]

The first major movement away from Massachusetts Bay took place in 1635, when groups of people pushed into the Connecticut Valley, either in search of furs to trade, fertile land to farm, or space to escape the oppressive rules laid down by the Puritan oligarchy of the Massachusetts Bay towns. Several new towns were quickly founded in Connecticut, and they promoted further movement on the inland frontier.[23] The propensity of the early settlements to reproduce themselves, in cellular fashion, was further reflected in the emergence of villages and towns in and around Narragansett Bay. Here, the momentum came from religious dissenters. In 1636, the Puritan minister Roger Williams established a settlement at Providence, together with supporters who followed him after his expulsion from the town of Salem. In 1638, two other religious dissenters, Anne Hutchinson and William Coddington, also split with the Puritan 'saints' in Massachusetts and founded their own town at Portsmouth; this then bifurcated when Coddington removed to found a town at Newport. The colonization of Rhode Island was further advanced in 1643, when the self-appointed preacher Samuel Gorton broke with Massachusetts town government and took his followers to establish the town of Warwick; later, in 1657, these dissenting groups were reinforced by the arrival of groups of Quakers who subsequently won converts among the settlers and thereby reinforced the colony's deviance from the Puritans of Massachusetts. Thus the settlements of Rhode Island were founded without authorization from a parent colony and without the support of either proprietors or merchants, and stemmed primarily from repudiation of the Massachusetts Bay communities' efforts to enforce conformity of religious belief and practice.[24] A third exodus from Massachusetts led to the development of New Haven, on the mainland of Long Island Sound and the region that lay around it. The principal motive for this movement was economic, since these were areas peopled by immigrants who found no suitable space for themselves elsewhere. Meanwhile, despite these movements away from Massachusetts, the Bay area remained the core of New England, with its major port, its largest population and its most prosperous and influential inhabitants.

The leaders of Massachusetts had arrived in 1630 with a royal charter that allowed them to construct a self-governing common-wealth, without intervention or supervision from England. Inspired by a desire to put their religious sentiments into practice and to preserve their churches against interference, community leaders consciously sought to create a new state, a 'New England' without the uncer-tainties and instability of old England. Such clarity of vision and strong sense of purpose allowed a firm structure of political and social order to emerge quickly and naturally, without direction from outside. Among Puritans, the first priority was to form an independent congregation of believers who agreed on fundamental religious issues and were ready to live and work together as a Christian community with shared ideals, closed off from the corruptions of the outside world. Composed of like-minded people who had joined together willingly, these communities had a firm basis for cooperation under their church leaders, and those who denied their authority were either expelled, or left of their own accord.[25]

The earliest unit of New England settlement was the nucleated village or town, where families were granted land on which to build a house and cultivate their subsistence, together with rights to share in common pastures and woodlands. Land grants were not of equal size, but depended on the status of community members and the size of their households. Some towns, such as New Haven, were formally laid out on a grid plan, but this was exceptional. Most simply adapted to the local landscape, with the first houses clustered in a village where the church or assembly hall served as a symbolic centre. Some, like Andover, retained this focused form, with community members working adjoining land that was organized in the open-field system still found in parts of early seventeenth-century England. Other settlements were less concentrated; as population grew and farming extended beyond the boundaries of the village, families dispersed into the countryside where they lived on their farms. While settlement did not fit a single, uniform pattern, Puritan settlers generally tended to cluster together in towns and adjacent neighbourhoods rather than disperse over the countryside, reflecting the habits and traditions of settlement in East Anglia, from which the majority of the first colonists came. This pattern also reflected the values of people whose religious beliefs intensified the importance of family and kin, and prescribed an ideal of life in orderly, self-regulating and fraternal communities which would nurture piety and preserve a stable and disciplined social order.

Sustaining this society was an agricultural economy which combined arable and animal husbandry in ways similar to those found in the English source communities. Several towns divided land into open fields for arable, and most had common pastures for grazing, thus looking back to customs which were under pressure from economic change in the mother country. The family farm with enclosed fields soon became the predominant unit of production, however, and farmers used an imported agrarian technology that rested on the use of the heavy English plough. Economic life initially offered little scope for the accumulation of great fortunes, as most markets for agricultural products were local. At its inception, New England was not in any case a capitalistic society, driven by the pursuit of profit. It is, perhaps, best described as 'an old-fashioned system of agricultural production, domestic industry and commercial exchange which bore the impress of East Anglian customs and Calvinist beliefs'. Such activity sustained communities which were much less economically and socially stratified than those of contemporary England and, for all the influence of English traditions, the Puritan settlements deviated from their past in one vital and deliberate way. Property and power were not concentrated in the hands of a few great families and, though the Puritans were certainly not social egalitarians, they decided to eliminate the highest and lowest rankings of the mother country. 'The result was a social revolution which . . . rose from religious ideals and social purposes of the founders.' In the absence of deep divisions of wealth and class, local influence rested on age and moral authority rather than on economic privilege or claims to nobility, which were explicitly repudiated.[26]

THE CHESAPEAKE BAY COLONIES: VIRGINIA AND MARYLAND

During the years when the remarkable society of New England was emerging, a different kind of social order was continuing to develop in the other principal area of colonization in English North America, in the region of Chesapeake Bay. There, population growth continued during the years of the Puritan migration to New England, but at a much less rapid pace. Between 1629 and 1640, Virginia's population tripled, from around 3,000 to roughly 8,500. This was a relatively slight growth compared to the population explosion in New England, but was nonetheless a demographic expansion that created a solid economic and political foundation for the later, larger migration from England to Virginia during the decades after 1640.

Population grew comparatively slowly in Virginia during the 1630s for two main reasons. First, Massachusetts was much more attractive to Puritans than the royal colony of Virginia, where the Church of England, which Puritans distrusted or abhorred, demanded conformity with Anglican religious practice.[27] More important, however, was the fact that migrants to Virginia were less successful in reproducing themselves: they were mainly single males, and suffered a heavy mortality from disease. Between 1625 and 1640 immigration into Virginia averaged about 1,000 per year, mostly indentured servants destined for work in tobacco cultivation, but death rates from maladies nurtured in the hot, humid summers of the Chesapeake cut a swathe through the newcomers. Thus, although some 15,000 immigrants arrived in Virginia in this period, they died off rapidly, and the population could be sustained only by continuing immigration.[28]

Government in Virginia differed notably from that of Massachusetts. Following Virginia's conversion into a royal colony in 1624, it was controlled by the crown rather than by a company. The King appointed a governor and council which ruled the colony in conjunction with an elected assembly. This assembly, first instituted by the Virginia Company, met informally and irregularly for many years, until it was formally recognized by the crown in 1629. Then, Charles I instructed the governor to call a representative assembly every year, and accepted that the assembly should play a role in the colony's affairs. In practice, however, the assembly was much weaker than the council, which was composed largely of rich tobacco farmers who were determined to protect and promote their own interests. While the council became a powerful local oligarchy that was capable of nullifying the authority of royal governors, prominent planters also controlled local administration, which was organized on the English model. The main unit of government was the county, whose court and sheriff enforced legislation, dealt with the less serious civil and criminal cases, collected taxes, and supervised elections. Below the county stood the parish, whose officers generally included the leading gentlemen of the area. Through the parish vestry, the gentry discharged an important function in enforcing the law at the local level, under the authority of the county court and assembly.[29] Indeed, during the seventeenth century, the parish became a crucial unit of both church and civil administration in Virginia, exceeding its English model in two respects. First, without an ecclesiastical hierarchy dominated by resident bishops, the Virginian parish was free of central control; second, the parish vestrymen acquired considerable power in the local affairs of both church and civil society, not only selecting ministers but also collecting tithes which were often larger than taxes raised by civil government.[30]

Despite the precipitious collapse of tobacco prices in 1630, economic life in Virginia continued to depend on tobacco. Planters reacted to the end of the boom by trying to restrict production, so that prices would be forced back to higher levels. The halcyon days of the 1620s were not recovered, however, and by 1642 the scheme had been abandoned. In another respect, Virginian agriculture was more successful. While the continuing cultivation of tobacco opened up new lands, the colonists also became better at producing their own subsistence. By sowing corn and keeping livestock, they produced provisions sufficient to feed the region's population and even to export a small surplus of cattle to Barbados. Their agricultural techniques were generally primitive. Rather than creating an ordered landscape of permanent fields, ploughed and manured to maintain their fertility, the settlers simply cleared the land of trees, planted it for a few years and then, when the soil was exhausted, moved on to uncultivated land.[31]

With such an open frontier for expansion, land held little value as property and the colony had a rather impermanent air, very different from that of Massachusetts. As the population grew, it straggled out over an increasingly wide area, out of proportion to its small numbers, spreading over the tidewater shores of the great estuary of Chesapeake Bay and westwards into the interior, along the James River and the other rivers that flowed into the Bay. Such spatial extension of settlement was further encouraged by the 'headright' system, whereby grants of land were given for every person brought to Virginia, a system that evolved into the concept that all indentured servants should receive a grant of fifty acres when they had completed their term of service. Appropriation of the land was not unopposed: the Indians who had been brought together in a confederacy by the chief Powhatan continued to resist encroachments on their lands after his death. The white advance was relentless, however, and after the massacre of whites in 1622, continuing conflict and harassment constantly eroded Indian numbers. As the Indians were pushed out of the coastal area, they were replaced by a rudimentary rural society. Insubstantial timber houses were scattered over the countryside; even the large planters had only small wooden dwellings to house themselves, their indentured servants and their tobacco crops. Few colonists lived in towns. Mid-century Jamestown, the capital, was a dilapidated place, for the tobacco economy had engendered a series of storehouses on the estuary rather than commercial towns.

Here, then, was a society which historians have long characterized as strikingly different from the settlements in New England. The difference derived from the character of the migrants and the setting in which they lived and worked. Virginia, it is said, attracted a particular type of English colonist, eager for economic opportunity and 'extraordinarily individualistic, fiercely competitive, and highly materialistic'.[32] Successful cultivation of tobacco then reinforced these values, for it not only enabled individuals to get rich quickly, but also undermined community by dispersing settlement.

This picture of a harshly competitive and materialist society, weak in its social institutions, has to some extent been modified by recent research. Before mid-century, Virginian agriculture diversified into arable and pastoral farming for local markets and wealth became rather more evenly distributed. Population growth also allowed for rather more concentrated settlement and this, together with the cultivation of kinship ties by people defending themselves from the constant ravages of death from disease, may have helped create a more stable and integrated society during the 1630s.[33] But if Virginia had lost its initially frenetic, 'get-rich-quick' atmosphere by the mid-seventeenth century, it was nonetheless still an immigrant society shaped more by individual acquisitiveness and competition than by any strong sense of community or shared religious and political values.

A significant development in the Chesapeake Bay region during these years was the creation of an entirely new colony north of Virginia, in Maryland. In its conception and early development, Maryland differed from Virginia. The colony originated with George Calvert, the first Baron Baltimore, who, after an abortive attempt to found a colony in Newfoundland in 1627, had visited Virginia in 1629 and conceived the idea of an American refuge for English Catholics.[34] His son, Cecilius Calvert, second Baron Baltimore, was given a grant of territory north of the Potomac River, and, calling it 'Mariland' in honour of Queen Mary, he sent two hundred people, led by his younger brother Leonard, to plant the first colony at St Mary's in 1634.

In fact, the colony was not exclusively reserved for Catholics; more Protestants than Catholics settled in its territory, and its government made a conscious effort at religious tolerance. Maryland was, nonetheless, a unique colony, with a political and legal status that differed substantially from those of other North American colonies. Baltimore's royal charter not only made him the proprietor and governor of the territory, but also endowed him with the powers of a medieval English frontier lord, able to dispense justice and administration independently of the King, and to grant land in feudal style. By using these powers, Baltimore intended to create a strongly hierarchical social order, based on a system of manors and manorial courts of a kind long in decay in England. Thus Maryland was something of a utopian project, designed to remake in the New World a society and religion which were rapidly being effaced in the mother country.

To underpin his social design, Baltimore sought to avoid the 'starving time' which had been experienced in early Virginia. He insisted that the small groups of first settlers should produce for their own subsistence and maintain good relations with the local Indians. When they had secured their own food supply, the settlers were then able to turn to tobacco planting, so that they might sustain trade with England. Baltimore's plans to create a feudal social order were, however, largely frustrated. Large landed estates were created, with lords of the manor and manorial courts, but they were rarely cultivated as single units and the idea of an aristocracy of great landowners did not survive amidst the realities of pioneering development in a new land.

In 1640, the population of Maryland consisted of only about 500 settlers; to induce immigration, land had to be made widely available and allocated in small parcels which poor migrants could afford. Thus, despite the programme of privilege planned by its proprietor, the characteristic unit of the Maryland economy soon became the small farm. Furthermore, with the move towards tobacco cultivation, Maryland increasingly came to resemble Virginia, on a smaller scale. Migrants and settlers sought to become independent farmers as soon as possible, and spread out over the surrounding riverbanks and estuaries of the Chesapeake region, raising their own food and growing tobacco for sale to the merchants who came to the Bay.

The political order in Maryland also eventually followed patterns established in Virginia, in spite of the peculiarities of the charter granted to Lord Baltimore and his determination to install a feudal form of government. In 1635, Baltimore was forced to concede an informal assembly to Protestants at Kent Island, and to allow the assembly to conduct itself in the manner of a local parliament when it first met in 1638. When more Protestants from Virginia entered the region, Maryland's Catholic proprietor came under mounting attack; indeed, during and after the English Civil War, Baltimore lost control of his colony to Puritan opponents. Although Baltimore was reinstated as proprietor in 1657, Maryland came increasingly to resemble Virginia, as a tobacco-producing colony of tidewater plantations, with its feudal 'hundreds' replaced by counties and parishes. In some respects, however, Maryland remained very different from the other colonies, including its near neighbour in Virginia: English Catholic emigrants established a network of families which intermarried with each other, sustained communications with their co-religionists in England or in exile in Europe, and provided a niche in English Protestant America where the Catholic church established its first ecclesiastical presence.[35]

THE WEST INDIES

If the years of the great Puritan migration before the English Civil War saw the creation of a new colonial society in New England, this was neither the sole nor the most important colonizing venture of those years: during the same period, a development of enormous significance for the future of the Anglo-American empire was taking place in the Caribbean. There, far from the North American mainland, substantial English settlements took root on the small islands of the outer arc of the Antilles, and attracted very large numbers of migrants. The islands of Barbados and St Kitts, first occupied in the 1620s, became the focal points for flourishing colonial societies which, during the 1630s, attracted possibly as many as 30,000 English emigrants.

Rapid growth in the English West Indies stemmed from speculative commercial ventures, in which London merchants sought to make quick profits from tobacco production. Spain claimed sovereignty over these islands but offered no opposition to their occupation by the English, and the first settlements were followed by a scramble for profits and privileges. Following their early development by merchant syndicates based in London along the lines of the Virginia Company, by the end of 1629 the islands were brought under the control of the Earl of Carlisle, who had been granted proprietary rights by King Charles I. Like Lord Baltimore in Maryland, Carlisle held quasi-feudal rights to land and government, could nominate governors and other officials, and draw an income from rents and customs dues. However, unlike Baltimore, Carlisle had no religious ideals and left colonization to be undertaken on a speculative, competitive basis, giving rise to poor government and bitter factionalism.[36]

Very little is known about the history of St Kitts and the other small islands during these early years, and comment on the English Caribbean during the early decades of colonization must therefore be based largely on the experience of Barbados, the most rapidly growing colony in the region. Here, the pattern of development is reasonably clear and, although it was much faster than in the neighbouring Leeward Islands, it set a course that the Leewards were to follow, albeit on a lesser scale.

Under Carlisle's proprietorship, land in Barbados was distributed in large blocks, creating an embryonic planter class from wealthy Englishmen with access to capital or credit. London merchants played a key part in developing the land: the London Merchant House received a grant of 10,000 acres, almost a tenth of the entire island, which it distributed in large units among tenants. Generally, land grants were relatively large, and land tended to concentrate in the hands of rich and politically well-connected individuals who often accumulated more than one grant to form estates of several hundred acres. Allocation of land in large units was for export rather than subsistence agriculture, and the emerging estates were dedicated to tobacco cultivation, using servant labour brought from England.[37]

Throughout these early years of colonization, indentured labour was of critical importance, as the islands had no alternative source of labour. During the 1630s, Barbados and St Kitts received a large influx of immigrants, mostly indentured servants drawn from London, the ports of western England and from Ireland. The exact number of these migrants and the size of the island's population are both uncertain, but it is clear that most were young males, with very few women and children.[38] This was, then, a migration similar to that which went to Virginia during these same years and, by the same token, radically different from the Puritan exodus which flowed into Massachusetts.

The cultural influence of Puritanism in the English Caribbean was negligible, though not entirely absent. In 1631, the Earl of Warwick, the Puritan proprietor of the Atlantic island of Bermuda, formed a joint-stock company with a number of high-ranking Puritan politicians in England; they then launched a daring plan to move into the western Caribbean, taking Providence Island off the coast of Nicaragua in the hope of turning it into a 'godly commonwealth' that would also be a commercial venture. In 1635, the company then decided to make the island a base for attacking the Spaniards on the Isthmus of Panama, while also organizing settlements on the nearby island of San Andrés and, further to the east, between Hispaniola and Cuba, at Tortuga. This aggressive Puritan venture was, however, to fail. Tortuga quickly became a pirate lair, and was retaken by Spain in 1635. The tiny English colony at Providence survived a little longer, but it too was recaptured by Spain in 1641.[39] Thus the English were forced back to the eastern Caribbean, to the starting points of their colonization in the Lesser Antilles.

There, on the islands of Barbados and St Kitts, the core of a tropical English America took shape during the 1630s, initially based in tobacco plantations producing for export to Europe. Their development as tobacco producers was short-lived. Like Virginia, Barbados suffered from the dramatic decline in tobacco prices from 1631, and its more enterprising planters shifted into the production of other crops. First they tried cotton, until in 1639 a glut on the London market ruined many planters. They then turned to indigo cultivation in the 1640s, but, more importantly, started to experiment with sugar-cane cultivation, thereby introducing the crop that was to sustain the Anglo-Caribbean economy throughout the colonial period. Brought to Barbados by Dutch merchants, sugar turned the island into the new boom colony of the nascent Anglo–American world, and set the pattern which the other West Indian colonies were to follow over the next half-century. Population continued to grow, helped by migration during and after the English Civil War. By 1650, the white population of Barbados was at least 23,000, and possibly as many as 30,000, with perhaps another 12,000 white people settled in St Kitts, 5,000 in Nevis, and close to 2,000 in Antigua and Montserrat.[40]

Like the settlers on the mainland, those in the English Caribbean islands established a system of government familiar to them from England. The aristocratic proprietors of the islands had wide-ranging powers and selected governors to enforce them. On Barbados, this initially produced an autocratic form of government, dictated by the governor and his council of prominent white planters. Government was, however, soon placed largely in local hands. The islands were divided into parishes, and the freemen of the parish elected officers to collect local taxes and to maintain order. Barbados also acquired a representative assembly in 1639, with delegates drawn from its parishes; the other islands founded assemblies after the English Civil War. But while the islands gradually acquired assemblies which matched those on the mainland, these did not become instruments for popular participation in politics. In the Caribbean, even more than in Virginia, power passed to rich planters who spoke for their own interests and controlled virtually all local government, including that of the Anglican church.[41]

Given the underlying equivalence of their early economic structures, these similarities between Virginia and the English Caribbean islands are readily understood. The societies of both regions were based on the cultivation of tobacco rather than family farming, this engendered a social order that was quite distinct from that of New England. In Virginia, most of the colonists were indentured servants who entered a hierarchical society which quickly became dominated by large planters. Social division was reinforced by the development of export agriculture, for although indentured servants could acquire land, the real fortunes were made by men with sufficient capital to create extensive estates. The same was true of the tobacco-producing islands in the Caribbean, where wealthy planters soon formed local elites that dominated society and government.

THE ENGLISH AND THE INDIANS

The English who settled in the Americas did not move into an empty landscape. Like the Iberian adventurers and settlers who were the vanguard of European colonization a century before, English settlers generally entered territories already occupied by indigenous peoples. The foundation of English colonies was therefore more than simply a process of planting offshoots of the mother country in foreign lands; it also thrust settlers into contact with cultures alien to them and raised questions concerning English rights to native land and obligations to native peoples. Like the Spaniards before them, the English sought to justify their intrusion into native territories as a spiritual mission for evangelizing and civilizing the American Indians.

The native cultures encountered by English settlers varied considerably from region to region, but generally the contexts in which English colonizers met with Indian peoples differed from those of Spaniards and Indians a century earlier. Nowhere did English settlers meet with native societies comparable to the densely populated tributary states of the Aztecs or the Incas, and they neither superimposed their colonies on native populations by military conquest in the style of Cortés or Pizarro, nor created institutions for exploiting Indian forced labour in the manner of the Spanish *encomienda* and *mita* systems. In the long term, English settlers also proved to be less concerned to persuade native peoples to convert to Christianity. There were no missionary endeavours in English America to compare with the great evangelizing enterprises of the Catholic religious orders in Spanish America, nor did English governments provide the consistent support for religious proselytizing that came from the Spanish monarchy. This more relaxed approach to native people did not reflect greater English tolerance. In their attitudes towards native peoples, English colonists and their descendants displayed the general European tendency to regard Indians as social and moral inferiors, with a corresponding disdain for the latter's rights to the lands that they occupied.[42]

That English attitudes towards American Indians showed the same basic proclivities as those of other Europeans is not surprising, since, like the Spanish before them, Elizabethan and Jacobean Englishmen denigrated Indians in order to assert title to their lands.[43] During the early years of Iberian discovery and settlement in the New World, some European writers had entertained a vision of America as an 'earthly paradise', peopled by innocent beings who enjoyed a life comparable to that of humanity before the Fall. But, if reports from the New World inspired a utopian literature (of which Thomas More's *Utopia*, written in 1517, is the striking English exemplar), idealization of Indians was chiefly a means of reflecting on the ills of European society and did not long survive the practical experience of colonization.[44] Reports of cannibalism, human sacrifice and other practices that deviated from European Christian norms soon shaped a negative view of Indians; both Spain and Portugal sought to justify their conquest and subjugation of Indian peoples as a providential mission for evangelizing heathens gripped by Satan's power. This did not preclude deep disputation over the character and treatment of Indians, most notably in Spain. At an early stage in Spanish colonization, missionaries denounced the enslavement and maltreatment of Indians and insisted on the primacy of the evangelical mission over the interests of state and settlers. Las Casas, the celebrated 'protector of the Indians', went further. He not only condemned the Spanish settlers' cruel and oppressive conduct towards the Indians, but also resisted the argument, supported by the authority of Aristotle's concept of 'natural slavery', that the Indians were a lesser form of humanity that was governed by base passions and incapable of a full, rational humanity. Indeed, having rejected this view that Indians should be subordinated to Europeans because they were incapable of 'civility', Las Casas finally reached the radical conclusion that the Spanish crown should renounce its dominion so that Indians might first embrace Christianity of their own free wills.[45] Other counsels and interests prevailed, however, and the task of converting Indians remained firmly identified with their subjection to Spanish sovereignty and their acculturation to European ways.

English perceptions of and behaviour towards the Indians was permeated by the same arrogation of religious, cultural and hence political superiority. When Richard Eden presented his English translation of Peter Martyr's *Decades of the New World* in 1555, he praised the Spaniards' 'merciful wars against these naked people', and declared that their Christianization meant that 'their bondage is such as it is much rather to be desired than their former liberty'.[46] Under Elizabeth I, such pro-Spanish propaganda was superseded by criticism of Spain's cruelty and tyranny, but the Spanish rationale, that conquest and colonization was essential for bringing the Christian message to the Indians, nevertheless remained an equally important element in English attitudes towards the American Indians. Now, helped by Las Casas's vivid denunciation of Spanish cruelty (translated into English in 1583 as *A brief narration of the destruction of the Indies by the Spaniards*), Elizabethan proponents of American colonization asserted that England also had a providential role to convert the Indians and, with it, an equal claim to their lands and allegiance. In 1565, the Bishop of Salisbury had argued that Spain's Catholic evangelization was but a prelude to England's mission and 'a stepping stone to the acceptance by the American Indian of the perfections of Protestantism'.[47] Two decades later, Hakluyt, Gilbert and Raleigh all took up this theme, asserting that England had a God-given duty to save the Indians from the errors of Spanish Catholicism and where necessary to save them from Spanish cruelty. By the time that English colonists established Jamestown, few, if any, doubts remained. England's prime task was, like Spain before it, to effect Indian conversion by taking Indian lands and, in pursuit of an evangelical and civilizing mission, to be rewarded with the resources of the New World.

Such exaltation of the Christian mission was to be no better guarantor of justice for the Indians in England's colonies than it had been in Spain's, either in the Caribbean or on mainland North America. In the Caribbean, English relations with native peoples were brutally simplified by the fact that most of the Indian population had disappeared before English settlers arrived in the region. The Arawaks had been virtually wiped out by disease and harsh exploitation on the islands settled by the Spanish; the arrival of English, French and Dutch settlers in the Lesser Antilles quickly killed off most of the small number who had survived the first onslaught of European invaders. Relations with surviving native groups were invariably violent, for the Carib peoples who lived on most of the islands of the eastern Caribbean mounted a fierce resistance to European invaders, slowing the advance of white settlement. Only Barbados was not populated by Caribs, a fact that helps to explain its rapid development following the first English occupation. Elsewhere, the problems of settling thickly forested and mountainous terrain were aggravated by Carib raids, and English relations with these people rarely extended beyond a pattern of savage attack and counterattack.

In the early years of settlement in the Lesser Antilles, English and French settlers put aside their differences to make alliances against the Caribs, who raided their settlements and forced them to retreat from several of the smaller islands. When European settlement was stabilized, the French made some, mainly abortive, efforts to evangelize the Caribs and occasionally succeeded in using them as auxiliaries against the English. The English, on the other hand, never established amicable relations with Carib groups or brought them under their control. Indeed, thanks to the Caribs' dedication to war and their ability to launch attacks from the sea in large war canoes, the surviving natives continued to harass European settlers in the Lesser Antilles throughout the seventeenth century. This did not save them from extinction. Although the Caribs successfully resisted subordination to Europeans, they became an increasingly marginalized people. Reduced to tiny, embattled redoubts on the outer fringes of a Caribbean society that was mainly composed of European and African immigrants, they were persistently persecuted by colonial settlers.[48]

In England's North American colonies, relations with Indian peoples were more complicated. When the English established their first settlements in Virginia and New England, they came into contact with native groups which, like the Caribs of the West Indies, already knew of Europeans, but unlike the Caribs generally received them peacefully. When the Jamestown colony was created, the many small tribes of the Chesapeake Bay region were loosely confederated under the leadership of chief Powhatan, who regarded the whites as potential allies and trading partners. Given their small number, the early colonists did not seem to threaten the much more numerous Indian tribes; under Powhatan's authority the Indians not only tolerated their presence, but also allowed them supplies essential to their survival. The Christian response was less generous. In its charter of 1606, the Virginia Company firmly proclaimed its commitment to the 'propagating of Christian religion to such people as yet live in darkness and miserable ignorance of the true knowledge and worship of God'.[49] But in practice neither company nor colonists brought any sense of urgency to this task. Among contemporary commentators in England, a negative view of the Indians, as uncouth and 'inconstant' savages, prevailed against ineffectual contestation; in the colony, settlers were suspicious and fearful of the Indians, and when Indians refused to trade they took to raiding their villages for food. Despite such armed clashes, an uneasy peace was preserved for several years, until the growth of the settler population and the demand for land on which to cultivate tobacco forced the Indians to defend themselves against the intruders.[50]

In 1618, Powhatan's successor, his brother Openchancanough, organized the Chesapeake tribes into a military alliance, and in 1622 killed about a third of the colony's population in an attack on outlying settlements. The attack precipitated a crisis in the Virginia Company, leading to its downfall in 1624, but did nothing to improve relations between settlers and Indians. On the contrary, it confirmed the settlers' distrust of the Indians and released restraints on those who wished to annihilate or enslave them. The Virginia government retaliated against the Indians with reprisal raids and determined to expel them from lands regarded as English property.

Indians were now routinely condemned as 'barbaric' and 'treacherous' people who, if they could not be controlled, should be exterminated. Preconceived ideas of Indians as 'savages' who were outside the moral laws governing white society were now used to justify their extirpation, while the continuing influx of settlers exposed the natives to an accelerating erosion of their numbers through epidemic disease. Driven to desperation, the Indians rose again in 1644 in an attempt to stem white encroachment on their lands. To end the violence, the Virginia government made a formal treaty with the Indians in 1646, providing displaced groups with lands in return for an annual tribute of beaver skins and military alliance.[51] However, by this time, the destruction and dispossession of the Chesapeake tribes was too far advanced to be halted. By mid-century, the balance of power in the region had definitively shifted towards the whites. As the settler population continued to grow, fed by flows of migration from England, the indigenous population underwent an equally sharp decline. Estimates of Virginia's Indian population on the eve of English colonization vary wildly (between 14,000 and 170,000), but it is certain that half a century after 1608, little more than a small remnant of Indian society remained.[52]

The Indians of New England suffered a similar fate at the hands of English settlers. When the first 'Pilgrims' arrived in 1620, they were favourably treated by the local Indians, the Wampanoags, who offered them land and trade in return for an alliance against the neighbouring Narragansett tribe. The lands they offered were unoccupied, most of the native population having already been decimated by epidemic diseases introduced by the Europeans who had long been engaged in the fisheries and fur trades of the northern region; surviving Indians were also eager to take advantage of the trade goods which the settlers offered in exchange for furs. So long as the settlers needed the food and furs provided by the Indians, friendly relations were sustained, but the tremendous increase in the white population that followed the establishment of the Massachusetts colony in 1630 soon produced a pattern of violence and Indian dispossession similar to that found in the Chesapeake region.[53]

Like their counterparts in Virginia, colonists in New England respected neither Indian culture nor Indian rights to land. The settlers came to America with a preconceived notion of indigenous people as heathens, whose beliefs and customs were evil simply because they did not conform to those of Christians, and they thought of Indians as 'savages' whose behaviour placed them beyond the normal standards of English law. Thus, in their patronizing presumption of cultural superiority, seventeenth-century Puritans differed little from most sixteenth-century Iberian Catholics. Indeed, Puritans were more intolerant of Indian ways. Among Franciscan missionaries in sixteenth-century Mexico, the first imperative was to baptize Indians, if necessary before they had been properly catechized. The Puritan approach to evangelization was more demanding. It required that Indians take up English ways, on the precept that 'in order to become Christians, they must first be made Men'. This dictum rested on the assumption (which paralleled the sixteenth-century Spanish opinion that Indians were 'natural slaves') that Indians were governed by passions rather than reason, and had to be trained in the arts of civilized life. The model of civility was of course that of English society, with the additional restraints imposed by Puritan theology. Puritans therefore wanted Indians to abandon completely their own beliefs and cultural practices, adopting English modes of settlement and farming, appearance and apparel, in order to prepare for their entry into the mysteries of Christianity. Thus, when the General Court of Massachusetts belatedly formulated a policy for proselytizing among the Indians in 1646, it sought to isolate neophytes from contrary influences by segregating them in 'praying towns', where they were subjected to draconian regulations formed more by cultural prejudice than scriptural precept. This missionary endeavour was largely the work of one man, the Puritan minister John Eliot, who played a major role in gathering a small population of natives in the fourteen 'praying towns' that were established in New England before the 1670s.[54]

After the 1670s, the advance of Christianity was apparently more rapid, but if few redoubts of paganism remained in southern New England at the end of the seventeenth century, this owed much to the fact that the few surviving Indians were simply culturally overwhelmed by a far larger white population. The Puritan missionary effort was slow partly because, unlike Catholic missionaries in Iberian America or the New Englanders' contemporary rivals, the Jesuits in New France, Puritan clerics believed that spiritual regeneration was brought about within the individual who accepted the gift of grace from God. Clergy could assist this process, but the effort required was intense and demanding of both minister and neophyte. Generally, however, English Protestants showed little real interest in evangelizing the Indians. Protestant pastors ministered to their own congregations and rarely ventured among the natives, except in a few doomed 'errands in the wilderness' that produced results far inferior to those achieved by Catholic missionaries in neighbouring Canada.[55]

A similarly convenient narrowness of outlook characterized the settlers' attitudes towards Indian lands. Although Indians in New England, like those of Virginia, engaged in subsistence agriculture and had their own clearly defined ideas and rules about property and the use of natural resources, English settlers insisted that the Indians were nomads and hunters who did not cultivate the land, had no property rights and no governments based on clearly-demarcated territories. On these grounds, leading colonists argued that the land was a virgin wilderness which could be taken over by Europeans who brought it under permanent cultivation. In English eyes, the Indians' hunting territories were simply wastelands over which the Indians had no property rights, and of which they could be dispossessed by any means convenient to the settlers, including war.[56]

In New England, as in Virginia, war between settlers and Indians was not long in coming, arising from competition for both land and furs. Two disputes converged to produce a war against the Pequot tribe in 1636–7. One was a dispute over land, arising from the colonization of Connecticut. This not only led to disputes between Indians and settlers, but also accentuated rivalries between the Puritan colonies of Connecticut and Massachusetts, both of which sought jurisdiction over Indian territory in order to gain access to land. The other dispute concerned the fur trade. The governments of Massachusetts and Plymouth were both concerned to keep the Dutch out of the fur trade and formed an alliance with the Narragansett Indians to achieve this goal. In the event, the Narragansetts were used to fight against their neighbours, the Pequots, who not only traded with the Dutch but also held lands that the settlers coveted. The result was a veritable war of conquest, in which large numbers of Pequots were either killed or sold into slavery and English control over southern New England was finally consolidated.

The Pequot war removed an obstacle to expansion and it gave Puritan merchants firm control over trade with the Indian tribes of a wide area. Both contributed to the continuing decline of Indian society throughout New England. By selling furs to the English, the Indians became increasingly dependent on European trade goods and increasingly involved in violent competition among themselves as the supply of furs dwindled. Thus inter-tribal wars between Indians compounded the destructive effects of epidemic disease and dependence on alcohol brought by contact with Europeans, drastically reducing the indigenous population. In 1620, there were at least 70,000 Indians in New England; by 1670, only some 12,000 remained.[57]

Establishing colonies on the coasts of North America and in the

Caribbean islands was, then, a process in which the English not only implanted cells of their parent society in the New World, but also destroyed Indian communities and cultures. When Indians resisted, they were treated with merciless contempt as 'savages' who could be plundered and enslaved; when peaceful, they were weakened, sometimes completely eliminated, by epidemic disease, territorial dispossession and cultural disintegration. The decay of Indian societies did not, of course, proceed at a uniform pace. Indian societies in the interior – most famously those of the Five Nations of the Iroquois Confederacy – entered into commercial and political relations with the whites, but preserved their independence by holding themselves apart from white society. The damage done to the Indian tribes in the lands along the Atlantic coast, on the other hand, was swift and irreversible. Where whites settled, Indians were displaced. While willing to use the Indians for trade and war, English settlers invariably regarded themselves as the superior ethnic caste and saw Indians as ignorant, brutish people who might be used for trade and war but had no place in white society. Rather than incorporating the Indians into the framework of colonial society, as the Spanish did in their American dominions, the English regarded them as an obstacle to colonization, fit only to be separated or removed.

ENGLISH AMERICA IN THE MID-SEVENTEENTH CENTURY

By the early 1640s, the first great surge of English colonizing in the Americas was over, its advance checked by the outbreak of civil war within the mother country. When war began in 1642, the tide of English emigration slowed and was even temporarily reversed, as some settlers returned to England to enlist in the struggle between King and Parliament. Then, for most of the ensuing decade, the colonies were left largely to their own devices, isolated from the great events taking place in England and little noticed by its governments. The great migration had, however, left an incipient empire in its wake, consisting of an archipelago of small, highly localized colonial societies that were as yet only loosely tied to the metropolitan power and contributed little to its economy.

Given the very different environments in which these colonies were established, it is hardly surprising that none was an exact replica of the English society from which their settlers were drawn. Like the

Spaniards and the Portuguese in Meso-America and South America, English settlers encountered new landscapes and peoples, and were forced to adapt, however unwillingly, to the conditions of their new worlds. Very few felt any sympathy or sense of fellowship with native peoples, and English colonists were no more ready to adopt the social practices and beliefs of Amerindians than were the Iberians who had spearheaded European settlement in the Americas. What, then, were the factors which shaped their first societies and, since they differed among themselves, how should we explain their variations? To what extent did they succeed in re-creating the societies which they had known in England, and which of the colonies most closely resembled that of the parent power?

Clearly, the nature of the new environment played a part in shaping the first Anglo-American societies. The fact that the Chesapeake and Caribbean colonists entered environments suitable for a tropical agriculture undoubtedly influenced their development, since these conditions spawned economies which allowed production and trade for overseas markets and individual enrichment for the fortunate. Migrants to New England, by contrast, entered an environment that was much less suited to economic exploitation of this kind, since it provided neither the mineral resources found by the Spanish in their territories, nor the fertile soils and sub-tropical climate required for cultivating exotic crops. It is, however, equally obvious that environmental differences are not of themselves sufficient to explain variations among the nascent colonies. Their character also derived from the organization of their Atlantic passage, from the social composition of the migrations that peopled them, and from regional cultures from which migrants emerged. Those who went to Virginia and the Caribbean entered a framework established and governed by companies and proprietors bent on economic innovation and exploitation of resources for private profit. The movements to New Plymouth and Massachusetts Bay, on the other hand, were influenced by religious and political rather than commercial purposes. The prime concern of New England settlers was to escape from a mother country where political and religious changes alienated Puritans and encouraged them to seek refuge overseas. Moreover, because Puritan migrants travelled in self-selecting groups that were predominantly recruited in East Anglia, and transplanted a society which closely reflected its progenitor in structure and beliefs, their colony bore a strong cultural resemblance to the society they left. Early Virginia was peopled differently, by adventurers and servants who were drawn from more diverse origins in southern England, who were thrown together in a search for economic opportunity, and who, due to the unbalanced age and sex ratios of migrations and the dispersed settlement and high mortality of settlers, were less able to create a coherent colonial order. Although research tells us less about early settlers and servants in the Caribbean islands, the available evidence strongly suggests that their pattern of development was very similar.

Which of these disparate societies most closely resembled that of the mother country has, until recently, seemed an easy question to answer. While acknowledging the effect of differences in settler intentions and American environments, historians have generally agreed that New England mostly closely replicated English social and economic traditions. T.H. Breen, for example, states that, while New England was not a complete monolithic 'fragment' separated from the mother country, migrants to Massachusetts had created a countryside which, at mid-century, 'appeared remarkably like the traditional English society which they had sought to preserve from Stuart intervention'. The Chesapeake colony seems, by comparison, to have been a much less complete reproduction of English society, since it 'did not represent a random sample of seventeenth-century English society or a cross-section of English values'.[58] There are, however, reasons for questioning this view. For, as J.P. Greene has observed, historians of early modern England are redrawing our picture of late sixteenth- and early seventeenth-century English society in ways which make it difficult to regard New England as its closest colonial expression. It is now less certain that English villages were composed of small, self-sufficient households built on a core of sturdy yeomen. Instead, amidst a rising population and an expanding commercial economy, we can discern the outlines of a rural economy in which large landowners played a dominant role, organizing large-scale, specialized production for the market and employing a workforce which relied on wages rather than subsistence farming. Small farmers, it seems, were also increasingly market-oriented and, with growing demographic and commercial pressures, economic and social inequalities were becoming more pronounced across the social spectrum. Far from being 'traditional' and 'paternalist', this was a 'modernizing' and 'fluid' society, in which geographical and social mobility became more common as labour moved around in search of work and the more prosperous sought to ascend the social scale by acquiring wealth. The commercialization of the economy was, in short, unsettling traditional structures of wealth and power, and giving English society a looser, more materialist cast.

From this revisionist perspective, Greene argues that 'the world established by the New England puritans was intended not to replicate but to move in precisely the opposite direction of the world they had abandoned in Old England'; Chesapeake society, on the other hand, 'was more expressive of the dominant features and impulses of contemporary English life than was the regressive world of orthodox puritan New England'. As he also finds that Bermuda and the Caribbean colonies resembled Chesapeake social and economic formations, Greene concludes that, far from representing the mainstream, 'the societies of orthodox New England . . . represented a deviant strain in English colonial history'.[59]

So, in its formative years, English colonization in the Americas was creating a disparate, heterogeneous social world, a world that reflected changes and tensions in the parent society, where entrepreneurial and commercial impulses were powerful forces promoting colonization, and where political and economic dislocations encouraged emigration. Compared to the American colonies of Spain and Portugal, those of England were insignificant in the mid-seventeenth century. Portugal's territories in Brazil were emerging as the world's largest producer of sugar, while the Spanish colonies were at the peak of their first great cycle of development based on the mining of precious metals. The Spanish empire was, it is true, greatly diminished in population. Its indigenous population had been catastrophically undermined by epidemic disease, and the energy of its mining centres was beginning to show signs of resource depletion. But it was still a formidable empire, with a population of about 10 million people distributed among its many provinces, an extensive network of urban centres, a highly productive agriculture, and a very valuable commerce conducted with Europe, Asia (via the Philippines) and between the colonies themselves. Spanish colonists were, moreover, still pushing forward their frontiers of settlement northwards from Mexico into North America. The basis of an English empire had nonetheless begun to take shape. As yet, none of the colonies was of great economic importance to the mother country, but a pattern for the future was starting to emerge.

From the English perspective, the islands in the Caribbean looked the most promising in economic terms, despite their small land area. In 1640, the population of Barbados was at least as large as that of New England and twice as big as that of Virginia, while St Kitts had a substantially larger population than Maryland. In their early years, these islands cultivated tobacco, but at mid-century they were beginning to go over to the production of sugar, the most valuable tropical crop of the age, using African slaves for labour. This new development, so important for the future, did not immediately benefit the English economy. First, it was inspired by the Dutch, who provided credit, technical help and markets for English sugar planters, and who, from the 1630s, virtually monopolized trade between Europe and those parts of the Indies that were not under Spanish control. Second, when the English Civil War began in 1642, England's government had neither formulated a colonial policy, nor built a unified political framework to contain the institutional and economic development of its nascent American possessions. Indeed, for all their differences, the new English colonies shared one common feature: they were not directly controlled by governments in England, nor ruled by a colonial bureaucracy of the kind which Spain had developed to govern its American dominions. Under the early Stuarts, England had succeeded in establishing colonies of settlements in the New World, but a stronger state was needed to bring those colonies into the framework of an empire. This was a development which awaited the resolution of internal conflict within the English state, a resolution achieved after England had passed through the calamity of civil war.

NOTES

1. Henry Gemery, 'Emigration from the British Isles to the New World, 1630–1700: inferences from colonial populations', *Research in Economic History* (1980) **5**: 179–231. See Table A.2, p. 212. Population figures in this and the next paragraph also draw on David H. Fischer, *Albion's Seed: Four British Folkways in America* (New York, 1989) pp. 226–7, and Edmund S. Morgan, *American Slavery, American Freedom: The Ordeal of Colonial Virginia* (New York, 1975) pp. 136, 159.

2. On the shift from 'engagement to flight' among English Puritans, see Stephen Foster, *The Long Argument: English Puritanism and the Shaping of New England Culture, 1570–1700* (Chapel Hill, NC, London, 1991) pp. 108–37. For a brief assessment of the historiography on social and economic change and religious divisions in England, and their relationship to political conflict, see Ann Hughes, *The Causes of the English Civil War* (London, 1991), especially pp. 95–116, 126–54.

3. The standard work on the 'great migration' is Carl Bridenbaugh, *Vexed and Troubled Englishmen, 1590–1642* (New York, 1967) especially pp. 394–473. A good introduction to the subject of early migration is Mildred Campbell, 'Social origins of some early Americans', in James Morton Smith (ed) *Seventeenth Century America: Essays in Colonial History* (New York, 1972 edition) pp. 63–89. A review of recent research on European migration to the Americas which places English migration in a comparative perspective is given in the editors' introduction to Ida

Altman and James Horn (eds) *'To Make America': European Emigration in the Early Modern Period* (Berkeley and Los Angeles, Calif, 1991) pp. 1–29.

4. On the origins and early use of indentured labour, see Abbot E. Smith, *Colonists in Bondage: White Servitude and Convict Labour in America, 1607–1776* (Gloucester, Mass., 1965 edition) pp. 3–20; David Galenson, *White Servitude in Colonial America: An Economic Analysis* (Cambridge, 1981) pp. 3–13.

5. Galenson, *White Servitude in Colonial America*, pp. 82–5; Henry A. Gemery, 'Markets for migrants: English indentured servitude and emigration in the seventeenth and eighteenth centuries', in P.C. Emmer (ed) *Colonialism and Migration: Indentured Labour Before and After Slavery* (Dordrecht, 1986) pp. 33–54.

6. T.H. Breen, 'Moving to the New World: the character of early Massachusetts immigration', in T.H. Breen, *Puritans and Adventurers: Change and Persistence in Early America* (New York & Oxford, 1980), pp. 46–67.

7. James Horn, 'To parts beyond the seas: free emigration to the Chesapeake in the seventeenth century', in Altman and Horn (eds) *'To Make America'*, pp. 85–130.

8. These observations are based on figures in Nicolás Sánchez-Albornoz, 'The population of colonial Spanish America', in L. Bethell (ed) *Cambridge History of Latin America*, vol. 2 (Cambridge, 1984) pp. 15–16; Maria Luiza Marcílio, 'The population of colonial Brazil', ibid., p. 47; Bernard Bailyn, *Voyagers to the West: Emigration from Britain to America on the Eve of the American Revolution* (London, 1987) pp. 24–5.

9. James Horn, 'Servant emigration to the Chesapeake in the seventeenth century', in Thad W. Tate and David L. Ammerman (eds) *The Chesapeake in the Seventeenth Century: Essays in Anglo-American Society* (Chapel Hill, NC, 1979); see p. 66.

10. Fischer, *Albion's Seed*. For a statement of his argument, see pp. 6–7.

11. Asuncion Lavrín, 'Women in Spanish American colonial society', in Bethell (ed) *Cambridge History of Latin America*, vol. 2, pp. 322–4. A recent estimate suggests that of legal and illegal migration to the Indies about 15 per cent were women in 1614–15; a study of emigration from two Extremaduran towns in the sixteenth century suggests that numbers of women and children increased over time. See Auke Pieter Jacobs, 'Legal and illegal emigration from Seville, 1550–1650', and Ida Altman, 'A New World in the Old: local society and Spanish emigration to the Indies', in Altman and Horn (eds) *'To Make America'*, Chapters 2–3, especially pp. 36–7, 80.

12. For material on settlers in early Spanish America, see James Lockhart, *Spanish Peru, 1532–1560* (Madison, Wis., 1968) especially Chapter 1. For comparison of the social types involved in emigration from France, Holland and England, see K.G. Davies, *The North Atlantic World in the Seventeenth Century* (Minneapolis, Minn., and London, 1974) pp. 63–140. On Dutch migration, see Ernst van der Boogaart, 'The servant migration to New Netherland, 1624–1664', in Emmer (ed) *Colonialism and Migration*, pp. 55–81. For more detailed information on the social composition and age and gender structures of French colonial migration, see Leslie Choquette, 'Recruitment of French emigrants to Canada, 1600–1760',

and Christian Huetz de Lemps, 'Indentured servants bound for the French Antilles in the seventeenth and eighteenth centuries', in Altman and Horn (eds) *To Make America*', Chapters 5–6.

13. For comparison between migrants to New England and the Caribbean, see Richard S. Dunn, 'Experiments holy and unholy, 1630–31', in Andrews, Canny and Hair (eds) *Westward Enterprise*, pp. 271–89.

14. For these different estimates of population, see Gemery, 'Emigration from the British Isles to the New World, 1630–1700', p. 212, and Fischer, *Albion's Seed*, p. 226.

15. The controversy is outlined in Ray Allen Billington (ed) *The Reinterpretation of Early American History: Essays in Honor of John Edwin Pomfret* (San Marino, Calif., 1966) pp. 45–52. For criticism of the terms of the debate, see Breen, *Puritans and Adventurers*, pp. 53–7. On local factors, see David Grayson Allen, *In English Ways: The Movement of Societies and the Transferal of English Law and Custom to Massachusetts Bay in the Seventeenth Century* (Chapel Hill, NC, 1981) pp. 163–204.

16. John Winthrop, 'A modell of Christian charity' (1630), in Edmund S. Morgan (ed), *The Founding of Massachusetts: Historians and the Sources* (New York, 1964) p. 203.

17. The classic study of the religious mentality in early Massachusetts is Perry Miller, *Orthodoxy in Massachusetts, 1630–1650: A Genetic Study* (Cambridge, Mass., 1933).

18. T.H. Breen, 'Persistent localism: English social change and the shaping of New England institutions', in Breen, *Puritans and Adventurers*, pp. 3–24; quotations from pp. 14, 17.

19. For an analysis of the English cultural roots of the Massachusetts colony see Fischer, *Albion's Seed*, pp. 13–49.

20. Gemery, 'Emigration from the British Isles to the New World, 1630–1700', Table B.3, p. 221.

21. Fischer, *Albion's Seed*, p. 31.

22. D.W. Meinig, *The Shaping of America: A Geographical Perspective on Five Hundred Years of History; Volume I: Atlantic America, 1492–1800* (New Haven, Conn., and London, 1986) pp.91–5.

23. Robert J. Taylor, *Colonial Connecticut: A History* (New York, 1979) pp. 3–19.

24. Sydney V. James, *Colonial Rhode Island: A History* (New York, 1975) pp. 13–74.

25. For an introduction to the political thought and politics of Massachusetts Puritans before 1660, see T.H. Breen, *The Character of the Good Ruler: A Study of Puritan Political Ideas in New England, 1630–1730* (New Haven, Conn., and London, 1970), pp. 1–86.

26. Quotations are from Fischer, *Albion's Seed*, pp.158, 177. For more detail on the early history of two New England towns, see Kenneth A. Lockridge, *A New England Town, The First Hundred Years: Dedham, Massachusetts, 1636–1736* (New York, 1970) pp. 3–90, and Philip J. Greven, *Four Generations: Population, Land and Family in Colonial Andover, Massachusetts* (Ithaca, NY, and London, 1970) pp. 21–99. Variations arising from differences in the regional origins of Puritan settlers are discussed by David Grayson Allen, *In English Ways*, pp. 8–160.

27. Fischer, *Albion's Seed*, pp. 233–4.
28. Morgan, *American Slavery: American Freedom*, pp. 158–63.
29. Wesley Frank Craven, *The Southern Colonies in the Seventeenth Century, 1607–1689* (Baton Rouge, La, 1970 edition) pp. 133–57.
30. W.H. Seiler, 'The Anglican parish in Virginia', in Smith (ed) *Seventeenth-Century America*, pp. 119–42.
31. Morgan, *American Slavery, American Freedom*, pp. 133– 45.
32. T.H. Breen, 'Looking out for Number One: the cultural limits on public policy in early Virginia', in Breen, *Puritans and Adventurers*, p. 109.
33. James R. Perry, *The Formation of Society on Virginia's Eastern Shore, 1615–1655* (Chapel Hill, NC, and London, 1990) especially Chapter 7.
34. On Calvert in Newfoundland, see Gillian T. Cell, *Newfoundland Discovered: English Attempts at Colonisation, 1610–1630*, Hakluyt Society, 2nd series, vol. 160 (London, 1982) pp. 46–56.
35. On the foundation and early years of Maryland, see Craven, *The Southern Colonies in the Seventeenth Century*, pp. 183–223; Russell R. Menard and Lois Greene Carr, 'The Lords Baltimore and the colonization of Maryland', in D.B. Quinn, (ed) *Early Maryland in a Wider World* (Detroit, Mich., 1982) pp. 167–215; Gloria L. Main, *Tobacco Colony: Life in Early Maryland, 1650–1720* (Princeton, NJ, 1982) pp. 9–48.
36. On the settlement of the Leeward Islands, and their early society, see Carl Bridenbaugh and Roberta Bridenbaugh, *No Peace Beyond the Line: The English in the Caribbean, 1624–1690* (New York, 1972) pp. 9–51. On Carlisle's methods of exploiting and ruling Barbados, see Gary A. Puckrein, *Little England: Plantation Society and Anglo-Barbadian Politics, 1627–1700* (New York and London, 1984) pp. 33–9.
37. Hilary McD. Beckles, *White Servitude and Black Slavery in Barbados, 1627–1715* (Knoxville, Tenn., 1989) pp. 13–35.
38. Richard S. Dunn, *Sugar and Slaves: The Rise of the Planter Class in the English West Indies, 1624–173* (London, 1973) pp. 49–59.
39. Arthur P. Newton, *Colonizing Activities of the English Puritans* (Port Washington, New York, 1966 edition) pp. 40–71, 272–82, 294–313.
40. Gemery, 'Emigration from the British Isles to the New World, 1630–1700', Table A.1, p. 211; John J. McCusker and Russell R. Menard, *The Economy of British America, 1607–1789* (Chapel Hill, NC, and London, 1985) Tables 7.1 and 7.2, pp. 153–4.
41. J.H. Parry, Philip Sherlock and Anthony Maingot, *A Short History of the West Indies* (London, 1989 edition) p. 180; Beckles, *History of Barbados*, pp. 10–12.
42. On English attitudes towards native peoples, see Francis Jennings, *The Invasion of America: Indians, Colonialism and the Cant of Conquest* (Chapel Hill, NC, 1975) pp. 43–82; also Paul Axtell, *The European and the Indian: Essays in the Ethnohistory of Colonial North America* (New York, 1982 edition) pp. 41–86.
43. The following account of English attitudes towards Indians during the sixteenth and early seventeenth centuries draws on two main sources: H.C. Porter, *The Inconstant Savage: England and the North American Indian, 1500–1600* (London, 1979), especially pp. 91–183, and Bernard W. Sheehan, *Savagism and Civility: Englishmen and Indians in Colonial Virginia* (Cambridge, 1980), especially pp. 9–143.

44. For a brief, illustrated discussion of early representations of America as utopia, see Hugh Honor, *This New Golden Land: European Images of America from the Discoveries to the Present Time* (London, 1975) pp. 3–27.

45. On the Spanish debate over the nature and treatment of the Indians, see Lewis Hanke, *The Spanish Struggle for Justice: Aristotle and the American Indian* (London, 1959). A detailed discussion of the application of Aristotle's doctrine of 'natural slavery' is given by Anthony Pagden, *The Fall of Natural Man: The American Indian and the Origins of Comparative Ethnology* (Cambridge, 1982) especially pp. 27–108.

46. Quoted in Porter, *Inconstant Savage*, pp. 26–7.

47. Ibid., p. 134.

48. Davies, *The North Atlantic World in the Seventeenth Century*, pp. 261–9; on English attitudes towards the Caribs and actions against them, see C.S.S. Higham, *The Development of the Leeward Islands under the Restoration, 1600–1688* (Oxford, 1921) pp. 122–42; also Philip B. Boucher, *Cannibal Encounters: Europeans and Island Caribs, 1492–1763* (Baltimore, Md, and London, 1992) especially Chapters 2–4.

49. Quoted in Porter, *Inconstant Savage*, pp. 277 8.

50. Ibid., pp. 310–417; also Morgan, *American Slavery, American Freedom*, pp. 71–9.

51. Porter, *Inconstant Savage*, pp. 459–83, 513–31; Sheehan, *Savagism and Civility*, pp. 144–76; Morgan, *American Slavery, American Freedom*, pp. 91–101, 231–4.

52. For recent estimates of pre-contact Indian populations, see James H. Merrell, ' 'The Customes of our Countrey': Indians and colonists in early America' in Bernard Bailyn and Philip D. Morgan (eds) *Strangers within the Realm: Cultural Margins of the First British Empire* (Chapel Hill, NC, and London, 1991) pp. 122–3.

53. For a brief comparison of Indian/white encounters in early Virginia and New England, see Gary B. Nash, *Red, White and Black: The Peoples of America* (Englewood Cliffs, New Jersey, 1982 edition) pp. 53–86.

54. The following discussion of Puritanism and Indian evangelization in New England is based on James Axtell, *The Invasion Within: The Contest of Cultures in Colonial North America* (New York and Oxford, 1986) pp. 131 78; quotation from p. 133.

55. Ibid., pp. 218–67.

56. William Cronon, *Changes in the Land: Indians, Colonists, and the Ecology of New England* (New York, 1983) pp. 54–81.

57. Jennings, *The Invasion of America*, pp. 178–222; for higher estimates, see Neal Salisbury, *Manitou and Providence: Indians, Europeans and the Making of New England, 1500–1643* (New York and Oxford, 1982) pp. 22–30.

58. Breen, *Puritans and Adventurers*, quotations from pp. 24, 108.

59. Jack P. Greene, *Pursuits of Happiness: The Social Development of Early Modern British Colonies and the Formation of American Culture* (Chapel Hill, NC, and London, 1988) pp. 28–54; quotations from pp. 38, 53.

PART TWO

Expansion and Consolidation,
1642–1713

CHAPTER FOUR
The Expansion of Empire

The great migration pioneered by Puritans had underpinned the first phase of English colonization in the Americas; the triumph of the Puritans who remained in England prepared the way for the second When England emerged from civil war in 1648, its political structure had been dramatically altered. The roots of this change lay, first and foremost, in the redistribution of power brought by revolution. Starting as the revolt of the nobility, the English Civil War released the accumulated tensions and conflicts of preceding decades in a revolution that eventually overwhelmed the monarchy. To fortify their cause, the King's opponents in Parliament had rallied popular support, promoting an unprecedented political mobilization of the lower classes, but the Civil War stopped short of becoming a popular revolution. When the propertied classes realized that their internecine conflicts left space for a challenge from below, they sought a return to stability under the monarchy. Consequently, in 1660 the Stuart dynasty was restored to power, in the person of King Charles II. A revolution in English government had nonetheless occurred. When the monarchy was restored in 1660, it came at the behest of Parliament into a political context where the personal power of the King could no longer be exercised without constraint. Henceforth, commercial interests carried more weight in politics and, in alliance with monarchs eager to increase their revenues, forged an aggressive commercial and colonial policy that was aimed at expanding England's trade and enlarging its empire.

These events in England had a decisive impact on the development of the colonies. During the latter half of the seventeenth century, the English presence in the Americas was consolidated and transformed. Gradually, a fragmented array of small agricultural settlements was expanded into a network of populous and prosperous colonies, increasingly integrated by currents of commerce, contributing more to the metropolitan economy and, though still enjoying considerable autonomy, subject to closer attention from the centre. These changes resulted from the convergence and interaction of two sets of forces: first, the development of a more forceful colonial and commercial policy in post-revolutionary England; second, the expansion of population and settlement within the colonies themselves.

REPERCUSSIONS OF THE ENGLISH CIVIL WAR IN AMERICA

During the Civil War, the great clashes which took place in England had muted but nonetheless distinct echoes in the colonies. While England was embroiled in revolution, the overseas settlements were of little concern to the contending parties, for whom England and its surrounding seas were the main arena of conflict. In 1643, Parliament affirmed its authority over England's overseas possessions by appointing the Earl of Warwick, a Puritan grandee, to head a commission to oversee the colonies and their trade. While war went on in England, however, Warwick's commission had no real weight; the already feeble grip of English government was further loosened as the absence of clear and undivided authority in the mother country left the colonies in a political vacuum, free to govern themselves and to trade with foreigners.

In New England, government proceeded along much the same lines as before. England's powerlessness allowed the colonists to strengthen local institutions, and the disruption of trade with the mother country encouraged New Englanders to open their ports and to develop commercial contacts with southern Europe, the Atlantic islands and the Caribbean. This did not bring about any great change in the colony's economy or society, but it did strengthen New England autonomy and hardened Puritan resolution to resist inter- ference from the English state, whether it be monarchist or republican. In Virginia, Maryland and the island colonies of the Caribbean, the Civil War had rather more disruptive political effects. In Maryland, the civil war had direct and violent reverberations, as Puritan settlers took advantage of the political turbulence in England to press their claims against the colony's Catholic proprietor, leading to armed disputes. In Virginia and the West Indies, there was no such violent upheaval during the war, and the colonies simply went their own way. While the war lasted, they enjoyed considerable political and economic freedom, with Virginia, Maryland and Barbados all opening their ports to foreign traders. This allowed Dutch merchants to move into positions previously held by English merchants, to the advantage of planters who found that the Dutch offered better prices for their tobacco. Thus, economic growth continued and the colonies maintained a wary neutrality towards the warring parties in England, while seeking to take advantage of the crisis for their own ends.

The first signs of a new, more forceful policy towards the colonies came after Charles I was executed in 1649. When the monarchy was replaced by the republican regime of the Commonwealth, the new government sought to assert its authority over all the territories of the deposed monarch, including the American colonies. At first, this evoked resistance in some areas of the Americas, for both political and economic reasons. On learning of Charles's execution, in 1649 the leaders of Virginia, Maryland, Antigua, Barbados and Bermuda proclaimed their loyalty to his royal heir. In these Chesapeake and Caribbean colonies, political resistance was stiffened by royalist exiles who detested the regicide government in England and opposed its authority as a matter of principle. Moreover, the planters in these colonies, who had deeply resented restrictions on their trade before the Civil War and had prospered from trade with the Dutch during the war, were loath to accept a government whose mercantile supporters in the City of London wanted to reimpose restrictions on colonial commerce.

Parliament responded to colonial defiance in 1650 with an Act that declared that all colonies were subordinate to the authority and laws of Parliament, all proprietary and chartered company rights were subject to parliamentary approval, and all colonies were prohibited from unlicensed trade with foreign shipping. The Act also authorized the Council of State to send forces against colonial rebels and to set up new governments where necessary. In the event, disintegration of the incipient English empire was avoided because colonial rejection of England's republican government proved brief and ineffectual. In Barbados, royalists resisted a fleet sent from England to subdue them; however, although the colony seemed close to breaking away from English rule, the leading planters capitulated when they saw that their trade might be ruined by war. Thus, in 1652, the Commonwealth was able to reduce Barbados to submission, imposing a new governor on the island, and reorganizing local institutions along lines favoured by Parliament. Virginia's resistance to the home government also dissolved without armed confrontation. In 1651, English commissioners restored the authority of the home government by negotiation, and secured Virginia's surrender on terms favourable to the colonists. Peace was less easily restored in Maryland, where conflict between Catholics and Protestants continued to provoke disturbances. The commissioners sent by the Commonwealth supported the opponents of the colony's royalist proprietor, and in 1655, Lord Baltimore was overthrown by an armed revolt. He regained his government in 1657–8 and, though faced with another brief revolt, was fully restored as proprietor in 1660.[1]

Thus, when England emerged from its internal conflicts, the home government soon secured the political submission of the American colonies. The assertion of England's authority was, however, accomplished more by diplomacy than force, and although parliamentary commissions were initially in power, did not bring any substantial alteration in the framework of colonial government. In Barbados, the rebellious planters were left with the right to trade with friendly nations and to refuse any taxation not imposed by their own assembly, while Virginians were still allowed to administer and legislate for the colony through their own assembly. The other colonies also retained their existing forms of government, keeping a large measure of local autonomy. But if the upheaval in England left the basic structures of government in the colonies largely untouched, the generation after 1650 did see the imposition of new measures to control and regulate colonial commerce which, initially promoted by republican imperialists in Parliament, in alliance with London merchants, were to have important long-term implications for the colonies' development and relations with the mother country.[2]

COMMERCE AND COLONIAL POLICY

The reorientation of English economic policy began during the Puritan ascendancy which immediately followed the Civil War, when England's republican regime initiated a new strategy for controlling and enlarging English trade. Before the Civil War, English merchants and statesmen had increasingly become convinced that England's economic problems arose largely from its unequal relationship with the Dutch republic. From the 1620s the Dutch had interposed themselves between England and its trading partners both in Europe and in the colonial world, and the displacement of English trade into foreign hands had evoked demands, and some measures, for protection of national commerce. As the disruption caused by the Civil War had further strengthened Holland's profitable intermediary position in English commerce, particularly in the colonial and long-distance trades, the republican government which came to power after the Civil War came under strong pressure to eliminate this competition. To do so, it introduced the Navigation Act of 1651.[3]

The Act had one simple aim: to strike at Dutch dominance over major lines of English trade, both in Europe and beyond. By ordering that imports into England were to be brought only from the country where they were produced, and carried only in either English ships or ships of the country of their origin, the Act sought to ensure that goods imported into England came directly from their producer or exporter, rather than passing through the hands of Dutch merchants or being conveyed by Dutch vessels. As part of this attack on Dutch shipping and the Amsterdam entrepôt, the Act also sought to cut Dutch inroads into English colonial trade by laying down that all goods imported from Asia, Africa or the American colonies be carried only in English ships. This marked a new departure in English commercial policy. Now, instead of forcing merchants to organize themselves in crown-chartered companies, the rules of the Navigation Act established a general framework for commerce in which merchants could operate freely within a closed system that was designed to build up English trade and shipping, and to keep foreigners out of colonial commerce.

In the short term, neither the first Navigation Act nor the first Anglo-Dutch war of 1652–4, which it helped to precipitate, produced the desired results. The Act could not be strictly enforced, and the conflict with the Dutch was inconclusive. But the Navigation Act of 1651 set a course that was to be followed after 1660 by the restored Stuart monarchy in a series of laws that shaped commercial policy for generations to come. Indeed, one of the first actions of Charles II's government, which retained many of Cromwell's key advisors in commercial and mercantile matters, was to strengthen the policy with further Navigation Acts that were directed towards the same goals. In 1660, Parliament passed a fresh Navigation Act which reiterated the provisions of the 1651 statute and, to make it more effective, introduced the policy of 'enumerating' certain colonial commodities which could be exported only to England or another colony. Such listed goods were sugar, cotton, tobacco, indigo, ginger and dyewoods, then the most valuable commodities of England's American trades; all of these, save tobacco, were produced in the West Indies. The purpose of 'enumeration' was to ensure that trade in these commodities was monopolized by the mother country, and, as in 1651, to hurt the Dutch while benefiting English merchants, industry and the crown. The 1660 Act was shortly followed by another law, designed to match the monopoly over colonial exports with a monopoly of colonial markets for the products of English trade and industry. The Staple Act of 1663 prohibited the colonies from importing any goods (with the exception of certain named items) which had not been made in England or carried through its ports by English merchants. A decade later, Charles II sought further to tighten the colonial commercial system with the Plantation Act of 1673. This law aimed at closing a loophole in earlier legislation which had allowed enumerated commodities to be shipped from one colony to another and then sent to England without paying duties; it did so by imposing duty on enumerated goods traded between colonies, and providing for customs officials to be appointed in all colonies to ensure enforcement. Finally, in 1696, another Navigation Act added to the powers for regulating colonial trade by imposing closer supervision over the movement of ships and goods through American ports.[4]

There has been much controversy concerning the origins and inspiration of the Navigation Acts. One interpretation, developed by Heckscher, presents the navigation laws as the embodiment of a 'mercantilist' economic ideology, a uniform body of ideas which English (and other European) governments embraced in order to strengthen state power.[5] An alternative interpretation relates the development of commercial regulations to the shift of political power brought by the Civil War. According to Christopher Hill, the Civil War not only removed a substantial segment of the landed upper class, but also gave commercial interests an unprecedented share of power which allowed them to use government as an instrument for furthering their own economic interests. Seen from this perspective, the first Navigation Act reflects a turning point in the development of English capitalism and the first stage of a new imperialism backed by commercial interests.[6] Other historians, by contrast, argue that the commercial regulation developed from the pragmatic responses of governments to short-term problems rather than from any clearly identifiable ideology or class interest.[7]

On balance, the progress of commercial regulation is probably best understood, as the latter formulation suggests, in terms of the responses of governments and mercantile groups to the periodic economic and financial problems which affected England and its governments after the Civil War. Robert Brenner has argued that the unprecedented influence of commercial interests in Parliament immediately after the defeat of Charles I was important in initiating the new trade policy, since the shift in power brought by the Civil War gave merchants, among them men active in the colonial trades, a chance to translate their private priorities into public policy.[8] But there were also other powerful reasons why Parliament passed the first Navigation Act. First, English commerce suffered a recession during and immediately after the Civil War which made Dutch commercial competition a matter for serious concern both to merchants and to a government concerned to improve its revenues and to sustain its defences against foreign attack. A second factor was the Commonwealth regime's determination to revive English trade with the Baltic, which had suffered deep disruption during the Civil War, and thereby to secure vital strategic supplies from that region. Its possession of a powerful navy, built up during the war, also gave government the instrument for enforcing commercial regulations that previous governments had lacked. Thus the new system of commercial regulation was born in the convergence of economic interests with political concerns, rather than deriving simply from the collective pressure of English merchants or from the state's enactment of a 'mercantilist' theory.

Similar interactions between governments preoccupied with defence and finance and economic interest groups lobbying for their own needs explain why the commercial policy initiated by republican government, and its aggression towards the Dutch, continued after the Restoration. Following the King's return, mercantile representation in Parliament was reduced, and the court and landed gentry again took precedence. But, although merchants became less politically prominent after the Restoration, elements of the landed aristocracy and gentry which filled the House of Lords and Commons were linked to trade, particularly with the colonies, and were consequently ready to promote policies congruent with their economic interests. Once again, private pressures for policies to protect and expand overseas trade blended with other concerns. The first of these was the crown's desire to enlarge its revenues, and thus to reduce its financial dependence on Parliament; the second was the larger concern of both the crown and the political classes with issues of national security. The navy was increasingly considered to be the essential core of England's defences, and a flourishing mercantile marine, nurtured by overseas trade, was accordingly regarded as the key element of the kingdom's defence against foreign enemies. For these reasons, Charles II not only advanced the commercial legislation started by the Commonwealth, but also followed its aggressive policy against Holland, using naval power in two further wars against the Dutch in 1664–7 and 1672–4. Indeed, under Charles II, the 'blue water' strategy adopted by the Commonwealth and Protectorate, in which the pursuit of commercial profit and naval power were regarded as mutually reinforcing, became a central tenet of policy, setting a course that was to be more vigorously pursued in the next century.[9] As for economic thinking and theorizing, their importance was not that they provided a precise, coherent blueprint for policy. It was rather that, with the buoyancy of commerce, the spread of market relations, and the increasingly frank pursuit of gain by England's upper classes during the latter half of the seventeenth century, economic thinkers responded to economic and social change by gradually constructing and disseminating a view of society in which profit, consumption and the expansion of trade were laudable goals, favourable to the nation as a whole and coterminous with the defence of the state.[10]

England's regulation of colonial commerce was not, strictly speaking, a colonial policy. As Charles Andrews observed, 'the famous navigation acts of the years from 1651 to 1696 were at bottom commercial not colonial, and England's interest in America during these years continued to be a matter of trade and not of organized control.'[11] Whereas Spain imagined its empire in terms of governing and civilizing, for the English trade was the heart of empire, and in the generation after 1650 the colonies were largely left to govern themselves. At first, the Navigation Acts threatened to damage England's relations with the colonies, as colonials protested against restrictions on their trade which they feared would drive down the prices of their exports. Gradually, however, planters in the West Indies and the American South learned that there were compensations in the closed system of trade, since it excluded competition from foreign producers in English markets. It also allowed trade between colonies, so that the producers of agricultural and other commodities which had no market in England were able to prosper by supplying the West Indian planters with vital foodstuffs and raw materials. Thus the body of commercial regulation built up in this period had important implications for the development of England's empire: they fostered a system of English colonial commerce which created economic ties between the colonies and England, and between the colonies themselves. As these trades prospered, they enhanced government interest in colonial affairs. In this sense, the navigation laws hardened economic and political bonds between colonies and the parent power, and thereby contributed to the growth and consolidation of the emergent English empire in the Americas.

Commercial considerations were not, however, the only influence on the development of England's colonial presence in the Americas after the Civil War. Cromwell's Protectorate (1653–8) also saw the resurgence of an older, anti-Catholic form of imperialism, which was aimed against Spain and at the acquisition of territory, and which, in its initial stages at least, was underpinned by a vision of an empire ordered by the state rather than organized simply for the convenience of commercial interests. If this vision was peculiar to Cromwell and his Puritan supporters, it nonetheless marked the start of a new wave of English colonization in the Americas which substantially enlarged England's colonial empire during the second half of the seventeenth century. This began with Cromwell's campaign to seize territory in Spanish America during the mid-1650s; then, for different reasons, it gathered momentum after 1660, when, under the restored monarchy, English governments promoted the establishment of new colonies in North America.

CARIBBEAN COLONIALISM: THE AGE OF THE BUCCANEERS

Under Cromwell, the prime target for English imperialist ambition in the Americas was in the West Indies. North America excited relatively little interest. Cromwell regarded New England 'with an eye of pity, as poor, cold and useless', and, reverting to an Elizabethan, anti-Catholic approach to empire-building, he was much more concerned to exploit the lands and the commerce of the Caribbean.[12] At first, Cromwell's strategy was to seek an alliance with the Dutch, based on mutual freedom of trade and a partition of the Iberian empires, through which the Dutch would take Asia, while leaving the Americas (except Brazil) as an English sphere of influence. However, as the English had little to offer the Dutch in return for such concessions, the dream of a grand Protestant alliance soon dissolved. Thus, following the first Anglo-Dutch war of 1652–4 – a war against fellow Protestants with which Cromwell had never been completely comfortable – the Lord Protector turned his attention to Spain's empire in the Americas, where he sought to establish a base in the Greater Antilles from which to attack Spain's colonial territory and trade.

Buoyed up by naval successes in the first Dutch war, urged on by Puritan demands for a crusade against Catholicism, and confident that Spain's colonial defences were weak, in late 1654 Cromwell took up the idea of a war against Spain in which he might profitably employ English naval strength.[13] His assault on Spanish power began in the Caribbean, with an attack on Hispaniola in April 1655. This was the first move in his 'Western Design', a strategy aimed at overthrowing the Spanish empire in the Indies and thereby enriching England, while also advancing the forces of Protestantism against the great bastion of Catholicism. In the event, the military expedition against Santo Domingo failed, no rich Spanish colonies fell to the English, and Cromwell's forces managed only to capture the poor, sparsely inhabited island of Jamaica.[14] Although at the time Jamaica seemed a poor return for the considerable loss of life incurred in Cromwell's Caribbean campaigns, the seizure of Jamaica nonetheless marked a new departure in English colonialism. It not only brought a permanent extension of English territory in the Americas, located at the maritime centre of Spain's empire, but also was the first of several territorial acquisitions which, under the restored monarchy, expanded the territory and authority of the English crown in North America.

At first, settlement of Jamaica was slow. Indeed, in its early years it was less successful as a colony than Surinam, the Dutch settlement in Guiana which the English colony had taken in 1651. Together with Jews driven from Brazil by the Portuguese and from Cayenne by the French, royalist planters from Barbados turned Surinam into a thriving settlement, run as a privately sponsored venture. The colonization of Jamaica, on the other hand, was undertaken by the state, in the first government-organized colonial enterprise of Anglo-America. This was not immediately successful. English government had had little experience in such matters, and the first soldiers sent from England to establish the 'plantation' of Jamaica were reluctant colonists. Not until experienced colonists arrived from the over-crowded islands of Nevis and Barbados, together with veteran soldiers from Cromwell's armies at home, did the English colony in Jamaica take on a firmer footing; even then, the island's governor had to cope with guerrilla attacks from Spaniards and their former slaves, and found it difficult to attract white settlers.

Ironically, however, it was the very weakness of Jamaica in its early years that was to transform it into the frontier for aggressive English imperialism in the Caribbean. For, while its military governors reorganized agriculture, in settlements subject to army discipline, Jamaica lacked adequate naval support. Jamaica's Governor-General D'Oyley therefore granted privateering commissions to the corsairs of nearby Tortuga, with their crews of lawless 'buccaneers'.[15] Tortuga was in French hands, but its corsairs were prepared to fight for any government that issued them with licences to privateer. Invited to settle in Jamaica, they were soon joined by English adventurers and settlers who were equally eager to profit from preying on merchant shipping and raiding enemy towns, and became Jamaica's navy.[16]

That Jamaica's first role in the Anglo-American empire was as a privateering station, rather than a plantation export economy, is readily understandable. In the 1660s, too many colonies were producing tropical goods, and privateering offered more profit than colonial agriculture, just as it had in the years of Elizabeth I. The Irish spy Sir Richard White explained this to Spain's Council of the Indies in 1671, when the council was trying to confront the English threat to Spain's colonies in the Caribbean region. There was, he said, no other way of making money in Jamaica than by robbing Spaniards. This was, moreover, an enormous temptation because there was a great deal of money waiting to be taken on the Spanish coasts, from Spanish colonials who 'have a great lack of courage with which to defend themselves, while amongst the aggressors there is an insatiable desire of riches, great courage, and total disdain of risk'.[17]

Even when officially sanctioned as privateering, such piracy was fundamentally a private enterprise, comparable to the *entradas* and *cabalgadas* (exploratory and plundering raids) made by the Spanish conquistadors into unknown territories during the early sixteenth century. The privateers recruited men of different social groups, ranging from gentlemen adventurers and impoverished planters and traders to lowly seamen, servants and the stateless, half-wild buccaneers of the islands. Like the conquistadors, these men went in search of plunder, they organized themselves on a military basis for the duration of an expedition under a particular leader, and they agreed to share the spoils according to prearranged rules, with bonuses for bravery and compensation for injury. Like the conquistadors, they could justify the personal pursuit of wealth and glory with the flimsy pretext of fighting for a national cause. Here, of course, the similarity ends, for the privateers often had no formal allegiance to the power for whom they fought, did not greatly discriminate between those whom they served, and were more concerned with pillage than with conquest. Nonetheless, the European privateers and buccaneers of the seventeenth century do bear some comparison with the Spanish conquistadors of a century earlier, since, like the latter, they were not a formal soldiery organized by the state, but groups of adventurers who, in their personal search for loot, could be mobilized for reasons of state. If the bands of conquistadors who conquered Spanish America were the first shock troops of European warfare in the Americas, the buccaneers were their heirs, fighting wars that were conducted at sea rather than on land, and were conflicts between Europeans rather than between Europeans and Indians.

For the English presence in the Americas, buccaneering had a twofold significance. First, it enabled England to hold Jamaica. During the 1660s, the buccaneers were Jamaica's only defence, and their employment enabled the island's authorities to keep their grip on what was later to become a vastly prosperous plantation economy. Second, buccaneering supplied the aggressive drive required to strengthen English sovereignty in the Caribbean and to develop bases for illegal trade with Spanish America, without any need for recourse to an expensive military or naval commitment by the state. For, although buccaneers were of little use in war against the Dutch or the French, they kept Spain on the defensive, and turned Port Royal in Jamaica into one of England's largest and most thriving towns in the New World.[18] Such was their importance as an instrument of English policy in the Caribbean that Henry Morgan, the most celebrated English buccaneer of his age, later became Lieutenant-Governor of Jamaica and was knighted for his services to the crown.

Morgan's fame and fortune rested on his extraordinary exploits of attack and rapine among the Spanish islands and along the adjacent mainland costs. To persuade the buccaneers to defend Jamaica, its governor had licensed them to attack Spanish shipping; Morgan, who quickly became their favourite leader, went much further. In 1668, he struck at Portobelo, one of Spain's strategic ports on the Isthmus of Panama, sacked the town and destroyed its fortifications. In 1669, he planned to attack Cartagena de Indias, the other great port for the Spanish galleons, and was prevented from doing so only by the accidental loss of his flagship. He sailed instead to Maracaibo, where he conducted a devastating raid on the town and then, against very unfavourable odds, defeated the Spanish warships sent to destroy him. The climax of his violent and bloodstained career came in 1670–1, when he set out from Jamaica with orders from its governor to conduct reprisals against Spanish American ports from which Spaniards had raided Jamaica in mid-1670. After raiding Rio de la Hacha and Santa Marta from Jamaica, Morgan subsequently sailed, in December 1670, towards the heart of the Spanish Main. First, he took Providence Island (previously a Puritan base which had been recaptured by Spain); then he sailed to the Isthmus of Panama, where he took the fortress at Chagres prior to crossing the Isthmus and sacking Panama, in a daring raid which dramatically revealed the weakness of Spanish defences in a strategic area.[19]

The plunder of Panama was the highpoint of English buccaneering, for in the Treaty of Madrid (1670) England and Spain agreed to end their wars of reprisal. This did not entirely eliminate the buccaneers. They continued to be used as an instrument of war by the competing powers, and their piratical depredations were stopped only when these powers found them more of a nuisance than an asset, and agreed on their suppression at the Treaty of Ryswick (1697). For the English, however, the buccaneers had served their main purpose by 1670, as the cutting edge of English imperialism in the Caribbean. The Treaty of Madrid reflected their achievement. The English position in the Caribbean was secure, entrenched in a series of islands of which Jamaica was to become the most important, from which it could conduct a growing contraband trade with Spanish America, and which it could develop as plantation economies producing sugar for the European market. After a decade of ferocious harassment by the buccaneers, Spain officially accepted what it had always previously denied: the English right to sovereignty over the lands and islands which they held in the Americas.

If the conquest of Jamaica came about as a result of Cromwell's 'Western Design', born from his vision of a coalition of Protestant powers arraigned against Catholic Spain, Cromwell's dream of empire did not entirely perish with him in 1658. After the Restoration, the links between commerce, colonies and war continued to fuel English aggression and expansion, directed particularly against the Dutch. These were years when the balance of the world economy created by European commercial and colonial expansion was beginning to shift significantly. From about 1620, Spain's American colonies were producing less bullion, or at least exporting less of it to Europe, and Spanish America was becoming less important to European trade. Now the Dutch, English and French wanted to exploit products for which there was a continuing high demand, such as tobacco and sugar, and they saw possibilities for doing this by exploiting their own overseas colonies, rather than merely interloping in the commerce of Spanish America. Continuing political conflict with Spain gave England an added incentive to support colonization in the Americas, at the same time that religious and political conflicts within European societies gave many people an incentive to emigrate.

The upsurge of English interest in the Caribbean was greatly stimulated by the development of the trade in African slaves, pioneered by the Dutch. Not only did the Dutch show the French and English settlers in the Caribbean that sugar could be a very profitable crop, but also showed them how to acquire the large supply of people required to produce it. Introduced from Brazil in the 1640s, sugar spread rapidly through the Caribbean, with black slavery in its wake. Taken together, sugar and slavery transformed the societies they touched, and made the Caribbean region a focus for European rivalry, of far greater interest than continental North America. For the Caribbean islands offered immediate returns. In sugar, they provided a valuable agricultural commodity which could be traded to Europe, fostering both the growth of a nation's trade and its shipping. As the sugar plantations were worked by African slave labour, national labour could be retained at home (allaying the fears of those anxious about domestic labour supply), while traffic in slaves also provided further valuable trade for English merchants.[20] Finally, the island colonies were easier to control politically. The planters were dependent on an import–export economy carried by sea and could accordingly be disciplined by the use of seapower, unlike such self-sufficient mainland regions as New England.

Once the race to develop sugar-producing colonies had started, England could not afford to lag behind its Dutch and French rivals, and competition to dominate the trade became a leading theme in international politics. Thus, during the later seventeenth century, the English colonies in the Caribbean became an engine for imperial growth, setting in motion economic forces that were to have a profound effect on the development of England and its American dominions.

ENGLISH EXPANSION IN NORTH AMERICA

Under Cromwell, territorial aggrandizement in the Caribbean also had a counterpart in North America. During the first Anglo–Dutch war, a small force was mobilized to attack the Dutch colony of New Amsterdam; when it was forestalled by the conclusion of peace with Holland, it was turned instead against the forts that defended France's incipient colony of Acadia (later Nova Scotia). A precarious settlement of only a few hundred settlers, Acadia seemed of little value and at the Treaty of Westminster in 1654, England agreed to return it to France. Thus, when Cromwell died, England had made no territorial gains in North America comparable to the capture of Jamaica in the Caribbean. The Dutch retained their colony at New Amsterdam and the French claim to Acadia had been acknowledged (though the forts taken in wartime remained in English hands), so that England continued to face competition from its leading European rivals on the American mainland. However, the continuation of an aggressive foreign policy by the restored monarchy, aimed mainly against the Dutch, was to bring important changes in English North America during the later seventeenth century.

In the three decades after 1660, fresh ventures of conquest and colonization filled the spaces between New England and the Chesapeake region, and spread English settlement southwards into regions contested with Spain. After the Restoration, Cromwell's initiative in Nova Scotia was abandoned and there was no movement into Canada, despite the fact that the French hold on these territories was extremely weak. In 1660, the French presence in North America was limited to a tiny population of about 2,500, but England's opportunity to expand into Canada was ignored. Instead, the gaze of colonial promoters fixed on more promising areas in the southern and middle reaches of North America's Atlantic seaboard. Between 1660 and 1681, four new colonies were founded in those regions, starting in the south. In 1663, the crown granted a charter for the foundation of Carolina; in 1664, New Amsterdam was taken from the Dutch and converted into the English colony of New York; together with neighbouring New Jersey, these territories were granted by royal charter to aristocratic proprietors in reward for their services to Charles II. Finally, in 1681, William Penn was given the right to found the colony that was named after him, as Pennsylvania. From the new colonies, others subsequently sprang: in 1701, Carolina was formally divided into two provinces, south and north; in 1702, part of what was originally Pennsylvania became the province of Delaware. Thus, during the later seventeenth century, England gained and consolidated a hold over the entire eastern seaboard between Maine and the Carolinas, greatly strengthening the English presence in North America in a network of colonies which became increasingly populous and prosperous. How, then, was this new wave of colonization launched, and what were its implications for the development of Anglo-America?

The first of the new colonies was set up in the region south of Virginia, which, under the name 'Carolina', was granted to a group of eight proprietors in 1663. Interest in the region was not entirely new. In 1629, Sir Robert Heath had obtained a grant from the crown for the area which he called 'Carolana', where he planned to resettle Huguenots exiled from France. But it was not until Charles II made his grant of 1663 that a real effort was made to settle the area, now renamed 'Carolina'.

The plan of the proprietors was not simply to imitate Virginia by cultivating tobacco, but also to promote the production of Mediterranean agricultural goods which England had to buy from foreigners, such as wine, olive oil and silk. They hoped to profit as speculators, developing lands in the new colony to furnish them with rents, but their scheme also embodied the new mood in England following the Restoration. The Carolina promoters were wealthy and powerful men who were widely involved in other commercial and colonial projects, and their interest in Carolina reflected a more general commitment to English economic and territorial expansion overseas.

The Carolina proprietors did not seek to people their colony with migrants from England, since colonists were readily available within the Americas. One of the leading promoters of the colony was Sir William Berkeley, the Governor of Virginia, who supported and helped organize settlement of Virginian colonists in the region just south of Virginia, around Albemarle Sound; this was to become the core of North Carolina. Another major figure behind the Carolina project was Sir John Colleton, a planter from the island of Barbados, who encouraged his fellow Barbadians to seek their fortunes in Carolina. Thus Barbados, whose people were already suffering from a shortage of land, was to be the major source of Carolina's colonists, focused primarily in the region south of Cape Fear. Reinforced by emigrants from New England, their first attempts at settlement during the 1660s met with little success, but after the foundation of Charles Town (modern Charleston) in 1670, the colony became firmly established under the leadership of a small group of Barbadians. Here the core of what later became South Carolina was created, as the 'colony of a colony'.

Initially, Carolina did not match up to the expectations of its proprietors, either politically or economically. They assembled elaborate plans for both its government and development, but these proved impossible to implement. In 1669, the English philosopher John Locke – then the secretary of Lord Ashley, one of the Carolina proprietors – drew up a constitution for the colony which envisaged a hierarchical social order of nobles and freeholders ruled by a political oligarchy. However, in this frontier society of settlers who followed their own interests, political practices learned in the colonies prevailed. Government in the Carolinas soon came to resemble that found in the other proprietary colonies, with a governor, a council and an elected assembly of freeholders. The single, unified government of Carolina was also formally superseded in 1701, when North Carolina was given its own governor.

The proprietors' hopes for the region's economic development were disappointed, too. Instead of becoming a source of Mediterranean crops for export to Europe, Carolina remained poor for many years, combining a subsistence agriculture with the production of foodstuffs and lumber for export to the Caribbean islands, particularly overcrowded Barbados. So, although formed as an offshoot of Caribbean plantation society, Carolina did not immediately reproduce the economic and social structure of that society. There was, however, an ominous sign that it would eventually follow this path, in that the settlers took Indians as slaves, both for their own use and for export to the West Indies. Later, in the eighteenth century, it was also to find a staple export crop in the form of rice; in South Carolina this was to enable a white elite to imitate the Caribbean pattern of development by creating a plantation economy based on slave labour imported from Africa.[21]

The establishment of Carolina exemplifies the motives and techniques behind colonial expansion under the restored monarchy. In the first place, it showed a determination to continue the expansive policy initiated by Cromwell, in this case by occupying lands that were claimed but not settled by Spain. Second, Carolina was granted to aristocratic proprietors, rather than to a mercantile company. This enabled Charles II to pay off political debts to his friends and supporters, to satisfy demands for land among those deprived of their estates during the Civil War, and to give incentives for occupying lands that might otherwise remain in Spanish or Dutch hands. This method of taking new colonial territory was continued shortly after the foundation of Carolina, when new colonies were founded in New York and New Jersey, in the mid-latitude area between New England and the Chesapeake colonies of Maryland and Virginia.

The creation of New York and New Jersey occurred in circumstances which differed from those of Carolina, since they involved the takeover of areas which were already partly settled by another European power. The Hudson River had been explored by the Dutch early in the seventeenth century, and the Dutch West India Company, founded in 1621, had created the colony of New Netherland in the Hudson Valley and on Manhattan Island. However, Dutch expansion in the Atlantic focused more on Brazil and Africa than on North America, and New Netherland remained a collection of trading posts rather than becoming a colony of any substantial Dutch settlement. Its main town, New Amsterdam, prospered from a flourishing fur trade with local Indians, but such was the Dutch neglect of the region's agricultural potential that in the 1630s the

Swedish were allowed to plant a colony in the Delaware River area of New Netherland. By the early 1660s, the European population of New Netherland was probably no more than about 10,000 people.

The English attack on New Netherland was in effect a continuation under the restored monarchy of the policy initiated by Cromwell. The first plan to take the Dutch settlement had been made during the Anglo-Dutch war of 1652–4, and was frustrated only by a lack of cooperation from Massachusetts, which had fatally delayed the assault envisaged by Cromwell's officers. A decade later, the project was revived during the second Anglo-Dutch war of 1664–7, under different circumstances but with more positive results. Neither Charles II nor Clarendon, his chief minister, favoured war with Holland. They were, however, forced to bow to pressures for war that stemmed from the self-interested search by courtiers and naval officers for profit and personal advancement, and from English merchants who were struggling to compete with the Dutch in the East and West Indies, and in the West African slave trade, where the Royal Africa Company (chartered in 1663) sought to take a share of this lucrative trade from the Dutch West India Company. As this was also a moment when the English economy was suffering a depression, the promise of personal enrichment was reinforced by the hope that war would stimulate economic and commercial activity. From this combination of pressures, English plans to attack Dutch overseas trade and to seize Dutch territory took shape.[22]

Harassment of Dutch trading posts in Africa and Dutch retaliation soon escalated into a full-scale war between England and Holland, with immediate repercussions in North America. Early in 1664, Charles II made his brother James the proprietor of a vast area encompassing both Dutch New Amsterdam and the huge tracts of land that stretched from the north of New England southwards, over all the territory between Connecticut and the mouth of the Delaware. By the end of the year a combined naval and military expedition had taken New Amsterdam without a shot being fired. Renamed New York, this new colony was buttressed to the south by the foundation of New Jersey, which Charles II ceded as a proprietary grant to two of his followers, John, Lord Berkeley and Sir George Carteret. When the second Anglo-Dutch war ended, Holland made no effort to recover these territories. In 1667, the Treaty of Breda left the two powers with the territories they had taken during the war, so that the Dutch effectively exchanged New Netherland for Surinam in South America, which they had taken from the English. By the same treaty, France, which had been Holland's ally during the war, finally secured the return of Acadia (which had been promised by the English in 1655) in return for captured territories in the Caribbean islands of St Kitts, Montserrat and Antigua. During the third Anglo–Dutch war, a Dutch fleet retook New York in 1673, but England's command of the New York and New Jersey regions was soon restored by the treaty that concluded the war in the following year. The Dutch had, then, been removed from North America, leaving the way clear for English colonization of the Middle Atlantic regions. The French remained, however, and, tenuous though its presence still was, France was now set to become England's great colonial rival in the Americas.

The early development of New York was to some extent simply a continuation of the past. Dutch place names were changed for English ones, but the title of Dutch landlords and tenants to their lands was confirmed, and the Dutch rural population continued to grow. The social heterogeneity of the colony was also sustained and developed under English rule, as the proprietor encouraged an influx of settlers from Europe, from New England and from England itself. Indeed, the defining characteristic of the region was its cosmopolitanism. English and Dutch elements were mixed with Huguenots from France and a variety of Protestant migrants from Flanders, Germany and Scotland, creating a mosaic of largely rural communities which clung to their own ethnic identities. The economies of both New York and New Jersey rested on the production of temperate food crops (mainly wheat, corn, oats and barley) for subsistence and, increasingly, for export to the West Indies and to southern Europe.

Politically, New York and New Jersey differed somewhat. While the New Jersey proprietors sought to attract settlers from other colonies by promising them freedom to trade, liberty of conscience, and rights to self-government through elected assemblies, in New York the royal proprietor stood out against the creation of representative government for many years. He was finally forced to concede it in 1683, after repeated protests and a refusal to pay taxes. This was then temporarily reversed between 1685 and 1689, when, as part of the King's plans to reorganize colonial government, New York was absorbed into the Dominion of New England, to be controlled by the crown without any representative assembly. However, after the fall of King James II in 1688, and a rebellion against its governor in 1689, New York finally settled into the institutional arrangements typical of other English colonies, with a royal governor, a council and an assembly presiding over its government.[23]

After these colonizing projects of the 1660s, nearly two decades then elapsed before another major new area of English colonization came into existence. In 1681, William Penn obtained from Charles II a proprietary grant to a large area of Middle North America, some 600,000 square miles standing between New York and New Jersey to the north and Maryland to the south. A leading English Quaker, Penn had already been involved in American colonizing projects for some years before 1681, as a consequence of his contacts with Quakers who had acquired West New Jersey. When he received Charles II's grant (made in payment for a debt owed to his father), he was eager to use it both as a means of bolstering his own fortunes and, more idealistically, as an opportunity for providing a religious refuge for his fellow Quakers, where they might build a model society governed by their religious and political values.

Pennsylvania started, then, with aspirations to become a 'Holy Commonwealth', just as Massachusetts had begun half a century before. But if Penn's central ambition was to engender a society ruled by Christian values, it was to be very different from that of Massachusetts. Unlike the self-righteous Puritans, Penn and his fellow Quakers believed that all people were intrinsically good, and they were committed to religious tolerance and the widespread dissemination of political and legal rights. Penn, moreover, conceived of his colony as a supra-national enterprise that would attract all European Protestants, particularly those fleeing from persecution. Thus, if New York was cosmopolitan by accident, Pennsylvania was made so by the will of its founder.

The result was remarkable. Within a few years, about 8,000 immigrants arrived in Pennsylvania, and the region rapidly became a colony of considerable importance. Most of those who went to Pennsylvania in these early years were Quakers, drawn from England, Wales and Germany, but in the succeeding decades, the colony attracted a growing stream of immigrants as it became renowned as the 'best poor man's country'. Penn himself took charge of the experiment between 1682 and 1684, and although his thorough planning for an orderly settlement based on careful land allocation was not systematically implemented, his achievement was extraordinary in several respects. First, he managed to avoid any conflict with local Indian tribes, always negotiating peacefully with them and paying for their lands. Second, thanks partly to the experience accumulated by colonists in the past, Penn presided over a colony that was a material success from the outset. It not only avoided the chaos and starvation which had attended the birth of earlier colonies, but also soon began a prosperous and flourishing agricultural economy. Finally, Penn's experiment in urban planning at Philadelphia created a town that was to become one of the major cities of eighteenth-century North America, rivalled only by New York and Boston as a focal point in England's burgeoning Atlantic economy.[24]

ANGLO-AMERICA AT THE END OF THE SEVENTEENTH CENTURY

By the end of the seventeenth century, the English presence in the Americas had been greatly strengthened. During this first century of colonization, more than 400,000 migrants had left Britain (principally from England, rather than from Scotland and Wales) for the West Indies and North America, a ratio of emigrants to domestic population that was much higher than that of any other European colonial power.[25] The development of sugar cultivation had converted the English Caribbean colonies into the economic core of a vigorous and growing system of imperial trade, and had obtained for England a strategic focus for commercial penetration of the Spanish empire. Meanwhile, in North America, the territory and population under English control had grown impressively. While the Caribbean colonies were being transformed by intensive economic change, in which large amounts of capital and labour were applied to small areas of land, North America had expanded extensively. Between 1660 and 1700, English North America grew steadily larger both in the extent of territory under English sovereignty and the size of its population. The territory under English rule had been enlarged along a north–south axis, extending over the whole of the eastern seaboard from Maine to the Carolinas. Settlement was still generally confined to the coastal hinterland, but these lands were occupied by a growing population, fed by both natural reproduction in the older colonies and continuing immigration from Europe.

In 1700, the total population of the British American colonies was still small in comparison to that of England. Whereas England (excluding Wales and Scotland) had a population of just over 5 million at the turn of the century, the population of English American colonies was at most about 500,000, which made it smaller than the population of London. It had, however, grown at a far faster pace than population in the mother country, increasing more than threefold between 1660 and 1710. The distribution of population between the colonies had also altered significantly, starting a trend which was to become much stronger during the eighteenth century. In 1660, the colonial population had been balanced roughly equally between North America, which had 52 per cent of total colonial population, both black and white, and the West Indies, which had 45 per cent. By 1710, North America had 67 per cent of Anglo-America's population, and the West Indies only 32 per cent.[26] Another distinctive feature of colonial demographic change was the growing proportion of black slaves. In 1660, African slaves formed just over a quarter of the English colonial population; by 1710, they were over a third. The expansion of the black population was mostly in the West Indies where it was driven by the imports of slaves to work the sugar plantations and where slaves became a majority that far outnumbered whites. But in the closing decades of the seventeenth century, the black population was reinforced by the increasing use of slave labour in the colonies of the American South, especially the tobacco-producing areas of the Chesapeake region.

The growth of the colonial population, particularly the enlargement of slave numbers, underpinned an expansion of the colonies' economies that contributed significantly to English commercial development during the latter part of the seventeenth century. In 1700 as in 1640, most English trade was with Europe, and London was still England's principal port. However, the scale and structure of English commerce underwent such tremendous change in the middle and later decades of the seventeenth century that historians speak of a 'commercial revolution'. During the second half of the seventeenth century, the overall value of English trade increased fourfold, and its composition became much more diverse. Expansion derived in large part from growth in trade with Europe, particularly in the export of cloth which, as English production shifted from the pure woollen cloth of the 'old draperies' to the lighter, cheaper and more colourful woollen fabrics of the 'new draperies', opened important new markets in southern Europe and the Levant. But during this period England escaped from its dependence on one major export. Whereas in 1640 about 90 per cent of London's exports were of woollen cloth sent to markets in Europe, by 1699–1701 woollens had fallen to less than 69 per cent of total English exports. This was in large due to the expansion of the re-exporting trades which transferred commodities imported into England to European markets. In 1640, London's re-exports were around 10 per cent of its total exports; by the turn of the century, re-exports from England constituted about 30 per cent of all exports. England had, in short, become a major European entrepôt, rivalling if not replacing Amsterdam.

Re-exports consisted mostly of commodities brought from the

colonies and tropical areas in Anglo-America, India and the east, and their growth reflects the growing importance of these long-distance trades. By the end of the century, almost a third of England's imports came from India and the American colonies, compared to about a fifth in the 1660s, while imports from Europe, especially north-western Europe, had concomitantly declined. In part, this reflected the huge expansion of internal demand for sugar and tobacco. In 1700, England imported nearly 38 million pounds of tobacco from North America, compared to about 1 million pounds in 1640; West Indian sugar imports expanded from 150,000 to over 370,000 hundredweight over the same period. As American production rose, so prices fell, and these previously luxury items became so widely used as to induce a veritable 'consumer revolution' in the mother country. Moreover, the change in English imports also brought a major change in English exports because, since domestic markets could not absorb all colonial production of these commodities, growing quantities were sold on to European markets.

The American colonies were not the sole source of tropical commodities in this burgeoning pattern of trade. Valuable cargoes of spices, silks and calicoes came from the east, channelled to England by the Levant and East India Companies. But in 1699–1701, the value of imports from North America and the West Indies, at nearly 19 per cent of the value of total English imports, was greater than the value of imports from the Far East, which stood at nearly 13 per cent. The cod fisheries of Newfoundland also supplied a valuable trade for England. Fishermen took their catches to both the Mediterranean, where fish was exchanged for Mediterranean products that were taken to England, and to the West Indies, where they provided food for the slaves who powered the sugar plantations. The demand for slaves in the colonies meanwhile underpinned the growth of a profitable English slave trade with West Africa which, though it provided only very small markets for English exports, inaugurated a trade that was to undergo a great expansion during the eighteenth century. The growth of American markets for English exports was much more marked in the eighteenth than in the seventeenth century, as we shall see in Chapter 8. Nonetheless, by 1700, American markets for English goods were taking about 13 per cent of English exports, mainly of manufactured goods, and thus contributed to the overall increase in England's trade. The growth of English trade with Spain and Portugal during the latter half of the seventeenth century also conceals an aspect of English commerce with the Americas which, though impossible to quantify, should not be ignored: namely, the re-export of English manufactures from Seville and Lisbon to the Iberian American colonies where there was a substantial demand for textiles of a quality and price which these colonial powers could not themselves supply.

The importance of the American trades was reinforced by their effect on English shipping. During the second half of the seventeenth century, England's mercantile fleet increased its tonnage by around 150 per cent, substantially strengthening the nation's power at sea. Here the American trades made an important contribution. In 1700, they employed 13 per cent of total English shipping employed in overseas trade; this was a proportion which competed with that of English shipping engaged in the Mediterranean trades, and was considerably larger than that employed in long-distance trade with the east. So, at the start of the eighteenth century, the Anglo-American colonies were already making a very valuable contribution to metropolitan commerce and acting as a dynamic element in its growth.[27]

From the English point of view, the arc of colonies which stretched from the West Indies to the Chesapeake Bay, in the American South, held England's most useful colonies: these were the regions which produced the profitable and expanding trades in tobacco and sugar, offered a growing market for English goods, and, as a secondary consequence of their development, a valuable trade in slaves. They therefore fulfilled what was for contemporaries the proper economic function of colonies, by acting as sources of primary commodities and markets for metropolitan finished goods and manufactures. Not all the colonies discharged this role, however. The new Middle Atlantic colonies produced grains of a kind that England could supply for itself, and in their early years only New York, with its access through the Hudson and Mohawk valleys to the huge fur-trapping regions around the Great Lakes, had a product which found valuable markets in Europe. New England also offered few exports of value to the home country. Its main markets were not in the mother country but in other colonies, among the West Indian islands that required lumber, livestock and provisions. In return for these exports, the New Englanders took sugar and molasses from both the English and French islands, some of which they re-exported to England in their own ships, and some of which they distilled into rum to supply their own mainland markets. In addition to these trades, which were perfectly legal, the New Englanders also evaded the Navigation Acts by exporting sugar and tobacco to continental Europe, thereby breaking the English monopoly and depriving the crown of revenue. Thus the economy of New England functioned in ways which did not directly benefit English commerce and were a periodic source of dispute

118

between the colony and the parent power. Indirectly, however, the development of intercolonial trade of the kind practised by New England strengthened English commerce and the English colonial presence in the Americas. For, by providing West Indian planters with a cheap and reliable source of foodstuffs and timber, it greatly facilitated the growth of the sugar trade and sustained the development of the English Caribbean Islands. By permitting colonial producers who had no markets in Europe to find outlets in other colonies (and allowing free immigration into its colonies), England also allowed English settlers to develop resources and markets in regions which might otherwise have been impoverished and marginal. This contrasts markedly with Spain's colonial policy which, by limiting intercolonial trade and restricting foreign immigration, left large parts of its empire undeveloped.

CONSOLIDATION AND CONFLICT

Although the Middle Atlantic colonies still held the lesser part of English North America's population in 1700 and were less economically developed than the older areas of settlement, the advance of settlement into these regions had important implications for the development of England's empire. It not only opened new spaces for colonization, but also converted English North America into a more coherent territorial entity. The extension of dominion in New York, New Jersey and Philadelphia was particularly significant, since it closed the gaps which had previously offered room for competitors and brought the whole of the eastern seaboard from Maine to the Carolinas under English control. This reflected a crucial victory over the Dutch, England's chief commercial competitor. With the Dutch removed from New Netherland, it became easier to build the closed commercial system by which England sought to profit from its colonies.

Taking New York and the Hudson Valley was also a significant step towards securing control of the interior, because it blocked the French advance towards the coast and challenged French domination of the fur trade. Albany now became a competitor with Montreal, and as English settlers pushed into the interior and joined in Indian wars, this competition led to increasingly frequent clashes with the French, foreshadowing the major struggle for territory that was to take place in the eighteenth century.

Although English America was much stronger at the end of the seventeenth century than it had been fifty years earlier, its frontiers were still insecure. Holland had withdrawn from North America and Spain had ceased to be an aggressive rival, but the English colonies still faced several dangers. For colonials in frontier areas of North America, a persistent peril lay among the native peoples of the interior, who were capable of mounting fierce resistance to the white advance. In the older colonies, years of contact with whites had decimated native peoples, diminishing the Indian threat. In Virginia, the native population in 1670 was less than a tenth part of what it had been when the English first planted their settlement there; in New England, disease and the advance of white settlement on to Indian lands had a comparably traumatic effect. Nonetheless, tensions between whites and Indians could still produce bloody confrontations.

In New England, white penetration of Indian tribal lands culminated in a major frontier war in 1675, when a confederation of Indian tribes joined in attacking white settlers, led by Metacomet, an Indian chief known to the English as 'King Philip'. Casualties were high. Forty towns were attacked, twelve destroyed, and several thousand settlers and Indians were killed. In the end, the whites prevailed. Metacomet was captured and executed, the rebellion collapsed, and the conquest of the native peoples of New England rapidly moved to completion, as Indians either accepted subordination or retreated from the region. In Virginia, war against the Indians was also still a fact of life in these same years. Indeed, in 1675–6 frontier planters organized indiscriminate hostilities against Indians, and, furious at the governor's refusal to support them, they turned their violence on government itself, in Bacon's Rebellion of 1676.[28]

Deeper in the interior, the Indians were much stronger. As their resistance was made more effective by alliances with competing white groups, and more lethal by the acquisition of firearms, they constituted both an obstacle to expansion and a threat to security. The most formidable grouping was that of the Iroquois Confederacy, an alliance of five Indian 'nations' which had grown enormously powerful during the seventeenth century. Competing for control of the fur trade with Europeans, the Iroquois had forced many other Indian tribes to accept their suzerainty and controlled a huge territory from the St Lawrence to the Ohio. Recognizing their power, the English and the Dutch had sought to remain on peaceful terms with the Iroquois, while the French sought alliances with their enemies, the Huron. In King Philip's War of 1675–6, Edmund Andros, then Governor of New York, formed an alliance with the Iroquois to fight the Indian insurgents of New England, and this formed the basis for the establishment of the 'Covenant Chain', an enduring partnership between the English and the Five Nations of the Iroquois against the French and their Huron allies. Henceforth, both the English and French used Indian allies in their conflicts with each other; in 1688, for example, the English used the Iroquois to attack Montreal, and the French retaliated by using the Abenaki Indians to raid English settlements in their territory.[29]

This use of Indian allies in conflicts between European settlers points to the second, greater source of danger threatening England's position in the Americas at the close of the seventeenth century. This was the challenge from France, which, after 1660, emerged as the most powerful European state. For England, the principal problem created by French expansion lay in Europe, where France seemed set to inherit the dominating position which the Habsburgs had held in the previous century. But conflict in Europe was also to lead inexorably towards conflict in the Americas, where England and France confronted each other from their respective bases in the Caribbean and North America.

Like the English, the French had long been concerned to establish colonies in the Americas, and early in the seventeenth century had put down roots in both the Caribbean and in North America. In the Caribbean, they had settlements in Martinique and other islands of the Windward group, together with Guadeloupe and several of the Leewards, and, like the English, France saw these islands as both plantation economies and bases from which to intervene in Spanish American commerce. In North America, French traders also uncovered the vast potential of the wilderness, penetrating deep into the interior from the mouth of the St Lawrence River and creating a highly valuable trade in furs. During the first half of the seventeenth century, France had been too embroiled in war and civil strife to pay much attention to these incipient colonies, but during the reign of Louis XIV (1643–1715) French colonial ambitions took on a more solid form. While Colbert was Louis's chief minister (1661–83), the French monarchy embraced the vision of a great Franco-American empire. It was born in 1663 with the adoption of a plan to combine French interests in Canada and the West Indies by establishing a great, state-sponsored *Compagnie des Indes Occidentales* which would link the northern and tropical colonies into a mutually reinforcing trade system. Inspired by Cromwell's capture of Jamaica, Colbert also wanted to seize a major Spanish island and, having established French authority over the buccaneers of Tortuga, he encouraged French settlement on

Spanish Hispaniola, thereby laying the foundations of St Domingue which, after it was officially ceded to France in 1697, later became the richest sugar colony in the world.[30]

Despite French colonial advances, England avoided conflict with France during the 1670s and 1680s, as both Charles II and his successor, James II, secretly sought alliance with France (and commitment to war against Holland) as part of their effort to establish royal absolutism in England.[31] But when James's political opponents joined with William of Orange to overthrow him and to place William on the English throne in the 'Glorious Revolution' of 1688, both the English state and its foreign policy entered a new era. Under William III, conflict with France became the dominant theme in England's foreign policy, setting a pattern that was to last for more than a century. Shortly after his accession, William went to war with France (in the Nine Years War of 1689–97) in order to stem the rising power of France on the Continent and to protect his succession to the English throne; this initiated a transformation in England's foreign relations and policy which, during the succeeding century, was increasingly to affect the Anglo-American empire.

In the Anglo-American colonies, conflict with France meant two things. The first was the intensification of European warfare in the Caribbean. During the later seventeenth century, the French West Indian islands became very successful sugar economies: by the 1680s, Martinique and Guadeloupe had a population of about 30,000, mostly black slaves labouring on highly productive plantations which fed a sugar trade that competed with that of the English islands. Now that France and England both had a major economic stake in the Caribbean, their island colonies became strategic targets in wartime, when each side tried to destroy the other's sugar trade. A second consequence of Anglo-French antagonism was felt in North America, where, despite difficulties in attracting immigrants to Canada, the French population increased substantially in the later seventeenth century, to about 25,000 people. French alliances with Indians meant that English colonials found their path to northern and westward expansion blocked; as confrontations between France and England intensified during the closing decades of the seventeenth century, clashes on these colonial frontiers began to merge into more general struggles for dominance between the two powers.

In the past, warfare had affected the Anglo-American colonies in different ways. In the Caribbean, English colonials were mostly in conflict with other Europeans, particularly with Spain. England had not only seized Jamaica and used buccaneers to assault Spanish colonies, but also continued to press for territory on the margins of the Spanish Main; indeed, in the 1690s, English ambitions to establish settlements in Spanish territory infected the Scots, who made an abortive effort to establish a colony at Darien on the Isthmus of Panama.[32] In North America, by contrast, colonial warfare was more often directed against Indians than Europeans, until France became England's major opponent during the 1690s. During the Nine Years War (known in the colonies as 'King William's War'), Anglo-French conflict extended into several North American campaigns involving the settlers and armies of the rival powers, as each side fought for ascendancy in Canada and its borders. France also challenged the English position in the south, where the establishment of Louisiana in 1682 threatened to strengthen French control of the interior and to add to the problems of defending the English frontier territories of the Carolinas.

At the turn of the century, then, France had already emerged as a major competitor in the American world, alongside England's old enemy, Spain; soon after the Treaty of Ryswick had ended the Nine Years War (in 1697), this pattern of enmities brought fresh conflict to the colonies. In 1700, Philip of Anjou, grandson of Louis XIV, succeeded to the Spanish throne, thereby forging a formidable Franco-Spanish dynastic alliance. Anxious to prevent Spain from becoming a satellite of France, England opposed the accession of Philip and, supported by the Dutch, entered into the long and bloody War of the Spanish Succession (1702–13) with France and Spain. Again, the conflict spread to the Americas, with fighting in both the Caribbean and in North America (where it was known as 'Queen Anne's War'), and English plans to spread war into the Pacific.[33] Again, these were minor theatres of a war that was fought mostly in Europe, and ended with neither side sufficiently powerful to overcome the other. The War of the Spanish Succession nonetheless marked a distinctive moment in the history of Anglo-America, in that it initiated the great three cornered struggle between France, Spain and England which, over the course of the eighteenth century, was to have a transfiguring effect on the empires of all the European powers in the Americas.

We shall return to the theme of English colonial expansion and inter-imperialist rivalry during the eighteenth century in Chapter 8. Before doing so, we must first focus on the economic, social and political structures that developed in the Anglo-American colonies during the period of expansion and consolidation which we have just described. For in the half-century after the English Civil War, two broadly different kinds of Anglo-American colonial society emerged, one in the tropical zone of the Caribbean, and another, of greater variety, in continental North America. To explore their characters and to identify their differences, we shall examine economy and society in the Caribbean first, then turn to the regions of North America. Finally, to complete our survey of colonial structures, we shall conclude this part of the book with a review of the political order which emerged under English rule.

NOTES

1. For a summary account of the repercussions of the English Civil War in North America, see R.C. Simmons, *The American Colonies from Settlement to Independence* (London, 1976), pp. 44–54. For a more detailed consideration, which stresses the colonial response to Parliament as a defence of local autonomy, see Robert M. Bliss, *Revolution and Empire: English Politics and the American Colonies in the Seventeenth Century* (Manchester, 1990) pp. 45–92. On Barbados, see Vincent T. Harlow, *A History of Barbados, 1625–1685* (Oxford, 1926, repr. New York, 1969) pp. 25–82, and Gary A. Puckrein, *Little England: Plantation Society and Anglo-Barbadian Politics, 1627–1700* (New York and London, 1984) pp. 91–123.
2. Robert Brenner, *Merchants and Revolution: Commercial Change, Political Conflict, and London's Overseas Traders, 1550–1653* (Cambridge 1993) pp. 577–632. Policies for colonial government will be covered in Chapter 7.
3. On the background and formulation of this policy, see Charles Wilson, *England's Apprenticeship, 1603–1763* (London, 2nd edition, 1984) pp. 57–65.
4. For a review of commercial policy towards the colonies throughout this period, see Charles M. Andrews, *The Colonial Period of American History*, 4 vols (New Haven, Conn., 1936) vol. 4, pp. 1–143.
5. For Heckscher and his critics, see D.C. Coleman, *Revisions in Mercantilism* (London, 1969).
6. Christopher Hill, *The Century of Revolution* (London, 1961) pp. 144–61.
7. Charles Wilson, *Mercantilism*, Historical Association Pamphlet, no. 37 (London, 1958) pp. 18–19; D.C. Coleman 'Mercantilism revisited', *Historical Journal*, (1980) **23**: 773–91; C.G.A. Clay, *Economic Expansion and Social Change: England, 1500–1700*, vol. 2 (Cambridge, 1984) pp. 182–222.
8. Robert Brenner, 'The social basis of English commercial expansion, 1550–1660', *Journal of Economic History*, (1972) **32**: 361–84; also Brenner, *Merchants and Revolution*, Chapters 10–12.
9. On the Commonwealth and Restoration periods as a turning point in British naval power and strategy, see Paul M. Kennedy, *The Rise and Fall of British Naval Mastery* (London, 1976), pp. 45–52.
10. For a detailed discussion of the interaction between theory, economic conditions and policy-making in England, see Joyce O. Appleby, *Economic Thought and Ideology in Seventeenth Century England* (Princeton, NJ, 1978) especially pp. 99–128. For a brief synthesis of the debate over

the formation of commercial policy and its relation to the colonies in this period, see W.A. Speck, 'The international and imperial context', in J.P. Greene and J.R. Pole (eds) *Colonial British America: Essays in the New History of the Early Modern Era* (Baltimore, Md, and London, 1984) pp. 384–98.

11. Charles M. Andrews, *The Colonial Background of the American Revolution* (repr. New Haven, Conn., 1961) p. 9.
12. Quotation from Richard S. Dunn, *Puritans and Yankees: The Winthrop Dynasty of New England, 1630–1717* (Princeton, NJ, 1962) p. 37.
13. One influence on Cromwell may have been Thomas Gage, a renegade English Catholic who had travelled in Spanish America as a friar, and who in 1648 published his *Travels in the New World*, a book which gives a fascinating glimpse of Spanish America (mostly Mexico) through the eyes of a seventeenth-century Englishman.
14. On the failure of the Western Design and the course of the war with Spain, see Bernard Capp, *Cromwell's Navy: The Fleet and the English Revolution, 1648–1660* (Oxford, 1992 edition) pp. 86–106.
15. The term 'buccaneer' was an English corruption of the French word *boucanier*, which described the foreign corsairs and contrabandists who settled on the uninhabited fringes of Hispaniola and Cuba and in the Lesser Antilles. These men lived by raiding passing ships and by hunting feral livestock, whose meat they dried in strips on a *boucan*. Tough, lawless and brave, they made excellent recruits as fighting crews for the privateers who infested Caribbean waters in time of war and who were equally ready to prey on shipping in time of peace. The standard historical work on the subject is C.H. Haring, *The Buccaneers in West Indies in the Seventeenth Century* (repr. Hamden, Conn., 1966).
16. An excellent account of the occupation and early government of Jamaica is given by Stephen Saunders Webb, *The Governors General: The English Army and the Definition of Empire, 1659–1681* (Chapel Hill, NC, 1979) pp. 151–210.
17. For this account of the privateers, see Peter Earle, *The Sack of Panama* (New York, 1981) pp. 49–53. Sir Richard White's comments are quoted on p 49
18. In 1692, shortly before it was destroyed by earthquake, Port Royal had a population of around 10,000. On the history of the city, see Carl Bridenbaugh and Roberta Bridenbaugh, *No Peace Beyond the Line: The English in the Caribbean, 1624–1690* (New York, 1972) *passim*.
19. Earle, *Sack of Panama*, pp. 155–249. A contemporary account which describes the life of the buccaneers, and recounts Morgan's exploits at length, was written by a buccaneer and first published in Dutch in 1678: see Alexander Exquemelin, *The Buccaneers of America*, trans. A. Brown (Harmondsworth, 1969). On Morgan's sack of Panama, see pp. 167–208.
20. On the background to and subsequent development of the English slave trade, leading to the establishment of the Company of Royal Adventurers to Africa in 1660, and the Royal African Company in 1672, see K.R. Davies, *The Royal African Company* (London, 1957) pp. 7–46.
21. Andrews, *Colonial Period of American History*, vol. 3, pp. 182–227; Wesley Frank Craven, *The Southern Colonies in the Seventeenth Century, 1607–1689* (Baton Rouge, La, 1970 edition) pp. 310–59; W. Stitt Robinson, *The*

Southern Colonial Frontier, 1607–1763 (Albuquerque, 1979) pp. 74–97.

22. For a discussion of English foreign policy during the period of the first and second Anglo-Dutch wars, see J.R. Jones, *Britain and the World (1649–1815)* (London, 1980) pp. 51–81.

23. On the English conquest of New Netherland, and the region's social and institutional development in the seventeenth century, see Robert R. Ritchie, *The Duke's Province: A Study of New York Politics and Society, 1664–1691* (Chapel Hill, NC, 1977) especially pp. 9–46, 155–79; also Michael Kammen, *Colonial New York: A History* (New York, 1975) pp. 73–127.

24. Edwin B. Bronner, *William Penn's "Holy Experiment": The Founding of Pennsylvania, 1681–1701* (New York and London, 1962) *passim*; Gary B. Nash, *Quakers and Politics: Pennsylvania, 1681–1726* (Princeton, NJ, 1960) *passim*.

25. Bernard Bailyn, *Voyagers to the West: Emigration from Britain to America on the Eve of the Revolution* (London, 1987) pp. 24–5.

26. Population figures for England from John Rule, *The Vital Century: England's Developing Economy, 1714–1815* (London, 1992) p. 5, and John Rule, *Albion's People: English Society, 1714–1815* (London, 1992) pp. 12–13. Colonial population statistics from Jack P. Greene, *Pursuits of Happiness: The Social Development of the Early Modern British Colonies and the Formation of American Culture* (Chapel Hill, NC, and London, 1988) pp. 178.

27. These statistics and comments on the expansion of English trade during the latter half of the seventeenth century are drawn from Ralph Davis, 'English foreign trade, 1660–1700', *Economic History Review*, 2nd series, (1954) **7**: 150–66; Wilson, *England's Apprenticeship*, pp. 160–84, and Clay, *Economic Expansion and Social Change*, pp. 141–82. Figures for tobacco exports from Russell R. Menard, 'The tobacco industry in the Chesapeake colonies, 1617–1730: an interpretation', *Research in Economic History* (1980) **5**: 109–77; see appendix.

28. Wars with Indians in frontier Virginia are described in Gary B. Nash, *Red, White and Black: The Peoples of Early America* (Englewood Cliffs, NJ, 1982 edition) pp. 116–26. Bacon's rebellion will be discussed more fully in Chapter 7.

29. Nash, *Red, White and Black*, pp. 224–30. On the foundation of the Covenant Chain, see Stephen Saunders Webb, *1676: The End of American Independence* (New York, 1984) pp. 355–404; also Francis Jennings, *The Ambiguous Iroquois Empire* (New York and London, 1984) pp. 147–71, 195–213.

30. On French policy towards America in this period, see William J. Eccles, *France in America* (New York, 1972) pp. 60–89.

31. Jones, *Britain and the World*, pp. 95–122.

32. On this project, see John Prebble, *The Darien Disaster* (London, 1968).

33. On the North American repercussions of the Nine Years War and the War of the Spanish Succession, see Simmons, *The American Colonies*, pp. 158–62; for English plans to attack Spanish possessions in the Pacific, see Glyndwr Williams, ' 'The Inexhaustible Fount of Gold': English projects and ventures in the South Seas, 1670–1750' in John E. Flint and Glyndwr Williams (eds) *Perspectives of Empire: Essays presented to Gerald S. Graham* (London, 1973) pp. 27–53.

CHAPTER FIVE
English Colonies in the Caribbean

English colonization in the Caribbean originally emerged from early seventeenth-century strategies for establishing footholds on the continental margins of Spanish America and conducting illegal trade with the Spanish colonies. On withdrawing from the Amazon lowlands during the 1620s, Englishmen had opportunistically annexed the Leeward Islands of St Kitts, Nevis and Barbados, small but fertile isles which displayed immediate potential. They were relatively close to Europe and had easy access from the Atlantic, but, because of the prevailing winds, could not easily be attacked from the Spanish colonies that lay to the west. By mid-century, the islands were important colonies despite their small size, attracting substantial white settlement and becoming producers of tropical export crops, especially tobacco. But their importance as an element in the emerging English colonial system became fully clear only after about 1650, when the islands' economies and societies were radically altered by the introduction of sugar and slavery, and when Jamaica, in the Greater Antilles, was annexed to provide England with a considerable addition to its Caribbean territories. From colonies of settlement, the English West Indies were turned into plantation societies that were dominated by the production of sugar for export, peopled by huge and growing forces of black slaves, and involved in complex interactions and conflicts with the larger culture of plantations and slavery which gradually spread among the colonies of the European powers present in the Caribbean.

ENGLISH TERRITORIES IN THE CARIBBEAN

After Cromwell had taken Jamaica from Spain in 1655, the territorial pattern of English sovereignty in the Caribbean remained virtually unchanged for more than a century. Apart from Jamaica, the principal English colonies were Barbados, St Kitts, Nevis, Antigua and Montserrat, all in that chain of beautiful and fertile islands of the Lesser Antilles on the eastern boundary of the Caribbean. Of these Barbados, though much smaller than Jamaica, was the most important of the English Caribbean possessions throughout the seventeenth century. It was renowned for its extraordinary fertility, and for the dense population and intense cultivation which made it seem, as Sir Richard Dutton said in 1681, like 'one great City adorned with gardens, and a most delightful place'.[1] During the second half of the seventeenth century, inter-island migration also brought a number of small islands under permanent English control: Anguilla, Barbuda and Tortola in the Lesser Antilles, and Eleuthera and New Providence in the Bahamas. However, like the older English colony on the Atlantic island of Bermuda, these attracted relatively little settlement and remained on the periphery of English colonial society.[2]

The English West Indies did not form a unified or concentrated insular cluster, nor did they develop at an equal pace. Apart from the Leeward Islands, they were separated from each other by considerable distances and varied considerably in topography and economic potential. Jamaica lay between the Spanish islands of Cuba and Hispaniola, a thousand miles west of the nearest English settlements in the Lesser Antilles, while Barbados was separated from its closest English neighbour by two French islands. The Leeward Islands of St Kitts (which the English shared with the French until 1713) were much closer together, but they were also part of a chain that contained several French and Dutch islands. The English colonies in the Caribbean were not, then, closely-interlocking parts of an integrated pattern of territorial sovereignty, clearly set apart from that of other colonial powers. They were, rather, scattered and disparate territories in a region where the leading nations of Europe were all concerned to hold territory and competed fiercely for commerce and influence, creating 'in miniature, a world of competing maritime empires'.[3]

Initially, English aggression focused on Spain, which claimed all territory and right to navigation in the Caribbean. However, once the Dutch, French and English had established their colonies, rivalry between these powers became the major cause of conflict in the region. Anglo-Dutch and Anglo-French wars were extremely destructive in the Caribbean, where clashes between rival settlers and naval forces mingled with the depredations of buccaneers and pirates to create a persistent climate of violence and warfare during the later seventeenth century. From the 1680s, the buccaneers were rarely used by the powers to fight their wars: their last appearance in a major attack was in the French assault on Cartagena de Indias in 1697. But their suppression did not guarantee the peaceful passage of merchant vessels through the Caribbean. Expelled from Jamaica, St Domingue and the central Caribbean, the remnants of the buccaneers moved north to the Bahamas islands and created pirate bases from which they attacked the shipping of all nations. In the early eighteenth century, piracy reached its peak, employing more than 5,000 men, using ports on the North American mainland, and ranging overseas as far north as Newfoundland. Such was the threat from piracy that the English government took concerted measures to close ports to pirate vessels and to hunt down and hang their crews, actions which helped greatly to reduce piracy by the mid-1720s.[4]

After 1660, the main cause of turbulence in the Caribbean was the growing conflict between England, Holland and France, and its main front was in the Lesser Antilles. The motive for war was not to acquire new territory, but rather to destroy enemy sugar production and commerce. When territory was taken, it was usually restored when war was over, and adjustments to the colonial holdings of the powers were accordingly slight. At the Treaty of Breda (1667), England returned Surinam, which it had colonized for fifteen years, to the Dutch; at the Treaty of Westminster (1674), England held all its territories; at the Treaty of Ryswick (1697), Spain formally ceded St Domingue to the French, but otherwise left Caribbean territories in their prewar pattern; finally, at the Treaty of Utrecht (1713), only one minor territorial change was made, when the French passed their half of St Kitts to the British. There was then no further change in the map of the English Caribbean until the Treaty of Paris (1763), when Britain acquired Dominica, St Vincent, Grenada, and Tobago from France. Thus, although the territorial pattern of English colonies in the Caribbean looked precarious in 1650 and was frequently threatened by war, it proved surprisingly stable. Furthermore, for all their individuality, the scattered islands had started to coalesce into a larger British West Indian economy, modelled on the first successful sugar producer in Barbados and bound to England and the North American colonies by the circuits of an increasingly sophisticated system of transatlantic and intercolonial trade.

THE SUGAR REVOLUTION

During the first two decades of their existence, English settlers in the West Indies searched for a staple crop which they could export to Europe, and experimented with varying degrees of success in the cultivation of tobacco, cotton, indigo and ginger. Of these, tobacco became the principal crop, and Barbados its major producer. At first, Barbados did not greatly differ from early Virginia. It was a struggling planter economy that depended on supplies of capital and indentured labour to promote and sustain growth. In the early years, black slaves were only a small element in Barbados society; most of the workforce consisted of indentured workers shipped out from England and Ireland. Lured by the promise of land, most of these workers lived and worked in harsh conditions, and the vast majority never fulfilled their hopes of becoming free landowners. In the long term, only those with the capital to buy large amounts of land and to hire substantial numbers of workers succeeded in profiting from export agriculture.[5]

Experimentation with plantation crops initially provided good profits, but hopes that Caribbean tobacco would rival that of Virginia soon foundered, because it was of much poorer quality, paid higher duties on import into England and fetched a lower price. As a result, Caribbean planters shifted into cotton, indigo and ginger production at the end of the 1630s, in a continuing search for a profitable staple export. These fuelled brief booms which prepared the way, particularly in Barbados, for the introduction of sugar cultivation based on servile labour and produced on large landholdings.[6]

The embryo of this important new development appeared in the 1640s, when the Dutch began to encourage and to subsidize sugar production by English planters in Barbados. During the previous decade, Dutch merchants had exported the island's tobacco and cotton to Amsterdam; now they sought to expand their role as intermediaries by providing planters with the credit and equipment necessary to promote sugar exports. At mid-century, this development was accelerated by the conjuncture of three independent events. First, in the late 1640s the island was afflicted by an epidemic that killed off a large proportion of the population, both rich and poor. From the subsequent sale of many landed properties, new and larger estates emerged, while the shortage of labour caused by white mortality encouraged a shift towards the use of imported black labour. Second, the Civil War in England forced a number of wealthy royalist families to take refuge in Barbados, bringing new capital, enterprise and commercial and political connections to the island. Third, revolt by

Pernambuco planters in 1645 forced Dutch traders to sell off slaves destined for Brazil in Barbados, at low prices and on generous credit terms. Thus, though an epidemic killed off thousands of Barbadians in 1647, the planters had a good supply of slave labour: by 1654, there were about 20,000 blacks on the island. The infusions of Dutch capital, trading skills and black slave labour evidently helped Barbados planters to pass quickly from experimenting with sugar to its large-scale production.

With this unexpected impetus, the economy and society of Barbados were revolutionized. In the decade between 1645 and 1654, the island experienced explosive growth, becoming the most populous, most congested and most specialized English colony in the Americas, with exports more valuable than those of all England's North American settlements. The unparalleled success of Barbados not only transformed its economy and society, but also created an archetype which was to be imitated throughout the English Caribbean in the century to come. The first sugar boom ended in 1654, when the Portuguese finally expelled the Dutch from their last stronghold in Recife and increased the flow of Brazilian sugar on to the European market. This competition, reflected in falling sugar prices, caused planters in some of the English islands to revert to producing crops other than sugar. But the reversal was temporary. The preliminary phase of plantation settlement, in which several commercial crops were grown, was complete; henceforth, sugar cane dominated over all others. In the later seventeenth century, sugar cultivation spread from Barbados into the Leeward Islands in a second stage of development; it then took root in Jamaica, taking English sugar production into its third great surge during the eighteenth century.[7]

The shift towards sugar transformed England's relations both with its Caribbean colonies and with its colonial settlements as a whole, forging economic links which turned the scattered American territories into an interconnected system which more properly resembled an empire. Barbados quickly came to be regarded as the gem among English overseas territories, its brilliance reflected in a web of commerce which not only spanned the Atlantic but also embraced the North American colonies. In the long term, the booming economies of the West Indies, New England and the Middle Atlantic found dynamic markets which enabled them to develop commercial production of commodities which had no outlets in Europe, turning outwards energies which might otherwise have been cramped and confined within much narrower boundaries. The islands played a crucial role in changing English North America in another respect too: they were the springboard from which African slavery was to be spread on to the mainland, where it was to transform the American South, shaping a society that long outlasted British rule. But what of the implications of sugar production for the evolution of English colonial society in the Caribbean? How did plantation agriculture and slavery evolve in the Caribbean, and what kind of social order did their liaison engender?

PLANTATION SOCIETY

In the Caribbean, Barbados was the prototype of plantation society producing sugar for export and using imported slave labour. Its advantages were manifold. Contact with Dutch merchants, knowledge of sugar-growing and refining techniques learned from the Brazilian plantations of Pernambuco, a fertile land well suited to sugar cultivation, and the absence of any competitor among the islands all helped to turn Barbados into the leading centre for Caribbean sugar production. The economic and social pattern which emerged from this conjuncture was not, however, simply a copy of the Brazilian plant-ations. Although sugar production in Barbados was similar to that of the Pernambuco estates, it differed in some important respects. The English did not follow the Portuguese seigneurial style, in which a *senhor de engenho* (sugar mill owner) controlled large amounts of land, slaves and animals, and from his *casa grande* (great house) presided over a largely self-sufficient and self-contained community of tenants, workers and slaves. The typical Barbadian estate was usually a smaller unit of land and was more dependent on imports of basic supplies to provide for its slave workers. Nor did the Barbados planters use the Brazilian technique of share-cropping, whereby the land was leased out to *lavradores de cana*, (the sugar cane farmers who lacked the capital or credit to build their own sugar mills, employed small numbers of slaves, and rendered a proportion of their crop to the *senhor de engenho*). From the outset, the Barbadian planters were concerned to make money rather than to become landed seigneurs, and they were accordingly less paternalistic and more capitalistic in their approach to cultivating sugar and organizing its workforce.[8]

In one vital respect, however, Barbados resembled Brazil. It quickly came to depend on black slave labour, transforming a white settler society into a slave society of a type that had not previously existed in the Anglo-American world. Once this process had started, its advance was inexorable. Although the price of sugar fell during the later seventeenth century, its market in Europe was huge and growing, as the consumption of sugar spread among all social classes.[9] Consequently, Barbados was followed by the other English islands in a drive towards specialization that gave sugar virtually unchallenged predominance in the Anglo-Caribbean economy. This pattern of activity was imitated by other nations with Caribbean territories, first by the French settlers in Martinique, Guadeloupe and St Domingue, and later by the Spanish, in Cuba and Puerto Rico. Barbados long remained in the forefront of producers, and it was not until the eighteenth century that its supply was outstripped, first by that of Leeward Islands, then by Jamaica, and finally, from the 1760s, by the French possession of St Domingue and the Spanish island of Cuba.[10]

In all these islands, black slavery became a crucial component of social and economic life. In Barbados and the English islands, the use of white labour did not die out immediately: sugar production created a huge demand for labour, and landowners continued to use indentured workers brought from the British Isles.[11] After the Civil War, some 12,000 prisoners of war from Cromwell's campaigns in Ireland and Scotland were deported to Barbados, and the supply of white labour was kept up by recruiting 'rogues and whores and such people' from among the poor in England's cities. That the character of these emigrants was different from those who had previously gone to the Americas can be judged from the description of Barbados in 1655 as 'the dunghill whereon England casts forth its rubbish'.[12]

By the 1660s, the flow of indentured labour to the islands began to fall off and was increasingly replaced by black slaves. Evidence from Barbados suggests that the switch to slavery is best explained in terms of supply and cost factors. It was difficult to recruit indentured labour because the conditions endured by white workers were often appallingly bad, and, as landowners expanded the area under sugar cultivation, white servants could not be attracted by the promise of free land. The supply of servants was further diminished in the 1660s, probably because the Chesapeake was more favoured by English emigrants; combined with the high mortality of indentured workers in the Caribbean and their failure to reproduce themselves, this pushed up the price of labour. As the African slave trade developed, black slavery offered a cheaper alternative. Barbados planters who visited Pernambuco around 1640 had seen black slaves manning sugar plantations, and, once they found their plantations sufficiently profitable to justify heavy investment, they passed easily from imported white servants to imported African slaves, supplied initially by Dutch and, from the mid-1660s, by English slave traders.

The change was rapid. In the mid-1640s, slaves were a minority in

Barbados: some 6,000 in a total population of 24,000; by 1676, the number had soared to more than 40,000 in a total population of 65,000. The white servant population, on the other hand, fell from over 13,000 in the early 1650s to fewer than 3,000 in 1680.[13] By the start of the eighteenth century, the inversion of white and black populations had reached the point where the black population (over 50,000 slaves) was about four times larger than the total of white inhabitants.[14]

In the Leeward Islands, this process began later. As Barbados was transformed from a white settler society into one with a black majority from around the mid-seventeenth century, landless freemen and small planters began to migrate to other English colonies, in streams which led towards Jamaica and the Leewards, and to Virginia and Carolina. But it was not long before the other Caribbean islands followed the Barbadian example. Until 1670, the colonists of St Kitts, Nevis, Antigua and Montserrat were still mainly small tobacco and cotton farmers, as they lacked the capital or credit required for large-scale sugar production, faced a less favourable geographical environment than the planters of Barbados, and suffered more from the vicissitudes of war. Nonetheless, during the 1670s, a nascent planter class was in place in the Leewards, growing wealthier and more powerful, and turning to black slave labour in imitation of Barbados.

Jamaica followed its own peculiar path of development. Initially peopled by soldiers who were turned into peasant proprietors by the island's military governor in the years after conquest, Jamaica's early agriculture was based on mixed farming which produced subsistence for settlers and provisions for the privateers who operated out of its ports, as well as a range of tropical goods for export.[15] But in the long term, Jamaican development followed the pattern previously laid down in the sugar islands. After privateering was outlawed at the Treaty of Madrid (1670), its settlers lost an important outlet for their food crops; primed by English mercantile capital, Jamaican agriculture was transformed from a mixed economy producing provisions, hides, tobacco, dyewoods and cloves into a highly commercialized and highly capitalized plantation economy based on sugar cultivation. The effect on the island's social structure was obvious at the end of the century, when the best lands were consolidated into large estates, the white population had declined, and the numbers of slaves imported had risen dramatically. In 1675, slaves were barely more than half Jamaica's total population of 18,000; in 1698, there were about 40,000 slaves in a population of some 50,000, so that slaves outnumbered whites by four to one.[16]

THE WEST INDIAN PLANTOCRACY

The development of slave-based sugar plantations underpinned a distinctive form of Anglo–American colonial society in the West Indies, in which small groups of wealthy planters formed a white ruling class, or 'plantocracy', that took command of transplanted institutions of English government and lorded it over their slaves and the rest of the population. By 1680, Barbados was dominated by a small group of rich land and slaveowners. Landownership was concentrated in the hands of 175 families, a group which formed only 7% of property holders but controlled more than half the island's land and slaves. The heads of these families were the richest men in Anglo–America, and they constituted a local aristocracy which dominated the island's political as well as its economic life. In the other islands, planter elites took longer to emerge, but the direction of social development was the same, leading to the concentration of property in few hands and the control of local government by planter oligarchies.[17]

In the style of life which they adopted, the rich planters of the West Indies mimicked the manners of the English gentry. Their housing, clothing and social pretensions were all those of the home society; they made little effort to adapt to the conditions of the tropics, or to identify with the territories from which they drew their fortunes. Being richer than most of the English gentry and less inhibited in their manners, the planters indulged in conspicuous consumption, lived idle lives, and were renowned for their copious consumption of food and drink. Among the poorer whites, diet was simple, and based, insofar as was possible, on the kinds of foods eaten in England. This, of course, posed a problem, since English food crops could not be grown in the Caribbean, and had to be imported from England, Ireland or North America. Even Jamaica, which had ample land on which to grow provisions, imported large amounts of food and drink, simply because the white population preferred European and North American products to the local variety. Among the planters, diet was rich and varied, frequently served in lavish circumstances, and invariably accompanied by heavy drinking. Rum was widely drunk among all social classes, though those who could afford to also drank wines and brandy from France and Madeira, as well as imported English beer and cider. Clothing conformed to English styles, with little concession to climate, and the rich tended to indulge in ostentatious display. The towns of the English West Indies looked rather like the smaller commercial ports of England, with some architectural adaptations to

135

deal with the threat of hurricanes and heavy tropical rainfall. Unlike the Hispanic American landed classes, who preferred city to rural life, the West Indian planters lived in country houses which, in their layout, decoration and furniture, imitated the manor houses of the English gentry.

The wealth of the planter elites was not achieved without some cost to themselves. Life expectancy among whites was short compared to England and notably shorter than that of whites in the mainland colonies of New England. Generally, the white population depended on constant immigration to sustain its size; white communities were also more unstable than their counterparts in North America, particularly those who lived in the temperate climates of New England, New York and Pennsylvania. In those regions, families tended to be large and closely knit, with a strong discipline based on the family. In the Caribbean, by contrast, death from tropical diseases kept families smaller and created instability by constantly dissolving them. While villagers of Andover in New England might routinely raise seven children and live to the age of 70, white people in Barbados usually had no more than two surviving children and died much younger.

The parishes of the West Indian islands were also more mobile communities than the New England village. In the latter, children tended to settle near their parents and to stay in the same locality; in the former, there was a constant movement among the population and a tendency for the rich to return to England as soon as they were able. Absentee landlordism was, indeed, one of the characteristics of West Indian society which clearly delineates it from other colonial societies in the Americas, including the English colonies of North America and the colonies of Spanish and Portuguese America. There were many reasons for planters to leave the islands where they owned estates, not least of which was an understandable desire to escape the dangers of a tropical climate and enjoy the income from their estates in England. In the short term, planter emigration to England offered one powerful advantage for the planters as a class: it created a powerful lobby for the sugar interest at the centre of the empire, where planters could directly influence government policy.[18] In the long term, however, absenteeism had its drawbacks. Estates left in the hands of salaried managers often deteriorated, capital which might have been used in the colonies was drained out for expenditure abroad, and the numerical imbalance of free whites to black slaves was worsened, making the islands more rigid, racist and unstable societies. Among whites, living in such societies tended to be culturally stultifying and brutalizing. Those who were sufficiently wealthy tended to forsake the colonies for a mother country, and the islands' white elites were thus depleted of their richest and most successful members; those who remained lived in a deeply materialist and divided society, where contempt for the blacks underpinned a vacuous sense of superiority.

SLAVERY

If sugar cultivation brought wealth and power to the rich planters, for the majority of the islands' peoples it brought misery and degradation, embodied in the servitude of the millions of Africans who were forcibly transported to the West Indies to work the sugar plantations. Barbados, the Leeward Islands and Jamaica had the unhappy distinction of being the pioneers of black slavery among the English colonies. By the end of the seventeenth century, about a quarter of a million African slaves had been landed in these islands: roughly half of them went to Barbados, about a third to Jamaica, and the remainder to the Leeward Islands. Their principal task was to sustain sugar cultivation and, secondarily, to meet most needs for manual labour in the towns and countryside.[19]

This was not, of course, the first time that African slaves had been used in the Caribbean, or in other regions of the Americas. Following the swift decimation of Indian populations in Hispaniola and Cuba in the early sixteenth century, black slaves had been introduced by Spanish settlers into these islands, and subsequently into the mainland colonies of Meso-America and South America. In Spanish America, however, black slavery was rarely a fundamental component of economic life. Slaves were employed in mining and agriculture in regions where there was a shortage of native labour or were used as personal servants by the rich, but the great majority of the Hispanic American labour force was recruited from among the native and *mestizo* populations. It was in Brazil that the employment of black slaves in commercial agriculture, coupled with the development of a large and regular African slave trade, first appeared when, with Dutch help, Portuguese landowners and merchants created the first great American sugar-exporting industry. But if the Brazilians showed the profitability of sugar cultivation using slave labour, the emergence of large-scale plantation agriculture based on slavery in the English and French colonies in the Caribbean during the middle years of the seventeenth century represented a new departure in the history of the New World. By 1660, Barbados had become the first colony in the

Americas where black slaves were a majority of the population, beginning a process which, when followed in the other Caribbean islands, created a vicious system of exploitation and oppression.

In the English islands, slavery was profoundly exploitative. Imported in large numbers, blacks could not be easily assimilated into the existing society and the slaveowners made no attempt to encourage their integration. Their principal concern was, rather, to mould the slaves into a disciplined and manageable workforce, over which they would exercise absolute control. Slaves were therefore quickly relegated to the status of mere pieces of property which might be sold off at the whim of their owners, and became members of a permanent underclass that was subject to an extremely harsh labour regime and deprived of basic legal and political rights.[20]

Cruel treatment of black slaves had some precedent in the planters' behaviour towards white indentured labour. After arriving in Barbados in 1647, Richard Ligon found 'much cruelty there done to servants, as I do not think one Christian could do to another', and he reported that 'some cruel Masters will provoke their servants so, by extreme ill usage, and often and cruel beating them, as they grow desperate and so join together to revenge themselves'.[21] However, if white servants suffered from oppressive masters, their position differed from that of black slaves in several important ways. The white indentured servant was a voluntary emigrant who generally had to be offered some protection and reward in return for his or her services; the servant was also covered by the laws and customs regarding bonded servants in the home country. The slave's position was much worse, since he or she was treated simply as an article of merchandise and, together with any children, was condemned to lifelong bondage. The status of slaves in English America was therefore governed by slaveowners who legislated in accord with their own socio-economic interests. While poor whites had legal and political rights which derived from their status as 'Englishmen', no such rights were extended to blacks. They were regarded as property and thus subject to the laws that governed property rather than persons. The slave code drawn up in Barbados in 1661 recognized that ordinary property laws were not entirely adequate to deal with slaves, since the latter were men rather than inanimate objects or animals. But if this meant that they required fuller protection than other kinds of property, they were nevertheless not to be treated as fully human. The Barbados law categorized them as men created 'without the knowledge of God in the world' and as 'an heathenish, brutish and an uncertain and dangerous kind of people' who could not be governed by English law.[22]

Throughout the English colonies, the laws framed by slaveholders were more concerned to protect masters from their slaves than slaves from their masters. No rules governed the diet or working conditions of slaves, or regulated the punishments which they might receive from their owners. Masters might be fined for wantonly killing their slaves, but, revealingly, were much more heavily fined for killing the slaves of another owner. Slaves were also subjected to far more draconian punishments than servants. Whereas indentured servants who ran away were punished by having their contracts extended, slaves might be whipped or mutilated. For crimes of murder, rape, arson, assault or theft of goods of more than small value, slaves could be executed; rebellion almost automatically involved a death sentence. The slave laws which developed out of the first slave code in Barbados did not move towards liberalization. On the contrary, as the black population grew and the white population diminished, fear of slave indiscipline and revolt drove the planters towards harsher and more restrictive measures. Among all the terrible measures that were introduced to police black slaves, the imbalance of the law is perhaps most strikingly reflected in a law of 1688. This stated that if a slave were executed for stealing food because he was starving, the sole punishment for the master who had starved the slave was to be refused compensation from public funds for the loss of his slave.

The Barbados slave law of 1661, with its subsequent modifications of 1676, 1682 and 1688, served as a model for the other islands. In Jamaica, the threat from the 'maroons' – the *negros cimarrones* who had escaped from their Spanish masters and taken refuge in the island's mountainous interior – encouraged severe punishments for undisciplined slaves, though in the early years of English colonization the relative scarcity of slaves on the island seems also to have promoted somewhat better treatment than that received by slaves in Barbados. Unlike Jamaica, colonial assemblies in the Leeward Islands did not adopt the Barbados slave code, but they enacted harsh laws of their own, and Jamaican planters often treated their slaves with unblinking brutality. Throughout the islands, the emphasis was on policing slaves, not protecting them. Indeed, the seventeenth-century laws which underpinned West Indian slave legislation legitimized a violent tyranny of whites over blacks which, though somewhat modified during the later eighteenth century, governed the treatment of slaves in the British West Indies until humanitarian pressures finally forced changes in the law in the early nineteenth century.[23]

The character and persistence of this cruel regime derived from the development of plantation societies in the context of English political and legal traditions which, ironically, were seen to guarantee the freedom of the subject. First, the tradition of representative government that was extended to the Anglo-American colonies ensured that slave laws were made directly by slaveowning elites who shaped them in accord with what they saw as the imperatives of the plantation system on which their wealth and power were based. Second, respect for property, which was an essential element of the English constitutional system as it developed during the late seventeenth and eighteenth centuries, allowed slaveowners great power over their slaves. English law viewed the slave as 'a special kind of property', rather than 'an inferior kind of subject', as in Spanish law. Thus the concern for the liberty of the subject which came to be regarded as the lodestone of the British constitutional system simply did not apply to slaves; on the contrary, it gave their masters freedom to create a whole system of law which curtailed liberty, while providing slaves with only minimal legal protections.[24]

Segregation between whites and blacks did not protect slaves from sexual exploitation by their masters. Like other Europeans in the Americas, Englishmen were ready to take advantage of their female slaves, producing mulatto children who formed the basis of an intermediate social group of people of colour who were neither black nor white. Occasionally, whites granted freedom to their concubines and their offspring, but most mulattos remained slaves who enjoyed a somewhat higher status than pure blacks. Even when they were free, they remained subject to slave law rather than English law, and were unable to vote, hold office, or own much land. Blacks were, moreover, excluded from the religious practices of white communities. Unlike Iberian and French America, where slaveowners had a formal responsibility to baptize their slaves and to supervise their evangelization as Christians, English planters were unwilling to admit slaves into the beliefs and rituals of Christianity. Not only did the planters exclude blacks from the benefits of white law, but also denied them any solace from what, for the whites, was the only true religion.

Behind this lay the fear of admitting any equality, however tenuous, between white and black. Richard Ligon, who in 1657 published an account of his experiences in Barbados, recalled that when he had asked a planter why he should not convert one of his slaves to Christianity, the planter had explained that, if he did so, 'he could no more account him a slave', and that, if such a practice were followed, the planters 'would lose the hold they had of them as slaves, by making them Christians'.[25] To teach slaves the precepts of Christianity would also mean teaching them English, something which the planters were reluctant to do because, as they explained to the Lords of Trade in 1680, 'the disproportion of blacks and whites, being great, the whites have no greater security than in the diversity of the negroes' languages which would be destroyed by conversion, in that it would be necessary to teach them English'.[26] So, just as the colonial state left the slaveholders to regulate their own social relations with slaves, so the slaveholders left the slaves to create their own cultures from the diverse mixture of traditions and values carried by individuals taken from many different regions and tribes in Africa. By deliberately reserving Christianity for the whites, the planters helped to nurture a sense of separateness and solidarity among all whites, both rich and poor, further polarizing their societies along bi-racial lines. Slavery was, then, to leave an indelible mark on the society and culture of the English West Indies. Not only did slavery create societies which were more African than European in their populations and cultures, but also it engendered a deeply racist social order in which, as a late eighteenth-century observer remarked, 'the leading principle on which government is supported is fear'.[27]

SLAVE RESISTANCE

The enslavement of Africans also produced its opposite: a struggle of slaves against their masters, mounted in ways which ranged from non-cooperation to overt rebellion. The islands' history shows that slaves used techniques of resistance which included refusal to work efficiently, sabotage, and suicide to deprive the owner of his property. Slaves also ran away, both collectively and as individuals. When individuals escaped, it was often for short periods, in a form of resistance which the French called *petit marronage*, a crime usually punished by flogging. Sometimes, however, slaves ran away from plantations with the aim of setting up their own independent communities in backland areas, beyond the reach of white society. The formation of such 'maroon' communities – known as *palenques* in Spanish America and *quilombos* in Brazil – started early in the West Indies. In 1647, it was reported that there were 'many hundreds of rebel negro slaves in the woods' in Barbados, at the time when the first large sugar plantations were being set up. As long the forests of the interior remained intact, runaway communities were also a notable feature of life in the Leeward Islands, particularly in Antigua. The maroon tradition was strongest in Jamaica, where the heavily forested

141

interior long remained a refuge for runaways who built their own communities, based on an African style of subsistence agriculture. Indeed, between 1725 and 1740, the 'maroons' presented a serious threat to order in Jamaica and defeated the white militias sent to subdue them. After fighting a prolonged and effective campaign, groups of Jamaica maroons forced the whites to conclude a treaty with them in 1739–40, conceding freedom and large grants of land for their subsistence. The maroons now ceased to subvert the slave regime and became its servants, helping to hunt down runaways and to suppress slave revolts.[28]

Small-scale rebellions, on individual plantations, were a frequent occurrence in almost every island, particularly before the mid-eighteenth century, but the repressive character of slave society and the high probability of terrible retribution made large-scale slave rebellion, embracing the slaves of whole regions, relatively rare. The greatest rebellions occurred in Jamaica, where revolts involving hundreds of slaves took place in the 1730s and in Tacky's rebellion of 1760. This is probably explained by the fact that in Jamaica the ratio of blacks to whites was particularly high, as was the proportion of African to locally born slaves; in a country with a forested interior which offered a possible refuge, the chances of successful insurrection were also better than in the smaller, more crowded islands.

Another aspect of the black response to slavery was the conservation and adaption of African cultural forms and traditions, creating distinct folk cultures which enabled the slaves to preserve their identities and order their own lives. Formed by slaves brought from many different African cultures, the character of such cultures naturally varied according to the origins of the slave population, so that each island, even regions within islands, developed their distinctive local variants. But, if it is difficult to generalize about slave culture for the whole of the British West Indies, it is nonetheless clear that slaves took many of their basic customs – of child-rearing, family organization, diet, music, funeral rites and so on – from African sources. Black religion also drew heavily on African origins. While the Christian clergy invariably confined their ministry to the whites, slaves were given little opportunity to embrace the religion of their masters, and turned instead to practices which whites regarded as dangerous witchcraft. Thus the 'obeah-man' (or woman), a priest-healer of an African kind who dealt in folk medicine and magic, became a key figure in shaping and expressing the slaves' religious life and, as a leader attributed with supernatural powers, was sometimes the medium for organizing resistance and revolt.[29]

142

For all the cruelties of slave society, confrontation between white and black was not absolute. Manumission and miscegenation between white and black produced groups of free people of colour, who came to form a small but growing proportion of the Anglo-Caribbean population by the end of the eighteenth century. Compared to the Iberian colonial world, manumission was relatively rare, however, and the free black population was correspondingly small. In Britain's slave colonies, the free coloured or mulatto population stemmed mainly from the concubinage of female slaves with whites or from reproduction among free coloureds, and began to grow substantially only from the end of the eighteenth century. The social position of free coloureds varied. Some worked in the agricultural economy, as small producers cultivating commercial crops such as coffee and pimento; most probably lived in the towns, where they worked as artisans and petty traders. Evidence from Jamaica suggests that most were poor, though some owned property and slaves. All were, however, subject to many restraints on their freedom, and, even where they formed a convenient social buffer between whites and black slaves, the free coloureds were far from enjoying an equality of status with whites.[30]

THE WEST INDIAN COLONIES: CHARACTER AND TRAJECTORY

By the start of the eighteenth century, the development of sugar plantations had converted Barbados, the Leewards and Jamaica, all of which had started as colonies of white settlement, into colonies of exploitation based on African slave labour. Meeting a growing demand for sugar and molasses, planters in the islands had doubled or even trebled their sugar production between 1660 and 1700; in the process, they passed from being slaveowning societies, where slaves were sometimes employed, into slave societies, where a large proportion of the population was enslaved and where slaves were fundamental to economic life.[31] The crucial role of slavery in the British Caribbean is clearly reflected in the demographic composition of West Indian societies: by 1713, the ratio of black slaves to free whites was about four to one in Barbados, and this pattern was followed and surpassed in the other islands. In the Leewards, there were more than three blacks to every white in 1713; by mid-century, the ratio was about seven to one. A similar plunge into slavery took place in Jamaica, starting in the closing decade of the seventeenth century: by 1713,

143

blacks outnumbered whites by about eight to one; before mid-century, the ratio had reached ten or eleven to one. Wealth meanwhile became increasingly concentrated in the hands of the few planters who could mount large-scale production and finance the labour needed for it, creating powerful plantocracies which played a dominant role in governing their societies, while also generating rich flows of trade for English merchants and shippers. Unlike the Spanish Caribbean islands, which were relegated to the periphery of Spain's colonial economy during the seventeenth century, the Anglo-Caribbean colonies had developed specialized plantation economies and slave societies, and their transoceanic trades in tropical staples stood at the core of a vigorous and expanding system of British colonial commerce.

Once established, the social and economic foundations of the West Indian colonies underwent no fundamental change until slavery ended in the nineteenth century. Indeed, in the eighteenth century the islands continued along the same general trajectory that they had entered in the preceding century, broadening and deepening a social world underpinned by the profits of sugar and marked by the inexorable spread of slavery. The islands' experience was not identical – differences in geography alone were enough to ensure that – but their development followed a similar pattern, characterized by the spread of sugar production and slavery, and the consequent Africanization of their populations. We shall return later, in Chapter 8, to examine the singular importance of West Indian production and commerce in the overall development of the British Atlantic system during the eighteenth century. For the moment, we need only note the words of an anonymous English commentator, who in 1749 observed that 'the extensive employment of our shipping in, to, and from America, the great Brood of Seamen consequent thereon, and the Daily Bread of the most considerable part of our British Manufactures, are owing primarily to the Labour of Negroes'.[32]

While the plantation complex continued to grow and flourish during the the eighteenth century, the regional balance of Britain's Caribbean colonial economy shifted as the frontier of sugar production moved through the islands.[33] At the turn of the century, Barbados, which had been the vanguard of the English sugar-plantation economy, was still the most populous island, the biggest producer of sugar, and had the largest number of black slaves. White immigration had, however, gone into a steep decline, as the growth of large estates for sugar production curtailed the supply of land, and the predominance of African slave labour greatly reduced the need for white indentured servants. Indeed, whites emigrated from Barbados to seek land and profit elsewhere, and thus spread the seeds of the slave society from which they came. This dispersion helped to propel sugar and slavery onto a new frontier, in the Leeward Islands of St Kitts, Nevis, Antigua and Montserrat, where the development of the slave-plantation complex took on fresh momentum and competed strongly with Barbados. Although Barbadian planters managed to sustain sugar production by employing intensive methods, during the eighteenth century Barbados ceased to be the major source of sugar which it had once been. As it adjusted to new economic circumstances, Barbadian society developed some distinctive features which set it apart from the rest of the British West Indies. After about 1710, its white population began to grow again, until by mid-century Barbados had a larger proportion of whites than the other main subregions of the West Indies (about 20 per cent in 1760, compared to 10 per cent in the Leewards and in Jamaica). Most of the Barbadian white population were creoles born on the island itself, who saw their society as a 'Little England' despite its black majority. Like the whites, the slaves of Barbados also became more 'creolized' than those of other islands; this coincided with the absence of any violent insurrection during the eighteenth century, though it did not necessarily curtail other forms of slave resistance.[34]

After Barbados, the Leeward Islands became the next major frontier for the British sugar–slave complex, with Antigua as the capital and core of the group. Although they had been settled early, the Leewards' development had been inhibited by Carib hostility and foreign attacks for much of the seventeenth century. However, during the 1730s, they became the major source of British sugar, and, through massive slave imports, were changed into highly specialized plantation economies where small white populations dominated large African majorities. By the closing decades of the century, the economy of the region had taken on a form that 'was perhaps beginning to resemble a nineteenth century industrial enterprise more closely than it did the settler societies developing elsewhere in colonial British America'.[35]

The Leewards were, in turn, surpassed by Jamaica, which became Britain's greatest single producer of sugar during the second half of the eighteenth century, when both Barbados and the Leewards had passed their peak. Jamaica had deviated from the Barbadian model at first. It did not phase through the tobacco planting phase, and, partly because Barbados and the Leewards absorbed much of the capital available for developing sugar, was slower to turn to sugar production. By far the biggest of all the English islands (with over 4,000 square miles Jamaica had a land area which was twenty-seven times that of Barbados and twelve times that of the Leeward Islands as a group), its settlers also had difficulty in taking the interior and controlling the maroons who took refuge from slavery amidst its mountainous landscape. But British settlers in Jamaica had a plentiful supply of land, and during the second half of the eighteenth century they used African labour to turn the island into the greatest of all England's sugar-producing colonies. By 1780, Jamaica was producing about 50,000 tons of sugar per year, which then constituted about half of all British sugar production. Despite the huge importance of its sugar plantations (which tended to be two or three times larger than the average plantation of Barbados and the Leewards), Jamaica's economy and society had some distinctive features. First, it never became such a specialized sugar monoculture: many of its plantations produced provisions, livestock and other staples; secondly, Jamaica had a broader white society than the small sugar islands (except Barbados), and, together with the huge inflows of African slaves, continued to attract immigrants from Britain (particularly Scots) throughout the eighteenth century.

While Jamaica flourished, the British West Indian sugar/slave complex continued to advance during the later eighteenth and early nineteenth centuries, as Britain took Dominica, St Vincent, Grenada and Tobago from France in 1763, and St Lucia from the French, Trinidad from Spain and the Guianas from the Dutch during the Napoleonic wars. More sugar plantations bred more slavery, and during the course of the eighteenth century the British islands became the world's greatest importers of African slave labour after Brazil. Between 1701 and 1810, slave imports climbed to about million and a half, with Jamaica taking the largest share. As most of the slaves died prematurely, the labour force had to be constantly replenished by fresh imports, and the population of the islands did not grow at a rate comparable to the scale of slave immigration. Thus, although African slavery met the islands' need for manpower, it did not provide them with a solid base for sustained demographic increase. Furthermore, the material success of the planters created a social order in which the mass of the population was alienated and repressed, and where the maintenance of social order depended on the constant threat and use of violence by white minorities against black majorities.

The West Indian social order saw only minor adjustments to its basic form in the eighteenth century. One current of change affected the slave labour force: during the later eighteenth century, the material conditions of plantation slaves were somewhat improved. From mid-century, life expectancy among slaves apparently rose, helped perhaps by improvements in food supply and by provision of better medical care from planters anxious to maintain a healthy and stable labour force. One visitor, returning to the West Indies in 1788 after a long absence, saw 'a wonderful change for the better' in the treatment of slaves in the islands; nonetheless, he accepted that this change was 'still far from complete', and admitted that slaves in Jamaica were generally 'overworked and underfed, even on the mildest and best regulated properties.' The rise in life expectancy was probably attributable mainly to growth in the proportion of creole slaves to imported Africans; locally born slaves were, it seems, more resistant to disease than African arrivals who, after suffering the trauma of captivity and transoceanic transportation, had then to be 'seasoned' to life and labour in the islands.[36] Furthermore, the fact remains that, throughout the eighteenth century, the plantation slaves who constituted the great majority of the black population were ill-fed, crudely housed and clothed, and very vulnerable to illness and disease. Indeed, the slaves' mortality remained too high, and the fertility of slave women too low, to allow the slave population as a whole to increase itself naturally; throughout the slavery period, replenishments had always to be found in Africa.[37]

A second development in eighteenth-century West Indian society was the emergence of a sense of local identity among the planter elites, notably in Barbados and Jamaica.[38] There, creole writers focused on the positive achievements of planter society, stressing the economic improvements it had brought to the islands, emphasizing the fundamentally English character of the local elites, and elaborating a negrophobic, pro-slavery ideology that was designed to reconcile the exploitation of slaves with metropolitan ideas of freedom and civilization. For a Jamaican planter–politician like Edward Long (1734–1817), the ideal planter was the scion of an established Anglican landholding family, and was modelled on the best kind of English country gentleman. In Long's vision of colonial society, the planter acted as a patriarch on his estates, stood as cultural arbiter for the merchants, professionals and artisans who formed the respectable elements of white society, and, as political leader, dedicated himself to the cause of public improvement in his home region. However, as Long himself recognized, the re-creation of British society in the West Indies, headed by a creole gentry, was constantly undermined by planter absenteeism. Unlike the elites of colonial North America, the cream of Jamaican planter society tended to forsake the colony for the metropole. Many abandoned the island to revel in London life or to live like the gentry in English country houses; those who remained added to the outflow by sending their children for education in

Britain, where many remained as permanent residents. Nonetheless, towards the end of the eighteenth century, whites began to show more commitment to their local societies by deploying their resources in developing towns, churches, schools and other public institutions; at the same time, an authentic creole culture was also emerging from the blend of European and African traditions, as crossovers of language, diet, music and dance formed distinctive local cultural styles and identities.[39]

The world which emerged from the complex of sugar and slavery was, of course, a very distinctive variant of colonial life in the first British Empire. Elsewhere in British America, on the North American mainland, a much more varied social world was created by British settlers and their creole descendants. Peopled by immigrants who enjoyed a wide range of economic and social opportunity, and led by elites with greater commitment to their colonial provinces, the North American regions were, as we shall see in the next chapter, to nurture Anglo-American societies of a kind quite different from those of the West Indies.

NOTES

1. For a description of the English islands during the seventeenth century, see Richard S. Dunn, *Sugar and Slaves: The Rise of the Planter Class in the English West Indies, 1624–1713* (London, 1973) pp. 25–39. The quotation is from p. 28.
2. Carl Bridenbaugh and Roberta Bridenbaugh, *No Peace beyond the Line: The English in the Caribbean, 1624–1690* (New York, 1971) pp. 195–229.
3. J.H. Parry, *Trade and Dominion: The European Overseas Empires in the Eighteenth Century* (London, 1971) p. 42.
4. Clinton V. Black, *Pirates of the West Indies* (Cambridge, 1989) pp. 21–5.
5. Bridenbaugh and Bridenbaugh, *No Peace Beyond the Line*, pp. 51–68, 101–28. On early Barbados, see Dunn, *Sugar and Slaves*, pp. 46–59; Gary A. Puckrein, *Little England: Plantation Society and Anglo-Barbadian Politics, 1627–1700* (New York and London, 1984) pp. 22–55.
6. Robert C. Batie, 'Why sugar? Economic cycles and the changing of staples on the English and French Antilles, 1624–1654', *Journal of Caribbean History* (1976) **8–9**: 1–41.
7. David Watts, *The West Indies: Patterns of Development, Culture and Environmental Change since 1492* (Cambridge, 1987) pp. 176–88.
8. Dunn, *Sugar and Slaves*, pp. 59–74; Richard B. Sheridan, *Sugar and Slavery: An Economic History of the British West Indies, 1623–1775* (Barbados, 1974) pp. 124–47; Philip D. Curtin, *The Rise and Fall of the Plantation Complex: Essays in Atlantic History* (Cambridge, 1990) pp. 53–5; 83.

9. On demand in seventeenth- and eighteenth-century England, see Sheridan, *Sugar and Slavery*, pp. 20–2.
10. On the regional spread of sugar production and expansion of production and exports, see Watts, *West Indies*, pp. 284–304.
11. Hilary McD. Beckles, *White Servitude and Black Slavery in Barbados, 1627–1715* (Knoxville, Tenn., 1989) pp. 36–58.
12. Ibid., p. 48.
13. Ibid., pp. 115–26.
14. For the ratio of slaves to whites in Barbados, see Watts, *West Indies*, p. 311.
15. On the early years of English colonization in Jamaica, see Stephen S. Webb, *The Governors General: The English Army and the Definition of Empire, 1569–1681* (Chapel Hill, NC, 1979) pp. 172–91.
16. Dunn, *Sugar and Slaves*, pp. 117–67, 312–13, Sheridan, *Sugar and Slavery*, pp. 148–225. For white to slave ratios in Jamaica, see Watts, *West Indies*, p. 311.
17. For the following, see Dunn, *Sugar and Slaves*, pp. 263–334; also Michael Craton, 'Reluctant creoles: the planters' world in the British West Indies', in Bernard Bailyn and Philip D. Morgan (eds) *Strangers within the Realm: Cultural Margins of the First British Empire* (Chapel Hill, NC, and London, 1991) pp. 324–38.
18. On the political activities of planters in England, see Sheridan, *Sugar and Slavery*, pp. 58–74.
19. These figures (and other statistics on the Atlantic slave trade cited in this book) are from Philip D. Curtin, *The Atlantic Slave Trade: A Census* (Madison, Wis., 1969).
20. The following account of the laws and treatment of slaves in the English West Indies during the seventeenth-century is drawn from Dunn, *Sugar and Slaves*, pp. 224–62.
21. Richard Ligon, *A True and Exact History of the Island of Barbadoes* (London, 2nd edition, 1673, reprinted 1976) pp. 44, 46.
22. Dunn, *Sugar and Slaves*, p.239.
23. For information on the treatment of slaves in the English Caribbean during the eighteenth century, see Michael Craton, *Sinews of Empire. A Short History of British Slavery* (London, 1974), pp. 155–237. For Jamaica, see Orlando Patterson, *The Sociology of Slavery* (London, 1967) pp. 70–92; for the Leeward Islands, see Elsa V. Goveia, *Slave Society in the British Leeward Islands at the End of the Eighteenth Century* (New Haven, Conn., and London, 1965) pp. 152–202. Late eighteenth-century efforts to reform oppressive slave codes are outlined in David Brion Davis, *The Problem of Slavery in Western Culture* (Ithaca, NY, 1966), pp. 255–61.
24. Elsa V. Goveia, 'The West Indian slave laws of the eighteenth century', in Laura Foner and Eugene Genovese (eds) *Slavery in the New World: A Reader in Comparative History* (Englewood Cliffs, NJ, 1969) pp. 113–37.
25. Ligon, *A True and Exact History of the Island of Barbadoes*, p. 50.
26. Quoted in Vincent T. Harlow, *A History of Barbados, 1625–1685* (Oxford, 1926, repr. New York, 1969) pp. 325–6.
27. Bryan Edwards, *The History, Civil and Commercial, of the British Colonies in the West Indies*, 2 vols (London, 1793) quoted in Craton, *Sinews of Empire*, p.176.

28. On the history of black rebellion and resistance in the eighteenth century, see Michael Craton, *Testing the Chains: Resistance to Slavery in the British Caribbean* (Ithaca, NY, and London, 1982) pp. 95–140; Mavis C. Campbell, *The Maroons of Jamaica, 1655–1796: A History of Resistance, Collaboration and Betrayal* (Granby, Mass., 1988); Hilary McD. Beckles, *Black Rebellion in Barbados: The Struggle Against Slavery, 1622–1838* (Bridgetown, Barbados, 1984) pp. 25–88; Patterson, *Sociology of Slavery*, pp.269–71; and Goveia, *Slave Society in the British Leeward Islands*, pp. 94–102. For further information on West Indian runaways and maroons, see the essays by Hilary Beckles, Gad Heuman, Richard Sheridan and Silvia W. de Groot in Gad Heuman (ed.), *Out of the House of Bondage: Runaways, Resistance and Marronage in Africa and the New World* (London, 1986).

29. For a brief outline of slave culture in eighteenth-century Jamaica, see Edward Brathwaite, *The Development of Creole Society in Jamaica, 1770–1820* (Oxford, 1971) pp. 212–39. For different views of obeah, see Craton, *Sinews of Empire*, pp. 218–9, and Patterson, *Sociology of Slavery*, pp. 182–95. On African influences in family and community life, see Barbara Bush, *Slave Women in Caribbean Society, 1650–1838* (London, 1990) pp. 91–110.

30. Gad Heuman, *Between Black and White: Race, Politics and the Free Coloureds in Jamaica, 1792–1865* (Oxford, 1981) pp. 3–15.

31. For the distinction between slaveowning and slave societies, and its implications, see Philip D. Morgan, 'British encounters with Africans and African Americans, circa 1680–1780', in Bailyn and Morgan (eds), *Strangers within the Realm*, pp. 163–80.

32. Quoted in Sheridan, *Sugar and Slavery*, p. 261.

33. The following comments draw on the succinct survey of West Indian economic and social development to 1760 found in Jack P. Greene, *Pursuits of Happiness: The Social Development of Early Modern British Colonies and the Formation of American Culture* (Chapel Hill, NC, and London, 1988) pp. 152–64.

34. Ibid., pp.154–157; on creole slaves, see Beckles, *Black Rebellion in Barbados*, pp. 52–7.

35. Greene, *Pursuits of Happiness*, p. 159.

36. Sheridan, *Sugar and Slavery*, pp. 244–5.

37. Craton, *Sinews of Empire*, pp. 187–99. For more detailed discussion of slave motherhood and infant mortality, see Bush, *Slave Women*, pp. 120–50.

38. For the following, see Jack P. Greene, 'Changing identity in the British Caribbean: Barbados as a case study', in Nicholas Canny and Anthony Pagden (eds), *Colonial Identity in the Atlantic World, 1500–1800* (Princeton, NJ, 1987) pp. 213–66; Michael Craton, 'Reluctant creoles: The planters' world in the British West Indies' in Bailyn and Morgan (eds), *Strangers within the Realm*, pp. 339–49; Gordon Lewis, *Main Currents in Caribbean Thought: The Historical Evolution of Caribbean Society in its Ideological Aspects, 1492–1900* (Baltimore, Md, and London, 1983) pp.103–16.

39. Edward Brathwaite, *The Development of Creole Society in Jamaica*, traces the emergence of this creole culture in Jamaica: see especially pp. 296–305.

On cultural encounters between black and white in the slave societies of British America, see Philip D. Morgan, 'British encounters with Africans and African Americans, circa 1680–1780', in Bailyn and Morgan (eds), *Strangers within the Realm*, pp. 203–11.

CHAPTER SIX

The North American Colonies

Like the Caribbean, colonial North America during the seventeenth century was a mosaic of European settlements. There was, however, a basic difference between the island and mainland regions. In the Caribbean, the spread of sugar cultivation shaped colonial societies that tended to resemble each other in their basic structures and relationships with Europe. North America, on the other hand, was a scene of great regional diversity. Not only did the colonies of England differ from those of France and Spain, but Atlantic Anglo-America was itself a mixture of several distinctive economic, social and cultural formations.

Spain was the source of the first European settlers in North America, but, finding nothing comparable to the rich Amerindian societies and precious mineral deposits of Meso-America, Spaniards had never effectively peopled the regions north of Mexico's silver-mining districts. The Spanish colonies of Coahuila and Texas were simply sparsely populated frontiers of settlement of little economic consequence. The colony of Florida was even less important in economic terms, and under Spanish sovereignty remained a military outpost rather than a colony of settlement. It centred on the garrison of St Augustine, which was positioned to protect Spanish shipping passing from the Caribbean into the Atlantic and had an economic base so weak that it had to be sustained by subsidies from Mexico.[1]

The French colonies in North America also encompassed large but economically undeveloped regions that failed to attract large-scale white settlement. Acadia, France's maritime colony in north-eastern North America, was largely neglected after the foundation of Quebec in 1608, when French efforts refocused on Canada. But even in Canada, the largest of France's American colonies, the settler population was small and unevenly distributed. A vast and ill-defined region in the lands bordering the St Lawrence River, Canada had two distinct parts, neither of which had any substantial French population. One reached deep into the interior, in a line of missions and trading outposts through which the furs taken in trade with Indian allies was relayed out to the coast. Near the coast lay the other, more European part of Canada, on the lower reaches of the St Lawrence. This attracted more settlement, mostly by immigrants from north-western France, and its social and economic order were organized in a government–inspired system of feudal land grants, known as *seigneuries*. By 1660, however, the population of New France was still tiny, at a mere 3,000 people. At the end of the century, the French also began to occupy the territory which they called Louisiana, but here their presence was even more tenuous. Designed to serve as a base for exploring and controlling a vast hinterland stretching far to the north, Louisiana was the southern counterpart to Canada. However, from the time that New Orleans was founded in 1718 and several thousand settlers were sent to Louisiana to settle along the river and on the coast, its population failed to grow. Despite some commercial development, Louisiana therefore remained a marginal province, largely dependent on government subsidies.[2]

The other European power with colonial ambitions in North America was the Dutch republic. After Henry Hudson's exploration of the Hudson River for the Dutch East India Company in 1609, Dutch traders started fur trading with Indians in the area before the Dutch West India Company established a permanent colony at New Netherland in 1624. The Dutch were, however, always more interested in trading bases than in agrarian settlements; the purpose of their inland fort at Albany and port at New Amsterdam was to enhance Dutch commerce, both by channelling furs to Holland and selling whatever commodities they could to the Indians. Helped by their Iroquois allies, they succeeded in diverting furs from the Great Lakes regions; the West India Company also tried to promote colonization by granting 'patroons', large riverside land grants given to proprietors on the promise that they would bring in migrants to develop agriculture. These did not take off, however, and when the English seized the area in 1664, the Dutch colony had a settler population of only about 10,000 people, not all of whom were Dutch.[3]

Of the European powers, the English developed the most complex and varied pattern of colonial settlements in North America. These occupied a relatively small territory but played a leading role in peopling the continent and developing its resources. The gap between the English colonies' population and resources and those of other European colonies on the continent was already wide by the mid-seventeenth century. In 1660, English North America had a population of over 70,000, compared to about 10,000 settlers in New Netherland, 3,000 in Canada, and even fewer in the Spanish territories of the Mexican borderlands and Florida. Gradually, this disparity deepened. In 1700, the English colonies' population reached about a quarter of a million, while the colonial populations of Spanish and French North America together did not exceed about 10,000 inhabitants. By the mid-eighteenth century, the English colonial population had passed the 1 million mark, while the French population of Canada had still not reached much more than 50,000 people, that of Louisiana was only about 5,000, and settlers in Spanish North America numbered fewer than 10,000 people. Clearly, then, the colonies of English North America showed far greater vitality during the seventeenth and eighteenth centuries than did those of the other European nations, and became the major force in the development of the continent's resources. They were, moreover, an increasingly important part of the English colonial system as a whole, displaying a remarkable capacity for growth and expansion.

ENGLISH NORTH AMERICA: REGIONS

Compared to the vast extent of Spain's possessions in the American continents, continental Anglo-America was small, being confined to the coastal plains which stretched along the eastern seaboard of North America. Like the Spaniards, who began their colonization of the American mainlands by establishing bases on islands and continental coasts, English settlers started their colonization with the establishment of tiny coastal footholds. However, unlike the Spaniards, who were soon drawn deep in the American interior and backlands in their search for native civilizations to conquer and precious metals to exploit, English colonists and their descendants remained a fundamentally maritime and rural people, clustered on a coastal strip that rarely extended more than about a hundred miles from the bays and river estuaries which were their first points of entry. Indeed, in terms of spatial distribution of settlement, seventeenth-century English North America was more akin to Portuguese America than to continental Spanish America. For, while the core areas of Spain's major colonies were focused on the high valleys and basins of mountainous interiors, the Portuguese colonies in Brazil were an archipelago of agricultural settlements on the fringes of a continent, and did not develop significant internal settlement until the turn of the century. The resemblance between Portuguese South America and English North America cannot, however, be carried far. In Brazil, the dominant form of colonial society was that of an export–oriented plantation economy using large numbers of African slaves to produce sugar for international markets, while its late colonial frontier settlements were built on gold and diamond mining. English North America, by contrast, remained a largely agrarian society which, despite the introduction of plantation slavery towards the close of the seventeenth century, was based mainly on settlers of European origin and had no mining frontier comparable to those of Iberian America. It was nonetheless far from being a homogeneous or unified entity. As the creation of new colonies added to the number and variety of political units under English rule, so, behind the increasingly complicated political map, we can trace the emergence and development of several distinctive macro-regions, marked by broad differences of economic, social and cultural character.

One such region was New England, where dissenting religious communities established corporate Christian settlements during the 'great migration' of the 1630s, as it grew from a core in Massachusetts, this 'Puritan America' embraced a region that gradually diversified from agriculture and fur trading into fishing, shipbuilding and maritime transportation.

A second region was that of the American South, built on an agricultural economy geared to production of tropical commodities for export overseas. This 'Plantation America' was formed of two parts. The oldest and most heavily populated of these was the Chesapeake Bay area, where the colonies of Virginia and Maryland encompasssed a rural economy of plantations and small farms devoted to producing tobacco for export and food for local consumption. In the Lower South, in the Carolinas, another variant of plantation economy developed towards the end of the seventeenth century. Influenced by settlers from Barbados, South Carolina evolved a type of economy and society that was quite close to that of the British West Indies. There, a slave plantation economy took firm root, growing rice and indigo in a North American variant of the Caribbean economies which, both geographically and socially, lay at the outer extreme of the spectrum of English colonies in the Americas.

In the latter half of the seventeenth century, a third major region developed in the Middle Atlantic colonies of New York, New Jersey and Pennsylvania. This region may be called 'Polyglot America'

155

because, although most migrants who entered these colonies by way of the Hudson and Delaware rivers were from Britain, a substantial number came from other European countries. Initially, these colonies resembled New England in their economic life, being sustained by small, self-sustaining agrarian communities of small white farmers, and a trade in furs. But they soon acquired a character of their own, quickly becoming commercialized as merchants and producers built connections with external markets in southern Europe and the West Indies.

A final region lay in the interior, again traversing the political boundaries that separated colonial provinces. This was 'Frontier America', located in the lands which lay west of the settled coastal plains, where fresh waves of migration opened new spaces for settlement in the eighteenth century.[4]

These regions shared some common features. All were, in differing degrees, demographically dynamic societies that formed part of a larger Anglophone culture based on English institutions and values. All were also increasingly oriented towards production for the market, and all were influenced by the economic and political development of a parent power which, during the later seventeenth and the eighteenth centuries, became a leading force in the world economy. Another common characteristic of these regions was their foundation in economies which rested heavily on agriculture. Although colonials created valuable trades in animal skins, furs and fish, in all regions the pillars of economic life rested on farming of one kind or another. However, beneath these broad similarities were important differences. In the first place, types of agriculture varied markedly from one region to another, arising not only from differences in soil and climate, but also from the scale and character of markets in which crops might be sold. The social organization of the regions was equally diverse, varying in accord with the timing of their colonization, the regional and cultural origins of their immigrant populations, and the systems of landholding which had arisen in the course of settlement. To understand these variants of British North America, we shall now examine each of the major regions in turn, defining the core elements of their socio-cultural structures and tracing the main trends in economic development and social change through the seventeenth and into the early eighteenth century.

PURITAN AMERICA: THE NEW ENGLAND REGION

The New England region may be loosely defined as 'Puritan America' because the core of its society long carried the imprint of the Puritan settlers who flocked to join the Massachusetts Bay colony during the 1630s. The immigrants who founded the colony exalted the family and the spiritual values of the community over the individual and the pursuit of material gain, and although these ideals were gradually diluted during the century after the first settlements, they continued to exercise a powerful influence over the social and cultural life of the region.

During the English Civil War, migration into New England came to a standstill, but this did not hinder the region's ongoing development. For by the 1640s, the Massachusetts Bay colony was already firmly established on the basis of immigration during the preceding decade. The number of towns had increased from 11 in 1630 to 21 in 1641, and 33 by 1647; moreover, while Puritan settlers spread along the coast of the bay and inland, dissidents from Massachusetts had also established fresh colonies in Connecticut and Rhode Island, and laid the foundations of settlement in the area which later became the province of New Hampshire. Though still small at mid-century, all these colonies were to continue to grow and develop during the succeeding years, building on early settlements to create a very distinctive form of English colonial society and culture.

A striking feature of New England's development was its rapid transition from an immigrant to a settled society. Large-scale migration to New England ended with the English Civil War, and immigrants henceforth made only a relatively small contribution to the region's development. However, although only about 10-12,000 newcomers arrived during the latter half of the seventeenth century, the region saw a large increase in its population. Abundant supplies of land and food, a balanced ratio of men to women, and a low incidence of epidemic disease made for high birth rates and low mortality, and the region consequently enjoyed a rate of population growth that was without parallel in either the Old World or most parts of the New. In 1660, New England had a population of about 33,000 people; half a century later, in 1710, the region's population had multiplied more than threefold, to over 115,000 people. Massachusetts benefited most from this demographic growth: by the early eighteenth century, it was still the most populous of the four New England colonies. In 1660, some two-thirds of New England's people lived in the Bay colony, and, as population grew and settlement expanded, Massachusetts'

157

demographic predominance was only partly diminished. In 1710, Massachusetts still held about half of New England's population; of the remainder, about a quarter lived in Connecticut, while the rest were divided between Rhode Island and New Hampshire. Throughout this period, New England was the most populous region in British North America, with more than a third of the total population of the mainland colonies.[5]

The outstanding cultural characteristic of New England was its dedication to a religious purpose. Before the Civil War, Governor John Winthrop's vision of the Massachusetts Bay colony as a society whose members would work together to create a community free from the corruptions of the Old World had brought the first settlers together under a government that was based on spiritual values, and devoted to enforcing the religious beliefs and moral code enunciated by Puritan theologians and ministers. Winthrop's efforts to build an authoritarian theocracy were soon modified by opposition from the towns outside Boston; in the mid-1630s, a constitution which enabled freemen who were also full church members to vote for their representatives allowed about half of the population to vote in elections to the colony's law-making general court, and in 1641 the general court allowed local congregations to elect their own officials, to decide on their own membership and, under the authority of Puritan ministers, to worship as they saw fit. The loosening of the reins of central authority did not however diminish the importance of religion in New England life. The religious congregation continued to be the heart of community, with the local church imposing doctrine on its members, nurturing a sense of collective identity and enforcing social discipline. Most New England towns and villages were inward-looking, corporate Christian communities in which the family, conceived in terms of the convenant theology central to Puritan religious belief, was the building block of the social order. Indeed, the idea of the 'convenanted family', in which all members were bound together by mutual obligations under the leadership of the father and imbued with a sense of collective responsibility, was so important an element in the Puritan conception of social order that, in early Massachusetts, Connecticut and Plymouth, all were compelled to live in family groups.[6]

The sense of community inspired by Puritanism combined with East Anglian social customs to exercise a powerful influence over New England's development. Accustomed to life in villages or towns in England, Massachusetts settlers clustered together in ordered rural communities, thereby creating the small towns which became the distinguishing feature of the New England landscape. Our picture of life in these communities as the work of pious, industrious people organized in a moral hierarchy and working towards a common destiny has taken much of its form and detail from studies of the Massachusetts towns of Dedham and Andover. In the records of Dedham, Kenneth Lockridge found a closed corporate community built on a utopian ideal and held together by shared religious beliefs, in Andover, Philip Greven saw a strong, stable community based on the patriarchal family, where sons did not acquire land until late in life and therefore long remained under the sway of their fathers. We must recognize, however, that not all New England towns fitted the mould or passed through the process of change described by Lockridge and Greven. Some diverged from the Puritan religious path at an early moment in New England history. Rhode Island, for example, was a separate colony of Baptists and Quakers who deliberately rejected Puritan dogma and discipline, and practised religious toleration. Stephen Innes has also disputed the idea that the closed, corporate community identified by Lockridge and Greven was typical of New England society as a whole. In his study of the river town of Springfield in Massachusetts (founded in 1636), Innes depicts a society that was dominated by a single family and characterized by inequality, and where materialism was always a more important force in structuring society than religious unity or utopian religious ideals.[7]

Despite these variations within New England society, it is nonetheless clear that the social order which the Puritans had established at the core of the region had some very distinctive features which, while they may have become less pronounced in the later colonial period, nonetheless clearly distinguish it both from the mother country and from other Euro-American colonies. In the first place, New England differed from its Old World progenitor in one vital respect: its founders eliminated the extremes of the English social order, with its nobility based in great landed estates and its mass of indigent rural poor. Although Puritans recognized and respected social distinctions based on wealth, they consciously rejected European notions of nobility and in their social ranking accorded more importance to age and moral character. Participation in political life was also much more widespread than it was either in England or in many of its colonies. In the seventeenth century, most adult males in New England had a good chance of owning their own land and were therefore eligible both to vote and hold office in the towns in which they lived. This did not produce democratic government; rates of participation in the routines of political life were often low, and the object of representation was to produce a community concensus rather to express and enforce the will of the majority. But the New England emphasis on the rights of community members to create their own rules, to live according to their own consciences, and to be free from want fostered a political tradition which, in its sensitivity to external interference, arbitrary government and social injustice, stood apart from both England and from most other colonial societies in the Americas.[8]

The development of New England's economic life during the later seventeenth century was shaped by two major forces. One was the remarkable rate of internal population growth which we have already noted: this ensured that New England's agrarian society had a firm basis for growth despite a low incidence of immigration. The other was the gradual development of external commerce and the consequent commercialization of New England's economy.

This process began slowly. Early settlers did not initiate purely extractive economies like those developed by French or Dutch fur traders in neighbouring areas, but aimed instead to establish farming communities producing foodstuffs for both subsistence and exchange. Conditions for agriculture on the small coastal plain where early settlement clustered were relatively poor: much of the soil was thin and stony, winters were long and hard, and, though the spread of settlement brought more fertile lands under cultivation, New England's crops were too similar to those of Europe to be suitable for export. Without a product which commanded an overseas market, early New Englanders developed an economy that was independent but backward. Some colonists focused on fishing, others even created a small manufacture of linen and hemp textiles, but the economy depended mainly on the work of small family farmers. In these circumstances, the development of manufactures for local use made little progress; with an open frontier of land and a preference for independence, labour could not easily be held in wage-earning occupations. New Englanders therefore imported many of their needs from overseas, and had to find a means to pay for goods brought from Europe. In the early years of the colony, this problem was solved by migrants who brought money with them, providing both markets for local farmers and a source of specie for buying imports. But when immigration fell off in the 1640s, New England's economy was plunged into depression and its inhabitants were forced back towards subsistence farming. In seeking a solution to the crisis, the Governor and General Court of Massachusetts adopted policies which were eventually to revive New England's economy, and to set it in a mould that was to last throughout the colonial period. The general thrust of this policy was simple enough: it aimed to reduce imports by promoting local manufactures and to increase exports by finding markets for New England products. The latter was much more successful than the former, reflecting the enterprise of local merchants, particularly those of Boston.

Fishing, rather than farming, became a central element in the development of New England's commercial economy during the later seventeenth century. The sea fisheries off Maine and the Newfoundland Banks had long attracted Europeans; indeed, they had played a part in attracting early colonists to the New England region. But New Englanders' exploitation of the fisheries' commercial potential did not begin to take off until the mid-1640s, when the activities of English fishermen were disturbed by the Civil War at home; then, during the decades that followed, the fisheries became a mainstay of New England's economy. Cod, the "beef of the sea", was more in demand in the Mediterranean countries than in England, and, ironically, Catholic Europe became an important market for the fisheries of Protestant New England. Growing quantities of fish were exported to the Spanish and Portuguese Atlantic islands, and to Spain and Portugal themselves, while, with the rapid growth of sugar planting in the Caribbean, the West Indies also became important outlets for the fisheries. The fish trade had important economic side-effects, in that it provided New England's merchants with channels through which they could send other local products abroad. Thus, livestock and timber products were sent to the West Indies, and barrels were exported to the Atlantic islands, particularly Madeira, in return for cargoes of wine. From the West Indies, New England's merchants also took sugar and its derivatives; molasses were particularly important as the raw material for rum distilleries which not only supplied mainland markets in North America, but also provided New Englanders with a means of buying slaves in Africa and trading them on to the West Indies.

Equally important was the fact that these trades encouraged the growth of New England's carrying and shipbuilding industries. Thanks to the energy and enterprise of local merchants, New England quickly developed its own mercantile marine, which was used on commercial circuits which led to Europe and the West Indies as well as being employed in a coasting trade along the North American shorelines. New England moved, then, from an economy geared largely to local self-sufficiency towards a diversified commercial economy, where the simplicity of early farming communities was increasingly counterbalanced by the relatively sophisticated commercial society of the trading ports.

By the turn of the century, demographic and economic growth were promoting social change and inducing social strains of several kinds. Population growth tended to weaken social and political cohesion, as those in search of land broke away from their parent society and formed competing communities; it also loosened the discipline of religion (though not necessarily its practice), as the spiritual elect became a diminishing proportion of the population. To these internal pressures was added another powerful force for social change when New England expanded its external trade and shipping activities. As commerce grew during the later seventeenth century, more towns became involved in production for local and external markets; together with population growth, this made them more complex and differentiated communities with greater disparities in the distribution of wealth and power, and a marked tendency to deviate from Puritan orthodoxy.[9]

The shift away from Puritan ideals was particularly marked in port and major river towns. Boston was the most striking example of such change. There, the rise of commerce was paralleled by the emergence of a merchant class which was outward-looking, urbanized and secularized, and, by the end of the seventeenth century, Boston was North America's principal port. In the process, it had become a society dominated by merchants who favoured religious toleration, closer contacts with England, and enjoyed a style of life which strayed far from the strict norms of early Puritan rural communities.[10]

Although demographic and economic growth made New England a more complex and contentious society, increasingly divided between those who clung fiercely to the simple virtues of the early Puritans and those who favoured commerce and conciliation with the mother country, the region nevertheless retained some of the basic features which had made it a very special component of English America. Undisturbed by the substantial immigration which went to other regions, the social order created by the early Puritans was shored up a high degree of cultural homogeneity and continuity. Commercial capitalism made headway in the main towns and ports, but coexisted with a deep conservatism which blunted the impact of social change in some areas of the countryside. Thus, by the early eighteenth century, the subsistence farming communities of New England still retained many of their original features, in the form of the small farm, the patriarchal family and the inward-looking religious congregation.[11]

PLANTATION AMERICA: THE CHESAPEAKE REGION

A society and economy very different from that of New England emerged in the American South, where the Chesapeake Bay became the entryway for the migrants who peopled the colonies of Virginia and Maryland. Although it had a population comparable in size to that of New England, in most other respects the Chesapeake region had little in common with the colonial society to the north. The estuary of the Chesapeake Bay and its river system offered a vast network of waterways which joined the ocean to the huge shoreline of a coastal plain rich in fertile alluvial soils; from their outset the Chesapeake colonies were based in cash crop production, organized on plantations producing tobacco for expanding European markets. In this environment, towns were few, as settlement tended to disperse over the countryside of the tidewater, in large plantations, small farms and loose rural neighbourhoods lined along on the banks of the bay and its main rivers.

The core of Chesapeake regional society lay in Virginia, which had a considerably larger population than neighbouring Maryland throughout the seventeenth century. (In 1660, the populations were of Virginia was 27,000 and that of Maryland, 8,400; in 1710, the populations were 78,000 and nearly 43,000 respectively.) The first forty years of Virginia's development were slow, hindered by heavy mortality among settlers and the instability of markets for tobacco, but during and after the English Civil War its society was transformed by a new wave of migration from England. The migration started as a direct result of the Civil War, as defeated royalists sought refuge from political persecution. Many went to Europe, others to the West Indies, but a significant group of "distressed cavaliers" were enticed to Virginia by the colony's royalist governor, Sir William Berkeley. There, in the congenial surroundings of a land governed by a man committed to the royalist cause and the Anglican church, younger sons of the English aristocracy and gentry founded a Virginian elite which was able to re-create important elements of the culture from which it originated. These men came from all parts of England, but were mainly drawn from the south and west, particularly from London, and, once established in Virginia, they created a kinship network which not only preserved ties with the English aristocracy and gentry but also gradually came to exercise a dominating influence over the colony's cultural and political life.[12]

Such patrician migrants were only a small part of a much larger movement to the Chesapeake, especially during the third quarter of the seventeenth century. Between 1645 and 1670, 40,000 to 50,000 English people migrated to Virginia and Maryland, providing the solid basis for growth that these colonies had lacked before the Civil War. Most migrants were poor people, and probably three-quarters were indentured servants, mostly young single males. Thus differences in pre-Civil War patterns of migration to Virginia and New England were sustained after the Civil War. Unlike the earlier migration to Massachusetts, which had been drawn largely from the middle sectors of eastern English society, the movement to the Chesapeake drew more heavily from the upper and lower ranks of English society, from the regions of the English south and west, and included far fewer women and children. Immigration also played a central role in Chesapeake development for much longer than it did in New England. More than half of the total seventeenth-century immigration into Chesapeake arrived between 1660 and 1700, especially during the 1660s and 1670s, and the continuing gender imbalance and high death rate of immigrants ensured that the society retained a fluid and unstable character. One consequence of high mortality was a family structure different from that of New England. Marriages were rarer and briefer, and families were smaller; moreover, in a setting where children were routinely deprived of at least one of their parents during childhood, parental control was weaker and the extended kin network a more important social institution than the nuclear family commonly found in New England.[13]

Chesapeake social values and behaviour were also more obviously imitative of English society than those of New England. In religion, the dominant group tended to discourage Protestant heterodoxy, and in society to foster the ideals of aristocracy. Virginia became a bastion of the Church of England in America. A well-educated clergy, sympathetic to the idea of social hierarchy, inculcated the liturgy and rites of Anglicanism into the white population, while paying much less attention than in New England to encouraging literacy and Bible-reading. Virginians also took the full range of social ranks from England, organized in a hierarchy of deferential relations that offered little room for social mobility. In colonial Virginia, few escaped from the social rank in which they were born. Compared to New England, this was a rigidly ordered society, where the mass of the common folk were clearly separated from and subordinate to the gentry.

Social hierarchy was paralleled by economic inequality. By the late seventeenth century, the top stratum of Virginian society consisted of about 10 per cent of adult males, who held between 50 and 75 per cent of the productive land and employed the bulk of the labour force. Next came a stratum of small freeholders, between 20 and 30 per cent of the population, who cultivated their own land, using family labour and one or two hired servants. The remaining 60 to 70 per cent was landless, owned little or no property, and worked for others. This group included tenant farmers working on large estates, the many indentured servants who had been drawn to Virginia by the hope of obtaining land, and the mass of poor labourers who furnished the rural and urban workforce.[14]

Social development and change in the Chesapeake region hinged on an economy which was highly commercialized from the early days of settlement. Virginia's tobacco exports started in 1616, and, after recession followed the first boom in the 1620s, tobacco production recovered to become the pivot of the Chesapeake economy. The first long period of growth spread over most of the seventeenth century, as tobacco exports rose steeply and steadily from about 60,000 pounds in 1620 to around 25 million pounds per year in 1690. After a short period of stagnation, exports then entered a second growth phase in 1715, underpinned by rising tobacco consumption both in the home country and in Europe, to which tobacco was re-exported in increasing volume. By 1727–8, the level of exports had almost doubled its seventeenth-century peak, reaching around 50 million pounds per year; in the succeeding half-century, growth continued unabated, until, on the eve of the American Revolution in the mid-1770s, tobacco exports reached around 100 million pounds per year.

An important feature of this form of economic development was its reliance on British merchants. Ships from England sailed far into Chesapeake Bay and its river system, to collect tobacco directly from the plantations. The smaller planters tended to enter into direct exchanges with British factors, who, financed by merchants in England and Scotland, bought their tobacco and sold them the imports they needed. The large planters, on the other hand, took to sending tobacco cargoes to England on their own account, for sale through agents, usually in London. By the early eighteenth century, most of their tobacco was sold in this way, and often included the crops which small planters sold to their larger neighbours. In return, agents in London organized transportation, finance and the export of European goods to the planters in Virginia. Both types of arrangements tended to lead to planter dependence on and indebtedness to British merchants, who provided advances on future crops.

Dependence on metropolitan trade was to some extent offset during the eighteenth century, when tobacco ceased to be the only item of Chesapeake exports. As the fertility of tidewater land was sapped by

165

tobacco cultivation, landowners began to diversify into producing food crops and livestock for the Caribbean market. At the same time, small farmers in the backlands began to sell food, including wheat, in the towns, and Baltimore became an important centre for the grain trade. Nonetheless, the region retained its essential character as an export economy, geared to overseas markets. This export economy also came increasingly to rely on African slaves to provide its labour force; the growth of the slave trade during the eighteenth century connected the Chesapeake region to another commercial circuit, which supplied slaves for its plantations.[15]

The economic realities of producing tobacco promoted the form-ation of large estates owned by a small elite of wealthy and powerful planters. Because tobacco quickly exhausted the fertility of the soil, planters with sufficient capital built up large landholdings in order to hold a reserve for future cultivation. This tendency became still more pronounced from the closing decades of the seventeenth century, when the flow of indentured labour slowed down and large plantation owners began to turn to black slaves rather than white servants for the bulk of their labour force. When tobacco exports declined temporarily in the 1680s, opportunities for the small planter virtually disappeared, and, as the myth of free land evaporated, white immigration declined sharply. The shortage of labour created by the downturn in immigration led in turn to a major change in Chesapeake society, as its economy shifted to a slave-based agriculture. English entry into the slave trade provided southern planters with a larger and cheaper supply of black slaves and, as the price of white labour rose, so the demand for blacks increased.

In 1650, the black population of Virginia was little more than 3 per cent of the population; by 1710, it had increased dramatically, to nearly 30 per cent. The growth of the slave population in Maryland was less obvious, but nonetheless quite pronounced, growing from nearly 5 per cent in 1660 to over 18 per cent by 1710. Henceforth, slavery advanced rapidly throughout the Chesapeake: by the mid-eighteenth century slaves made up 40 per cent of Virginia's population and 30 per cent of that of Maryland. So, having put down its first roots in the Caribbean, slave society began to spread during the closing decades of the seventeenth century, moving to the continental mainland where it was to transform the society of the American South. In 1700, blacks were still a minority in the North American colonies, but having been solidly installed in the old colonies of Virginia and Maryland, slavery was set to become a vital and enduring element of Chesapeake society during the century that followed.

In social and political terms, the Chesapeake colonies became more stable from the end of the seventeenth century. A land which had previously had a high turnover of immigrants was henceforth increasingly populated by native-born people, led by planter elites who showed a greater commitment to, and held firmer control over their provincial societies. Important differences nonetheless continued to distinguish the Chesapeake region from New England and other British mainland colonies. For slavery brought a major social transformation, turning the Chesapeake into a society organized along racial lines. Henceforth, the society of the South was one that was controlled by small numbers of planters who dominated a white tenantry and a large and expanding slave labour force. Conflict within the society was, however, counteracted by several factors. Although opportunities for social advance were blocked by the high concentration of landownership in old settled areas, the opening of an internal frontier provided space for small farmers, and economic growth raised the standard of living among free whites. The shift towards the employment of slaves also helped the planter elites to cope with tensions between whites, by promoting the idea of racial solidarity. With the rapid growth of slave numbers, the principal social division was increasingly perceived as that separating black from white; shored up by pressures towards white solidarity, the planter families who controlled power legitimized their position with an ideology of paternalism.[16]

PLANTATION AMERICA: THE CAROLINAS

While the plantation economy of the Chesapeake was shifting towards slavery in the late seventeenth and early eighteenth centuries, another variant of American plantation society was taking shape in the Carolinas. Settlement in these areas differed from that of other colonies, as most migrants came from within Anglo-America rather than directly from the metropolitan country. North Carolina began as an extension of Virginia in the 1650s, when settlers first started to move into the Albemarle Sound area, close to the southern boundaries of Virginia. South Carolina was peopled from 1670, initially by migrants from Barbados. By 1710, the population of North Carolina had grown to about 15,000 people, while South Carolina had nearly 11,000. Both areas saw spectacular demographic growth over the next half-century: in 1760, the population of the Carolinas was nearly 205,000, divided more or less evenly between North and South.

North Carolina gradually developed an economy and society which broadly resembled that of the Chesapeake. It exported tobacco, grains and meat products, naval stores and wood products, plus some rice and indigo from the country bordering South Carolina, in the Cape Fear Valley. When the shift to slavery took place in the eighteenth century, North Carolina also became similar in ethnic composition to the Chesapeake, with blacks making up 30 per cent of its population in 1760. A different picture emerged in South Carolina. From the earliest years of their settlement in the 1670s, the white immigrants who peopled South Carolina searched for a staple crop which they might profitably export. Initially, they had some success with stock-raising, as cattle and hogs found a favourable ecological niche in the area's rich grasslands and the West Indies offered markets for meat and timber products. It also seemed that trade with the Indians might provide a staple for trade with Britain, as Carolina-based traders found a valuable export in deerskins acquired from Indians in the interior. However, by the end of the century, South Carolina discovered a staple export in the form of rice, a crop that was to make a very distinctive mark on the economy and social structure of the region.

The expansion of rice exports in the early eighteenth century was rapid, rising from 1.6 million pounds in 1710 to 18 million pounds in 1730, and continuing to rise, albeit less steeply, for the remainder of the colonial period. With rice came African slavery, which became the basic system of labour in the burgeoning export economy. The area's orientation towards export was further reinforced when indigo cultivation was introduced in the 1740s. Indigo complemented rice perfectly, since it was grown on higher lands to a different seasonal rhythm of production, and it gradually became a major export, supplying the growing English textile industry with a prized dyestuff. The export of rice and indigo created an economy in South Carolina which resembled that of the West Indies. Like sugar, rice generated a strong tendency towards monoculture, and some areas of South Carolina were dedicated exclusively to rice production. South Carolina's economy was nonetheless more diverse than that of the Caribbean islands, and it never depended on food imports to the same extent as the West Indies. Instead, the region produced most of its own food; its livestock farmers even exported food, generally beef and pork, to the Caribbean islands.

Slavery quickly took root in the new colonies of the Carolinas. Shortly after 1700, blacks outnumbered whites in South Carolina, and by the 1730s, they made up more than two-thirds of its population. In the richest rice-growing areas, the concentration of slaves was so striking that, to a foreign traveller in 1737, 'Carolina looks more like a negro country than like a country settled by white people'.[17] When the slave plantation economy was reinforced by the development of indigo exports, which started in the 1740s and boomed in the years prior to the American Revolution, the society of South Carolina seemed increasingly to imitate that of the British West Indies, from which many of its founding immigrants had originated. Economies of scale encouraged the formation of large, specialized plantations which absorbed smaller landholdings and consolidated a wealthy and dominant planter class whose power rested on slavery. Trade was largely in the hands of British and New England merchants, so that, like the West Indies and the Chesapeake region, South Carolina did not develop a strong merchant class of its own, but depended on outsiders to organize its commerce. Meanwhile, within the colony 'prosperity rested on a brutal, exploitative system of slavery and plantation agriculture thoroughly dominated by a confident and class conscious local gentry.'[18]

POLYGLOT AMERICA: THE MIDDLE ATLANTIC COLONIES

Another, quite different pattern of economy and society based in agriculture arose in the colonies of New York, New Jersey, Pennsylvania and Delaware. Here, in the Middle Atlantic region, the wide coastal plain was highly suitable for farming and its rich soils, equitable climate and plentiful land attracted European immigrants in large numbers. In a relatively benign disease environment, white settlers flourished, and the region as a whole saw very rapid population growth, beginning in the last decades of the seventeenth century and gaining momentum in the eighteenth. In 1710, the region's total population was about 63,000; half a century later, in 1760, spectacular growth rates had raised the total to nearly 400,000. New York and New Jersey had grown around fivefold, to over 100,000 and 87,000 respectively; Pennsylvania increased eightfold to 180,000, while Delaware had multiplied its population ten times, to over 33,000. Thus, a century after the English had first secured a position in the region, the Middle Atlantic region held about a quarter of the total European population of British North America and had become a prosperous agricultural zone, in which the production of grains and livestock flourished. The character of development in these colonies varied, but shared one common feature: an early involvement in overseas trade, and a mixed agriculture which provided plentiful surpluses for export.

New York and the Hudson Valley, an important sub-region of the Middle American area, had already been partly developed as the Dutch colony of New Netherland before the English seized control of the region in 1664. The port of New Amsterdam, which became the city of New York, had never been more than a small commercial entrepôt in the Dutch empire, however, and much of the interior remained empty. At first, change was slow. Although place names were altered, Dutch proprietors and tenants generally retained their lands, and the Dutch merchants engaged in the fur trade in the Upper Hudson Valley, at Albany, were left undisturbed in their commerce with the Indians. The region's development was, moreover, inhibited by the English proprietor's policy of granting vast tracts of land to a few individuals who had neither the capital nor the enterprise to exploit it. In the Hudson Valley large, semi-feudal estates worked by tenants were created, some of which survived into the eighteenth century, but attracting settlers was difficult, as other colonies offered them better terms. Much land was thus left in the hands of speculators, and was unsettled and uncultivated until the population began to grow at a rapid pace during the first half of the eighteenth century. The area around Albany remained solidly Dutch, reinforced by further Dutch immigration, but in the lower Hudson a bewildering variety of Europeans, including English, Dutch, Swedes, Norwegians, Germans, French Huguenots, as well as African slaves, came into the region to create a population of extraordinary diversity, in which no single religious or ethnic group held a dominant position. The European ethnic groups generally lived in separate clusters, mostly within a day's journey of the port of New York, and independent, family-based farms became the typical feature of the landscape.[19]

During the later seventeenth century, New York's trade was small. Under English rule, the economy shifted from reliance on the fur trade towards an agrarian economy, in which farmers produced foodstuffs which were increasingly exported to the English Caribbean islands, and flaxseed for Europe. The rise of New York was, however, a phenomenon of the eighteenth rather than the late seventeenth century, as settlers searching for lands poured into the region from Europe and from densely settled New England. Despite the influx from New England, which was to lead to sharp conflict later, New York remained very different from the neighbouring colony. In the eighteenth century, New York merchants and shippers made their port

a major clearing point for a growing commerce in agricultural commodities from the whole Middle Atlantic region, and the city and
colony became a prosperous commercial society, dominated by
patrician mercantile and landowning families. The sheer diversity of
New York, with its layers of ethnic groupings built on and around the
Dutch colonists, its mixture of large estates and small freehold farmers,
and a strongly individualistic and materialist character contrasted
markedly with that of early New England.[20]

An even more distinctive culture developed to the south of New
York, in and around the Delaware Bay. There, the Delaware River
provided the point of entry for the third major British migration of
the seventeenth century, consisting largely of Quakers from England's
northern Midlands and from Wales. Quakers had moved to the
Americas shortly after the foundation of the 'Society of Friends' in
1649, but their first large and organized movement started in 1675,
when a shipload of Quakers founded Salem in West Jersey, on the
shores of the Delaware Bay. This was followed by a wave of immigration into the Quaker colony of Pennsylvania, founded in 1682.
Between 1675 and 1715, as many as 23,000 colonists moved into the
Delaware Valley, most of them Quakers or people with Quaker
sympathies; in the early eighteenth century, they multiplied so rapidly
that, by 1750, Quakers constituted the third largest religious
denomination in British America.[21]

When Penn established his colony, he intended to create a benign
social order which would avoid the extremes of wealth and poverty
found in England, and replace the English system of hereditary social
ranks with a system where status rested on individual merit and moral
worth. In the event, he suffered many setbacks and eventually became
disillusioned with his colonial creation; nevertheless, while its founder's
ambitions were not entirely fulfilled, Pennsylvania's Quaker origins
were to make it a colony with highly distinctive traits.

One distinguishing feature of Pennsylvania was its relatively
egalitarian agrarian society: most land holdings in Pennsylvania were
independent farms of modest size, and the Delaware region long had a
more equitable distribution of land than any other colony in British
America. Indeed, despite the fact that commercial growth accentuated
economic inequalities after the mid-eighteenth century, the region
long retained its reputation as the 'best poor man's country' in the
world.

Another singular feature of the colony was its political life, which
was deeply influenced by Quaker ideals. Quaker migration, like
Puritan migration to New England, was based in a religious purpose,

171

and motivated by a desire both to escape religious intolerance at home and to construct a new society based on religious principles. Less restrictive than the Puritans, the Quakers' Christianity was a positive and inclusive creed, with a system of church government opposed to clerical hierarchy and ceremony. Quakerism was, moreover, an evangelical, embracing movement which ignored the boundaries of race and nation, so that English Quakers welcomed like-minded immigrants from other countries into their colonies. Indeed, such was their openness that, by the mid-eighteenth century, English Quakers had become a minority in the colonies they had founded in Pennsylvania, West Jersey and Delaware, and Quakers had been displaced from political control in Philadelphia by non-Quaker merchants and their allies. But the political culture created by the Quakers, with its concept of a 'loving neighbourhood' of farmers regulated by principles of respectable, honourable Christian behaviour between neighbours, left an enduring mark on Pennsylvania's political culture, promoting a disposition towards equality, autonomy and quietism. From Quaker insistence on religious freedom, there also stemmed a deep concern with individual political liberty, resolutely opposed to interference from the state and established Church but ready to protect the individual against oppression by others. The Quakers were, in short, remarkably consistent in translating their principles into practice. Once established, they did not hesitate to extend to others the rights they wanted for themselves and, though they used black slaves, they even questioned the propriety of slavery at a time when slave-ownership was becoming more common in British North America.[22]

Pennsylvania saw relatively little progress as a commercial economy during the late seventeenth century, when its agrarian foundations were being laid down by incoming settlers. However, the agrarian environment and opportunities to market cash crops, combined with the anti-authoritarian cast of Quakers, meant that any tendency towards forming a closely knit, community-oriented society was gradually counterbalanced by acquisitive and individualist aspirations. Easy availability of land and outlets for trade in foodstuffs with the West Indies and southern Europe gave a strong momentum to economic growth during the eighteenth century. Large number of immigrants were drawn to Pennsylvania, adding to its cultural mosaic, and by mid-century Philadelphia had become a leading colonial port, on a par with Boston and New York. Here, as in the other regions of Middle Atlantic America, the outstanding features of economic life were diversity of trade, a wide diffusion of prosperity and a strong market orientation among settlers.[23]

Although there were marked differences among the Middle Atlantic colonies, particularly between the Hudson and Delaware regions, by comparison with other British colonial regions the colonies of the Middle Atlantic shared some outstanding features. One shared characteristic of life in the Middle Atlantic region was the family farm. In some areas of New York and New Jersey, land speculators formed large estates where they leased land to small farmers, creating sharp social divisions between rich rentiers and their tenants. But in other parts of these colonies, as well as in Pennsylvania and Delaware, the prevailing system of landholding was based on freeholders with small and medium-sized farms directed towards production for the market, using family labour and sometimes wage labourers and slaves. The family farm had indeed quickly become the central cell of regional society. On the rich soils of the coastal plain, smallholders with one or two hundred acres derived a good income from working family farms, competing with many others within a rapidly-evolving market economy. Their prosperity in turn attracted growing numbers of new immigrants and settlers who spread into the lands of the interior, beyond the coastal plains.[24]

Another general feature of the Middle Atlantic colonies was their ethnic and cultural heterogeneity. Unlike New England, which remained relatively homogeneous, or the South, which moved towards a bi-racial hierarchy of blacks and whites, the Middle Atlantic colonies became the diaspora of peoples from many cultures. From their early years, both New York and Pennsylvania were complex mixtures of ethnic and religious groups. Immigrants from England and New England mingled with the Dutch settlers left over from the New Netherland colony, and to this combination were later added French Huguenots, Central Europeans, and, in the eighteenth century, waves of migrants from Ulster and Scotland. In similar vein, Pennsylvania encompassed groups from many European regions, as Quakers mixed with the members of Protestant sects drawn from a remarkable range of nationalities and religious persuasions. It is not surprising, then, that experience of life in the Middle Atlantic colonies gave rise to Crèvecoeur's famous remark that the people of the British continental colonies were 'a mixture of English, Scotch, Irish, French, Dutch, Germans, and Swedes' and that, 'from this promiscuous breed, the race now called Americans have arisen'.[25]

FRONTIER AMERICA

Settlement of the interior was largely a phenomenon of the eighteenth century. For, as land became scarcer in the well-settled areas, both colonials and migrants from Europe moved to areas where land was more generally available, until, after mid-century, 'a seemingly bound-less proliferation, a new population, utterly different from the original native peoples whose territory this once had been, was spreading over a vast inland arc curving irregularly west and south from Nova Scotia to Florida, far removed from the coastal ports.'[26] From New England, settlers went north along the Connecticut and Hudson rivers; in New York, new settlements spread upriver to the juncture of the Hudson and Mohawk rivers; in Pennsylvania, settlers poured south-westwards into the Appalachian uplands and the Ohio Valley, as well as spreading beyond Pennsylvania through the Cumberland Gap into west Virginia and the backcountry of the Carolinas. In all these regions, the van-guard of settlement, particularly on the farthest frontiers, was formed by immigrants, most of whom came not only from England, the traditional source of colonists, but also from other areas in the British Isles. Searching for escape from difficult economic circumstances at home, people from northern England, from Scotland and from northern Ireland pushed into the backcountry of the interior and, over the course of the century, founded another distinctive variant of Anglo-American colonial society.

The scale of the exodus is difficult to measure accurately, but on a conservative estimate it seems that, between 1718 and 1775, about 50,000 people entered North America from northern England, together with over 75,000 from Scotland, and some 150,000 from northern Ireland. This was in several respects a different kind of migration from those of the seventeenth century. In the first place, it was more British than English, as the bulk of migrants came from the Scottish highlands and lowlands, and from the Protestant Irish communities of Ulster. Second, unlike the Puritan migrations to New England or the Quaker movements into Pennsylvania, it was motivated more by hopes of material improvement than by flight from religious or political persecution, or the pursuit of utopian spiritual ideals. Emigrants from the peripheral areas of Great Britain left their homes to escape from hunger, deprivation and exploitation by landlords and governments, and were lured to America by the hope of free land in a new country. Theirs was also mainly a movement of families, and, although they included small numbers of gentry and independent farmers, the migrants consisted mainly of people of lowly social origin, drawn from the ranks of poor tenant farmers, farm labourers, artisans and petty traders. Many were, moreover, people drawn from cultural contexts which differed significantly from those of earlier colonists from Britain, being from borderland societies where traditional ties of blood and kin were the foundations for social organization.[27]

The cohorts of British border peoples generally entered America through the Delaware River, but moved quickly into the interior in search of unoccupied land. Going westward from Philadelphia, they also spread south and west into the mountains of Maryland, Virginia and the Carolinas, extending settlement over an area roughly equivalent in size to western Europe. Here land was plentiful, but life was far from easy. Amidst conflict and periodic warfare with native tribes, the backcountry offered few comforts. Settlers lived in primitive wooden cabins on isolated farmsteads which provided little more than a bare subsistence, while landownership was often concentrated in the hands of landlords who became wealthy by renting their lands to settlers. Backcountry society was therefore one of extremes, divided between a small cohort of great landowners and a mass of tenants or squatters who, though living amidst vast tracts of uncultivated territory, often owned no land of their own.

Government and politics in these lands were rudimentary. The writ of provincial governments ran thin on the frontier; there, justice was frequently administered in extra-legal ways, by men called 'regulators' who imposed their rules without reference to the formal processes of law. Feuds and banditry were common, and violence routine. Not surprisingly, politics in such settings lacked finesse. There was little interest in the kind of systematic thinking about the social order which had been found among Puritans or Quakers; on the frontier, personal leadership by forceful, charismatic men carried more weight than formalized political institutions. For backcountry people, political liberty was not based in ideas of tolerance or notions of community, nor ordered by internalized concepts of deference. On the frontier, far from centres of government on the coast, freedom from government and its agents was more important than freedom within the state, exercised through the apparatus of government and its institutions.

SLAVERY IN NORTH AMERICA

For most of the seventeenth century, socio-economic development in England's North American colonies diverged from that of the

Caribbean colonies in one obvious respect: it depended on European settlement rather than African slavery. Whereas a large proportion of the labour force in the continental colonies came from voluntary European immigrants who provided a temporary form of coerced labour as indentured servants, the workforce for plantations in the West Indies was increasingly composed of involuntary African migrants, forced into perpetual servitude as slaves. However, at the turn of the century, this distinction between continental and island colonies begins to blur, as the institution of African slavery penetrated North America and set the southern colonies on to a path of development which in some respects converged with that of the Caribbean colonies.

African slavery was known on the mainland from early in the seventeenth century, but by the start of the eighteenth century, it began to assume a new dimension and meaning. The transition began in the last quarter of the seventeenth century; slavery then grew rapidly over the next hundred years, as Table 6.1 shows.

Table 6.1   English slave imports into North America, 1676–1780.

Years	Southern Colonies	Mid-Atlantic Colonies	New England	Totals
1676–1700	10,000	——	——	10,000
1701–20	28,000	2,000	——	30,000
1721–40	64,000	4,000	2,000	70,000
1741–60	63,000	1,000	1,000	65,000
1761–80	80,000	2,000	——	82,000

Source: Richard S. Dunn, "Servants and Slaves: The Recruitment and Employment of Labour", in Jack P. Greene and J.R. Pole (eds) *Colonial British America: Essays in the New History of the Early Modern Era* (Baltimore, Md, and London, 1984) p. 165.

The impact of slavery on the American continental colonies was, however, much more uneven than in Britain's Caribbean colonies. Slave ownership was found throughout British North America, but the transition from slaveowning to slave societies took place only in regions of plantation agriculture, in the American South. Of all the slaves imported into the mainland, the vast majority went to the southern colonies, and the classic forms of North American slave society took shape in the plantation economies of the Chesapeake and Carolinas. As early as 1700, about 25 per cent of Virginia's population was black; after 1750, it exceeded 40 per cent. Maryland's black population followed a roughly similar trend, rising from 20 per cent in 1720 to over 30 per cent for the remainder of the colonial period; in North Carolina, the proportion of slaves rose from 20 per cent in 1720 to 34 per cent by 1780. South Carolina, with the smallest white population of these southern colonies, was a slave colony virtually from its outset, and had the largest percentage of blacks throughout the period. In 1700, blacks were already over 40 per cent of its population; by 1720, they formed 70 per cent of the population, declining gradually thereafter to about 50 per cent at the time of the American Revolution. At the other extreme stood New England, where slaves never exceeded about 3 per cent of the population, while in the Middle Atlantic region the proportion of slaves was around 7 per cent throughout the eighteenth century.[28]

Generally speaking, the growth of black numbers was matched by the degradation of the black individual. Prejudice against blacks was already strong in North America before slavery became firmly entrenched during the eighteenth century; as the numbers of slaves increased and blacks became a common form of property, so white slaveowners degraded their legal status, tightened restraints of their freedom, and institutionalized slavery into a dehumanizing system of domination and control.[29] In this sense, North American slavery resembled that created by English slaveowners in the Caribbean islands.

Some historians have argued that English law deprived slaves of fundamental human rights by treating them as mere property, making slavery a more oppressive institution in British America than in the Iberian American dominions, where the tradition of Roman law recognized the obligations of masters as well as the duties of slaves. It is true that, because representative government for colonials allowed slaveowners to construct their own laws for slaves and their treatment, the legal codes of North American slave societies provided scant protection from the masters' arbitrary exercise of power and offered few opportunities for the slave to obtain freedom. But differences in the legal and political traditions of Anglo-America and Iberian America should not be accorded too great an importance. Legal and religious principles were one thing; their implementation in practice was another. In reality, differences in legal and cultural norms were less important in influencing the status and treatment of slaves than were specific local conditions, such as the type of economic activity in which the slave was employed, the size of the productive unit in which he or she lived and worked, and the market conditions for the

177

commodity which he or she produced. Field hands on large plantations, for example, particularly those producing sugar, were probably most vulnerable to inhuman treatment, especially when high prices for the commodity they produced encouraged slaveowners to treat their slaves as an expendable factor of production which could simply be replaced by fresh imports from Africa. Thus, differences in the character of slave regimes cannot be attributed solely to broad cultural differences between host societies; regional and temporal variations were of equal if not greater significance.[30]

In North America, the treatment of slaves was undoubtedly harshest in those regions where slaves were most numerous, and where whites consequently lived in greatest fear of indiscipline and insurrection. The slave system that came closest to that of the West Indies was found in South Carolina. When large numbers of slaves were concentrated on plantations and blacks often outnumbered whites in rural areas, white fears of slave indiscipline and insurrection led to draconian laws that tightened political controls over blacks, and sanctioned cruel and dramatic punishments to force slaves into submission. Virginia and Maryland also developed oppressive slave codes, but the regime of slavery was generally less brutal. As the tobacco plantation reached its mature form during the eighteenth century, the large planters came to regard their estates as complete entities, micro-societies in which they ruled as the patriarchs of an extended family. Chesapeake slavery was thus coloured by a paternalism which, however pyschologically suffocating for blacks, generally protected them from the worst abuses of slavery. Conditions were least inhumane in Puritan New England and Quaker Pennsylvania, where slaves were a far less important element in economic life and were employed as artisans and servants rather than as agricultural labourers. It is, then, impossible to talk of slavery in North America as though it were a homogeneous institution; the slave system of South Carolina differed from that of the Chesapeake, and neither much resembled the conditions of slavery in the farm colonies and towns to the north.[31]

There was, however, one striking general difference between the slave societies of the British continental colonies and those of the English Caribbean islands: this was the tendency of black slaves in North America successfully to reproduce themselves. The extent of the difference is clearly revealed by comparing the scale of slave imports with changes in the size of the black population. In 1700–80, the British West Indies imported 950,000 slaves, but by 1787 had a slave population of only about 350,000; during the same period, the North American colonies imported around 250,000 slaves, but by 1790 had a slave population of around 750,000. This was not entirely due to better treatment of slaves in North America; other factors must also be taken into account, such as the ratio of male to female slaves imported, the disease environment and conditions affecting the formation of slave families.[32] It is clear, however, that enslavement in British North America offered black slaves a much better chance of survival than their counterparts in the British Caribbean.

Black cultures born in slavery in North America naturally varied, depending on the rate of slave importation and the local conditions in which slaves lived. In the Chesapeake region, high rates of importation in the early eighteenth century created a black population with a high proportion of young African males, who implanted strong African traditions. By the 1770s, however, only 10 per cent of annual growth in Virginia's slave population came from imports, and black society had become a more balanced, family-based society with its own kinship networks, and closer affinity to the local American culture. In the large plantations of South Carolina, on the other hand, blacks were more isolated from whites and constant importation produced a black culture which retained strong African traditions in language, religion and social relations. In the north, where slaves were more commonly employed as servants and artisans than as agricultural workers and were more widely dispersed, they were more exposed to the norms of the white society in which they lived and worked, and hence more closely assimilated into it.

One final general difference between slavery in the British mainland and island colonies was the greater degree of resistance and rebellion found in the Caribbean. While slaves everywhere found means to resist the demands of their masters, there was much less overt, violent opposition from slaves in North America than in the Caribbean. Slave rebellions in North America were rare and generally small, and there was no 'maroon' tradition of escaped slaves of the kind found in Jamaica or the French islands. Again, this is not necessarily attributable to better conditions or greater passivity on the part of North American slaves, but was probably more closely related to differences in the field of power surrounding them. In North America, slaves generally faced formidable odds from majority white societies, and had less easy access to backland areas in which rebels could take refuge and create their own, alternative communities outside the slave order.[33]

NORTH AMERICAN SOCIETY: CHARACTER AND TRAJECTORY

It is obviously hazardous to generalize about English North American society as a whole; regional economic and social structures and cultural traditions were too varied to permit simple categorizations. Nonetheless, seen in comparison with Europe or with the Iberian American colonial world, there are some general features of this disparate, multifaceted social world which, as it continued to mature into the eighteenth century, distinguish it sharply from contemporary European societies and from the colonies built by the Iberian powers in Latin America.

First, the North American colonies shared a tendency to develop more open, less rigid structures than the societies of contemporary Europe or Iberian America. Although migrants brought to America the customs, values and practices which they had known in the mother country, adaption to the American environment prevented any simple replication of European socio-economic systems. Not only did immigrants usually enter into an undomesticated landscape which they had to shape to their needs, but land was often plentiful, labour was scarce, and the apparatus of the state generally weak. Availability of land and scarcity of labour were particularly important in shaping the character of seventeenth-century English North America, favouring a relatively wide diffusion of economic gains among the white population and precluding the emergence of great gulfs between rich and poor. The weakness of church and state meant that institutional economic demands were also slight. For the freeholders who formed a preponderant group in English North America, the product of their land and labour was almost entirely their own. This was, of course, very different from conditions in European societies and in the Spanish colonies, where landlords, church and government took a large proportion of the peasant farmer's surplus, in rents, tithes and taxes.

Another characteristic of social life in England's continental colonies which distinguishes it from that of other European colonies in the Americas, particularly those of Spain, was the diversity of religious belief and practice found among colonials, and the concomitant weakness of the established church. Religion undoubtedly played an important part in the formation of Spanish American societies: their early development would be incomprehensible without reference to the activities of missionaries among the native peoples. Religion was no less important in the foundation and formation of English colonies, but played a very different part in social life. It was, first, an important force in the settlement of several colonial regions. In New England, the Puritans did not simply import the orthodox beliefs and practices of the national Anglican church, but sought to create a new, regenerated church, free of the corruptions of the established Church of England. Religious aspirations also played an important part in shaping the social order of the Middle Atlantic colonies, where another heterodox Protestant group, the Quakers, formed the colonizing vanguard in New Jersey and Pennsylvania. Nor were these the only heterodox groups in the colonies. During the eighteenth century, Central European and Scotch-Irish Protestants brought still more churches and sects into North America, with Mennonites, Moravians and Presbyterians, to name but a few, adding to the spectrum of Protestant religious belief and practice.

While religious belief encouraged the immigration and settlement of European Protestants in North America, laying the foundations of a Protestant American tradition that stands apart from the Catholic tradition which dominated the Iberian and French colonies, it was also significant in shaping the social and political life of the colonies. Religious congregation provided an important focus for social and political organization, offering a forum for collective action, supplying leadership, and shaping attitudes towards matters of public policy. Religious issues tended, furthermore, to drive a wedge between the colonies and the mother country. In England, Protestants who dissented from the Anglican church were a small proportion of the population, and were largely excluded from positions of power within the state. In North America, the reverse was usually true. Although the Church of England was stronger in the south than in other regions, and although its membership increased during the eighteenth century, Anglicans remained a minority without much political influence. Thus religion occupied a position in North American society which differed significantly from that which it held in Spain's colonies. In Spanish America, religious life was firmly controlled by a single established church which was intolerant of heterodoxy and strongly supportive of the colonial state. English America, on the other hand, was characterized by ideological pluralism. Most religious practice developed outside the confines of the Church of England, rejected control by an ecclesiastical hierarchy imposed from without in favour of autonomous local congregations, and tended to be critical of the metropolitan state.

This is not to say that the English in North America nurtured a society that was born prosperous and free; far from it. Indians and blacks were of course relegated to inferior and servile positions within colonial societies, but white society was also divided by hierarchical ranking and differences in wealth. One group which evidently suffered inferiority was that of indentured servants: their contractual servitude often imposed severe discipline and poor conditions of life. Social divisions were, of course, most marked in plantation economies, where for most of the seventeenth century the production of staples for export required large numbers of indentured servants. But they were certainly not absent elsewhere. Plentiful land did not always make North America a land of opportunity, even on the internal frontier, and colonial societies did not easily cast off the concepts and categories of hierarchy known in the Old World. Moreover, with rapid demographic and economic growth during the eighteenth century, differences in wealth and power tended to become more marked, particularly in the plantation colonies and the major port cities. In the Chesapeake, the heirs of the English elite which had arrived after the Civil War became the core of a gentry imbued with the hierarchical values of the mother country, and came to form a political oligarchy whose power rested on the wealth generated by tobacco plantations. In the northern and middle colonies, wealthy local merchants also formed provincial elites which held a disproportionate share of power and influence in their regional societies.

The social structure of colonial North America was, nonetheless, still significantly different from that of the European countries that were the sources of its immigrants, or from the American colonies of Spain. Two major differences stand out. First, British North America lacked an hereditary aristocracy; though the Virginia gentry strove to emulate the lifestyle of the English gentry, the colonies remained without a formal nobility, even on the small scale that the Spaniards created in their colonial realms. Second, colonial conditions allowed upward social mobility of a kind that was very rare in Europe. Such mobility was not always easy to achieve, particularly in plantation societies and in the larger towns. However, the possibility of acquiring a small plot of land remained good in many areas for most of the colonial period, thereby creating a very substantial 'middling' group of small independent farmers and precluding the emergence of the large landless groups that formed the impoverished underbelly of society in Britain and other European societies.

In terms of racial stratification, English North America was less complex than Latin American colonial societies. In Latin America, miscegenation between the races had produced complex ethnic mixtures, elaborately stratified on a scale of racial types created by mixture between Indians, blacks and whites; North American societies saw less racial mixture. Generally, Indians were simply pushed aside; where racial stratification occurred, as in the south, it tended to be a simpler division in which whites assumed a general superiority over the growing numbers of blacks who were forced or born into slavery.

A final, vital trend to note in North American societies during the late seventeenth and early eighteenth centuries is their remarkable capacity for population growth. Demographic increase reached its most spectacular levels after 1700, but a fast upward trend was clear before then, bringing with it a change in the demographic balance of England's American empire and laying the foundations for a future in which the Caribbean colonies were relegated to a secondary position.

For most of the seventeenth century, the Caribbean and North American colonies both attracted white settlers, with roughly equal numbers going to the islands and to the mainland. In the eighteenth century, this pattern was greatly modified, as the stream of emigrants to the Caribbean islands declined and European migrants made the colonies of North America their principal destination. Although the scale of eighteenth-century migration to the colonies was probably lower than that of the previous century, the North American colonies nonetheless attracted large and swelling streams of European immigrants, especially to the newer Middle Atlantic colonies of New York, New Jersey, Pennsylvania and Delaware. Plentiful land acted as a powerful pole of attraction, and the pulse of migration was assisted by the permissive policy of English governments. While Spain closely regulated migration to its American colonies, and both Portugal and France discouraged the immigration of Protestants into their dominions, England imposed no such restrictions. Emigration from England was open to all who could find a means of paying their passage to the Americas, and the colonies were allowed to attract immigrants from wherever they could find them. Thus, in the eighteenth century they drew substantial numbers of migrants from Central Europe, particularly from the Rhine Palatine, Austria and the Swiss cantons. Such immigration added to an already rapidly expanding population. In 1660, the English colonies in North America had about 70,000 inhabitants; a half-century later, in 1710, their population had grown to over 300,000.

This growth marked a major shift in the demographic balance of English colonial America as a whole, as the North American colonies overhauled their Caribbean counterparts in size of population. One estimate suggests that the proportion of the total Anglo-American population (black and white) in the West Indies fell from about 51 per cent in the mid-seventeenth century to 32 per cent in 1700; another traces a comparable downward shift, from about 45 per cent in 1660 to about 32 per cent in 1710.[34]

During the eighteenth century, the shift in the demographic balance of English America away from the Caribbean and towards the mainland colonies was paralleled by a change in the economic balance of the Anglo-American empire. Despite the spectacular growth of the Caribbean plantation societies during the latter half of the seventeenth century, the mainland colonies were ultimately to prove much stronger, mainly because they were more balanced societies in which a prosperous and growing labour force multiplied rapidly and continuously. Plentiful land and low rents produced cheap food and underpinned growing communities, thereby creating larger markets for both local products and imports. To pay for imports, colonials had to find a means of earning an income from overseas trade, and they generally did so by exporting staple commodities. The export of tobacco had, of course, been the mainstay of the Chesapeake economy from the early years of colonization; in the eighteenth century, other tropical staples were added to North American commerce, including rice and indigo from South Carolina. The colonies in the cold and temperate climates to the north meanwhile found staples of a different and more varied kind, ranging from fish, fur, timber and shipping services in New England, to wheat, maize, beef and pork in the Middle Atlantic colonies.

These trades did not follow any single course, nor was their growth uniform. Depending on their source, exports went to Britain, the Atlantic islands and southern Europe, as well as to the West Indies and to Spanish America. But, if the development of British North America during the eighteenth century was uneven, the colonies nonetheless shared a general tendency to commercialize their sources of wealth and to enlarge their external trade. From these trends stemmed a process of growth which was gradually to transform the character of North American society and, as we shall later, to alter its relations with the metropolitan power.

NOTES

1   On Spanish frontiers in North America, D.W. Meinig, *The Shaping of America: A Geographical Perspective on Five Hundred Years of History; Volume I: Atlantic America, 1492–1800* (New Haven, Conn, and London, 1986) pp. 191–3; 202–5; on both Spanish and French explorations and colonization, see Carl O. Sauer, *Seventeenth Century North America* (Turtle Island, Berkeley, Calif., 1980).

2   Marcel Trudel, *The Beginnings of New France* (Toronto, 1973) pp. 93–267. For an introduction to French Acadia, see Naomi E.S. Griffiths, *The Contexts of Acadian History, 1686–1784* (Montreal and Kingston, 1992) pp. 3–32. On Louisiana, see Meinig, *Atlantic America*, pp. 193–202.

3   Meinig, *Atlantic America*, pp. 119–20; Francis Jennings, *The Ambiguous Iroquois Empire* (New York and London, 1984) pp. 47–57.

4   The following account of the main socioeconomic and cultural regions of British North America draws on the approaches and information found in the following works: Meinig, *Atlantic America*; Jack P. Greene, *Pursuits of Happiness: The Social Development of the Early Modern British Colonies and the Formation of American Culture* (Chapel Hill, NC, and London, 1988); David Hackett Fischer, *Albion's Seed: Four British Folkways in America* (New York, 1989); James Henretta, *The Evolution of American Society, 1700-1815: An Interdisciplinary Analysis* (Lexington, Mass., Toronto and London, 1973).

5   For these and other population figures given in this chapter, see Greene, *Pursuits of Happiness*, Table 8.1, pp. 178–79.

6   Fischer, *Albion's Seed*, pp. 68–87.

7   Kenneth A. Lockridge, *A New England Town: The First Hundred Years. Dedham, Massachusetts, 1636-1736* (New York, 1970); Philip J. Greven, *Four Generations: Population, Land and Family in Colonial Andover, Massachusetts* (Ithaca, NY, and London, 1970); Stephen Innes, *Labor in a New Land: Economy and Society in Seventeenth-Century Springfield* (Princeton, NJ, 1983).

8   Fischer, *Albion's Seed*, pp. 103–11; 166–80; 189–205.

9   These changes are traced at the community level in Lockridge, *A New England Town*, pp. 93–164, Greven, *Four Generations*, pp. 175–251, and Richard Bushman, *From Puritan to Yankee: Character and the Social Order in Connecticut, 1690–1765* (Cambridge, Mass., 1967), Parts 1–3.

10 Bernard Bailyn, *New England Merchants in the Seventeenth Century* (Cambridge, Mass., 1955).

11 Michael Zuckerman, *Peaceable Kingdoms: New England Towns in the Eighteenth Century* (New York, 1970), especially pp. 46–84; 187–220.

12 Fischer, *Albion's Seed*, pp. 207 46.

13 On the Virginia family, marriage, sexual mores, and child-rearing, see Fischer, *Albion's Seed*, pp. 274–320. For a more detailed analysis of mortality and family structure in Virginia, see Darret B. Hutman and A.H. Rutman, 'Now wives and sons-in law: parental death in a seventeenth-century Virginia county', in Thad W. Tate and David L. Ammerman (eds) *The Chesapeake in the Seventeenth Century: Essays in Anglo-American Society* (Chapel Hill, NC, 1979) pp. 153–82. Demographic and family structures in Maryland are analysed in Russell R. Menard, 'Immigrants and their increase: the process of population growth in early colonial Maryland', in Aubrey C. Land, Lois G. Carr & Edward C. Papenfuse (eds) *Law, Society and Politics in Early Maryland* (Baltimore, Md, and London, 1977) pp. 88–110, and in Lorena S. Walsh 'Till death us do part': marriage and family in seventeenth century Maryland", in Tate and Ammerman (eds) *The Chesapeake in the Seventeenth Century*, pp. 126–52.

14 Fischer, *Albion's Seed*, pp. 374–89.

15 Figures for tobacco exports are from Russell R. Menard, 'The tobacco industry in the Chesapeake colonies, 1617–1730', *Research in Economic History* (1980) **5**: 109–17. For a summary of Chesapeake economic development, see McCusker & Menard, *The Economy of British America, 1607–1789* (Chapel Hill, NC, and London, 1985) pp. 117–43. For a full account, see Morgan, *American Slavery, American Freedom*, Chapters 11–18.

16 Greene, *Pursuits of Happiness*, pp. 81–100.

17 Quoted in Peter H. Wood, *Black Majority: Negroes in Colonial South Carolina from 1670 through the Stono Rebellion* (New York, 1975 edition) p. 132. Part One of this book offers an excellent introduction to the development of colonial society in South Carolina.

18 For a broad survey of economic development in the colonial Carolinas, see McCusker & Menard, *Economy of British America*, pp. 169–88; quotation from p. 188. On the major features of its social development in the eighteenth century, see Greene, *Pursuits of Happiness*, pp. 141–51.

19 Meinig, *Atlantic America*, pp. 119–29.

20 On economic growth in New York, see Kammen, *Colonial New York: A History* (New York, 1975) pp. 161–90; on the agrarian structures of the colony, see Sung Bok Kim, *Landlord and Tenant in Colonial New York: Manorial Society, 1664–1775* (Chapel Hill, NC, 1978) especially pp. 1–43, 129–61.

21 This and the following paragraphs on Quaker Pennsylvania draw on Fischer, *Albion's Seed*, especially pp. 418–45, 455–62, 566–603.

22 On Quaker relations with Indian peoples, see Urs Bitterli, *Cultures in Conflict: Encounters between European and Non-European Cultures, 1492-1800* (Cambridge, 1993 edition) pp. 109–32; on Quaker attitudes and opposition to slavery, see David Brion Davis, *The Problem of Slavery in Western Culture* (Ithaca, NY, 1966) pp. 299–332.

23 Greene, *Pursuits of Happiness*, pp. 47–50; McCusker & Menard, *Economy of British America*, pp. 187–208.

24 Greene, *Pursuits of Happiness*, pp. 125–130.

25 J. Hector St John de Crèvecoeur, *Letters from an American Farmer* (London, 1971 edition) p. 41.

26 Bailyn, *Voyagers to the West: Emigration from Britain to America on the Eve of the Revolution* (London, 1987) p. 10.

27 For this characterization of frontier society, see Fischer, *Albion's Seed*, especially pp. 608–39, 747–82. For additional material, see Bailyn, *Voyagers to the West*, Parts IV and V. On the relationship between European settlers and Indian peoples on the eighteenth-century frontier, see Jennings, *The Ambiguous Iroquois Empire*, pp. 347–66.

28 Statistics from Jim Potter, 'Demographic development and family structure', in Jack P. Greene and J.R. Pole (eds) *Colonial British America: Essays in the New History of the Early Modern Era* (Baltimore, Md, and London, 1984) pp.137–38.

29 For the evolution of English attitudes towards blacks during the sixteenth and seventeenth centuries, see Winthrop D. Jordan, *White over Black: American Attitudes towards the Negro, 1550-1812* (New York, 1977 edition) especially pp. 44–100.

30 The seminal essay comparing slave systems in Anglo-American and Iberian America is Frank Tannenbaum, *Slave and Citizen: The Negro in the*

Americas (New York, 1947). For further comparison and a critique of Tannenbaum's thesis, see David Brion Davis, *The Problem of Slavery in Western Culture*, pp. 223–61. A succinct comparison of the impact of Protestant and Catholic traditions on slaves and their religious experience is found in Eugene D. Genovese, *Roll, Jordan, Roll. The World the Slaves Made* (New York, 1976 edn) pp. 168–83.

31 For a review of differences in slave systems in North America, see Ira Berlin, 'Time, space and the evolution of Afro-American society in British mainland North America', *American Historical Review* (1980) 85: 44–78. Comparison of slavery within the wider Anglo-American world is facilitated by Philip D. Morgan's vivid essay 'Three planters and their slaves: perspectives on slavery in Virginia, South Carolina, and Jamaica, 1750–1790', in Winthrop D. Jordan and Sheila L. Skemp (eds) *Race and Family in the Colonial South* (Jackson, Miss. and London, 1987) pp. 37–79, and by his 'British encounters with Africans and Afro-Americans, circa 1600–1780' in Bernard Bailyn and Philip D. Morgan (eds) *Strangers within the Realm: Cultural Margins of the First British Empire* (Chapel Hill, NC, and London, 1991) pp. 157–219.

32 For the debate over these differences in slave reproduction, see McCusker and Menard, *Economy of British America*, pp. 231–4.

33 The most serious slave uprising of colonial North America – the Stono uprising of 1739 in South Carolina – is analysed in Wood, *Black Majority*, pp. 308–26. On slave flight and its meaning, see Philip D. Morgan, 'Colonial South Carolina runaways: their significance for slave culture', in Gad Heuman (ed) *Out of the House of Bondage: Runaways, Resistance and Marronage in Africa and the New World* (London, 1986) pp. 57–78. For a general interpretative analysis of slave resistance and the factors conducive to slave rebellion, see Eugene D. Genovese, *From Rebellion to Revolution: Afro-American Revolts in the Making of the Modern World* (Baton Rouge, LA & London, 1979) especially Chapter 1.

34 Percentages calculated from McCusker and Menard, *Economy of British America*, p. 54, and Greene, *Pursuits of Happiness*, pp. 178–9.

CHAPTER SEVEN
Government and Politics

In Chapters 4–6 we have seen that the Anglo-American world entered a fresh phase of expansion during the latter half of the seventeenth century, as previously small colonies grew and prospered, and new territories were brought under English rule in North America and the Caribbean. We have also seen that, for all their variety, the lands peopled by English settlers entered upon two broadly different paths of social and economic development. On the continental mainland, English migrants created colonies of settlement which, though they formed regions with distinctive socio-economic and cultural characteristics, were clearly distinguishable from the colonies of exploitation in the Caribbean. Whereas the West Indies depended on sugar prodution for overseas markets and were peopled mainly by Africans carried into slavery, the mainland colonies were more economically self-reliant and predominantly European in their demographic and cultural composition. But, though the social and economic development of the Anglo-American colonies followed different paths, their institutional development conformed to a broadly similar pattern.

Each colony constituted a discrete political entity, subject to governments that operated independently of each other and had their own local configurations of power and politics. All shared, however, in the development of a peculiarly English form of colonial governance which differed markedly from that found in other European colonies in the Americas. Whereas the Iberian monarchies, especially Spain, established secular and ecclesiastical institutions designed to impose centralized authority and religious orthodoxy, the English state was less concerned to exercise close control over its colonies and allowed them a large measure of autonomy. In principle, the English system of colonial government accorded wide powers to London. In practice, however, colonials took the initiative in their government, to the point where the responsibilities and powers of internal government belonged largely to colonials; by the start of the eighteenth century, the colonies had become virtually self-governing entities under the sovereignty of the English monarchy.[1]

This movement towards self-government within the empire did not everywhere proceed along precisely the same lines, nor was it uninterrupted. Indeed, during the latter years of the restored monarchy, especially under James II, the English crown made a determined effort to reduce the colonies' autonomy and to centralize imperial rule. However, by the end of the seventeenth century, following James's deposition and his replacement by William and Mary in 1688, colonials had generally asserted their right to play a central role in their own government, as subjects with equal status and equal rights to those held by Englishmen in the mother country, and with governing bodies that they regarded as equivalent and in some vital respects equal to the English Parliament. This development was of enormous significance, for it was eventually to end in the struggle for power between colonies and metropolis from which the first independent American state emerged. What, then, were the elements which went into the making of colonial government, what were the policies by which England sought to weld its colonies into a unified empire, and why were the English colonies able to achieve a degree of formal autonomy unparalleled among European settlements in the American world?

FOUNDATIONS OF COLONIAL GOVERNMENT

During the first phase of colonization which took place before the English Civil War, during the reigns of James I and Charles I, the English monarchy had no policy for directly governing its American colonies. The creation of English colonies was always the result of private initiatives. Nowhere was a colony founded and controlled by royal government from its outset, and the early colonies developed without aid, or much intervention from the crown. This was not unusual in European America. All monarchs sought to avoid the risks and costs of colonization by delegating rights to enterprising individuals, giving them territorial grants and governing powers in return for extending the royal realms. So, like other European monarchies, the English crown claimed sovereignty over territories settled by its subjects, and granted charters to individuals and groups, authorizing them to take possession of these lands in the King's name. When they settled a colony, charter holders then became the governors of the territory that they claimed, subject to the sovereignty of the monarch and the terms of the charters which they held.[2]

In a general sense, the charters granted by the English crown were similar instruments to the *capitulaciones* granted by the Spanish monarchy to the explorers and conquerers of Spanish America, or to the grants to proprietary 'captaincies' which the Portuguese crown used to promote colonization in Brazil. In the English case, however, early colonial grants were made in several different ways, all of which allowed settlers a greater measure of private initiative than the Iberian monarchies had allowed their subjects in the New World. One peculiar feature of English colonization was the part played by private trading companies and proprietors who sought to enrich themselves from commerce in tropical commodities. In Virginia and the Caribbean, the organization of colonies by companies and proprietors backed by merchants gave early seventeenth-century colonizing projects a markedly commercial character, imbued with ideas of mercantile profit and the expansion of trade.[3] The colonists who went to New England had of course a larger purpose than that of mere profit. Nonetheless, though the colonies of New Plymouth and Massachusetts were more than simply trading ventures, they were also founded on the format of the joint-stock company. Indeed, the Massachusetts Bay Company's charter was modelled on Virginia's charter of 1612, with rights given to a small group of investors to form a corporation that controlled and governed all the land granted by the King. Because companies were self-governing and self-financed bodies, their employment in colonizing ventures was to nurture a form of colonial government in which the English state played only a minor role. Spanish colonization in the Americas had also been an affair of private enterprise, to which the state contributed very little in terms of finance or military support. However, although the Spanish monarchy initially granted generous contracts to the leaders of colonizing expeditions, it quickly replaced them with an apparatus of centralized royal government, as well as supporting an extensive missionary effort for evangelizing and protecting native peoples who were treated, and taxed, as subjects of the Spanish state.[4]

The pattern set down in the English colonies was to be very different. In Virginia, Massachusetts and the West Indies, the crown generally refrained from interfering in the affairs of the companies and individuals to which it granted charters for colonial settlement, and did not assume responsibilities for shaping the administration of settlers and

Indians. In the case of Virginia, the grant made to the Virginia Company was revoked in 1624, when the crown took direct control as a result of a crisis in company affairs. But Virginia's conversion into a crown colony was a response to crisis in the company's government of the colony, not a blueprint for a system of colonial administration, and government in the other colonies was devolved on companies and proprietors who were left to pursue their own interests with little interference from the mother country. The Massachusetts Bay Company was the extreme case of such autonomy, because it transferred the company headquarters from England to the colony, quickly transformed a trading company into a colonial government, and went on to absorb into its jurisdiction the previously founded colony of New Plymouth, which had never received a formal charter from the King. Other regions were also granted charters that allowed them corporate self-government. The colonies of Rhode Island and Connecticut were unusual, in that they obtained corporate charters which gave them rights of self-government after they were established, thereby legitimizing the de facto colonies created by breaking away from Massachusetts. In Maryland and the Caribbean islands, on the other hand, charters went to personal proprietors rather than companies; as these charters were granted to individuals in the manner of a feudal fief, they also ensured that colonial government functioned without interference from the crown.

Equally at variance with the Spanish experience was the political role of religion in Anglo-American colonization. In one sense, Spaniards and Englishmen shared a religious perspective on colonization in the New World, in that both justified their intrusion into American lands by claiming that God had granted them a special role in evangelizing and civilizing heathen peoples. However, whereas Spain imposed one religion and one church on its colonies, and thus provided a means of unifying its American possessions with the mother country, England did not enforce religious exclusivism in its colonies, nor endow them with an established church that supported the state. So, instead of becoming a platform for a single church dedicated to sustaining a disciplined orthodoxy of religious belief and practice on both settlers and native peoples, English colonial settlements contained a powerful element of religious dissent which both enhanced the settlers' sense of separation from the parent society, especially in New England, and divided them from each other.[5]

Another feature of political development that distinguished the English colonies from other European colonies in the Americas was the early development of representative institutions, known as 'assemblies', which gave colonials a strong voice in their own government. The first such assembly took embryonic form in Virginia in 1619, when the directors of the Virginia Company in London decided to establish a government in the colony itself and to provide a forum in which leading settlers might express their views on important questions. When responsibility for the colony was taken up by the crown in 1624, the assembly survived the change from private to royal government. Indeed, it not only continued to exist under the new royal governor but also gradually extended its power, as it transformed into the House of Burgesses, with rights to initiate and to authorize laws for the colony.

Other early English colonies followed a similar path towards autonomous and representative government, some faster than others. Settlers in Bermuda created their own assembly in 1620, to govern in conjunction with the governor and council appointed by the island's proprietor, the Somers Island Company. Early Massachusetts was initially governed by an authoritarian Puritan oligarchy which ruled through the Bay Company's General Court, but in the 1630s the General Court became a representative general assembly which drew deputies elected by freeholding church members in all the towns within its jurisdiction. The other New England colonies followed their own patterns, but they too created forms of government which gave rights to representation to the freemen of their towns, both to elect local officials and deputies to be sent to a general colonial assembly. Even Maryland, where Lord Baltimore held princely powers, acquired an assembly in 1638, after settlers had pressed their claim to give or withhold consent to the laws made by the proprietor.[6] In the West Indies, the autonomous government of the proprietor of the 'Caribbee islands' (Barbados and the Leewards) initially concentrated power in the hands of governors and their councils, and several decades passed before assemblies were established. Barbados's first representative assembly met in 1639 and secured the right to initiate legislation in 1642; assemblies appeared in Antigua and St Kitts in the 1640s, and Nevis and Montserrat finally acquired similar representation in the 1650s and early 1660s.[7]

The inclusion of a representative element in colonial government meant that the political order in the Anglo-American world deviated sharply from the Spanish model. This divergence derived in large part from the disparity between English and Spanish political structures and traditions at the time of colonization. When the Spanish monarchy was building its empire in the late fifteenth and early sixteenth centuries, it was also enlarging its authority in Spain, at the expense of both the great territorial aristocracy and the medieval representative institution of the *cortes*. The Catholic monarchs were determined to ensure that the constraints on royal power which these forces imposed at home would not be replicated in the colonies; under their successor, Charles V, the Spanish crown continued with policies designed to prevent the emergence of a feudal aristocracy or representative institutions in the Americas. After crushing the Castilian Comunero revolt of 1520–1, Charles V effectively terminated the development of representative government in Castile, and went on to curtail the emergence of powerful and independent elites in Spain's major colonies. As royal authority became increasingly entrenched, so the *cabildos* (town councils) of Spanish America were also relegated to relative obscurity, and royal officials successfully ensured that the elites which controlled them were increasingly confined to managing only municipal affairs.

When Englishmen were establishing their first colonies, on the other hand, they came from a state where traditions of local and corporate autonomy, and a matching belief in the rights of individuals and communities to freedom from arbitrary royal interference, were still strong. Thus the incorporation of a representative element in colonial government was partly an extension of political practice at home, reflecting contemporary English beliefs in the liberty of the King's subjects and their right to consent in their government. It was also a practical expedient, necessary to encourage settlement. If English colonists were to be attracted to the Americas, they had to be afforded at least the same rights that they enjoyed at home; settler participation offered, moreover, a means of instilling some sense of cooperation among settlers, while ensuring that colonists were able to protect their interests and contribute to the costs of their own administration.

Representation in the colonies was not of course democratic in the sense of being based in universal suffrage. Rights to vote for representatives to an assembly, or to act as a representative were restricted to free males with appropriate qualifications as property holders; in Massachusetts, it was subject to church membership. The introduction of the principle of representation was nonetheless a crucial feature of political development in English America. Once established, it became an element in colonial government that was impossible to eradicate, even under the post-Civil War governments which sought to exercise a greater degree of control over England's nascent empire. We shall return to the character and workings of the institutions of colonial government shortly. For the moment, the important point to note is that, from their inception, the English colonies enjoyed a large measure of autonomy, with governments that included representative institutions of the kind not found in the other European-American empires.

Such autonomy was reinforced by the crown's lack of concern with directing, even supervising, the affairs of its colonies. It is true that, in 1625, Charles I asserted that there should be 'one uniforme course of Government in, and through Our whole Monarchie', and that, in 1634, he attempted to assert his authority over the colonies by creating a permanent 'Commission for Regulating Plantations', with powers to make laws for the colonies, to impose punishments, appoint and remove officials, and review charters. But the Commission achieved very little before it was dissolved in 1641 by a Parliament anxious to curb the growth of royal power. Had Charles's personal rule continued, he might have developed a clearer imperial policy; as it was, his reign did not produce coherent administrative or economic policies for the colonies. Thus, although the English monarchy asserted its sovereignty over the colonies and established the principle that they were part of England's political order, rather than being formally autonomous polities, it did little to assert close control over their affairs during the early years of their formation.[8]

Under James I and Charles I, the poverty of the colonies ensured that their affairs were overshadowed by more pressing political matters at home and in Europe. For, unlike the territories discovered by Spain a century before, the lands colonized by the English simply did not offer rich resources worthy of the monarch's close attention. Spain's monarchy had had a strong incentive to affirm its authority in the Americas, because, following the discovery of gold in the Caribbean islands and continental shorelines, and the subsequent development of silver and gold-mining enterprises in Mexico and South America, the Spanish Indies offered rich potential sources of royal revenue. Early English America offered no such fiscal cornucopia to the monarch, and accordingly ranked low in the priorities of governments at home. The weakness of royal government in the nascent colonies was then compounded by the fact that, without sources of colonial revenue under its control, it could not finance the construction of a royal bureaucracy for overseeing the colonies' government in the manner of the Spanish monarchy. Government in the English colonies was therefore in the hands of local agencies, established under the terms of the charters granted to colonizing companies and proprietors.

So, when the English Civil War started in 1642, a pattern of self-government had been established in the English colonies under a monarchy which did not yet attach great importance to its overseas dominions, had no immediate ambitions to govern them directly, and, in any case, lacked the resources to construct and finance a system of royal administration. This monarchy was, however, defeated and overthrown during the great political upheaval of England's Civil War. In its wake, new men took power in the republican regimes of the Interregnum, before the monarchy was restored in 1660. How did these shifts in power in England impinge on the political life of the colonies and their relations with the parent power?

COLONIAL GOVERNMENT AFTER THE ENGLISH CIVIL WAR

We saw in Chapter 4 that the Interregnum brought two important changes in England's empire in the Americas. One was the territorial expansion of the empire inaugurated by Cromwell's capture of Jamaica from Spain in 1655; the other was the introduction of a body of legislation designed to harness colonial resources and markets for the metropolitan power, initiated by the Navigation Act of 1651. Both changes were consolidated after the Restoration. Not only did Charles II hold on to Jamaica despite powerful pressure from Spain, but his government sought further expansion with the conquest of New Netherland from the Dutch, and gave support to other colonizing projects in North America. The monarchy meanwhile carried forward the regulation of colonial commerce started by the Navigation Act of 1651, reinforcing it with other navigation laws designed to tighten England's hold on American trade. Thus the Civil War marked the beginning of a new phase in England's presence in the Americas and its relations with the American colonies, in that, after 1650, English governments pursued policies aimed at both extending colonial territory and controlling colonial commerce.

The Interregnum and Restoration saw the first efforts to bring the colonies under closer political control from the centre. According to Stephen Saunders Webb, this shift in policy sprang from the experience of social and political breakdown during the Civil War, when Parliament and Protector sought to strengthen an executive authority weakened by the struggle between Parliament and the King, and, having learned the effectiveness of military force and military forms of government during wartime, also used them to impose central authority during peacetime. Thus, he asserts, the spread of 'garrison government' extended to the Americas, where new colonies were created by conquest in Jamaica, New York and New Jersey, where England assumed new responsibilities for defence, and where government by military men was reflected in the increasing tendency of London to appoint army officers as colonial governors. In Webb's view, this determination to exert authority, coupled with the introduction into the colonies of professional military men as garrison governors and military commanders, altered the outlook and practices of imperial government, and engendered a process of imperial centralization which gradually took clearer shape following the Restoration.[9]

This concept of colonies as subject territories ruled by an imperial authority did not immediately alter the character of colonial government; during the generation after 1650, relations between England and its American dominions were primarily shaped by the commercial system which regulated trade while leaving the colonies to govern themselves. When the Stuart monarchy was restored to power in 1660, Charles II introduced some new measures affecting colonial government, particularly in the West Indies, and in the years that followed military men were more widely employed in the colonies, in both their administration and defence. But these measures wrought no great change to existing arrangements.

The colonies accepted the reversion to monarchy – by 1662, all had proclaimed Charles II as their King – and in return the crown generally accepted the status quo in the colonies. In Maryland, Lord Baltimore's status as proprietor had already been restored by Cromwell, and this was confirmed by Charles II. In Virginia, the royal governor who had been removed by the Commonwealth commissioners was reinstated by the colony's assembly early in 1660, and Charles II renewed his commission and left the assembly in place. In some parts of New England, particularly New Haven, there was local opposition to the monarchy, fed by fears that the return of the Stuart dynasty would restore Catholicism and absolutism in England. But Charles II's government refrained from immediate interference with Puritan autonomy, except in trying to curb the worst excesses of intolerance towards the Quakers, and attempting to bring Massachusetts law into line with that of England. Rhode Island and Connecticut also had their corporate charters renewed, thereby reaffirming their right to choose their own governing officials. Change was more apparent in the West Indies, where both the republican regime and the restored monarchy made stronger efforts to assert authority. Following the restoration, the crown retained Jamaica in spite of strong Spanish pressure, and considered that the island, as the fruit of conquest, should be governed according to royal discretion. Thus Jamaica became a royal colony in 1662, with a governor appointed by the crown. In Barbados and the Leeward Islands, the crown took advantage of the planters' opposition to proprietary government to convert the islands into royal colonies in 1663. However, although royal governors (or in the smaller islands, lieutenant-governors) were henceforth installed in place of the governors supplied by proprietors, the islands' assemblies were left in place; in return for a commitment to pay a fixed duty on their exports, they were conceded the right to veto legislation that was not to their liking.[10]

Aside from these rearrangements, Charles II did not attack colonial autonomy, nor create effective institutions for exercising central control. In 1660, he appointed a special committee of the Privy Council to deal with colonial questions, endowing it with responsibility for overseeing the colonies and their trade. But this responsibility was subsequently devolved among a series of subcommittees, councils which had short lives of four or five years; until 1675 they lacked executive powers and so had little impact on policy or practice regarding the colonies.[11] As for government within the colonies, this continued along familiar lines, with the conventions of representative government being extended to the new colonies that were established after 1650. In 1663, Charles II allowed that his free subjects in Jamaica should have the same privileges as all Englishmen, and conceded them the right to an elective legislative assembly. In the new colonies of North America, the crown delegated its powers to proprietors, following a pattern which differed from that of the early seventeenth century insofar as these grants were all made to individuals rather than to corporations. In New York, New Jersey, the Carolinas and Pennsylvania, royal charters conferred extensive rights on private proprietors, who were given title to vast areas of land and wide powers of government with few reciprocal responsibilities to government in England. But there, too, representative government was soon established. Just as colonial proprietors received generous concessions from the crown, they also conceded participation in government to colonists, mainly to attract people to the new territories and to ensure their political stability. Even the Duke of York, who was to show a strong aversion to parliamentary institutions when he became King James II, decided in 1683 to allow the convocation of an assembly in his proprietary colony of New York, so that its colonists might be persuaded to remain in the colony and to pay the taxes required to sustain its government.

The Stuart monarchy did, however, seek to tighten royal control over colonial government in the later decades of the seventeenth century, when stricter regulation of the colonies' commerce (by the Plantation Act of 1673) was matched by attempts to impose more central control over their government. The first step in this direction was taken in 1672, when detailed instructions were given to the Council for Plantations which Charles II had set up in 1670, with a view to rationalizing colonial government and subjecting the colonies to the executive authority in London. Instructed to collect information about the colonies and to make sure that they conformed to English law and commercial regulations, the council established principles for a colonial policy, and prepared the way for a concerted effort to bolster royal authority in America. This came after 1675, the year when the council was succeeded by a more powerful body, the Lords Commissioners of Trade and Plantations. As a standing committee of the King's Privy Council, this council had powers to make and enforce decisions, and was the most effective body for colonial administration yet seen. From 1676, this body sought to reconstruct the political relationship between England and its colonies not only by enforcing colonial trade legislation, but also by attempting to build a uniform system of colonial government. This was reflected in its attempts to eliminate the charters which gave autonomy to proprietary and corporate colonies, to curb the powers of local institutions, especially the assemblies, and to expand the crown's jurisdiction over internal colonial affairs by installing royal governors.[12]

REBELLION AND ROYAL GOVERNMENT IN THE LATE SEVENTEENTH CENTURY

The first task which faced the Lords of Trade and Plantations was to resolve a crisis of government in Virginia. In 1676, an armed rebellion was triggered by disagreements between settlers and the colony's royal governor over taxation and the conduct of policy towards Indians. The quarrel over taxation sprang from the imposition of a new levy on tobacco which aggravated existing resentments over the inequitable distribution of political power and fiscal burdens in the colony. Anti-tax protest was reinforced by opposition to Governor William Berkeley's military policy on the frontier. As English plantations had spread away from the old frontier near the tidewater, expansion of white settlement had provoked conflict between whites and Indians in the interior; when hundreds of whites died at the hands of the

Susquehannock Indians in early 1676, the question of how to deal with Indian attacks became a burning political issue.[13]

Governor Berkeley favoured a defensive strategy of building forts to protect settlers, rather than launching retaliatory raids that might provoke a general Indian war. His policy did not meet with popular approval, however, and an active opposition emerged under the leadership of Nathaniel Bacon, a young, well-educated and wealthy Englishman who owned a plantation on the frontier. Backed by frontier planters, Bacon called for aggressive reprisals against the Indians; in direct opposition to the governor, he organized volunteer forces which launched indiscriminate attacks on Indians. The quarrel over Indian policy and Bacon's defiance of the governor's order acted as a catalyst for the release of various discontents among Virginia settlers. When the governor convoked an assembly in June 1676, Bacon's bold opposition to Berkeley encouraged its members to attack the power and privilege of the self-seeking oligarchy which ruled with the governor. Its members accordingly enacted measures aimed at widening the electorate for the colonial assembly and sharing offices more widely, in order to reduce the governor's grip on local government and to end the exemption of the ruling clique from taxation. The governor then declared Bacon and his followers as rebels against royal authority. In response, Bacon reoccupied and sacked Jamestown in September 1676, took effective control of Virginia, and sought alliances with settlers in Maryland and Carolina. The threat to royal authority did not last, however. When Bacon died suddenly in late 1676, the rebellion dissolved as quickly as it had started in the previous April; by the end of the year, Governor Berkeley had restored royal control over the colony.

The Virginia rebellion was partly a dispute between factions within the colony's landed gentry, involving tensions between those who controlled central authority and those who represented local interests, and between ordinary planters and the privileged group favoured by Governor Berkeley's patronage.[14] But, to widen his support, Bacon turned the quarrel into a rebellion of the poor against the rich and 'reminded Englishmen in Virginia of republican alternatives'. Thus, the rebellion took on the character of a revolution, in which Bacon sought to rally other colonies in a general resistance to English authority.[15] Though it failed, the rebellion nonetheless had an important long-term political significance. By sending troops to Virginia to repress the rebels, the crown showed its determination to control American affairs, and brought an end to the autonomous form of government practised in Virginia before 1676. After the rebellion, the crown not only repealed the laws passed by the assembly during the rebellion, but also punished the assembly by reducing its powers and enhancing those of the royal governor and council. Thus the concern with colonies which had previously been expressed through commercial legislation now entered the political realm, where, over the next decade, it left a mark not only on Virginia but on other colonies too.

The policy of tightening royal control over colonial government was part of a wider political pattern, based on the desire of the Stuart monarchy to exercise greater power over its subjects and to increase its revenues, coupled with the interests of powerful politicians who were personally interested in the colonies and their trade.[16] Assisted by permanent staff and by officials whom they placed in the colonies, the Lords of Trade were the primary agency for implementing a more rigorous colonial policy. In the royal colonies of Virginia, Jamaica, Barbados and the Leeward Islands, the committee tried to make royal governors more efficient and responsible agents of the crown, while reducing their dependence on elected legislative assemblies. It also sought to convert the existing private colonies into royal colonies, and to prevent the foundation of any new private colonies. Thus, in 1679, it ensured that New Hampshire was detached from Massachusetts, and made a royal colony; it annulled the charters of Massachusetts and Bermuda in 1684, and, though unable to prevent the grant of personal proprietorship of Pennsylvania to William Penn in 1681, it limited the powers accorded to Penn by his charter.

The effort to extend the crown's power over the colonies was most strongly felt in New England; as in Virginia, it was facilitated by a crisis in settler relations with Indians on the frontier. Relations between whites and Indians had steadily deteriorated as settlers moved inland, and in 1675–6 broke into open warfare when Metacomet (a tribal chief known to the settlers as King Philip) responded to aggression from Plymouth by launching Indian warriors into assaults on settler families. The struggle between Metacomet and Plymouth soon extended to include whites and Indians throughout New England, leading to many deaths among the settlers and the virtual extinction of the Algonquin Indians. The war also marked a significant moment in New England's history in a more general sense, marking the end of a long period of political autonomy. For 'it sapped the physical (and psychic) strength of puritanism, limited the territorial frontiers of New England, and dramatically reduced the corporate colonies' ability to resist the rising tide of English empire either politically or economically'.[17]

In 1676, the Lords of Trade sent Edward Randolph to Massachusetts to inquire into the colony's government and to report on observance of the Navigation Acts. When Randolph reported that the rules of colonial commerce laid down by the Acts were routinely evaded, that Massachusetts had illegally extended its government over Rhode Island and New Hampshire, and that the Puritans' religious intolerance prevented members of the Church of England from voting, sometimes even from worshipping, this persuaded the crown to reform the colony's government. The Lords of Trade began legal proceedings against Massachusetts which led to the revocation of its charter in 1684, so that Massachusetts became a royal colony. When James II took the throne in 1685, this opened the way for implementation of a plan to rescind the charters of Rhode Island and Connecticut, and to bring all the New England colonies, together with New York and New Jersey, into a single administrative unit known as the 'Dominion of New England'. Behind this lay the larger ambition for 'the reduction of the remaining independent governments overseas, and their regrouping, with the royal provinces, to form viceroyalties comparable in size to the Spanish territories to the South and greater in military strength than the French power to the North'.[18]

From 1686, the Dominion of New England felt the firm hand of royal government for the first time. Governor Edmund Andros restricted the rights of town governments, enforced the Navigation Acts, insisted on religious toleration, and reformed the courts to make them conform with English legal practice. But if it was intended as the first step towards grouping all of England's colonies into similar administrative units, the Dominion of New England did not become a new model for English colonial government. In 1688, dramatic political change in England ended Stuart ambitions to assert monarchical power, when James II's Whig opponents joined with William of Orange, King of Holland, to overthrow the King in the 'Glorious Revolution' of 1688. Suddenly, King James was toppled from his throne and forced into exile in France, 'his whole strength, like a spider's web . . . so irrevocably broken, with a touch'.[19]

The fall of James II and his replacement by William of Orange gave colonials a chance to express openly their antipathy to direct English rule and to recover their threatened autonomy, while presenting both as a loyal defence of England's Protestantism and liberty. No sooner had the *coup d'état* in England asserted the rights of Parliament against arbitrary royal power and reversed James II's attempt to restore Catholicism, than colonials seized the chance to side with English opponents of the Stuart monarchy. In 1689, New Englanders toppled their governor and overthrew the Dominion of New England, created by James II. In the same year, there were popular rebellions in New York and Maryland, fuelled by both fervent anti-Catholicism and by popular antipathy towards proprietary governments which had become increasingly oligarchic and authoritarian in character. Thus the Stuart attempt to imitate a Spanish model of empire was subverted from within the metropolis itself, with colonials enthusiastically following where English opposition to absolutism and popery had led.[20]

THE GLORIOUS REVOLUTION AND THE COLONIES

If the Glorious Revolution allowed colonials to express their resentment at central authority and desire for local autonomy, the political settlement between colonies and home government left underlying tensions between colonial and metropolitan governments unresolved. Colonial elites believed that they won the same rights to self-government as Englishmen, and saw their assemblies as equivalents of the English Parliament. In fact, their assemblies did not have the same status as Parliament, whatever they believed. However, as William III tolerated colonial autonomy, conflict over this issue was deferred. He was neither opposed to colonial assemblies on principle, as James II had been, nor did he continue his predecessors' efforts to consolidate colonial government under royal control.

In the agreements that were reached after the Glorious Revolution, the crown approved the calling of assemblies and left them with a large measure of power. Neither King nor Parliament, however, conceded that the colonial assemblies had the same powers as the legislature in England. King William and his successors took the view that they held the same powers over the colonies as the Stuart monarchy, with the difference that this power was henceforth exercised through the English Parliament rather than directly by the King. If colonial politicians saw themselves operating within a federal empire composed of governments with equal rights, English government continued to see the colonies as subordinate provinces, subject to the overriding authority of a home Parliament which might legislate for the colonies as it pleased and without their approval. Thus, although the Glorious Revolution had given colonials the opportunity to reassert local interests against central government, and nurtured their belief that they had the same rights as Englishmen, it had not altered England's claim to precedence and dominance over its colonies.[21]

Where change occurred, it affected colonial commerce more than colonial government. The Lords of Trade retained some influence and momentum during the early years of William's reign, and managed to ensure that Massachusetts was converted into a royal colony in 1691. In 1696, the crown also introduced a new Navigation Act (the 'Act for Preventing Frauds, and Regulating Abuses in the Plantation Trade') which not only tightened controls over colonial commerce, but also provided for the establishment of Admiralty courts in the colonies. While the Treasury sought to expand revenues from customs on colonial trade and the Admiralty established Vice-Admiralty courts for curbing contraband, the Board of Trade was created and charged with overseeing colonial affairs and recommending legislation for the colonies to Parliament. For the next eighty-six years, this task was discharged by a small committee whose work was all too frequently confounded by competition with the other agencies – the Customs, the Admiralty, the War Office, the Secretary of State for the Southern Department which also had interests in the colonies.

The Board's fundamental aim was to uphold and enforce the Navigation Acts which subordinated colonial economic interests to those of the metropolitan power, and it generally favoured stricter control over the trade and administration of the colonies. The Board of Trade did nonetheless do something to reaffirm metropolitan political authority in the colonies. For it steadfastly opposed the existence of the privately chartered or proprietary colonies, temporarily ended the proprietorship of Lord Baltimore in Maryland, and confirmed New York as a royal colony. Maryland later reverted to its proprietor, though he was left with greatly reduced powers. New Jersey was made a royal colony in 1702, the two Carolinas were brought under royal rule in 1728, and Georgia was added in 1754. While the Board of Trade acknowledged that assemblies were a necessary element of colonial government, it consistently upheld the view that the colonies were subordinate to Parliament and subject to the power of governors acting on instructions issued by the crown.[22]

Conflict between metropolis and colonies was avoided, however, for two main reasons. First, although Parliament legislated frequently for the colonies, it confined its activities to supervising colonial trade and refrained from intervening in matters of colonial government. This was partly a matter of simple inefficiency. Close study of New England's government in the decades after the Glorious Revolution uncovers 'the familiar debris of Stuart bureaucracy, of overlapping and often contradictory instructions, of projects floated but never fulfilled, and orders given but never carried out – the knots in a string of endless expedients.'[23] A second factor influencing metropolitan–colonial relations was the fact that, by the start of the eighteenth century, colonials were increasingly conscious of the threat from foreign powers, notably France and Spain, and thus tended to perceive a closer community of interest with the mother country. Exposure to foreign attack had of course long ensured the political quiescence of the Caribbean colonies, but after the Glorious Revolution fear of foreign assault also helped bond the North American colonies to Britain.[24]

Thus, during the three-quarters of a century after the Glorious Revolution, Britain settled into a closer but relaxed relationship with its American colonies. In Britain itself, a monarchy which claimed authority as a divine right had been replaced by a parliamentary monarchy, in which kings had to learn to cooperate with a Parliament that was extending its powers. In the colonies, these consequences of the settlement of 1688 convinced colonials that their own government mirrored that of the mother country, with assemblies replicating Parliament in their responsibilities and powers. Despite pressures for clarification, colonials never succeeded in extracting any explicit recognition of this view from Parliament; however, lax administration of colonial affairs from the centre, which was particularly obvious during Walpole's long ministry (1721–42), encouraged a creeping decentralization of power, and a tendency to equate colonial prosperity with freedom from metropolitan intervention. Indeed, such was the autonomy of colonial governments by the mid-eighteenth century that one worried British commentator lamented that they were becoming more like 'pure Republics'.[25]

Parliament did not of course accept colonial claims to autonomy, but in practice British governments refrained from active intervention in the colonies' internal affairs, and imposed only slight burdens on them throughout the first half of the eighteenth century. The Board of Trade made some efforts at reform, but exploitation of patronage to dispose of colonial offices by metropolitan political factions undermined such efforts, leaving colonial policy to be determined by the 'blind interaction of private interests'.[26] Instructions from England were, moreover, often simply ignored, since the small colonial bureaucracy was generally inefficient and corrupt. Caribbean planter interests were represented by the West India lobby in Parliament, and North American colonies by agents who resided in London to campaign on their behalf, but for most colonials, imperial government meant little. What counted was that the government of their own colonies should be run by local men in accord with local interests, and in each colony government was in the hands of social elites which put their own needs before those of the parent power.

GOVERNMENT IN THE COLONIES

By the end of the seventeenth century, the system of colonial government had become more or less standardized. The powers of government once vested in companies and proprietors had generally come to rest in the hands of a governor who acted as the chief executive officer and who was, by 1700, generally appointed by the King. He exercised authority together with a council, which resembled a board of directors, and an elected assembly, which represented the colonists. Thus, a basic institutional pattern spread to all of England's colonies, though with variations in local political practice which stemmed from differences of custom and tradition.

Each colony was a separate entity, with its own governor, council and assembly; each made its own laws, subject to the approval of the governor in his capacity as representative and guardian of the rights of the sovereign. At its simplest, colonial government consisted of two branches. On one side stood the governor and his council, representing the prerogative of the crown and acting as the executive power. On the other was the colonial legislature, with an upper house made up of the governor's council, and an elected assembly, chosen by and from the colony's freeholders. Only Connecticut and Rhode Island stood outside this framework of an English-appointed executive and an American-elected assembly. After the dismemberment of the Dominion of New England in 1688, they returned to their prior status as corporate colonies, where voters chose the governor and his council as well as the assembly, and where the governor's powers were more limited than elsewhere.

In formal terms, the leading power in the colonies was held by governors, who held commissions issued by the King and acted as his principal representative, on secret instructions drawn up by the Board of Trade and approved by the crown. Colonial governors were usually Englishmen and sometimes Americans; they had wide-ranging powers in civil, military and judicial spheres. The governor had the right to convoke and dismiss assemblies and to veto any of the assembly's legislative acts. As the executive head of civil administration, the governor could grant lands, appoint officials, regulate the colony's trade and conduct its external relations with other colonies, with

Indian tribes and even, on occasion, with foreign powers; as commander-in-chief of local military and naval forces, he was responsible for the defence of the colony. Finally, the governor played an important role in the colonial judiciary, with the right to appoint and dismiss judges and magistrates, and a responsibility to form the colony's court of appeal, together with his council.[27]

In practice, the powers of colonial governors were less formidable than they appeared in theory. First, governors had to work with their councils, generally consisting of twelve members appointed by the King, often on the advice of colonial governors and usually serving for life. The colonial council had three functions. It acted as an advisory board to the governor in his executive duties; it constituted the upper house of the legislature when sitting as the council in the assembly; its membership acted, together with the governor as the highest court of appeal in the colony. By sharing in the governor's powers, the council could act as a check on the governor and hinder his government. Usually, however, councils did not present an obstacle to a governor who elicited their cooperation. For reasons of social position and political ambition, councillors were generally disposed to work with royal authority rather than opposing it, although where a governor failed to treat council members with sufficient tact his advisors could become his opponents.[28]

Much more severe limitations were placed on the governor's powers by the lower house of the assembly, which, after the Glorious Revolution, colonials tended to regard as an American version of the English House of Commons. All the colonies had such legislative bodies, chosen by a colonial electorate. Generally, the right to vote was associated with rights to property, and was conferred on all free adult males who owned property of a specified size or value. Property qualifications (and their enforcement) varied between colonies and changed over time, but in North America, unlike the West Indies, the potential electorate was quite large. While it excluded women, servants and small property owners, as well as Indians and blacks, the relatively easy availability of land meant that the franchise was generally wide, incorporating between 50 and 80 per cent of the white adult male population.[29]

Seen from England, the role of the assembly in government was to support the executive power of the governor and his council. English authorities did not allow colonial executives the exclusive right to make laws or raise taxes, but nor did they concede full parliamentary status to the assemblies. The right to representation was regarded as a favour from the crown, and in principle government was by royal command, conveyed to the colonies through the instructions given by the King to his governors prior to their departure for the Americas. As the King's representative, the governor had the power to convene, suspend and dissolve assemblies as he saw fit; he might also suggest legislation and veto laws passed by the assembly, while the crown retained the right to disallow any laws passed in the colonies. The assembly was also obliged to provide the governor and his council with tax revenues to meet the needs of government. In theory, then, the role of the assemblies was simply to participate and cooperate with the governor and his council in matters of legislation, and to provide the executive power with the funds required to support the administration and defence of the colony.

The assemblies took a quite different view of their functions, and increasingly behaved in ways that were at variance with the model of colonial government envisaged by the crown. Their members held that, far from being dependent on royal favour, the assemblies embodied the rights of Englishmen to government by consent and should function without royal interference. Seen from the Americas, the model for colonial government was that of England itself. The governor and his council were regarded as the colonial equivalents of the King and his Privy Council, while the lower house of the assembly was the coeval of the English House of Commons, upon which assemblies modelled their procedures. In particular, the assemblies claimed control over the raising and expenditure of taxes, in the manner of the House of Commons, and they refused to supply revenues or to approve expenditures which they did not control.[30]

The assemblies' insistence on their right to control financial administration was a powerful political lever because colonial governors had no substantial source of revenue other than that supplied by the assembly. This situation was very different from that of Spanish America, where colonial government had its own fiscal base. In the Spanish colonies, the colonial bureaucracy drew revenues directly from Indian tribute payments and from a wide range of taxes on production and trade; colonials had no formal institutional machinery through which they might control the raising and expenditure of taxation. Taxes were levied at the command of the King and collected by the officials of the *Real Hacienda* (royal treasury), both for remittance to Spain and for the expenses of colonial government and defence. Using the revenues raised by taxation, the crown created a bureaucracy of officials which carried out royal orders and depended on royal authority. In English America, by contrast, there was no separate fiscal apparatus designed to collect taxes in the manner of the Spanish *Real*

Hacienda, nor was there an extensive bureaucracy supported by royal revenues and dependent on the crown. Instead of being concentrated in a bureaucratic hierarchy, the tasks of government were shared between officials and colonials, and, through the formal right to representation through their assemblies, colonials came to play a key role in making laws for their own governance.

Most important was the practice of allowing the assemblies the right to consultation in matters of taxation, as this gradually became institutionalized into a practice whereby the assemblies controlled taxation and its expenditure. Because English kings had insufficient colonial revenues to pay their officials, they insisted that each colony levy taxes to pay its governor. In Virginia, Maryland and the West Indies, governors' salaries were paid from permanent taxes on exports. Elsewhere, governors depended on assemblies to provide them with an income, often on a year-to-year basis.[31] This gave the assembly a powerful political weapon: by delaying or reducing governors' salaries, or by rewarding cooperative governors with large incomes, the assemblies used their power to vote taxes as an instrument for bending the executive to their will. By the mid-eighteenth century, they had secured a firm place in appointing officials, and further influenced policy-making by determining the areas in which taxes were spent. In these conditions, the assemblies became a powerful counterweight to governors. They could prevent governors from following the instructions they received from the crown, and force them to accept constant encroachments upon their prerogatives and powers. They also provided a vehicle for colonial elites to exert a strong, sometimes commanding influence over their local affairs.[32]

THE DISTRIBUTION OF POWER

If government in colonial English America is distinguished from its counterparts in other Euro-American colonies by this powerful element of representation, with its characteristic insistence on the 'liberties' of English subjects, we should not assume that such government was 'democratic' in the modern sense. In fact, popular participation in government was limited by a number of factors. First, although the scope of the electoral franchise was broad, especially where land was cheap, many individuals – women, blacks, Indians, servants and small property owners – were excluded from voting. Second, the practice of politics depended on social context. In

Massachusetts, for example, the extension of the right to vote to large numbers of white Protestant males did not necessarily mean that government rested on the democratic principle of a free choice between contending groups or policies. The early Puritan leadership had permitted a widening of the franchise in order to ensure that town leaders could compel obedience to authority by supporting themselves with the concensus of the community, rather than because they wished to allow voters freely to choose between competing ideas or political groupings. Voting was designed to consolidate the community around decisions already negotiated before elections were held, rather than to express a plurality of opinions.[33]

Throughout the colonies, those elected to office also tended to represent the upper echelons of society, concentrating local political authority in the social and economic elites. This was partly because the pursuit of a political career required wealth. Property and other qualifications were more stringent for office-holders than for voters, and both seeking and holding office generally involved greater monetary costs than benefits. But elite political predominance also owed much to habits of deference among voters, who normally regarded the wealthy and educated as the 'natural' spokesmen of the community as a whole.[34] The political position of landed elites in the colonies differed from that of the English landed aristocracy, however, in certain important respects. For, as Bernard Bailyn argues, the landed gentry in Virginia and other colonies lacked the continuity and concentration' of social and political power which the device of entailed estates (combined with the practice of primogeniture) gave the English aristocracy, by allowing it to pass land and its related political power through successive generations. In Virginia, where land was relatively easily available and wealth alone gave eligibility for political office, political influence tended to become diffused over a wider range of leading families and was not, as in England, a prerogative of birth. In the colonies, there was also a divergence between social and political leadership at the apex of government. London conferred power on governors who were rarely members of local society, who came and went, and who consequently could not provide a continuous identification between colonial elites and external authority.[35]

The tendency for political influence to gather in the hands of the wealthy was particularly clear in the West Indies, where the imitation of English government – with the governor in place of the King, the council in place of the House of Lords, and the assembly in place of the House of Commons – was shaped by the nature of slave societies.

Superficially, the evolution of West Indian government followed a pattern similar to that found in the other colonies. Whites regarded themselves as Englishmen overseas who enjoyed the same political rights as those at home, and their assemblies tended to gain power at the expense of the governor, to secure control over public finance, and so on. But in reality the assemblies expressed only the interests of very small groups; the outwardly representative character of government cloaked the concentration of power in the hands of narrow oligarchies. Those who were elected to the assemblies were not all great planters, but the planters predominated; they controlled all the main offices of government in the islands that were not held by non-residents, ranging from the council, through the courts, down to the parish level.[36]

Government by members of landed elites was also found in North America, particularly in Virginia, where the landowning gentry dominated the assemblies and formed a broadly based ruling class which ran government in its own interests. There was, however, an important difference between the politics of the continental and island colonies. Government on the North American mainland was generally more representative than in the Caribbean islands, because there was a broader electorate to whom office-holders had to appeal and respond. Thus, although there was a close correlation between wealth and power in most colonies, the political life of the North American colonies was very different from that of the Anglo-Caribbean societies, where the great majority of the population, being slaves, were entirely excluded from the legal and political system.

At the end of the seventeenth century, English government of the Americas was a balance of power which tended to tilt towards the colonies. On one side stood a metropolitan authority which was concerned to subordinate the colonies to the interests of English commerce, and which reserved to itself the power to make laws for the colonies and to supervise their administration. It was, however, without an effective machinery for doing so. Unlike the Spanish crown, the English monarchy had failed to create agencies of central government which had clear and comprehensive authority over colonial government. Even when the crown sought to improve its command of colonial policy by establishing the Board of Trade in 1696, central control of the colonies remained weak and divided. For, though the Board of Trade was given responsibility for overseeing colonial administration and improving commerce between England and its colonies, it did not have the authority of Spain's Council of the Indies. Its main concern was simply to defend and extend English trade, and, although it was the leading central agency dealing with colonial affairs, the Board of Trade had to coordinate its activities with several other departments of state, such as the Treasury, the Admiralty, the War Office and the Southern Department, all of which diluted its capacity to make and enforce policy.

Counterbalancing the agencies of royal government in London were the governments of the colonies themselves, where elective assemblies tended to oppose the power of the executive authorities which represented imperial government. Colonials did not question the sovereignty of the English crown, but they were strongly conscious of themselves as members of autonomous communities with rights to self-government and to the pursuit of their own interests, and colonial assemblies and courts tended to gain legitimacy at the expense of the metropolitan power. While lawyers in London might insist that the colonial assemblies were subordinate to Parliament, in practice there was little that London could do to enforce its will over refractory colonials because, with their power over local finances, the assemblies effectively controlled the colonies' governments.

Although the Anglican church improved its position in some colonies after the Restoration, the monarchy did not succeed in promoting its authority by establishing a single colonial church, even in the new colonies founded during the second half of the eighteenth century.[37] Because in Britain's colonies, 'there were no elaborate bureaucracies, no bishoprics, no deaneries, no prebends, few regular army or navy posts, and not much to speak of in the way of crown livings', the crown had a limited ability to use the power of patronage as a means of securing political support loyalty as it did at home. As Gordon Wood has pointed out, however, the meagre power of patronage at the disposal of royal officials may have been more influential than historians have generally allowed. For, in societies where growing economic prosperity blurred the calibrations of social rank, offices in the gift of royal governors were coveted by colonials desperate 'for any little distinction in title or name' which might confirm their social standing and raise them above their fellows.[38]

The ability of the crown to bind the colonial elites to metropolitan government was nonetheless weak. At the heart of colonial government lay a permanent tension, based in the discrepancy between royal governors who were under instructions to implement orders from the metropolitan centre, and colonial assemblies which were convinced that they had rights analogous to those of the British Parliament. So long as colonial matters remained a low priority for the crown and Parliament and metropolitan governments left the colonies to manage their own internal affairs, this tension and the frictions it caused could be sustained without inflicting permanent damage on relations between Britain and the colonies. Conflicts occurred, but colonials regarded clashes with the executive power as part of normal politics, not as challenges to the legitimacy of British rule. Political conflict within the colonies was, moreover, largely a struggle of factions, competing for local official influence, or asserting rival regional interests of town and countryside, coasts and interiors. Generally, colonial institutions provided a stable framework for absorbing and resolving such conflicts; for almost a century after the Glorious Revolution, colonial politics was free from any disturbance sufficiently serious to disrupt or endanger British rule. It was only after 1763, when Parliament took a more active and interventionist approach to colonial affairs, that the framework of imperial rule finally came under severe strain. To explain this shift, which ultimately led to a great fracture of empire, we must now examine the remarkable advance of British power during the eighteenth century, and the equally striking expansion of the economies and societies of Britain's American colonies.

NOTES

1. For a succinct survey of the political relationship between metropolis and colonies over this long period, see Jack P. Greene, *Peripheries and Center: Constitutional Development in the Extended Polities of the British Empire and the United States, 1607–1688* (Athens, Ga, 1986) Chapters 1–2.
2. Francis Jennings, *The Invasion of America: Indians, Colonialism and the Court of Conquest* (Chapel Hill, NC, 1975) pp. 105–9.
3. Carole Shammas, 'English commercial development and American colonization', in K.R. Andrews, N.P. Canny and P.E.H. Hair (eds) *Westward Enterprise: English Activities in Ireland, the Atlantic and America, 1480–1650* (Liverpool, 1978) pp. 151–74.
4. On the development of the Spanish colonial state, see J.H. Elliott, 'Spain and America in the sixteenth and seventeenth centuries', in L. Bethell (ed) *Cambridge History of Latin America*, vol. 1 (Cambridge, 1984) pp. 287–339; also Mario Góngora, *Studies in the Colonial History of Spanish America* (Cambridge, 1975) Chapter 3.
5. Patricia U. Bonomi, *Under the Cope of Heaven: Religion, Society and Politics in Colonial America* (Oxford and New York, 1986) pp. 12–24.
6. The special features of Maryland government are brought out in David W. Jordan, *Foundations of Representative Government in Maryland, 1632–1715* (Cambridge, 1987) especially pp. 11–33.
7. F.G. Spurdle, *Early West Indian Government, Showing the Progress of Government in Barbados, Jamaica and the Leeward Islands 1660–1783* (Palmerston North, New Zealand, n.d.) pp. 7–24.
8. For an exposition of Charles I's attitude and approach to the colonies, see

Robert M. Bliss, *Revolution and Empire: English Politics and the American Colonies in the Seventeenth Century* (Manchester, 1990) pp. 17–44; quotation from p. 19.

9. Stephen Saunders Webb, *The Governors General: The English Army and the Definition of Empire, 1659–1681*, (Chapel Hill, NC, 1979) especially Chapters 2–3. A brief statement of his thesis is given on pp. 442–70.

10. Bliss, *Revolution and Empire*, pp. 132–60; Spurdle, *Early West Indian Government*, pp. 28–85; A.P. Thornton, *West India Policy under the Restoration* (Oxford, 1956) pp. 25–66. A full account of Jamaican government in the decade after the Restoration is given by Webb, *The Governors General*, pp. 196–258.

11. Thornton, *West India Policy under the Restoration*, pp. 5–15.

12. For a statement of these trends, see R.C. Simmons, *The American Colonies from Settlement to Independence*, (London, 1976) pp. 50–6.

13. The following account of the rebellion draws on Wilcomb E. Washburn, *The Governor and the Rebel: The Story of Bacon's Rebellion and its Leader* (Chapel Hill, NC, 1957), and Stephen Saunders Webb, *1676: The End of American Independence* (New York, 1984) pp. 13–163. For a brief outline, see Edmund S. Morgan, *American Slavery, American Freedom: The Ordeal of Colonial Virginia* (New York, 1975) pp. 250–70.

14. Bernard Bailyn, 'Politics and social structure in Virginia', in J.M Smith (ed) *Seventeenth Century America* (Chapel Hill, NC, 1959) pp. 102–6.

15. The interpretation of Bacon's Rebellion as a 'first American Revolution' is found in Webb, *1676: The End of American Independence*, quotation from p. 66.

16. On the latter, see Bliss, *Revolution and Empire*, pp. 191–200.

17. Webb, *1676: The End of American Independence*, p. 412.

18. Philip Haffenden, 'The crown and the colonial charters, 1675–1688', *William and Mary Quarterly*, 3rd series (1958) **15**: 297–311.

19. For a concise analysis of the Glorious Revolution, see Geoffrey Holmes, *The Making of a Great Power: Late Stuart and Early Georgian England, 1660–1722* (London, 1993) pp. 160–91; the quotation, from the contemporary historian Gilbert Burnet, is from p. 176.

20. For a detailed analysis of the antecedents and consequences of the Glorious Revolution in the North American colonies, which concludes that the political settlement did not create political equality between colonies and mother country, see David S. Lovejoy, *The Glorious Revolution in America* (New York, 1972). See also his 'Two American revolutions, 1689 and 1776', in J.G.A. Pocock (ed) *Three British Revolutions, 1641, 1688, 1776* (Princeton, NJ, 1980). A succinct statement of the repercussions of the Glorious Revolution in both the West Indies and North American colonies is given by K.G. Davies, 'The revolutions in America', in Robert Beddard (ed) *The Revolutions of 1688* (Oxford, 1988).

21. A narrative of colonial policy in William's reign is given by G.H. Guttridge, *The Colonial Policy of William III in America and the West Indies* (London, 1966) pp. 44–178.

22. For a full account of the Board of Trade and its activities, see Oliver M. Dickerson, *American Colonial Government, 1696–1765* (New York, 1962) especially Chapters 3–4.

23. Richard R. Johnson, *Adjustment to Empire: The New England Colonies, 1675–1715* (Leicester, 1981) p. 408.
24. For this view, see Philip S. Haffenden,, *New England in the English Nation, 1689–1713* (Oxford, 1974).
25. On British colonial government during the first half of the eighteenth century, see Greene, *Peripheries and Center*, pp. 43–54; quotation from p. 33.
26. James Henretta, *'Salutary Neglect': Colonial Administration under the Duke of Newcastle* (Princeton, NJ, 1972) pp. 374.
27. Leonard W. Labaree, *Royal Government in America: A Study of the British Colonial System before 1783* (New York, 1958) pp. 92–133. On the system of government in the Leeward Islands, see C.S.S. Higham, *The Development of the Leeward Islands under the Restoration, 1660–1688* (Cambridge, 1921) pp. 211–43.
28. Labaree, *Royal Government in America*, pp. 134–71.
29. Simmons, *The American Colonies*, pp. 247–8.
30. Labaree, *Royal Government in America*, pp. 172–89, 269–75.
31. Ibid., pp. 312–27.
32. Ibid., pp. 427–34.
33. Michael Zuckerman, 'The social context of democracy in Massachusetts', in Stanley N. Katz (ed) *Colonial America: Essays in Politics and Social Development* (Boston, Mass., and Toronto, 2nd edition, 1976) pp. 271–90.
34. J.R. Pole, 'Historians and the problem of early American democracy', *American Historical Review* (1962) **LXVII**: 626–46; Jackson Turner Main, 'Government by the people: the American Revolution and the democratization of the legislatures', in Jack P. Greene (ed) *The Reinterpretation of the American Revolution, 1763–1789* (New York, 1968).
35. Bailyn, 'Politics and social structure in Virginia', pp. 106–15.
36. Richard S. Dunn, *Sugar and Slaves: The Rise of the Planter Class in the English West Indies, 1624–1713* (London, 1973) pp. 91–100; Elsa V. Goveia, *Slave Society in the British Leeward Islands at the End of the Eighteenth Century* (New Haven, Conn., and London, 1965) pp. 51–102; Edward Brathwaite, *The Development of Creole Society in Jamaica, 1770–1820* (Oxford, 1971) pp. 9–49.
37. On church and state in the colonies during the seventeenth century, see Philip S. Haffenden, 'The Anglican Church in Restoration colonial policy', in Smith (ed) *Seventeenth Century America*, pp. 166–91. For an explanation of continuing religious pluralism after the Restoration, see Bonomi, *Under the Cope of Heaven*, pp. 30–7.
38. Gordon S. Wood, *The Radicalism of the American Revolution* (New York, 1992) pp. 77–92; quotations from pp. 78, 80.

PART THREE

Transformations of Empire, 1713–1815

War, Trade and Empire, 1713–1776

During the eighteenth century, Britain and its empire in the Americas entered and experienced an extraordinary phase of its evolution. This phase was marked by the rapid rise of Britain to the front rank of European powers, by vigorous economic growth in both the metropolis and its transatlantic colonies, and by a tendency for the Anglo-American empire to become more closely bound to a parent power that was frequently embroiled in war with its great colonialist rivals. These developments were in turn succeeded by another, more remarkable change. Just as the British empire seemed to have acquired an unswerving forward momentum, it was suddenly disabled by internal breakdown, when, in 1776, thirteen of its North American colonies joined in rebellion against the mother country and, in the American Revolution, fought the successful war for independence that led to the foundation of the United States.

The crisis of empire caused by the American Revolution we shall examine in Chapter 9. The purpose of this chapter is to identify the forces which shaped the development of the colonies during the three-quarters of a century before the American Revolution. These were, first, the development by the British state of foreign and military policies aimed at enlarging its colonial commerce and territory through war; second, the expansion of the British Atlantic economy and the growth of commerce with the American world; and third, the rapid demographic and economic growth that took place within the British colonies themselves. We shall also examine the workings of the British colonial system and, by way of conclusion, consider the condition of the Anglo-American empire after the end of the Seven Years War, in which Britain achieved its greatest victory over its colonialist rivals and the empire moved towards its meridian.

THE EXPANSION OF BRITISH POWER

Central to any understanding of the changes which affected the Anglo-American empire during the eighteenth century is the political and economic evolution of the metropolitan power itself. While Spain, England's oldest competitor in the Americas, was struggling to recover control over its colonies and to recuperate from the decline suffered under the later Habsburgs, Britain entered the eighteenth century as a freshly consolidated and vigorous state that was increasingly bent on expanding its overseas commerce and colonial influence, and increasingly capable of waging war with its great continental rivals.[1]

In 1707, the Act of Union joined Scotland to England and Wales, finally bringing the long-divided island into political and economic unity as the United Kingdom of Great Britain; then, in 1714, the throne passed from Queen Anne to George I, the Elector of Hanover, thereby consolidating the constitutional monarchy defined by the 1688 Bill of Rights (translated into law in 1689) and the Act of Settlement of 1701. The principle that the crown could exercise its powers only through Parliament was now firmly entrenched; although the monarch still retained some freedom for action, by 1720 British monarchs became more fully accountable to Parliament and retained little scope for pursuing personal policies. Furthermore, as Britain's governing class became increasingly committed to the struggle for mastery with France, so in the quarter-century after the Glorious Revolution, 'the British state underwent a radical transformation, acquiring all the main features of a powerful fiscal-military state: high taxes, a growing and well-organized civil administration, a standing army and the determination to act as a major European power'.[2]

The transformation of the British state, the revolution in its foreign policy, and the formation of financial mechanisms which allowed Britain to wage prolonged and successful wars against more powerful competitors, all had important long-term implications for the Anglo-American empire. For although concern to prevent French hegemony on the continent and to preserve the Protestant succession at home were the leading goals of policy, commercial expansion and colonial acquisitions assumed a growing significance for both British government and the landed and mercantile interests represented in Parliament, and made the Americas an increasingly important arena for action. Kings and their ministers were interested in expanding Britain's colonial commerce because it provided important sources of revenue for the state, and made a major contribution to supplying the ships and sailors essential for defence of the realm. At the same time, their need to persuade Parliament to approve and finance state foreign policy helped powerful mercantile groups to enhance their political leverage. In this context, the crown's concern to curb the growth of French power, combined with private ambitions for enlarging British overseas trade, nurtured a more aggressive commercial and colonial expansionism both in the Americas and in the Far East, and gave British foreign policy a sharper, more bellicose edge as the century progressed.

So, while England had succeeded in establishing and consolidating a place in the Americas and a share in their resources during the seventeenth century, in the eighteenth century Britain's governments entered into a prolonged competition with France and Spain for dominance in overseas trade and empire. Between 1689 and 1815, Britain fought seven major wars against France, five of which also involved Spain, France's Bourbon ally. The great struggle between Britain and France, sometimes called the 'second Hundred Years War', was not confined to the western hemisphere. French and British commercial interests also competed for the rich commerce of the east, particularly in India, and sought to extend control over the slave trade by creating territorial enclaves on the coasts of West Africa. But the greatest attention was given to the Americas, where the colonies created by European migrants and their descendants held large populations and abundant resources, and provided some of Europe's most valuable commodities and markets. Indeed, Britain's ability to defend its new status among the powers came increasingly to depend on commercial and colonial expansion at the expense of France and Spain. As a result, the Anglo-American colonies become much more exposed to the effects of international conflict over the course of the century, as the armies and navies of the rival powers conducted campaigns on colonial frontiers and in American waters, usually with the support of forces recruited from the colonies themselves.

The impact of such conflict on the very different colonies that lay between Nova Scotia and Barbados was never uniform, but war was to be an important catalyst for change in British America. This was especially true of North America, where the effects of international conflict interacted with rapid demographic and economic growth to bring about changes in the shape and character of the empire which were ultimately to contribute to its rupture. So, let us now trace Britain's growing involvement in imperialist conflicts for trade and dominion, and examine their implications for the Anglo-American colonies.

IMPERIALIST RIVALRIES AND COLONIAL WARS

The first sign that conflict over colonial trade and territory was to play a major part in eighteenth-century wars between the European powers came in the War of the Spanish Succession (1702–13). Commercial calculations had little part in the Nine Years War, when William III had fought against Louis XIV in order to defend his succession to the English throne and to provide the Dutch United Provinces with an ally against France. But when the accession to the Spanish throne of Philip of Anjou, grandson and protégé of Louis XIV, created the prospect of a Franco-Spanish alliance in which Spain would become a French satellite, commercial and colonial considerations began to play a more prominent part in shaping British foreign policy. For the union of France and Spain threatened to impair English trade not only with the Mediterranean world, but also with Spanish America and the West Indies. At the same time, any accretion to French influence in the Americas threatened the strategic security of England's colonies in North America, where French aspirations to control the great arc of territory that stretched from Canada to Louisiana jeopardized the safety and future growth of the English Atlantic colonies.

To block French ambition, Britain joined with Holland and Austria in a Grand Alliance and, by fighting the War of the Spanish Succession, forced France to abandon its plans for creating a Franco-Spanish 'super state' based in Bourbon dynastic alliance. At the Treaty of Utrecht (1713), France, Spain and Britain negotiated a compromise which brought an Anglo-French détente that lasted for more than two decades. Philip V, first of the Spanish Bourbons, remained on his throne, but renounced any claim to the throne of France, thereby formally pre-empting the union of the French and Spanish monarchies which the other European powers so feared. In return for recognizing the Bourbon succession to the throne of Spain, Britain made some important gains in territory and trade. From France, Britain acquired Newfoundland, Hudson Bay, Acadia (Nova Scotia) and Port Royal, so strengthening the boundaries of England's empire in northern North America. From Spain, Britain took territory in Europe (Gibraltar and Minorca), thereby confirming its power in the Medi- terranean. Britain also gained an important commercial concession from Spain at Utrecht, by securing the *asiento de negros*, the thirty-year contract which gave the South Sea Company the monopoly of the Spanish American slave trade, together with related rights to trade directly in specified Spanish American ports. This forestalled French domination of Spanish colonial commerce, and gave British merchants the direct entry to Spanish American markets which they had long coveted. Britain's access to Latin American resources was further strengthened by the concessions made at Utrecht to Portugal, which had become firmly linked to Britain by the Methuen Treaty of 1703. The terms agreed at Utrecht confirmed Portugal's title to the Colônia do Sacramento on the River Plate, and this provided an additional channel for contraband trade with Spanish colonial markets. Thus Britain secured important economic advantages at Utrecht, and the pursuit of commercial and colonial concessions which figured in the Utrecht settlement set a pattern for the future: all the peace treaties which Britain concluded during the next half-century were to include clauses relating to commerce and colonies.[3]

The Treaty of Utrecht preserved the balance of power in both Europe and the Americas: Britain and France achieved a rapprochement which lasted for the next three decades, and Spain retained sovereignty over its colonies. The concessions made at Utrecht had, however, sharpened British appetites for gaining access to Spain's colonial markets; conflict over colonial trade helped to lead Britain into minor wars with Spain in 1718 and 1727. These wars had muted echoes in the colonies. In the West Indies, Spanish seizures of British vessels disrupted trade and led to small-scale protective naval deployments, but no major engagement. In North America, Anglo-Spanish hostilities also occurred in the borderlands between Florida and South Carolina, where Spain sought to guard its territory against the intrusions of settlers from neighbouring British colonies. The scale of conflict was small, involving petty raiding rather than substantial military campaigns; dispute over territory in this region did however help to ensure official support for the new colony of Georgia, which received its royal charter in 1732. This new colony not only provided a project for settling the poor of London, whom its founder, James Edward Oglethorpe, wished to benefit, but also provided a bastion against the threat of Spanish military incursions from Florida.

While contention between Britain and Spain worsened during these wars, France continued to harbour ambitions for expansion in both the Americas and India, and thereby increased the chances of Anglo-French confrontation over colonies and commerce. Throughout the 1730s, Anglo-Spanish relations continued to deteriorate, and the Family Compact (1733) consolidated a Franco-Spanish alliance which was henceforth to ensure that France and Spain were jointly drawn into colonial warfare against Britain. In these circumstances, war between the powers henceforth took on an increasingly American dimension, with much blood and treasure expended in struggles for trade and territory in the regions between Canada and Cape Horn.

The shift towards full-blooded colonial conflicts began in 1739, when Britain went to war first with Spain, then, from 1744, with France too. This was not a European war which spread to the colonies, but a war rooted in competition over American resources. Several issues were involved, including Spanish resentment at British encroachments on Central American coasts, in the log-cutting settlements of Honduras, and on the borders of Florida, where the new colony of Georgia was founded in 1733. But the major source of contention arose from British violations of Spanish commercial laws in the Americas, and Spain's seizures of British vessels suspected of smuggling into Spanish colonies. Searches and arrests of British ships in the Caribbean provoked angry responses in England, and a campaign in Parliament and the press not only carried anti-Spanish feeling to a high pitch, but also revived in the public mind old dreams of British Protestant conquests of a decadent Catholic empire. An incident in Caribbean waters, when a Spanish coastguard seized an English vessel and allegedly cut off its captain's ear, provided a convenient focus for warmongers. Playing on popular patriotic sentiments, anti-Catholic prejudices, and the cupidity of mercantile and manufacturing interests, a belligerent opposition whipped up widespread support for extraordinary projects of imperial aggrandizement. Thus Britain entered the 'War of Jenkins' Ear' (1739) amidst a clamour of anti-Spanish rhetoric, and with a clutch of grandiose schemes for overturning the Spanish empire by seizing important Spanish American towns and inciting Spain's colonial subjects to break away from their metropolitan power, so that they might share in British liberty.[4]

This vision of imperial conquests in Spanish America was soon revealed as an illusion. Hopes for swift military successes were dashed when Admiral Vernon's successful assault on Portobelo in 1740 was followed by defeat at Cartagena de Indias and Santiago de Cuba, and when misplaced hopes of creole and Indian uprisings against Spain came to nothing. Nor, when France entered the war in 1744, did British military performance secure any great advantage. Although the British navy inflicted considerable damage on French wartime forces and trade in the Caribbean, little direct damage was done to France's West Indian colonies. The only major attack on French territory was in North America, where Britain captured the fort at Louisbourg on Cape Breton Island, at the entrance to the St Lawrence River. This was not decisive, however, and the war eventually terminated in a stalemate. At the Treaty of Aix-la-Chapelle in 1748, Britain returned

Louisbourg to France in return for Madras in India, and made no territorial gains in the West Indies. Spanish America was also left intact, and Britain took nothing from Spain to compensate for the large human losses incurred by British forces in attacks on Spanish colonial strongholds. Thus the underlying causes of conflict were left unchanged, and the powers retired to prepare for another round of the struggle.

Britain's aggressive stance was generally popular among its colonial subjects, since it accorded with their interests. Planters in the West Indies applauded attacks on French colonies because they curbed competition from the French Caribbean islands, which were becoming formidable sugar producers. Having more land and more fertile soils at their disposal, French sugar planters, particularly in St Domingue, produced sugar at lower costs and sold it at lower prices than their British counterparts, thereby limiting their markets and squeezing their profit margins. Unable to compete economically, the West India sugar interests used their influence in the British Parliament to pressure home governments to protect its trade by artificial means, and welcomed wars which crippled French competition. At the same time, settlers and land speculators in North America also favoured war with France and Spain because it provided armed support for expansion on western and southern frontiers, and gave merchants and shippers from the northern colonies opportunities to profit from interloping and privateering in the Caribbean[5] Many colonials therefore joined enthusiastically in the wave of jingoistic patriotism that swept Britain during the 1740s, gladly embracing the vision of Britain's destiny as a great maritime empire that was expressed in James Thomson's refrain, 'Rule Britannia, rule the waves, Britons never will be slaves'. Thus, by the mid-eighteenth century, the colonies seemed set to become the enduring pillars of a great empire, celebrated by a militant nationalism which, in both Britain and the Americas, proclaimed the special status of the British monarchy as a 'cradle of liberty' with an imperial mission and destiny.[6]

As the attractions of aggression gained ground, supported by a vociferous nationalist outcry both at home and in the colonies, a return to war was virtually inevitable after the standoff in 1748. In fact, fighting on North American frontiers continued during the early 1750s, and British determination to break the barriers to westward expansion formed by French forts and Indian protectorates prepared the way for a resumption of war with France in 1756. This, the Seven Years War (1756–63), marked a new stage in the struggle for empire, in which Britain and France engaged in combat on a global scale.

Fought in Europe, India, West Africa, the West Indies and North America, the 'Great War for Empire' differed from the preceding war in that it involved a contest for territory in both the Caribbean and the North American continent, and ended with a treaty that redrew the map of European colonial dominion in the Americas.

At the outset of the war, Pitt determined on destroying France as a colonial power, using the British navy to stifle resistance in the French American colonies. This strategy was successful in both North America and the Caribbean. By the end of 1759, Britain had not only taken the strategic French fortress at Louisbourg, but had also destroyed French outposts in the Great Lakes and captured Quebec. Together with successful naval operations in Europe, these actions isolated and neutralized French forces in Canada, and left Pitt free to concentrate on taking the military initiative in the Caribbean, focusing attack on the French islands. In 1758, Britain had already damaged the French plantation islands by seizing the slave stations of Senegal, and subsequently went on to inflict more direct damage by taking Guadeloupe, Martinique, Dominica, St Lucia and St Vincent in the French West Indies. When Spain entered the war as an ally of France in 1762, British forces also deprived Spain of important colonies, taking Havana in Cuba, and Manila in the Philippines.

After delivering these crushing blows, Britain was able to secure unprecedented territorial gains at the Peace of Paris in 1763. Even after returning some captured areas to France and Spain, Britain obtained huge concessions from its rivals. Spain suffered the loss of Florida, which was ceded to Britain in return for Havana and Manila. France suffered much greater losses. In the Caribbean, France retained St Domingue, recovered St Lucia, Martinique and Guadeloupe, but lost the smaller islands of the Grenadines, Tobago, St Vincent and Dominica. But it was in North America that France suffered the most devastating territorial blow to its empire: Britain took the whole of Canada and the right to all lands east of the Mississippi River, thereby reducing French possessions to a couple of tiny islands off the shores of Newfoundland, conceded to France as landing places for its fishermen.

This dramatic change in the balance of colonial power was to have momentous implications for the British empire in the Americas. Although Britain's gains from the Seven Years War seemed to present tremendous opportunities for the extension of empire, colonial aggrandizement was not without risks and costs. In the short term, however, victory in the Seven Years War appeared to be a triumphant vindication of Britain's 'blue water' strategy. Not only had it produced a stunning territorial aggrandizement, but also, as the first war in which British overseas trade had expanded, the 'Great War for Empire' had reinforced an expansion of British Atlantic commerce which, since the start of the century, had paralleled (and to some extent powered) the struggle between the leading European powers for ascendancy over American trade and territory.

EXPANSION IN THE BRITISH ATLANTIC ECONOMY

Throughout the first half of the eighteenth century, the great contest for empire which began in the War of the Spanish Succession and culminated in the Seven Years War interacted with a notable expansion of Britain's extra-European trades. This does not mean that British policies were driven simply and solely by the interests of a commercial capitalism grounded in overseas trade. As we have already noted, British foreign and military policies were initially shaped in response to the rising power of France, and the related concerns of British kings and their ministers to protect the European balance of power against the threat of French hegemony. It is nonetheless impossible fully to understand Britain's aggressive stance and its determination to expand its influence in the Americas without taking account of the growth of its extra-European trades. For growth in the long-range trades that were conducted eastwards to India and westwards to the Americas strengthened the political influence and pressure which mercantile interests exerted on government policy, and helped to ensure that the colonies occupied a key position in British military and diplomatic strategy.

Growth in Britain's American trades took two major forms during the eighteenth century. One was the enlargement of Britain's direct and indirect commerce with the colonies of the Iberian powers; the other, more important area for growth was in Britain's commerce with its own colonies in the Caribbean and on the North American continent. Both these developments fuelled British ambitions to be the major power in the Americas, contending for the lion's share of all European colonial commerce with the western hemisphere.

One element of British commercial expansion with the American colonies of other European powers is found in trade with Portugal and Brazil. Thanks to the Methuen Treaty of 1703, Portugal became an economic satellite of Britain and, because Portugal was unable to supply sufficient manufactured goods for Brazil's markets, Britain was a major beneficiary of the Brazilian gold boom (c. 1690–c. 1760). British exports to Portugal, many of which were trans-shipped to Brazil, doubled in 1700–40, providing new outlets for English manufactures, especially cheaper and lighter textiles, and giving Britain a valuable supply of gold in return. When gold production declined from around mid-century, so too did trade with Portugal, though Britain continued to benefit from trade with Brazil for the rest of the century.[7]

Another element of Britain's trade with American regions outside its own colonies was commerce, legal and illegal, with Spanish America. Like the trade with Brazil, this was primarily a means of expanding markets for British goods, in return for gold and silver, rather than a means of securing tropical staples. British goods entered Spain's colonial markets by various routes. Some were carried through Spain, to be taken to the Americas on Spanish ships sailing out of Spanish ports, together with manufactures from other regions of Europe. Between 1713 and 1739, the British South Sea Company also funnelled goods into the Spanish colonies under cover of its monopoly contract for supplying slaves, acquired under the terms of the Treaty of Utrecht. Meanwhile, British goods were also smuggled to the coasts of northern South America and the Isthmus of Panama by contraband traders who operated out of the British West Indies in search of gold and silver from New Granada and Peru. This trade is difficult to quantify accurately, but it was sufficiently large to confound Madrid's efforts to revive Spanish Atlantic commerce during the first half of the eighteenth century, and provided such potent competition that the Bourbon monarchy had to reorganize the system of Spanish commerce with South America during the 1740s.[8]

The third and most important component of British transatlantic commercial expansion was found in trade with Britain's colonies in North America and the Caribbean, which provided both a surging flood of tropical staples and a swelling market for metropolitan manufactures. There was, first, a notable increase in British imports from the Americas in the three-quarters of a century before the American Revolution. Between 1700–1 and 1772–3, American colonial exports (from both North America and the Caribbean) became a growing component in Britain's import trade, rising from 19 to 38 per cent of all British imports (see Table 8.1).

While producers in the Americas were supplying Britain with ever larger amounts of their resources, the markets of the Americas were also absorbing growing quantities of goods sent from the metropolis. Table 8.2 shows how, between 1700–1 and 1772–3, Britain's exports to its North American and West Indian colonies increased from 10 to 38 per cent of total British exports, with particularly rapid growth after 1750.

Table 8.1   British imports from North America and the West Indies, 1700–73.

Years	Value (£000)	Percentage of total British imports
1700–1	1,157	19.7
1730–1	2,241	30.1
1750–1	2,361	30.0
1772–3	5,199	38.2

Note: Figures for years before 1772 for England and Wales only
Source: B.R. Mitchell, *British Historical Statistics* (Cambridge, 1988) p. 496

Table 8.2   British domestic exports to North America and the West Indies, 1700–73.

Years	Value (£000)	Percentage of total British exports
1700–1	461	10.3
1730–1	725	13.9
1750–1	1,420	15.6
1772–3	3,875	38.0

Note: Figures for years before 1772 for England and Wales only
Source: Mitchell, *British Historical Statistics*, p. 496

Clearly the colonies were becoming increasingly valuable to Britain, both as sources of primary commodities and as markets for British goods, with the North American colonies making a growing contribution to trade from the American world. Indeed, perhaps the most arresting aspect of the eighteenth-century expansion of British commerce is the emergence of the colonies, particularly the North American colonies, as major customers for British manufactures. But we should not forget that the West Indies still made the greatest contribution to Britain's trade with areas outside Europe. In 1768–72, they provided 17.7 per cent of the total value of Britain's extra-European trade, compared to the contribution of 16.6 per cent made by North America, 12.1 per cent by Asia, and 3 per cent by Africa.[9] The continuing importance of the Caribbean colonies to British trade, despite North American growth, also points to the fact that the expansion of eighteenth-century British colonial commerce was to an important degree sustained by an expansion of slavery and the slave trade. Indeed, Eric Williams argued that the trade and the system of slavery which it fed made a crucial contribution to the progress of British capitalism, in that the profits obtained provided one of the main streams of that accumulation in England which financed the Industrial Revolution.[10] 'The slave trade', Williams observed,

> kept the wheels of metropolitan industry turning; it stimulated navigation and shipbuilding and employed seamen; it raised fishing villages into flourishing cities; it gave sustenance to new industries based on the processing of colonial raw materials; it yielded large profits which were ploughed back into metropolitan industry; and, finally, it gave rise to an unprecedented commerce in the West Indies and made the Caribbean territories among the most valuable colonies the world has ever known.[11]

The Williams thesis – that the colonial trades in slaves and the profits produced by slaves in the British West Indies made a vital contribution to financing Britain's Industrial Revolution – has been much criticized.[12] In the broader debate concerning Britain's economic growth and transformation, there has been a strong tendency to attach greater importance to the expansion of domestic rather than overseas markets, and thus to downplay the significance of the colonial trades. A current re-evaluation suggests, however, that, while Williams exaggerated the importance of slavery in generating economic growth and change in Britain, slavery and the slave-based economies of the West Indies did play a vital part in expanding the British Atlantic economy. To Barbara Solow, revised estimates of the pace and pattern of British economic growth in the eighteenth century confirm the importance of exports to industrial growth, and point to 'a solid connection between slave production in the Americas and British production of industrial goods'.[13]

This is not, of course, to claim that slavery powered the Industrial Revolution. It does, however, emphasize the importance of sugar and slavery as the heart of the British Atlantic trading system, and draws attention to the fact that, as a growth-pole within that system, the slave-based economies of the West Indies made a singularly important contribution to British development. This point is reinforced by David Richardson's examination of the direct and indirect contributions made by the slave trade and the West Indian economies to broadening markets for British industrial products. In West Africa, the trade in slaves underpinned a rising demand for British manufactures; more important, the growth of West Indian sugar production based on slavery generated demands for livestock, lumber and foodstuffs which stimulated North American colonial economies, and thus allowed the colonies north of the Delaware to enlarge their markets for British manufactures. Richardson's calculations indicate that, from the late 1740s to the early 1770s, the direct and indirect effects of growing purchasing power in the Caribbean may have accounted for as much as 35 per cent of the growth in total British exports. He therefore concludes that, during the third quarter of the eighteenth century, the 'West Indian and related trades . . . played a more prominent part in fostering industrial changes and export growth in Britain . . . than most historians have assumed'.[14]

The debates about the role of overseas trade and slavery in generating metropolitan growth raise complex issues in British economic history which lie beyond the compass of this study, which is concerned with developments within the colonies themselves.[15] What is nonetheless clear is that British trade in the Atlantic world grew impressively during the eighteenth century, and that the expansion of the metropolitan economy and its trading networks was a major stimulus to the growth of the colonial economies in both North America and the West Indies. Colonial growth did not depend wholly on British trade and the expansion of metropolitan markets for staples, however. The colonies also derived vitality from a demographic explosion whose causes and characteristics we shall now briefly outline.

COLONIAL POPULATION GROWTH

One of the most striking structural developments within the Anglo-American empire during the eighteenth century was the tremendous increase in population, with rates of increase in the North American colonies which were without parallel in the western world. The continental colonies of settlement were the main demographic growth area: their population increased almost eightfold between 1700 and 1770, from about 300,000 to 2.3 million. The Caribbean colonies saw slower growth from a smaller base: during the same period, the population of the West Indies trebled, from approximately 150,000 to almost 480,000. One obvious effect of these different rates of growth was to alter the demographic balance of the Anglo-America empire: by 1770, the mainland colonies had 82 per cent of the population of Anglo-America, while the West Indies' share had fallen back to a mere 18 per cent.[16]

In the West Indies, demographic growth was almost entirely driven by the import of African slaves. Between 1701 and 1780, nearly 1 million slaves were landed in the British Caribbean colonies, with Jamaica receiving by far the largest single input (about 38 per cent of the total).[17] With this great wave of forced African immigration went the continuing transformation of the islands' ethnic structure. At the turn of the century, blacks already constituted about 82 per cent of the islands' population; by 1770, they composed close to 90 per cent. The huge increase in slave imports did not provide a strong basis for sustained population growth, however, since slave mortality was extremely high. Disease, overwork and undernourishment, together with the planters' brutal belief that it was more economical to import slaves than to improve conditions in ways that might encourage their natural increase, ensured that the slave population increased much more slowly than slave importation. In Barbados, for example, the slave population increased by less than 25,000 between 1712 and 1768, despite slave imports of at least six times that number.[18]

Heavy mortality among the white population of the West Indies also persisted throughout the eighteenth century. Although there were variations between the islands, the death rate invariably outpaced births, so that the white minority was, like the black majority, able to increase only through immigration. It generally failed to do so. Between 1650 and 1712, the white population of Barbados fell from 20,000 to 12,500, and despite subsequent growth never recovered its mid-seventeenth-century level. In Antigua, the white population declined by about 50 per cent in the half-century from 1723 to 1774, and the other Leeward Islands saw a similar pattern of contracting white numbers accompanied by rapidly growing slave populations. In Jamaica, by contrast, the white population did grow (by about 27 per cent in 1741–74), but there, too, demographic growth among whites was completely overshadowed by a great increase in the population of black slaves.[19]

Population growth in British North America was much faster than in the West Indies; it was also a more complex phenomenon, encompassing high rates of white immigration and black slave imports, as well as rapid rates of natural increase among both groups. As regards immigration, the largest single ethnic group of newcomers to arrive during the eighteenth century was that of Africans carried into slavery: about a quarter of a million were landed in North America between 1700 and 1780. Unlike the West Indies, however, the growth of the black population did not rely on imports alone. There was also a high rate of natural increase among the slave population, particularly in the

Chesapeake region where there were fewer tropical diseases to cause mortality and depress fertility, and where the conditions of plantation slavery allowed slaves a more stable family life.

Blacks were, then, a significant element in the demographic revolution that was transforming eighteenth-century North America. By 1770, they constituted about 20 per cent of total population in the continental colonies, and were especially prominent in the South, where the vast majority were concentrated, living mostly as slaves.[20] Indeed, in the British American colonial system as a whole, slavery became increasingly prominent. In 1660, when slavery was primarily connected to sugar cultivation in the Caribbean, slaves had made up about 25 per cent of the total population of colonial Anglo-America. By 1710, this proportion had risen to 36 per cent, and slavery was firmly established in the continental colonies. Despite the very high rate of white population growth in North America, through the middle years of the eighteenth century slaves continued to constitute close to a third of the total number of people (excluding Indians) in the British American colonial world. Thus, the British American empire was to an important degree built on black slavery, and by mid-century 'slavery was everywhere an integral and accepted component of British American culture'.[21]

Africans carried into slavery and their African-American offspring were one component of the continental colonies' demographic explosion, but by far the greatest growth was among whites, whose numbers were swelled by both immigration from Europe and high rates of natural increase. The precise number of European immigrants entering North America in 1700–83 is not known, but recent estimates suggest that it was between 330,000 and 450,000 people.[22] A prominent and novel feature of this immigration is that it was more British than English. The single biggest group of migrants were Protestant Irish from Ulster. Between 1717 and 1783, at least 150,000 such people, who were known as the Scotch-Irish, migrated to North America. Most entered via the Delaware River, from whence many pushed westwards and southwards to establish themselves as small farmers in the interior. During the same period, between 70,000 to 80,000 migrants also left Scotland for North America. These were what we would now call 'economic refugees', seeking to escape the hardships of life in countries where land was scarce, rents were high, and economic opportunities generally very limited. Another novel feature of eighteenth-century immigration into North America was the presence – alongside the substantial proportion of the migrants who still came from the London and Home Counties area – of a new element of English migration, composed of about 50,000 people from the counties of northern England.[23]

Most of the other immigrants were from Central Europe with possibly as many as 100,000 from German-speaking territories. People from various regions of Germany and Switzerland sailed to America to escape the effects of war and religious persecution, and made very distinctive contributions to the social development of certain regions, particularly in the Middle Atlantic colonies.[24] The presence of German-speakers was strongest in Pennsylvania. Benjamin Franklin estimated that, in 1766, about a third of Pennsylvania's population was composed of German-speakers, and he complained that they would 'shortly become so numerous as to Germanize us instead of our Anglifying them', turning Pennsylvania into a 'a colony of Aliens'.[25] British North America was, then, already showing signs of that capacity to attract foreign immigrants that was to reach such astonishing proportions a century later, long after the colonies had become the United States.[26]

While immigration propelled demographic growth, population increase was mainly driven by an extraordinary rhythm of natural increase. Rates of growth varied between colonies, but they were generally extraordinarily high by contemporary European standards. In New England, the average increase of population was around 2.4 per cent per year from 1670 to 1780; in the Chesapeake colonies of Virginia and Maryland, it was about 2.7 per cent; in the Middle Atlantic colonies, it was even higher, with a remarkable annual average growth rate of about 3.4 per cent between 1690 and 1780. Most people (about a third) lived in the South, where Virginia was the single largest colony of North America (and of Anglo-America as a whole), but the most striking development of the eighteenth century was the very rapid growth of population in the Middle Atlantic region, particularly in Pennsylvania. Allowing for variations between regions, British North America as a whole showed an annual average growth rate of 3 per cent in 1660–1780, a rate of growth which increased the population by about a third every decade. This was twice as high as the growth rate in the British Caribbean islands for the same period, as well as being much higher than that of most European countries, where the rate was generally less than 1 per cent per year even at the time of rapid growth during the later eighteenth century.[27]

A number of factors lay behind this phenomenal reproductive capacity, but the key influences were a plentiful supply of cheap land and a broader horizon of economic opportunity than that found in the old societies of Europe. Access to land encouraged people to marry earlier than they did in Europe, while cheap and abundant food enhanced female fertility and reduced infant mortality. Cheap food may also have helped fortify people against the effects of epidemic diseases, for, though less prone to epidemics than European countries, the North American colonies were not free of this scourge. Smallpox, diphtheria, yellow fever, influenza and malaria struck in several regions at different times during the eighteenth century, killing large numbers, and cities such as Boston, Charleston and Philadelphia were especially prone to the ravages of epidemics. Mortality from epidemics was nonetheless much lower than in Europe, probably because plentiful food created a healthier population with greater resistance to disease, and because a more widespread dispersion of settlement inhibited the rapid transmission of contagion. Certainly contemporaries were in no doubt that the high standard of living in the North American colonies was the cause of their population increase. Adam Smith, for example, concluded that 'the great multiplication of the species' in North America was due to the fact that high wages, low food prices and the absence of dearth encouraged early marriage, large families and a long lifespan.[28]

Whatever the causes of rapid population growth, its consequences are plain enough. First, it led to greater density of settlement in populated areas, where neglected lands were brought into cultivation; second, it pushed the frontier of settlement into new lands, previously untouched by white farmers. All the continental colonies saw movements on their frontiers, with the largest internal migrations stemming from Pennsylvania and New England. Before mid-century, farmers and land speculators were already reaching inland into Pennsylvania and beyond, into the Carolina hills; so, too, were land-seekers from Virginia and Maryland.

The western frontier settlements had different economies from those of the older coastal societies, and differences in the economic interests and political concerns of established and frontier communities produced tensions between them. The gap between coastal and frontier societies was particularly obvious in the Carolinas, where the planter/slave society of the coast was counterbalanced by a backcountry peopled by small farmers. Geopolitical strains were often reinforced by cultural differences, as many of those who ventured in the interior were German and Ulster immigrants who formed communities that had little in common with the English societies closer to the Atlantic shore. Movement from New England, the other major source of internal migration, also created new communities which brought conflict in their wake. After the British acquisition of

Canada in 1763, New England settlers surged northwards and westwards, into Nova Scotia, the Connecticut Valley and the Upper Hudson Valley. In the latter, they disputed for territory with New York, which claimed prior jurisdiction, leading to sporadic border warfare between whites, and between whites and Indians.

Movement into the interior was also driven by land speculation. Since the early days of English colonization, possession of land had been regarded as a key to wealth, and the great proprietors of colonies such as Maryland, New York and the Carolinas had sought and obtained huge grants of land from the crown in the hope of future profit. As the rising influx of immigrants added to local demands for land, such speculation in land became more common in the eighteenth century. Both individuals and companies bought up land as a commodity for future sale, awaiting or promoting its settlement as a means of bringing a good return on their investment. A famous instance of such speculation was the Ohio Company, organized in 1747 by a group of wealthy Virginia and Maryland planters in order to acquire vast tracts of land across the Allegheny Mountains, where, they argued, their venture would secure the land against the French, who also claimed the territory. In this case, as in others, movement on the frontier arose from the plans of rich men to acquire land in strategically sensitive regions, taking advantage of British animosity towards France as a means of drawing central governments into supporting private profit-making ventures. In this manner, land companies became a significant factor in the politics of frontier expansion and conflict, interacting with the larger struggle between Britain and France.

COLONIAL COMMERCE AND ECONOMIC GROWTH

If rapid demographic growth was one motor for colonial economic growth during the eighteenth century, the other was the expansion of external trade. Seen as a whole, Anglo-American colonial commerce retained the basic structure developed in the previous century, when it had been grounded in the export of agricultural goods and raw materials, particularly tropical and semi-tropical products. However, over the course of the eighteenth century, this pattern of trade changed in both scale and composition, as existing circuits of commerce were greatly enlarged, and new products and markets developed.

Throughout the eighteenth century, sugar and its derivatives were the most valuable exports produced by Britain's colonies. After a slow start in the early decades of the century, the trade in sugar, which had long been the central commodity in British colonial commerce, grew rapidly from the early 1730s. During the first half of the eighteenth century, the volume of Britain's sugar trade doubled; it then doubled again between mid-century and the mid-1770s.[29] The basis for this growth lay mainly within Britain, which consumed a growing proportion of the sugar produced by the West Indian colonies. English people of all social classes took to using sugar to sweeten tea, which during the eighteenth century was becoming a national addiction, and coffee, which was popular among a narrower segment of society; they also became increasingly fond of rum, which became a substitute for French brandy and an alternative to gin.

These demands of metropolitan consumers ensured that, though the continental colonies held most of the British colonies' population, the West Indies remained Britain's most valuable colonial possessions. At the start of the century, they were already supplying about 13 per cent of British imports; by 1772–3 they were contributing about a quarter of all trade entering Britain. The Caribbean islands were less important as a market for goods exported from Britain, but here, too, they occupied considerable weight in the balances of British commerce. At the start of the century, the West Indies took about 5 per cent of total British exports; by 1772–3, they took 12 per cent.[30] Table 8.3 indicates the general course of West Indian commerce before it was disrupted by the onset of the American Revolution.

Table 8.3 British imports from and exports to the West Indies, 1700–73 (in £000 and as a percentage of total British imports and exports).

Years	Imports	% of total	Exports	% of total
1700–1	785	13.4	205	4.6
1730 1	1,586	21.4	374	7.2
1750–1	1,484	18.8	449	5.0
1772–3	3,222	23.7	1,226	12.0

Note: Figures for years before 1772 for England and Wales only
Source: Mitchell, *British Historical Statistics*, p. 496

The growth of sugar exports was associated with both continuity and change in West Indian patterns of production and commerce.[31]

Continuity was evident in the continuing trend towards export monoculture: during the eighteenth century, the Caribbean islands became increasingly geared to sugar production and dependent on exporting to Britain. Change was reflected in the emergence of Jamaica as the greatest single sugar producer in the British West Indies from around 1720, and in alterations in the direction and composition of the sugar trade. The latter changes were prompted by the planters' need to cope with the effects of growing competition in the international sugar trade. Following the War of the Spanish Succession, sugar prices declined for twenty years, confronting the planters with economic difficulties to which they had to adjust. One method of adjustment was to seek protection, by persuading the home government to prevent the import of foreign (mainly French) sugar, molasses and rum into Great Britain, Ireland or the North American colonies. This the planters achieved with the Molasses Act of 1733, which placed higher import duties on foreign sugar and its derivatives. This measure did not succeed in keeping foreign sugar out of North American markets, where merchants colluded with customs men to evade the law, but the Act did give the planters some protection to compensate for their losses to French competition in the European sugar trade.[32] West Indian planters also responded to growing competition by developing markets for sugar derivatives in North America, thereby enlarging their trade with the continental colonies. Between 1726–30 and 1773–4, the value of West Indian exports to North America increased threefold, as part of a general pattern of growth in trade between the island and continental colonies.[33] Finally, planters responded to changing market conditions by processing sugar into forms other than the traditional brown muscovado that was produced by their competitors, and thereby opened new markets for refined white sugar. Their ability to increase production at a time of falling prices also suggests that they achieved gains in productivity by innovation in the organization of production.[34]

The periodic difficulties which planters experienced during the early decades of the eighteenth century were generally replaced by good times in the years between mid–century and the start of the American Revolution in 1776. Prosperity was of course occasionally threatened by war. On the whole, however, international conflict hurt French more than British sugar interests, because British naval supremacy protected the West Indies while simultaneously hindering the trade and production of French rivals.[35] The long–term tendency for sugar prices to fall, due to the massive increases in Caribbean sugar production, also failed to harm West Indian producers. For, while prices fell, the size of the market grew at a much faster pace due to the tremendous growth of demand in Britain and the North American colonies, where growing populations with larger incomes and a taste for tea, coffee and rum pushed up the consumption of sugar and its derivatives. This was, then, the 'silver age' of the British West Indies, when the planters reached the peak of their prosperity. Recent estimates of the per capita wealth of whites in the islands, compared to their continental counterparts, provide a striking measure of that prosperity. In 1771–5, West Indian whites had an average net worth of between £878 and £1,000, a level many times higher than that found among whites and free people in any of the continental colonies, where average worth per white person was £74 in *c.* 1770–4.[36]

The commerce of North America also underwent a striking expansion during the eighteenth century. As Table 8.4 shows, exports from the continental colonies to Britain gradually increased their share of total British imports about 6 per cent in 1700–1 to over 14 per cent in 1772–3.

Table 8.4 British imports from and exports to the North American colonies, 1700–73 (in £000 and as a percentage of total British imports and exports).

Years	Imports	% of total	Exports	% of total
1700–1	372	6.3	362	7.7
1730–1	655	8.7	559	6.8
1750–1	877	11.2	1,179	9.4
1772–3	1,977	14.5	3,254	19.0

Note: Figures for years before 1772 for England and Wales only
Source: Mitchell, *British Historical Statistics*, p. 496

Tobacco retained its place as the most valuable of North American exports, as its continuing growth was sustained by a great enlargement of re-exports to Europe. But British North America was far from depending on the export of a single commodity. As Table 8.5 indicates, rice and indigo from the Lower American South were important exports, while the Middle Atlantic colonies exported valuable cargoes of bread and flour, and New England exported large quantities of fish. Together with tobacco, these five commodities represented 63 per cent of the total value of North American exports in 1768–72. The rest of the trade comprised a large variety of primary commodities, in which deerskins, naval stores, whale oil, iron and flaxseed figure as the most important items in a large spectrum of minor exports.

Table 8.5 Principal North American exports, 1768–72 (annual averages).

Export	Value (£)
Tobacco	766,000
Bread and flour	410,000
Rice	312,000
Fish	154,000
Indigo	113,000

Source: Gary M. Walton and James F. Shepherd, *The Economic Rise of Early America*, p. 81

The expansion of North American colonial commerce derived partly from increased consumption of agricultural staples in British markets, but the continental colonies had a much more varied pattern of trade than the colonies in the Caribbean. While some 58 per cent of North American exports went to Britain in 1768–72, the remainder found markets outside the parent power. A major outlet, especially for New England and the Middle Atlantic colonies, was in the Caribbean, which took 27 per cent of North American commerce; the countries of southern Europe also provided markets for foodstuffs, and took 14 per cent of North American exports. Dependence on Britain varied between regions, of course. The American South depended heavily on the British connection, which took about three-quarters of Chesapeake and Lower South exports. For both the New England and Middle Atlantic colonies, Britain was much less important, since it took only about 20 per cent of their exports, while the remainder went to markets in the West Indies and to southern Europe.[37]

Shipping and transportation services were another aspect of North American commercial activity which contributed substantially to the colonies' earnings and prosperity. Mainly organized by merchants and seamen from the New England region, and to a lesser extent by men from the Middle Atlantic ports, North American ships carried goods to and from Europe, Africa and many regions in the Americas, including those under British, French and Spanish control. The importance of this activity can be gauged from the fact that, in 1768–72, earnings from this maritime carrying services probably outstripped those from the sale of tobacco, North America's single largest export.[38] Thus, though most of the trades of the West Indies, and to a lesser extent the American South, were controlled by British merchants, the northern colonies' trade, some of the slave trade, and the intercolonial and southern European commerce were mainly managed by North American merchants and shippers, who brought earnings from trade to their home regions.

The regions of British North America did not all participate in, or benefit equally from overseas trade. The largest export earnings went to the Chesapeake colonies, which in 1768–72 earned over £1 million per year from their exports (£1.82 per capita). The Lower South and the Middle Atlantic region each earned about £0.5 million on annual average during the same period (£1.78 and $1.03 per capita respectively), while New England took annual export takings which averaged about £440,000 (£0.84 per capita).[39] Although the continental colonies evidently did not have the same opportunities to gain from commerce, all participated in overseas commerce, and contact with external markets was everywhere an important impulse for economic growth.

The growth of North American exports was matched by an increase in the continental colonies' capacity to import goods from abroad. Imports grew considerably during the eighteenth century, not only because the population grew larger but also because North American whites generally enjoyed a high standard of living which made the continental colonies an attractive market.[40] Thus the total value of British imports into North America increased ninefold between 1700–1 and 1772–3 (see Table 8.4), while per capita imports from Britain rose by about a third over the same period. Expansion was particularly rapid from the 1740s, bringing a 'consumer revolution' to continental American markets.[41]

Most imports (about 78 per cent in 1768–72) came from Britain, and consisted almost entirely of manufactured and semi-manufactured goods. These were mainly textiles of various kinds, particularly English woollens and Irish linen. Hats and metalware were also items, followed by a miscellany of products covering a range of household goods, such as glassware and tableware, and, to a lesser extent, paper, gunpowder, tea, pepper and drugs. Leaving aside imports of slaves from Africa, the remaining 22 per cent of imports came from foreign and colonial sources. Southern Europe supplied about 2 per cent of North America's imports, of which wine from Madeira was the most valuable. Far more important, as the source of about 20 per cent of North American imports, were the West Indian islands: these provided molasses, rum and semi-refined sugar, exchanged against the increasingly large quantities of foodstuffs, livestock, timber products, tallow and oil which North Americans exported to the Caribbean.[42]

THE COLONIES AND THE COLONIAL SYSTEM

The vitality of colonial commerce during the eighteenth century testified to the success of the British colonial system which, for all its mercantilist restrictions, allowed colonial producers and merchants to thrive. The navigation laws imposed restraints on colonial production and commerce, but the burden of restriction was slight. Indeed, the British colonial system was a huge area of free trade which embraced over 7 million people at mid-century, governed by laws which, by combining freedom and protection, provided a basis for economic growth in all the major colonial regions.

One way to appreciate the advantages of the British colonial system is to contrast its flexible regulations with the rigid rules that imperial Spain imposed on its American colonies. For most of the colonial period, Spain imposed strict controls over the trade of its American dominions in ways that tended to curb rather than to cultivate the commercialization of colonial resources. The great bulk of Spanish colonial trade was canalized through a single monopoly port in the peninsula and a few entrepôts in the Americas; with a few minor exceptions, transatlantic traffic was confined to a system of fleets which sailed at prearranged intervals between these ports. To compound these constraints, the Spanish crown granted a small group of peninsular merchants a virtual monopoly over transatlantic trade, thereby allowing them to profit from exchanging high-priced (and heavily taxed) European imports for precious metals, while giving them little incentive to develop colonial exports. Finally, Spain also restricted intercolonial commerce and prohibited trade with foreigners, thus depriving the colonies of outlets for goods for which Spain had no markets. The British system was, by contrast, more open and pliable. The navigation laws allowed trade within the empire to all British subjects, including colonials, and authorized merchants and shippers to move freely between all British and colonial ports. The laws also permitted colonials to trade with foreigners in non-enumerated goods, thereby providing vents for goods for which Britain itself had little or no need. Unlike Spain, Britain avoided burdening its colonial commerce with a heavy weight of taxation, and sought instead to promote the interests of traders and producers within the colonial system.

The relatively relaxed rules of the British colonial system had important implications for the development of the Anglo-American colonies. In the first place, they allowed colonial producers to trade with foreign markets in Europe, as well as foreign and colonial markets in the Americas, all of which gave them outlets for temperate agricultural commodities which would otherwise have had only small local markets. Contacts with markets in the Caribbean, where the sugar-producing islands offered a dynamic demand for foodstuffs, were particularly important for New England and the Middle Atlantic colonies, linking them indirectly with growth in Britain. The Spanish Caribbean islands failed to function in the same way for Spain's continental colonies. For most of the colonial period, the islands of Cuba, Puerto Rico and Santo Domingo were poor, largely self-sufficient agricultural economies, rather than prosperous specialist monocultures of the kind found in the British and French islands. Even when Cuba began its rapid development as a sugar producer in the later eighteenth century, it took relatively few of its foodstuffs from neighbouring Spanish colonies on the mainland; by the end of the Spanish colonial period, Cuba became enmeshed in the networks of British North American trade, through which the newly independent United States supplied growing amounts of basic food-stuffs, and shipping services.[43] Second, the British system permitted colonials to participate fully in their own trade, both as merchants and carriers. This encouraged the development of independent merchant groups in the major North American ports, and enabled some colonies to become major centres for shipbuilding and shipping services. Indeed, although British merchants controlled most of the trades of the West Indies and to a lesser extent the American South, North American merchants and shippers managed virtually all the northern colonies' trade, some of the slave trade, and most of the intercolonial and southern European commerce and thus brought earnings from trade to their home regions. Third, British tariff policies tended to promote the growth of metropolitan industry, and hence, in the long term, provided the colonies with relatively cheap sources of manufactured goods.

Britain did of course impose restrictions on colonial production which cramped some areas of economic enterprise and development. The Hat Act of 1731, for example, discriminated against colonial manufacturers by prohibiting the export of colonial-made fur hats to Britain in order to protect London hatters, while the Iron Act of 1749 prohibited the finishing of iron and steel in the colonies. Generally, however, such restrictions were of little consequence. The Iron Act did not prevent the continuing operation of iron mills in colonies such as Pennsylvania and Delaware, nor did it inhibit the creation of new ones. Meanwhile, other kinds of industry were unaffected by legal constraints, and during the eighteenth century responded to growing colonial demand for processed and manufactured goods. Rum distilleries, sugar refineries, flour mills, sawmills, shipbuilding, and textile and shoe manufacturing all found room for growth; in their development some historians detect a process of proto-industrialization in late colonial North America.[44]

If manufacturing industries did not develop on a scale which might compete with those of Britain, it was not simply because mercantilist restrictions impeded the growth of colonial industry. Much more important was the fact that land was plentiful and cheap in the colonies, while labour and capital were relatively dear. This was clearly understood by Adam Smith, who pointed out that the supply of cheap land in the continental colonies inhibited manufacturing in the colonies because, by allowing many Americans to achieve personal economic independence as farmers, it pushed up the cost of labour.[45] At the same time, agricultural producers in North America profited from expansion of markets for their products both within the British colonial system and outside it. Britain took growing quantities of tobacco and rice, mostly for re-export to Europe, while growth in the West Indies' sugar trade enlarged the islands' demands for North American grain, meat, fish and timber products. American shipbuilding and shipping also boomed, thanks to the general growth of commerce with Europe, the Caribbean, and between the continental colonies themselves. While prices for their products tended to increase more than those for goods bought from Britain, colonial consumers benefited from metropolitan economic growth. For, as British manufacturing expanded rapidly in response to home and overseas markets, colonials could obtain a broad range of manufactures from Britain at affordable prices; as purchasing power rose, common people were increasingly able to buy goods previously regarded as luxuries. Finally, rising living standards and the 'consumer revolution' were reinforced by the inflows of capital which Britain made available to North Americans during the eighteenth century, as its successful banking system enabled British exporters to supply American planters, merchants and shopkeepers with abundant credit.[46]

THE ANGLO-AMERICAN COLONIES AFTER THE SEVEN YEARS WAR

In 1760, Benjamin Franklin remarked that 'the foundations of the future greatness and stability of the British Empire lie in America. . . . All the country from the St. Lawrence to the Mississippi will in another century be filled with British people'.[47] After Britain's triumph in the Seven Years War, sealed at the Peace of Paris in 1763, his prediction seemed ready to be fulfilled. Spain, England's old enemy, and France, its great contemporary rival, had both been forced out of the eastern half of the American continent; now that Britain had vanquished its European competitors, the growing North American colonies seemed to have unprecedented opportunities for expanding their settlement and trade. For more than a decade after the war, the broad upward trends in trade and production were sustained in most of the colonies. The import of slaves from Africa into the Caribbean islands grew at a fast pace after 1763, and West Indian trade with both Britain and the North American colonies reached its zenith in 1768–75.[48] The trade of the continental colonies meanwhile followed a similar, though more regionally varied pattern of expansion. Rising demand for grain in southern European markets favoured farmers in the Middle Atlantic colonies; rice and indigo planters in South Carolina saw their overseas markets expand; and the shippers and traders of the major North American ports continued to enlarge their business to the point where they carried the bulk of the mainland colonies' trade. Population also continued to grow at a fast pace. After 1760, streams of emigrants poured out of Europe, drawn by the prospects of cheap or free land. Between 1760 and 1776, close to 140,000 new migrants may have disembarked in North American ports: some 55,000 came from Ulster, 40,000 from Scotland and 30,000 from England and Wales, while around 12,000 German-speaking migrants followed the routes traced by others of their kind earlier in the century.[49] The rate of reproduction in colonial families also remained very high and, when combined with immigration, pushed up the white population of North America by nearly half a million within a decade after 1765. Thus the remarkable growth in population and economic activity which had characterized the first half of the eighteenth century extended into the years that followed the Seven Years War, and Britain's 'empire of goods' continued to prosper. When he published his *Wealth of Nations* in 1776, Adam Smith observed that, 'though North America is not yet as rich as

England, it is much more thriving, and advancing with greater rapidity to the further acquisition of riches'.[50]

These long-term trends in demographic and economic growth enriched Britain's empire, and brought a measure of convergence in the social and cultural development of metropolis and its American dominions, as the colonies became more structurally similar both to each other and to the mother country. Culturally, the elites sought to imitate metropolitan institutions and values, shared a sense of Protestant solidarity against Catholic France and Spain, and, buoyed up by both Britain's rise to power and their own rapid economic progress, tended to identify strongly with the mother country. Experience of war, to which colonials contributed both money and men, had probably reinforced their sense of 'Britishness'. For colonials not only fought on their own borders, but also participated in war outside their homelands. North American soldiers had, for example, been present in Vernon's attacks on Spanish possessions in the Caribbean in the early 1740s, and during the Seven Years War, colonial militiamen also fought alongside British troops, participating, for example, in the famous capture of Quebec. At the same time, economic growth created complex, confident and volatile societies, which were more internally differentiated and urbanized than in the past, more marked by inequalities of wealth and status, and led by self-confident provincial elites who asserted their right to local rule. Thus, it has been said that the mainland colonies were becoming increasingly 'Europeanized'.[51]

If the gulf between metropolitan and colonial societies was being reduced, so in some respects were differences between the Anglo-American colonies. An obvious point of colonial convergence is found in the regions of plantations and slavery. The Lower South came closest to the type of economy and society found in the British Caribbean. South Carolina depended heavily for its growing wealth on the export of tropical staples (rice and indigo), and, as the only continental colony with a black slave majority, seemed to be developing into a society comparable to those of the West Indies. The colonies of the Chesapeake region were also strongly influenced by dependence on export-oriented plantation agriculture, built on black slavery.

We should not exaggerate these similarities, however, for although the regions of the American South were deeply engaged in plantation agriculture for export, their economies were more diverse and self-sufficient than those of the West Indies. As tobacco production moved into the interior during the eighteenth century, the

Chesapeake region began to diversify its agricultural production, particularly into grain cultivation for local and export markets.[52] The economies of the American South also relied less on slave imports than the West Indies, as their slave populations were replenished by natural reproduction. If South Carolina planters showed a tendency towards absenteeism, the great planters of the Chesapeake region formed self-conscious, confident elites who were closely identified with their localities, and exercised political power based on a broad spectrum of support from substantial white communities of tenants, farmers and smaller planters.

The divergence of North American from Caribbean patterns of development was even more evident in the colonies of the Middle Atlantic and New England regions. In the former, rising grain prices brought prosperity to large numbers of family farmers who formed the backbone of society. In Pennsylvania and New York particularly, flourishing trades in grains and livestock accompanied demographic and territorial expansion, together with the rapid growth of ports, petty manufacturing, shipping and shipbuilding. New England, which had fewer exportable agricultural commodities, benefited less from commercial expansion, but there, too, trade in the products of farms, forests and fisheries, together with a flourishing shipbuilding and shipping industry, supported the continuing development of an increasingly commercialized and urbanized society, with widespread participation in the market economy. If, however, the North American colonies showed a more obvious trend towards Europeanization than their Caribbean counterparts, they nonetheless remained very different from the parent power. They were, moreover, passing through an exceptionally intensive period of social and economic change, so that, as Gordon Wood points out, 'just at the moment when some parts of American society seemed to be becoming more like England's, powerful forces were accelerating and changing everything'.[53]

These forces of demographic and economic growth had a more disruptive impact in most regions of North America than they did in the colonies of the West Indies. In the Caribbean islands, the expansion of the sugar trades spread and deepened the influence of slavery, which in turn discouraged conflict between whites, and hardened the region's dependence on the mother country. In the continental colonies, by contrast, demographic and commercial expansion produced more internally differentiated and mobile societies which showed symptoms of disruption and stress. Population growth greatly increased the demand for land, leading to feverish land speculation, disputes over land rights, and internal migrations that tended to weaken the ties of family and community in the older settled areas. Movement and instability in the countryside was paralleled by growing inequalities in the cities, where wealth became more concentrated in landowning and mercantile elites, and the numbers of the poor multiplied.[54]

The colonies' deepening engagement in overseas trade also created instabilities and tensions, because it exposed them to cyclical fluctuations that brought periodic recession. The first of these occurred at the end of the Seven Years War, when reductions in British wartime expenditures, a contraction of business credit, and curbs on the issue of paper money (imposed by the Currency Act of 1764) caused sharp deflation in the continental colonies. A British banking crash caused further economic disruption in 1772, leading to bankruptcies among planters in the Chesapeake as well as the West Indies (where economic problems were exacerbated by the effects of the severe hurricane of that same year). These periodic problems brought complaint from the producers and traders who were most closely involved in external trade. Planters in the Chesapeake resented their reliance on British merchants who extended them credit at high interest rates; unlike West Indian planters who benefited from British legislation which protected their markets, they chafed at laws that forced them to sell tobacco in metropolitan markets at lower prices than they might have obtained by exporting directly to Europe. Similarly, farmers and merchants in the New England and Middle Atlantic colonies disliked curbs on their trade with foreign colonies in Spanish America and the French West Indies, and showed their impatience with such restraints by seeking to evade them, even when Britain was at war with Spain and France.[55]

Britain's success in supplying its colonies with cheap manufactured imports also provoked envy and complaint in some quarters. From mid-century, colonial merchants who wanted to share in the profits of trade with Britain resented the sharp commercial practices of British merchants, who undercut them by selling goods at auction and dealing directly with shopkeepers on liberal credit terms.[56] On the other hand, the spread of commercialism among the common people, who strove to increase their incomes in order to purchase consumer goods, also elicited objections from social conservatives and religious leaders who saw such materialism as a threat to social hierarchy and morality.[57]

These tensions did not of themselves endanger the colonial connection with Britain. However, in the aftermath of the Seven Years War, internal frictions within North American societies were matched by disharmony in their external relations with Britain. This discord sprang directly from the great extension of British colonial dominion brought about by the Seven Years War. The 1763 settlement at Paris seemed to have strengthened the empire, bringing new territory and resources. But it had also brought unforeseen complications, confronting British governments with new burdens of administration and of defence against enemies who were preparing for an opportunity to recoup their losses. To cope with these burdens, British governments, like those in Spain and France, began to consider ways of tightening administrative and economic control over the colonies. In so doing, they entered into conflict with colonies which, with the demographic and economic growth of previous decades, had become more expansive societies led by elites whose sense of autonomy was buoyed up by confidence in the economic potential of their lands. Indeed, by exalting the virtues of the British constitution and the rights of 'free born' Englishmen, the patriotic rhetoric of wartime had tended to strengthened colonials' convictions of their rights to self-government within the empire. Thus, once freed from the threat of French attack, these elites tended to become more insubordinate in their attitudes towards the metropolitan power.

In the West Indies, reliance on the British market, combined with the continuing military threat from France and fear of rebellion among the slave populations, encouraged loyalty among the islands' elites. But such dependence was much weaker in North America. After the French threat had been removed from North America by British victory in the Seven Years War, the peoples of the continental colonies became more conscious of the constraints of empire, and when metropolitan governments began to demand that they bear a heavier share of its responsibilities, they joined first in protest, then in open rebellion against the mother country. To the origins and outcome of that rebellion, which was to bring a protracted war of secession and a partial disintegration of the Anglo-American empire, we must now turn our attention.

NOTES

1   For a comprehensive, balanced outline of Britain's rise to power at the turn of the century, see Geoffrey Holmes, *The Making of a Great Power: Late Stuart and Early Georgian England, 1660–1722* (London, 1993) pp. 212–65.

2 John Brewer, *The Sinews of Power: War, Money and the English State, 1688–1783* (London, 1989) p. 137.

3 For an analysis of the European context of King William's War and the War of the Spanish Succession, and their implications for Britain, see J.R. Jones, *Britain and the World (1649–1815)* (London, 1980) pp. 133–78. On the importance of commercial considerations, see Holmes, *The Making of a Great Power*, pp. 248–53.

4 For a brief account of the issues and events of the 1739–48 war, see Jones, *Britain and the World*, pp. 195–206; for a more detailed account, see Richard Pares, *War and Trade in the West Indies, 1739–1763* (London, 1963) pp. 65–127.

5 On North American interests in contraband trade with the Spanish colonies before and during the War of Jenkins' Ear, see Peggy K. Liss, *Atlantic Empires: The Network of Trade and Revolution, 1713–1826* (Baltimore, Md, and London, 1983) pp. 27–8.

6 Robin Blackburn, *The Overthrow of Colonial Slavery, 1776–1848* (London, 1988) pp. 69–77. On the emergence of British nationalism, see also Linda Colley, *Forging the Nation, 1707–1837* (New Haven, Conn., and London, 1992) pp. 1–100; on growing American identification with British culture and politics, see Ian K. Steele, *The English Atlantic, 1675–1740: An Exploration of Communication and Community* (New York, 1986) pp. 229–71.

7 On the Brazilian gold boom, see A.J.R. Russell-Wood, 'Colonial Brazil: the gold cycle, c. 1690–1750', in L. Bethell (ed) *Cambridge History of Latin America*, vol. 2 (Cambridge, 1984) pp. 547–600, especially pp. 594, 598–9; on Anglo-Portuguese trade, see H.E.S. Fisher, 'Anglo–Portuguese trade, 1700–1770', in Walter Minchinton (ed) *The Growth of English Overseas Trade in the Seventeenth and Eighteenth Centuries* (London, 1969).

8 For some statistics on British trade with South America and the foreign West Indies, see B.R. Mitchell, *British Historical Statistics* (Cambridge, 1988) pp. 492–4. Its effects on Spanish American commerce are detailed in Geoffrey J. Walker, *Spanish Politics and Imperial Trade, 1700–1789* (London, 1979).

9 For these figures, see Seymour Drescher, *Econocide: British Slavery in the Era of Abolition* (Pittsburgh, Pa, 1977) Table 2, p. 21; for comparison of West Indian and North American shares of British exports to, and imports from the extra-European world, see Tables 3 and 4, pp. 22–3.

10 Eric Williams, *Capitalism and Slavery* (London, 1964 edition), especially Chapters 3 and 5; quotation from p. 52.

11 Eric Williams, *From Columbus to Castro: The History of the Caribbean, 1492–1969* (London, 1970) p. 166.

12 Rebuttals of Williams's contention are found in Roger Anstey, *The Atlantic Slave Trade and British Abolition, 1760–1810* (London, 1975) pp. 49–51; Stanley L. Engerman, 'The slave trade and British capital formation in the eighteenth century: a comment on the Williams thesis', *Business History Review (1972)* **46**: 430–43, and J.R. Ward, 'The profitability of sugar planting in the British West Indies, 1650–1834', *Economic History Review*, 2nd series (1978) **31**: 197–213.

13 Barbara L. Solow, 'Capitalism and slavery in the exceedingly long run', in Barbara L. Solow and Stanley L. Engerman (eds) *British Capitalism and*

Caribbean Slavery: The Legacy of Eric Williams (Cambridge, 1987) pp. 51–77; quotation from p. 73.

14 David Richardson, 'The slave trade, sugar and British economic growth, 1748–1776', in Solow and Engerman (eds) *British Capitalism and Caribbean Slavery*, especially pp. 124–33.

15 For a view of the debate, see R.P. Thomas, 'Overseas trade and empire, 1700–1860', in Roderick Floud and Donald McCloskey (eds) *The Economic History of Britain since 1700: Volume I, 1700–1860* (Cambridge, 1981) pp. 87–102. An excellent recent reassessment, which accords greater importance to the role of overseas trade, is given by Pat Hudson, *The Industrial Revolution* (London, 1992) pp. 181–200.

16 Population figures from Greene, *Pursuits of Happiness*, pp. 178–9, and from John J. McCusker and Russell R. Menard, *The Economy of British America, 1607–1789* (Chapel Hill, NC, and London, 1985) p. 54.

17 Jamaica took nearly 38 per cent of the total slaves imported in this period, some of which were re-exported to other destinations. See Philip D. Curtin, *The Atlantic Slave Trade: A Census* (Madison, Wis., 1969) Tables 40 and 65, pp. 140, 216.

18 Selwyn H.H. Carrington, *The British West Indies during the American Revolution* (Dordrecht, 1988) Tables 1 and 16, pp. 8, 26. An even higher estimate of slavery mortality in Barbados, suggesting that slave imports were ten times greater than slave population increase, is given in J.H. Parry, Philip Sherlock and Anthony Maingot, *A Short History of the West Indies* (London, 1969 edition) p. 88.

19 Carrington, *The British West Indies during the American Revolution*, Tables 3 and 11, pp. 10, 19.

20 McCusker and Menard, *Economy of British America*, p. 54.

21 Greene, *Pursuits of Happiness*, p. 176.

22 Estimates from Jim Potter, 'Demographic development and family structure', in Jack P. Greene and J.R. Pole (eds) *Colonial British America: Essays in the New History of the Early Modern Era* (Baltimore, Md, and London, 1984) pp. 135–6; and Ida Altman and James Horn (eds) *'To Make America': European Emigration in the Early Modern Period* (Berkeley and Los Angeles, Calif., 1991) p. 3.

23 David Hackett Fischer, *Albion's Seed: Four British Folkways in America* (New York, 1989) pp. 608–9, note 8; Altman and Horn (eds) *'To Make America'*, p. 3.

24 Marianne Wokeck, 'Harnessing the lure of the "Best Poor Man's Country": the dynamics of German-speaking immigration to British North America, 1683–1783', in Altman and Horn (eds) *'To Make America'*, pp. 204–43; A.G. Roeber, '"The origin of whatever is not English among us': The Dutch-speaking and the German-speaking peoples of colonial British America"', in Bernard Bailyn and Philip D. Morgan, *Strangers within the Realm: Cultural Margins of the First British Empire* (Chapel Hill, NC, and London, 1991) pp. 237–83.

25 Leonard W. Labaree (ed) *The Papers of Benjamin Franklin*, vol. 4 (New Haven, Conn., 1961) p. 233.

26 On the importance of non-British immigration in the late colonial period, see T.L. Purvis, 'The European ancestry of the United States population, 1790', *William and Mary Quarterly*, 3rd series (1984) **41**: 85–101.

27 McCusker and Menard, *Economy of British America*, pp. 229–30.
28 Adam Smith, *The Wealth of Nations, Books I–III* (Harmondsworth, 1986) p. 173.
29 Richard B. Sheridan, *Sugar and Slavery: An Economic History of the British West Indies 1623–1775* (Barbados, 1974) Tables 18.1 and 19.2, pp. 418, 450; also Appendix I, pp. 487–9.
30 Ibid., Appendix VIII, gives annual figures for West Indian imports from Britain for 1697–1775.
31 Ibid., pp. 415–59, gives an account of trends in sugar trade and production from the Treaty of Utrecht to the early 1770s.
32 Ibid., pp. 54–74, for the political campaigns by planters which secured this measure.
33 Ibid., Table 14.3, p. 315.
34 Ibid., pp. 342–59; McCusker and Menard, *Economy of British America*, pp. 157–68.
35 For the effect of the 1739–48 war on British sugar planters, see Pares, *War and Trade in the West Indies*, pp. 469–516.
36 Peter A. Coclanis, 'The wealth of British America on the eve of the Revolution', *Journal of Interdisciplinary History* (1990) **21**: 245–60.
37 Gary M. Walton and James F. Shepherd, *The Economic Rise of Early America* (Cambridge, 1979) pp. 79–82.
38 Walton and Shepherd, *Economic Rise of Early America*, p. 100.
39 James F. Shepherd and Gary M. Walton, *Shipping, Maritime Trade and the Development of Colonial North America* (Cambridge, 1972) pp. 44–7.
40 For estimates of growth in income and production during the colonial period, see McCusker and Menard, *Economy of British America*, pp. 55–7.
41 T.H. Breen, 'An empire of goods: the anglicisation of colonial America, 1670–1776', *Journal of British Studies* (1986) **25**: 467–99.
42 Walton and Shepherd, *Economic Rise of Early America*, pp. 83–6; McCusker and Menard, *Economy of British America*, pp. 276–94.
43 Jacques Barbier and Allan J. Kuethe (eds) *The North American Role in the Spanish Imperial Economy, 1760–1819* (Manchester, 1984) *passim*.
44 See the essays by James Henretta and Jacob Price in Ronald Hoffman, John J. McCusker, Russell R. Menard and Peter J. Albert (eds) *The Economy of Early America: The Revolutionary Period, 1763–1790* (Charlottesville, Va, 1988) pp. 45–87, 303–22.
45 When the American artificer (artisan) had acquired capital from his business, Smith observed, 'he does not, in North America, attempt to establish with a manufacture for more distant sale, but employs it in the purchase and improvement of uncultivated land. . . . He feels that an artificer is a servant of his customers . . . but that a planter who cultivates his own land . . . is really a master, and independent of all the world': Smith, *Wealth of Nations*, p. 482.
46 Walton and Shepherd, *Economic Rise of Early America*, pp. 96–143; 170–1; Marc Egnal, 'The economic development of the thirteen continental colonies, 1720 to 1775', *William and Mary Quarterly*, 3rd series (1975) **32**: 199–215.
47 Quoted by Angus Calder, *Revolutionary Empire: The Rise of the English-Speaking Empires from the Fifteenth Century to the 1780s* (London, 1981) p. 633.

48   On West Indian trade in this period, see Carrington, *The British West Indies during the American Revolution*, pp. 22–47.

49   Bernard Bailyn, *Voyagers to the West: Emigration from Britain to America on the Eve of the American Revolution* (London, 1987) p. 26.

50   Smith, *Wealth of Nations*, p. 173.

51   On this process of convergence, see Greene, *Pursuits of Happiness*, pp. 170–206.

52   The extent of such diversification can be gauged from the fact that tobacco fell from over 77 per cent of Virginia's exports in the 1730s to 61 per cent in 1773. See McCusker and Menard, *Economy of British America*, pp. 130–1.

53   Gordon S. Wood, *The Radicalism of the American Revolution* (New York, 1992) p. 124.

54   Gary B. Nash, 'Urban wealth and poverty in pre-revolutionary America', *Journal of Interdisciplinary History* (1976) **VI**: 545–87; James Henretta, 'Economic development and social structure in colonial Boston', *William and Mary Quarterly*, 3rd series (1965) **XXII**: 75–92; Jackson Turner Main, 'The distribution of property in colonial Connecticut', in James Kirby Martin (ed) *The Human Dimensions of Nation Making: Essays on Colonial and Revolutionary America* (Madison, Wis., 1976) pp. 54–107: Gloria L. Main, 'Inequality in early America: the evidence from probate records of Massachusetts and Maryland', *Journal of Interdisciplinary History* (1977) **VII**: 559–81.

55   On the growth of North American trade with Spanish and French America between 1748 and 1776, see Liss, *Atlantic Empires*, pp. 29–32.

56   Marc M. Egnal and Joseph A. Ernst, 'An economic interpretation of the American Revolution', *William and Mary Quarterly*, 3rd series (1972) **29**: 3–32.

57   Wood, *Radicalism of the American Revolution*, pp. 134–6.

CHAPTER NINE
Crisis of Empire

While success in the Seven Years War had shown the strength and resilience of Britain's fiscal-military state, coping with its consequences was soon to reveal the limitations of British imperial power. The war had involved a massive financial outlay, far larger than that required in previous wars; faced with a ballooning national debt, postwar British government looked to the colonies for a larger contribution to imperial expenditures. Raising new taxes from Americans was, however, to prove far more difficult than raising taxes at home. Within Britain, an efficient state, backed by a solid system of public finance and by ministries that legitimized their fiscal demands through parliamentary statute, was able to deliver huge sums without provoking great political instability. In the colonies, especially the North American colonies, conditions were different. There, the power of the state was attenuated by distance and traditions of lax government, people were accustomed to low taxes, and colonial assemblies demanded a right, parallel to that of the British Parliament, to consent to their taxation. Thus, when British governments sought to exert their power at the periphery, they were to face strong resistance from colonials who challenged their right to do so. After a decade of protests, resistance turned into rebellion, and, in 1776, the American Revolution began. How, then, did this conflict develop, why did it affect the continental but not the island colonies, and why, finally, did it escalate into the fratricidal war that ruptured Britain's American empire? To approach these issues, we must first trace the events which, unfolding between 1763 and 1776, poisoned Britain's relations with its North American subjects.

IMPERIAL REORGANIZATION

Immediately after the Seven Years War, the first preoccupation of the British government led by George Grenville was to bring the new American territories acquired by war under British administration and defence. To integrate territory taken from Spain, the new provinces of East and West Florida were established in the south. In the north, the French territory south of the St Lawrence estuary was attached to the British colony of Nova Scotia, while French lands further up the St Lawrence, around Montreal and Quebec, were brought into the new colony of Quebec. The French *habitants* who had been abandoned by their mother country were treated cautiously. The system of French colonial government at Quebec and at other centres of settlement was simply replaced by a British military governor and his lieutenants, and the French population otherwise left in peace. Schemes to tighten Britain's hold on the annexed territories by promoting schemes of emigration into Canada from neighbouring colonies came to nothing; though Canada was now under British sovereignty and open to British trade, it was left as a fundamentally French society, with its social and cultural instititions generally intact. This essential continuity was later formally recognized in the Quebec Act of 1774, by which the British Parliament guaranteed the laws and customs of the French in respect of their legal system and religious life, while nursing the hope that the Quebecois would ultimately become anglicized.[1]

This left British governments with the problem of governing the wilderness west of the Upper St Lawrence and the Appalachian mountains, a vast frontier where the French had previously used Indian allies to block the intrusions of British colonials. Here, government in London faced an immediate dilemma. Indians who had previously used rivalry between France and Britain to defend their territorial and trading interests now feared that the disappearance of the French would open their lands to unchecked settler expansion from the British side. When disputes with unscrupulous traders exacerbated their discontents, Indians attacked outlying settlements in the Great Lakes region in May 1763 and, in the ensuing uprising known as 'Pontiac's Conspiracy', spread terror and death throughout the frontier regions of Virginia, Maryland and Pennsylvania during the months that followed.

To deal with these disturbances in the interior, Parliament passed the Proclamation Act in October 1763. Setting a 'Proclamation Line' or boundary which ran from the Gulf of St Lawrence down the ridge of the coastal mountains to Florida, Parliament decreed that the great territories to the west of the line were reserved to Indians, whatever the claims made by North American colonies and their settlers. The boundary was artificial, since whites and Indians continued to live on both sides of it in some areas, and, because there were insufficient funds to police it rigorously, white settlers continued to drift on to lands which the Indians regarded as theirs. But even though it could not be completely enforced, the Proclamation Act created as many problems as it solved. Colonials disliked it for obstructing the expansionist aspirations of settlers and land speculators; they were also reluctant to pay the costs of maintaining garrisons in the Indian country of the interior. These costs were, moreover, only one part of the larger burden of defence in North America. Britain also had to guard the sparsely inhabited northern and southern provinces which it had taken from France and Spain, and which those powers were expected to try to recover at the earliest opportunity.

British government thus faced new administrative and military problems after the Seven Years War, and to solve them the crown had to find fresh sources of finance. The British treasury was, however, exhausted by war, which had left a huge national debt and had pushed tax rates to unprecedented levels. Within Britain itself, there was strong opposition to any increase in taxation. The British were already the most heavily taxed nation in Europe, and the landed class constantly bewailed the fiscal burdens that it was forced to bear. Governments in London were therefore wary of imposing new taxes at home, for fear of the political consequences. Seen from London, there was in any case an obvious alternative at hand. If the colonies had to be defended, why should not colonials pay more towards their defence?

Americans paid little in taxes compared to people in Britain. The expenses of provincial governments were low because bureaucracy was small, and colonial legislatures consequently voted only small sums for government services. One estimate of provincial taxes during the late colonial period suggests an average payment of between 2 and 4 shillings per person, which represented about 1.5 per cent of estimated per capita income. In England, by contrast, the national tax rate levied by Parliament was between 12 and 18 shillings per person, or about 5 to 7.5 per cent of per capita income.[2] Immediately after the Seven Years War, the disparity was striking. A modern index of relative per capita tax burdens in 1765 in Britain and North America suggests that, if per capita tax in Britain is rated at 100, the equivalent in the major continental colonies was less than 4.[3] Now, even if British ministers were not fully aware of this glaring disparity between national and colonial taxes, they certainly knew that colonials were lightly taxed, and, in the extraordinary financial circumstances that followed the Seven Years War, Grenville, George III's new prime minister, felt fully justified in asking the colonies to contribute to the costs of forces needed for their defence, especially since the Pontiac uprising and the Proclamation Act demanded the presence of British troops on North American territory. But, if British ministers found just cause for taxing the colonies more heavily, their view was widely rejected by colonials.

At first, Grenville decided that the colonies should pay more duties on their trade in order to defray the expenses of their defence. In 1764, he introduced a new Act of Trade which reorganized duties on certain imports into the colonies, and took steps to ensure that customs duties were efficiently collected in colonial ports. Known as the 'Sugar Act' because it affected the import of molasses into North America from the West Indies, this new legislation angered sections of colonial society, particularly rum distillers, who claimed that it would destroy their industry, and coastal shippers whose trade was impeded by new customs regulations associated with the Act. The Currency Act of 1764, which prohibited the issue of paper money, also caused discontent because it threatened to hinder trade at a time when the huge cash injections made by Britain during wartime had dried up, bringing short-term recession. Dislike of these measures was dwarfed, however, by the wave of outrage that followed the introduction of the Stamp Act which, in 1765, imposed duty on legal and commercial documents, newspapers, pamphlets and playing cards. To the British government, this statute seemed an entirely reasonable expedient: its apologists argued that colonials had no reason to complain, since much of the stamp tax would be paid by British merchants, and the revenue it raised would be spent in America. North Americans, on the other hand, were enraged by the new measure and took violent collective action to show their displeasure.

COLONIAL RESISTANCE TO REFORM

The Stamp Act aroused a storm of protest. In May 1765, the Virginia Houses of Burgesses passed a series of resolves against the Act; other colonial assemblies soon followed their example, on the grounds that the new tax violated the rights of Englishmen to freedom from taxation not voted by their own representatives. In October 1765, a number of colonies sent delegates to a 'Stamp Act Congress' which reaffirmed this principle and set out to coordinate opposition. The delegates agreed to boycott British imports and to suspend debt payments to British merchants; with this sanction, the campaign against the Act took energetic and violent form. Rioting urban crowds attacked the persons and property of tax-collectors, prevented the arrest or trial of rioters, and a network of protest groups, made up of men from a cross-section of colonial society who joined together as the 'Sons of Liberty', organized a concerted campaign to ensure that the tax was unworkable.[4] Such was the impact of this defiance that American stamp tax collectors were forced to renounce their posts, and the crown was showered with petitions to repeal the measure, both from colonials and British merchants who found the disruption in the ports seriously damaging to their trade.

Confronted with widespread disobedience and disruption, Grenville declared the colonies to be in rebellion and seemed ready to restore order by force. In the event, British government decided that caution was the better part of valour; when George III replaced Grenville with Rockingham, confrontation gave way to conciliation and both King and Parliament were persuaded to repeal the Stamp Act in March 1766. However, on the same day that the repeal became law, Parliament passed the Declaratory Act, stating that it had 'full power and authority to make laws and statutes of sufficient force and validity to bind the colonies and peoples of America . . . in all cases whatsoever'. To avoid provocation, the Act did not mention taxation, but this did not blind thoughtful Americans to its significance. Parliament had declared its right to legislate for the colonies 'in all cases whatsoever', thereby asserting its power with greater clarity than ever before.

Revocation of the Stamp Act was followed by some further concessions. The Sugar Act was altered, and in 1766 Parliament passed the Free Port Act in order to encourage an inflow of specie to the American colonies through the West Indies. The damage inflicted on the relationship between Britain and the North American colonies was not so easily repaired, however. While colonial assemblies voted thanks for repeal, the leaders of colonial resistance to the Stamp Act realized that Parliament had not abandoned its claims. They therefore loudly reaffirmed their right to freedom from parliamentary intrusion in matters of taxation, sought to maintain the organizations which had opposed the stamp duties, and remained vigilant for any fresh assault on their self-proclaimed political rights. Thus the end of the Stamp Act eased political strains but did not eliminate their cause. To colonials, the Act had raised a fundamental issue of political principle.

In their eyes, it transgressed against the long-defended right to vote their own taxes without interference from Parliament. Resistance to the Stamp Act thus assumed a deeper significance than a simple reluctance to pay new taxes; it raised a political issue of prime importance to Americans, crystallized in the doctrine that there should be 'no taxation without representation'. By seeking to levy taxes directly, Parliament had challenged the autonomy that had become an article of faith among colonials and, in their resistance, encountered a defiance of parliamentary sovereignty that was impossible to overlook.

The Stamp Act was thus the catalyst of a dangerous division in colonial relations, for, by arousing debate over the the rights of American subjects, it forced each side to clarify underlying political views and positions, and to see their fundamental divergence. Even so, further conflict might have been avoided had Britain's government remained in the hands of moderates who were ready to avoid confrontation on the issue of taxation and thus at least to sustain an appearance of consensus. But when Rockingham's ministry fell, British government was taken over by men who were no more inclined to yield on a point of principle than were their colonial opponents. Within a year of the repeal of Stamp Act, a new ministry, headed by William Pitt, Earl of Chatham, but effectively led by Charles Townshend, his Chancellor of the Exchequer, returned to the political offensive and again set Britain on a collision course with its North American colonies.

FROM RESISTANCE TO REBELLION

The second act of the political drama that had started in 1765 opened in 1767. First, Townshend insisted that the colonies observe the Quartering Act of 1764, which required them to provide housing and supplies for British troops. When faced with New York's stubborn refusal to comply, Parliament suspended the New York legislature in 1767, thus forcing it to render grudging obedience. In the same year, Townshend returned to the fiscal offensive: he launched a programme for raising revenues in the colonies by levying customs duties on a variety of American imports, and simultaneously created a new machinery to ensure that these duties were properly collected. Townshend made a feeble effort to justify this to colonials by insisting that customs duties were an 'external' tax collected on trade at the ports, and so did not interfere with the colonies' procedures for levying of 'internal' taxes. His argument carried no weight, however, and his plans stirred fresh agitation in North America. In fact, colonials had not accepted the distinction between 'internal' and 'external' taxes. They rejected to Parliament's claim to levy any taxes that raised revenues in the colonies rather than simply regulating trade; they also strongly objected to Townshend's plan to use new revenues to pay the salaries of colonial governors, since this would release such crown officials from dependence on funds voted by the American assemblies. Thus the Townshend Acts brought constitutional conflict back to the boil, by reviving American fears that the crown planned to whittle away the liberties that they, as Englishmen, had won in the Glorious Revolution of 1688.

The Massachusetts legislature led opposition to the Townshend Acts, by calling for a general boycott of British imports, especially tea. So successful were the non-importation agreements that government in London was forced to retreat once more. By March 1770, all the Townshend duties on imports were suppressed, except that on tea. Once again, the British government's fiscal manoeuvres had incurred high political costs without achieving any financial benefits. Not only did opposition to Townshend's legislation revive strong and coordinated opposition in the North American colonies, but growing anti-British feeling heightened when British troops fired on a rioting crowd in Boston, killing five people in the 'Boston Massacre' of 5 March, 1770. In these circumstances, the rhetoric of American radicals – who portrayed the British government as a despotism intent on destroying American liberty – found a sympathetic echo among a colonial public that was becoming increasingly politicized. Divisions and doubts remained, however. Among merchants and rich men who had colluded in opposing British policy, enthusiasm for opposition waned as the blockage of imports hampered their business, and political disturbances endowed obscure radicals with a political influence previously reserved to the upper classes. Thus the partial repeal of the Townshend Acts provided a respite in conflict with the British government, and opened a space for reconciliation.

Conflict was not easily resolved, however. Popular participation in organized opposition to British policy had brought new, often poorer men into politics; as some of these individuals found their political vocations and careers in arousing and orchestrating opposition to Britain, the issues that divided metropolis and colonies were not allowed to fade away. Meanwhile, ministers of the British crown failed either to understand the depth of colonial opposition or to appreciate the character of the political conflict in which it was involved. Lord

North's government, initiated in 1770, soon stumbled into trouble. In 1773, Parliament passed the Tea Act, designed to ease the British East India Company's financial difficulties by allowing it to sell tea imports in the Americas through its own agents, while also asserting Parliamentary authority by retaining the tax on tea sales. Seen from London, there seemed no reason why colonials should not accept this measure, since it reduced the price of tea paid by consumers. In fact, the Tea Act rallied a fresh coalition of protesters. Not only did the Act threaten to ruin American merchants who held stocks of tea bought at higher prices, but, because it revived Parliament's attempts to impose taxation on the colonials, it also allowed radicals to revive the spectre of British encroachment on American freedom.

Resistance centred on the port of Boston, where the defence of economic interest and constitutional principles brought merchants and urban crowds together in direct defiance of the Tea Act. In the famous 'Boston Tea Party' of 16 December, 1773, tea ships were boarded by protesters dressed up as Indians and their cargoes emptied into the harbour amidst public celebration. Responding to this insolent disregard for English property and government authority, Lord North decided to punish Boston and the colony of Massachusetts. In 1774, his administration passed a series of measures that Americans called the Coercive or Intolerable Acts: these closed the port of Boston and transferred the seat of provincial government to Salem, amended the charter of Massachusetts to give the crown governor greater powers, revised judicial procedures, and provided for billeting British troops wherever civil disorders occurred.

This effort to force colonial submission soon proved counter-productive. While North attempted to target retribution on Massachusetts, his coercive laws encouraged other colonies to unite in sympathy, turning a provincial protest into a general movement of opposition. The Quebec Act of 1774 had meanwhile further reinforced the general aversion to royal policy and helped solidify an alliance against Britain. By extending the boundaries of the province of Quebec south and westwards, the Quebec Act confirmed colonial fears that the crown was intent on infringing their freedom. In the fevered political atmosphere of these years, the Act appeared as a deliberate attempt to people western lands with French Catholics who, having no representative institutions and being governed directly by the crown, seemed to be subject to the very royal despotism that colonials abhorred.

With the constitutional issue of Parliament's power over the colonies once again firmly in the forefront of colonial politics, resistance quickly extended beyond Boston. By seeking to isolate and intimidate Massachusetts, Lord North achieved the opposite. His opponents in the thirteen colonies saw the threat to one colony as a challenge to all, and, burying their differences, the colonies rallied to support Massachusetts. In September 1774, a Continental Congress was convened at Philadelphia to devise a common policy for confronting British government. Events now moved towards a climax that resulted in a final rupture with the mother country.

Preceded by much political activity within the colonies themselves, the first Continental Congress reflected the gravity of the political situation that had developed since the first British efforts at colonial reform a decade earlier. Throughout the colonies, local political organizations – most of them extra-legal assemblies, committees and conventions established to resist British policy – elected delegates to represent them at the Congress, and all the old colonies except Georgia duly sent their representatives. During the deliberations of the Congress, the gulf between the colonies and Britain widened, despite efforts by a minority which sought to persuade the British government to create a federal system for the empire, embodied in a 'Plan of Union' put forward by Joseph Galloway. This plan called for the creation of a new American legislature elected by the colonial assemblies, and empowered to approve all American legislation together with the British Parliament, subject to the veto of a president-general appointed by the crown, while leaving the existing colonial legislatures with control over local affairs.

Lack of confidence in the British Parliament ensured that this compromise was rejected. Instead, the delegates adhered to a more radical plan: they accepted the restrictions of the Trade and Navigation Acts, but insisted on the repeal of the Quebec and Coercive Acts, and petitioned George III to redress as grievances all legislation regarding trade and taxation passed since the Sugar Act of 1764. Condemning Parliament for its attack on the constitutional principles of colonial government, the delegates also formed the colonies into a Continental Association, organized to block trade with Britain, to prevent the consumption of British goods, and thus by peaceful means to persuade the crown to redress American grievances.

Proposals for conciliation were discussed in the House of Commons in early 1775, but failed: although influential voices called for concessions, the response from Lord North and King George III was uncompromising.[5] Parliament's right to tax the colonies was firmly restated, and preparations were made to send troop reinforcements to back the royal will with force if necessary. Political contestation now shifted towards armed conflict, starting with military skirmishes at Lexington and Concord, near Boston, in April 1775, followed by fighting on the western frontier of the colony of New York in May. When delegates from the assemblies reconvened for the Second Continental Congress in May, the colonies were already effectively at war with Britain; in June, the Congress voted to create and finance a Continental army, with George Washington as its Commander in Chief.

As royal government in the colonies broke down amidst these events, the political initiative passed to those who wanted independence and who organized for power. While colonial officials were everywhere under attack, radicals appealed to Congress for permission to form their own state governments. Congress finally complied in May 1776, when it declared that royal government should be entirely suppressed, placing 'all the powers of government . . . under the authority of the people in the colonies.'[6] Having effectively declared independence with this resolution, it remained only for Congress to formalize the replacement of royal by independent government. In June 1776, Richard Henry Lee of the Virginia assembly presented the Congress with resolutions which declared the independence of the united colonies, called for a plan of confederation, and stated the need to seek foreign alliances for war against Britain. After debating these proposals, the delegates decided to draw up a document explaining and justifying their actions. The result was the Declaration of Independence of 4 July, 1776, a statement of principle and intent that confirmed the rejection of British rule which was already under way. War now followed, to decide whether the colonies would capitulate to British authority or overthrow it.[7]

ORIGINS OF REVOLUTION

The open repudiation of British sovereignty by the North American colonies in 1776 did not extend to the whole of the British American empire; the island colonies of the Caribbean remained loyal to the crown, as did Nova Scotia and the newly acquired French territories of Canada. Why, then, did British rule prove so vulnerable in precisely those regions where, by sweeping aside its foreign rivals in 1763, Britain seemed to have established its ascendancy so completely? What transformed a sizeable section of North American colonial societies from enthusiastic advocates of imperial expansionism during the Seven Years War into determined adversaries of imperial rule?

To understand the reaction of the North American colonies against British government after 1763, it is important, first, to recall the character of political and economic relations that had previously prevailed. Since the late seventeenth century, colonials had not experienced any attempt at rigorous, centralized imperial control of a kind that systematically subordinated the interests of the colonies to those of the metropolitan power. Quite the contrary. Following the Glorious Revolution of 1688, the new monarchy in Britain abandoned the efforts of its Stuart predecessors to assert crown authority through a redesigned structure of colonial government, and had instead allowed the colonies both a high degree of autonomy over their internal affairs and a wide margin of tolerance for their commerce. Relations were not, of course, entirely free of friction. There was constant bickering over the payment of governors' salaries, as the lower houses of the colonial assemblies jealously defended their rights to control internal finances, and controversies over other issues, such as the right of the Anglican church to appoint bishops for the Americas. But Parliament had never become sufficiently concerned with these issues to carry them to conclusive decisions, and on the whole political relations between metropolis and colonies remained on an equitable plane. Nor (as we noted in Chapter 8) did North Americans suffer significant hindrance to their economic interests from the restrictions imposed upon them by the British Navigation Acts. The commercial regulations imposed by the navigation laws presented no serious impediments to the development of the colonies' external commerce and, by linking producers and traders in a matrix of expanding markets, helped to bind the empire together. Colonials periodically complained about constraints on trade, but the English commercial system had never been an economic strait-jacket of the kind that Spain imposed on its American colonies. Britain's colonies could trade directly with foreigners in certain commodities, and a wide range of European and intercolonial outlets ensured that, by the mid-eighteenth century, they were among the most thriving economies in the American colonial world. Both politically and economically, then, the British colonial system functioned without serious strains for more than half a century after the Glorious Revolution. So why did relations suddenly deteriorate in the dozen years after 1765, leading to the fracture of empire in 1776?

Analysis of this political transformation must start at the point at which the empire had reached its eighteenth-century apogee, following the Peace of Paris in 1763. Historians generally agree that the conflict between Britain and its North American colonies began because the policies which the metropolitan power adopted in the wake of the Seven Years War disrupted the status quo that had long governed their relations. For some historians, these policies reflected a basic shift in the attitude of Britain's governing elite, from a mercantilist concern simply to regulate the colonies' commerce to an imperialist preoccupation with territory and the exercise of authority. Others believe that policy change entailed a shift in tactics rather than a fundamental change in strategy, involving new methods rather than new goals.[8]

On balance, Britain's postwar policies are probably best understood as a response to short-term needs, rather than the conscious elaboration of a new imperial strategy, designed to replace previous pragmatic, ad hoc arrangements with an entirely new and rationalized structure of colonial government. The fact is that British statesmen were forced to take a greater interest in colonial policy after the 'Great War for Empire' because the sudden extension of colonial territory, combined with the financial crisis left by the war, presented them with decisions that were difficult to avoid. After the war, the British government had a huge national debt, faced an international situation that remained dangerous, and confronted a British public already subject to a heavy burden of taxation; it therefore had a powerful incentive to mobilize colonial resources and, in so doing, to impose a stricter system for extracting revenues.

Whether British government intended fully to rationalize the system of colonial government or merely to tap colonial resources for immediate returns is, however, less important than the fact that North Americans were unwilling to comply with new fiscal demands. Their reasons become clearer if we compare the situation of the British colonies in North America with that of the British colonies in the Caribbean. There, the threat of external attack from France and Spain, both of which continued to hold important territories in the Caribbean, ensured that colonials were heavily dependent on maritime and military force supplied by the mother country for their defence. In North America, by contrast, the threat from France and Spain had apparently been removed, so that colonials could relax their guard and pursue new opportunities for expansion. Colonial leaders felt that they had made a significant contribution to the war; when France had been expelled from the continent, they had no pressing reason to enlarge their share of defence costs. Indeed, they expected to be given full scope for pursuing their interests, particularly through westward expansion, while Britain went on providing and financing defence as it always had.

North American readiness to resist new British policies was not, however, rooted simply in refusal to bear a larger share of the costs of empire, or in objection to policies which offended specific colonial economic interests. Although protest against new taxes involved the defence of local and sectional interests, conflict quickly assumed a wider political dimension because North Americans became convinced that Parliament was not simply trying to take more money from them, but was launching an assault on their fundamental political rights. They saw their societies as overseas extensions of the mother country, and regarded themselves as British citizens who were entitled to exactly the same rights as the King's subjects in Britain itself. This was made transparently clear by the 'Address to the People of Great Britain' issued by delegates to the Continental Congress. In this document, the delegates placed Americans on a par with 'fellow-subjects in Britain', asked 'why English subjects who were three thousand miles from the royal palace should enjoy less liberty than those who are three hundred from it', and robustly declared that colonials would 'never submit to be hewers of wood or drawers of water for any ministry or nation in the world'.[9] Thus the North American movement towards independence began as a defence of established practices within the political system created under British sovereignty, rather than as an immediate repudiation of that system. Indeed, it seems that the colonials' very sense of identity with the political traditions of the mother country helped to promote their separation from it.

Colonial defence of the principle of 'no taxation without representation' was, as Jack Greene observes, also an assertion of the right to 'no legislation without representation'. This insistence on the right to government by the consent of the governed was grounded in political practice, rather than in any clearly formulated legal principle or explicit guarantee of constitutional rights. In practice, the colonies had developed their own governments, embodied in elected assemblies which colonials had come to regard as American equivalents to the British Parliament, bodies which, like Parliament, shielded Britain's American subjects against the arbitrary deployment of executive power. Parliament had, however, never formally acknowledged the equality of colonial governments, and when confronted by resistance to new taxes it simply asserted its constitutional supremacy. This revealed a previously latent split in colonial and metropolitan views of the very constitution of the empire, showing that Parliament did not share American views of the empire as a federal political system of equal parts, a system described by one American commentator in 1766 as 'a confederacy of states, independent of each other, yet united under one head'.[10]

Discovery of this divergence was a shock to North Americans and, influenced by traditions of political thought which emanated from Britain itself, they came to see British policy as not simply a set of administrative adjustments designed to improve the efficiency of the empire's government and defence, but as a dark conspiracy to deprive them of basic rights. Indeed, according to Bernard Bailyn's study of colonial political ideas on the eve of Revolution, Americans held a view of politics which persuaded them to see the actions of British government as a calculated attack on basic freedoms. It was, says Bailyn, 'the fear of a comprehensive conspiracy against liberty throughout the English-speaking world [which] lay at the heart of the Revolutionary movement'.[11]

The American perception of the behaviour of British government as a fundamental violation of constitutional liberties was, as Bailyn has shown, shaped by a configuration of ideas and attitudes which were mainly drawn from the metropolitan culture itself. One important influence derived from the body of English Common Law, which stressed the rights of the individual against the state and, through such procedures as trial by a jury of ordinary citizens, provided means of defending individual freedom against the encroachments of the powerful. Another influence, one which was particularly powerful in New England, came from Puritanism, with its notion of covenant between community and God, and its belief that colonization had been a special event in the Divine Plan, the meaning of which still awaited full revelation. A third, more important element in American political thinking derived from the ideas and principles of republicanism, which educated Americans learned directly from their familiarity with the classical texts of the ancient world and, more importantly, by indirect transmission through their reading of the works of eighteenth-century English Whig radicals. Indeed, radical English thought provided Americans with their central medium for understanding the dispute with Britain. During the early eighteenth century, radical political thought developed since the Civil War was persistently recalled and developed in pamphlets and tracts written by the 'real Whig' opponents of the corrupt and oligarchical governments of the Hanoverian monarchy. Widely read in the colonies, this literature provided a powerful conceptual framework both for explaining the behaviour of British government and exciting opposition to it. Rooted in the conviction that human nature was fundamentally corrupt and self-seeking, this tradition presented politics

265

as an unending struggle between liberty and tyranny, in which aggressive, power-hungry men constantly struggled to turn their fellows into servile dependents. Its ideas encouraged Americans to exalt their simple provincial virtues against corruption at the centre of power, reinforced the view that the best form of polity was one in which citizens ruled themselves warned of the constant dangers that civil societies faced from the inherent tendencies towards despotism found in any state, and, during the 1760s and 1770s, provided them with compelling analogies to their own times. In short, the radical Whig and republican strains in eighteenth-century English political thought provided Americans with a vital catalyst for forming a complete theory of politics which united the disparate strands found in the classics, in Renaissance and Enlightenment thought, in common law and in Puritan covenant theology, and which provided the conceptual filter through which colonials analysed and responded to the new policies imposed by Britain after 1763.[12]

Informed by these ideas, North Americans were quick to detect ulterior motives in the actions of British governments, and, once convinced that there was a pattern behind its acts, they came to see them as parts of a cynical, disguised attack on American freedom. This 'conspiracy theory' was neatly encapsulated by Joseph Warren in 1766, when he reported that the Stamp Act had led some people to imagine that it was designed, not to raise taxes, but 'to force the colonies into a rebellion, and from thence to take occasion to treat them with severity, and, by military power, to reduce them to servitude.'[13] Once established, this attitude was further sharpened by all the subsequent actions of British government, however innocent its ministers might have been of the malevolent intentions attributed to them. Whether or not Americans misunderstood the constitutional issues and the thinking behind British policy is still debated.[14] What is clearly of central importance, however, is the fact that colonials' perception of the political meaning of British policy encouraged them to challenge and eventually to overthrow British authority.

In his influential study of the ideological origins of the American Revolution, Bernard Bailyn has insisted that it was 'above all else an ideological, constitutional and political struggle and not primarily a struggle between social groups undertaken to force changes in the organization of the society or the economy'.[15] Studies of late colonial America suggest, however, that a social interpretation of the Revolution cannot be dismissed so summarily. First formulated by Carl Becker, for whom the Revolution was not only a dispute over 'home rule' but also a struggle over 'who was to rule at home', the interpretation of the Revolution as a conflict within American society, rather than simply a struggle against an external power, has been revived by historians who have explored the relationship between social tensions and political conflict in late colonial America. In their view, the struggle with Britain was a radical revolution that was bound up with the transformation of American society and involved a vision of social change, rather than being simply a political conflict based primarily in constitutional issues.[16]

An important contribution to this historiography has been made by those who argue that rapid demographic and economic expansion during the first half of the eighteenth century brought the existing structures of America's colonial societies under severe strain, leading to inter-regional and inter-class conflict.[17] Evidence of the interaction between social strain and political conflict is found in both rural and urban areas. In the older, more densely populated areas of settlement in New England, demographic growth caused land shortages which, by constricting opportunities for individual independence and prosperity, created tensions between the landed and the landless. In newer colonies, such as New York and New Jersey, the concentration of landed property in the hands of great proprietors also occasioned conflict, as resentments against large landlords occasionally erupted in violent confrontations, such as the riots and uprisings that took place in central New Jersey at mid-century and in New York's Hudson Valley in the 1750s and 1760s. In addition, the spread of settlement into new areas led to conflict, often because settlers in the interior resisted government by elites who, being based in older centres of power, had different economic and political interests. Such rural violence (which occurred in frontier areas of all the colonies except Virginia) had complex roots, involving taxation, titles to land, Indian policy, relations between landlords and tenants, and the distribution of political power between settled and frontier regions; it was usually on a small scale or took place in areas distant from centres of government, and involved purely local political targets and intentions. It did nonetheless unsettle the rural society of the regions affected, and, by mobilizing country people in challenges to the authority of provincial elites and government, ensured that issues of local power and property were to interact with the struggle against Britain.[18]

Even more striking symptoms of social division and conflict have been found in the larger colonial cities. In his study of the three leading colonial cities of Boston, New York and Philadelphia, Gary Nash presents a portrait of urban societies where the rich were becoming richer, while the poor became both poorer and more numerous. While tax lists show wealth concentrated in fewer hands at the top of society and records of poor relief show a spreading poverty among the lower orders at the bottom, Nash also detects a greater economic insecurity among the middling sectors in these cities, in the ranks of their artisans, shopkeepers and petty merchants. He contends, furthermore, that these animosities, reflected in periodic riots, tumultuous local electoral battles and in the receptivity of city dwellers to the radical evangelists of the Great Awakening, show that 'a rising tide of class antagonism and political consciousness, paralleling important economic changes, was a distinguishing feature of the cities at the end of the colonial period'.[19]

For Nash, as for like-minded historians who have focused on the larger cities and their regions, economic distress and difficulty induced a growing restlessness among city folk which, when inflamed by the factional politics of competing elites, contributed to politicizing ordinary people even before opposition to British reforms created a new arena for political dispute and debate.[20] So, when the conflict with external authority began in 1765, lower-class crowds were ready to respond to the leadership of first the 'Sons of Liberty', the network of urban radicals which organized popular resistance to the Stamp Act, and then to the popular committees which took power from royal officials between 1774 and 1776. In this process, radicals merged social and constitutional issues, fusing Whig political ideas with a popular ideology and formulating demands which went beyond the issue of parliamentary sovereignty to embrace broader questions about the internal distribution of wealth and power. Thus, it is said, the Revolution was not simply a political conflict between colonial elites and metropolitan governments; it also involved a struggle between underprivileged groups and wealthy elites, a clash between classes which changed a colonial rebellion into a popular revolution.

Although the expansion of population and settlement, urbanization and economic growth undoubtedly induced strains and divisions in the colonies, particularly in the major seaports, the notion that colonial societies were riven by deepening class conflicts is open to question. For, as Jack P. Greene reminds us, 'it is by no means clear that the increase in poverty . . . was a linear process or was yet leading to the creation of a substantial underclass of residual poor among the free population'.[21] In fact, agricultural tenancy and employment as free wage labour were often only temporary conditions for the younger generation in rural and urban areas, and therefore did not necessarily relegate the property-less and poor to permanent dependence and deprivation. Land was undoubtedly more difficult to find in the older colonies, but western frontiers afforded space where both immigrants and colonials could acquire land; at the same time, the growth of population and commerce opened markets that expanded employment opportunities in service, mercantile and industrial activities in the towns. In these economic circumstances, colonial society did not divide into well-defined social classes; the crucial social distinction was instead between two broad categories, consisting of those with sufficient property or occupations to allow them economic independence, and those who, as servants, labourers or slaves, depended on others for their living. Moreover, what was remarkable about late colonial society was that the independent population was very large. Although Britain's North American colonies were very far from being classless societies which had abolished poverty, they were nonetheless still 'the best poor man's country in the world', offering prospects of property, prosperity and social mobility that were extraordinary by contemporary European standards. Indeed, as the economy became more commercialized around and after mid-century, the free population generally benefited from opportunities to participate in the market economy, both as producers and consumers. In this setting, Greene argues, free white males were still able realistically to aspire to

> the achievement of personal independence, a state in which a man and his family and broader dependents could live 'at ease' rather than in anxiety, in contentment rather than want, in respectability rather than meanness, and perhaps more important in freedom from the will and control of other men.[22]

Seen from this perspective, the social origins of the Revolution are not to be found in poverty and economic frustration; they are instead associated with the aspirations of the free, independent whites who formed the majority of the colonial population at a time of rapid and disturbing social change. Thus, as Gordon Wood has persuasively argued, political instability arose not from the conflict of social groups in an increasingly class-based society, but rather from the rapid disruption of the paternalist and monarchical order to which Americans had become habituated under British political and cultural hegemony.[23]

At mid-century, Wood argues, Americans still saw their society in terms taken from the monarchical order of the mother country. In this society, social distinctions were not measured by wealth and occupation alone; designations of 'quality' derived from birth were a far more important measure of social status. Within this context, the principal social difference was the distinction that separated the gentleman from the commoner, the patrician from the plebeian. This division was, moreover, underpinned by a conception of society which took the patriarchal family as a paradigm for a hierarchical social order bound by reciprocal ties of dependence between superiors and inferiors. Within the family, authority was exercised by the father who, as 'natural' master in his personal domain, determined the disposition of family property and resources. Beyond the family, public authority derived from private social position. Thus, political power was primarily the domain of wealthy gentry and merchant families, and political life was governed more by personal connections between patrons and their clients than by competition between social groups. Colonial politics was, in short, based in 'vertical' rather than 'horizontal' social relations and alliances. This social and political order was, however, weakened during the eighteenth century when demographic explosion, the rapid spread of settlement, and economic growth all contributed to reshaping and destabilizing a predominantly rural society.

One source of instability arose from shortages of land in older areas of colonization on the coast. This encouraged geographical mobility and as people migrated in search of land or other economic opportunities, established structures of patriarchy, community and political authority decayed. At the same time, the spread of settlement to frontier areas created communities which outran established institutions, since they stood outside the networks of political patronage and control commanded by the elites of the older settlements of the eastern seaboard. The expansion of commerce further contributed to altering social values and social relations. Commercialization of production stimulated a shift from subsistence towards production for the market, bringing a rise in money incomes which, aided by the spread of paper money, underpinned a 'consumer revolution'.

Such changes corroded the norms of traditional society. Distinctions of social rank were blurred by the new mobility, and social deference declined as the small and middling farmers who formed the majority of the free white population sought independence from their social and economic superiors. In the process, the bonds of traditional colonial society were loosened, accentuating the underlying contradictions of a colonial society where a relatively high degree of equality coexisted with values and institutions taken from a class-based parent society to which the colonies bore little real resemblance.

The repercussions of rapid demographic and economic change had particularly powerful force in North American societies because the authority of the monarchical state was much weaker than in the mother country. Americans shared with the British a conception of the British constitution as an admirable confection of monarchical and republican elements, combining freedom and firm government in a unique system. Colonials tended, however, to emphasize the republican strains in British political discourse. Some, such as Scots and foreign immigrants, had no firm loyalty to the English crown; others, such as New Englanders, proudly recalled anti-monarchist sentiments from their past; indeed, being so distant from the centre of royal government, Americans were generally unimpressed by the dignity and majesty of the crown. Instead, their conception of government was shaped by experience of decentralized and localized institutions which were not closely integrated with the metropolis and which they jealously guarded against external intrusion.

If royal authority was weakened by this inherited opposition between central and colonial government, it was further attenuated by the fact that the social hierarchy and institutions of the mother country were imperfectly replicated in North America. As we have seen, royal authority in the colonies lacked the support of an established church and an aristocracy comparable to that of Britain; it also existed within the context of a far more egalitarian social structure, quite different from that of the metropolis. In Hanoverian England, most of the population was landless and huge numbers lived in a precarious poverty, dependent on the gentry and the church for charity. In America, on the other hand, most of the white population held freehold land and enjoyed a standard of living that contemporary visitors invariably found amazing by European standards.

The unsettling effects of economic and demographic expansion in this setting first became apparent during the 'Great Awakening', the religious revivalist movement that swept through the colonies in the mid-1730s. With its emphasis on salvation through spiritual rebirth, the movement undermined existing churches and their clergy, and in its wake left new denominations which, by emphasizing individual piety and freedom, challenged constituted authority.[24] In political life, too, previously accepted authority was challenged, partly because, when factions within the gentry jockeyed for local power, they courted votes from common folk and thereby widened the arena of political life. Now, greater popular participation in politics did not of itself constitute a threat to imperial authority. But it did further weaken networks of kinship and patronage that were being damaged by economic change and, by arousing a reaction from conservatives who deplored popular intrusion into politics, created new oppositions and antagonisms.

Thus, Wood concludes, it was not the inequalities caused by economic and demographic change that produced political instability;

271

the social sources of political strain arose from the anxieties and aspirations generated by opportunities for social advancement and freedom from dependence. In a society where the calibrations of traditional society were being replaced by a simpler dichotomy between freemen and dependents, and where the presence of slavery and servitude reminded the free population of the perils of sub-ordination and dependence, Americans became acutely sensitive to threats to their freedom and predisposed to regard Britain's attempts to impose its authority as a conspiracy against their rights. In this unstable setting, it becomes easier to understand why Americans should, as Burke said, 'augur misgovernment at a distance and snuff the approach of tyranny in every tainted breeze.'[25]

THE OVERTHROW OF BRITISH GOVERNMENT

As the conviction among colonials that Britain had decided to deprive them of their liberties grew steadily stronger between the passage of the Stamp Act in 1765 and the Coercive Acts of 1774, so a movement first to defy and then to overthrow British government gathered force and momentum. This was not a single movement, grounded in a pre-existing nationalist ideology which had already envisaged a political life outside the colonial system. It was, rather, a series of alliances which arose from successive responses to British actions, and which gradually brought disparate regions and social groups into a coordinated movement. The creation of these alliances was a crucial element in the process that led to American independence, since no single region or social group was capable of confronting British power alone.

Before 1765, there was no clearly articulated American nationalism. Left to a large extent to their own devices by a distant metropolis, enjoying considerable political autonomy and growing economic strength, Britain's colonial subjects in the Americas had long sensed important differences between their societies and that of the mother country, but this sense of difference did not of itself generate a desire for political self-determination. Indeed, the colonies were deeply divided both between themselves and within themselves. Insofar as they were aware of an identity, it was primarily regional. Colonials tended to see themselves as Pennsylvanians or Virginians, rather than 'Americans', and their governments were rarely prepared to act in any cooperative or coordinated fashion. The colonies were also divided internally in a number of ways. Religious differences separated groups professing the various strands of Protestantism practised in America; ethnic divisions set the descendants of English settlers apart from non-English immigrants, and frontier settlers in the west were frequently alienated from the established societies of the coast, where government was based. Consequently, after the Seven Years War, 'Americans were still very far from being a people bounded by a shared sense of purpose and identity'.[26]

These differences were not suddenly swept away by opposition to Britain. British policies did, however, create a political situation in which colonial differences were increasingly superseded by a general antagonism towards the metropolitan power, and a sense of shared identity against an external adversary. The shift from diversity to unity began in 1765, with the organization of a general congress of colonies to oppose the Stamp Act. It took much more tangible form after 1773, when the Virginia assembly called on the other colonial assemblies to participate in forming a Committee of Correspondence to coordinate their response to British policy, paving the way for the creation of the first Continental Congress, which met at Philadelphia in 1774. Twelve colonies sent delegates to the Congress, where they formed an association to oppose British policy jointly, by preventing imports, exports and the purchase of British goods. Henceforth, the term 'American' took on a wider currency, being used to express both general opposition to Britain and commitment to a new, proto-national confederation.

While the colonies were entering a formal network for orchestrating opposition to Britain, another development that was taking place among the wider public made colonial opposition increasingly widespread and effective. This stemmed from the raising of political consciousness among the many people who had previously played little active part in political life, through the creation of organizations which enabled them to articulate their grievances and combine their protests. The basis for such mass politicization lay initially in the mobilization of urban crowds which, acting within an established tradition of popular action against local abuses of power, protested against the Stamp Act. But the crucial additional element of this mobilization came from the political work done by the groups known as the 'Sons of Liberty', which orchestrated protest in New York, Boston, and other major towns. These organizations created a militant, cross-regional movement which linked popular grievances into a wider political movement and kept opposition to Britain alive after the repeal of the Stamp Act. A vital, culminating popular upsurge came with the organization of local committees to enforce the economic boycott of Britain between 1774 and 1776, which spread opposition to Britain in a veritable explosion of political participation.[27] Thus, in August 1775, when George III declared the colonies to be in open rebellion and his government took steps to suppress it by force, an existing organizational framework was ready to expand its activities to meet the emergency. Clandestine committees now came into the open, and often expanded their membership as communities elected men to deal with the crisis. In places, the committees assumed the functions of government, and everywhere they made preparations for war, forming militias, organizing armament and amassing military stores. Popular mobilization through the committees transformed the colonies' political life, bringing farmers, small traders and artisans to the centre of public life and giving them confidence in their cause.

The popular upsurge was further boosted by the publication and widespread dissemination in 1776 of the pamphlet *Common Sense*, written by the English radical Tom Paine. Aligning himself with the lower ranks of society rather than the elites, Paine spoke in plain terms, readily understandable by common people; he called for the foundation of a simple republic, free of British monarchical rule, with a broad democratic base. Paine's call for independence reverberated throughout the colonies. Colony after colony instructed its delegate to vote for separation, culminating in the formal declaration of independence at the Second Continental Congress in July 1776. In his draft of the Declaration of Independence, Thomas Jefferson echoed Paine's sentiments. Like Paine, he rejected the argument that the colonies should appeal to a beneficent monarch over the head of a corrupt Parliament, and exhorted Americans to fight together to throw off English government and to replace it with a state of their own. Thus the stage was set for the final and decisive contest, fought with arms rather than words.[28]

BREAKING BRITISH POWER: THE AMERICAN WAR OF INDEPENDENCE

At first sight, the odds were heavily loaded against the North American rebels. Britain had overwhelming military and naval supremacy, great economic and financial resources, and long experience in war. The Americans, on the other hand, had only a small, ill-trained army, and little military experience. They did have some advantages, however, in a defensive position some three thousand miles from Britain, a terrain ill-suited to European methods of warfare and a rural population accustomed to and expert in the use of firearms. In the opening stages of the war, the British government seemed fully capable of overcoming these obstacles. Its strategy for retaking the colonies hinged on taking control of the eastern seaboard at three strategic points, from which British forces would reach inland to divide and crush the rebels. The first objective was to break resistance in New England by isolating it from the Middle Atlantic colonies, and to dominate the Hudson Valley so that New York could be reinforced from Canada; another aim was to establish a stronghold in the south. Thus the pivots of the campaign were to be at Newfoundland, Nova Scotia and Canada in the north; at East Florida, Georgia and South Carolina in the south; and in the centre, at New York, where Britain planned to drive a wedge between New England and the other colonies.[29]

These objectives were never fully secured. The northern approaches to the continent were taken without difficulty, and a key naval and military base established at Halifax in Nova Scotia. In the Carolinas, however, rebel opposition proved too strong; after an abortive assault on rebel fortifications at Charleston in mid-1776, the British concentrated their forces on the New York region. A powerful force did succeed in taking New York in late 1776, and defeated General Washington's army. But, having forced Washington into retreat, the British failed to finish him off. This cost them dear. A year later, Washington scored a major victory by smashing General Burgoyne's army when it advanced south from Canada in an attempt to link up with British forces in New York. In October 1777, British forces under Burgoyne were surrounded and forced to surrender at Saratoga.

Washington's success at Saratoga marked a turning point in the war, not because it established any American military superiority, but because it persuaded France to enter the war against Britain in 1778, providing the Americans with arms, supplies and naval support, and transforming a local into a global conflict. Britain now had to deploy its naval and military forces over a much broader front, diverting resources from the North American theatre of war and distracting from the main task of suppressing the colonial rebellion. The British West Indies had to be protected against French attack, and naval forces had to be devoted to coping with the maritime threat from France. Henceforth, 'a shadow hung over the British path of conquest: the shadow of the French fleet'.[30]

Despite the defeat at Saratoga and the distractions of war against France in the Caribbean, at this stage the war was still far from over. British naval power ensured that North American commerce was crippled, and in 1779 there were some military successes in Georgia and South Carolina. But Britain was unable to dominate the southern backcountry; when Spain entered the war in June 1779, as an ally of France, a new threat appeared in Florida. Enfeebled by the economic repercussions of war, the Americans were still suffering many setbacks, but as Britain's enemies multiplied, its increasingly disjointed military strategy slowly disintegrated under manifold pressures. First, Britain found that it could not break American resistance by controlling a few urban centres along the coast, since most of the colonial population did not depend economically on such cities. Furthermore, in the extensive interior behind the coast, where transport and communication were difficult, it proved impossible to conquer and police territory effectively, or to provide protection and aid for those substantial elements of the colonial population that remained loyal to Britain. The American rebels, on the other hand, were at home in their environment, and free to use guerrilla tactics to harry British forces which ventured into the interior. Finally, after France (and later Spain) entered the war, Britain faced increasing difficulty in maintaining the very extended transatlantic supply lines on which its armies relied.

Thus, British strategy eventually foundered under the mounting pressures of American military force and French maritime intervention. In 1780, following a series of costly but indecisive engagements in the Carolinas, Britain shifted its main army from South Carolina to Virginia, so that it might combine more effectively with the forces that still held New York. However, when Washington responded by shifting his forces from a planned attack on New York and marching southwards to Virginia, the British plan rapidly unravelled. Learning that General Cornwallis had moved his army to Yorktown, where he had encamped on a peninsula near the mouth of the Chesapeake Bay to await a British fleet, Washington called on the French to blockade the mouth of the Bay while he used his large army to cut off Cornwallis's retreat by land. Beseiged by Washington's superior forces, and unable to escape by sea, General Cornwallis was left with little choice but to capitulate, which he did in October 1781.[31]

Over-extended in its global conflict, a war-weary Britain opted to make terms with the American rebels. After lengthy negotiations, a formal treaty was concluded in September 1783, separating the thirteen continental colonies from Britain and acknowledging their

existence as the independent United States of America. Britain kept
Canada and managed to keep the French out of the continent, but
returned Florida to Spain in order to retain possession of Gibraltar.
The rich colonies of the eastern seaboard, the cradle of English
colonization in North America, as well as the recently acquired
territory in the south, were permanently lost. Colonials who had
begun by resisting reforms to imperial policy ended by achieving that
which they had not originally claimed: an independent state, delimited
by borders on the Great Lakes and the Mississippi in the north and
west, but with boundless possibilities for future expansion in the vast
lands that lay in the interior. For the first time in the history of the
Euro-American world, colonial peoples had permanently overthrown
the government of their parent power through a revolutionary
struggle.

THE EMERGENCE OF THE UNITED STATES

When they had achieved independence in 1783, the colonies of the
North American Atlantic seaboard entered into a new phase of their
history which, being outside British colonial rule, lies beyond the
compass of this study. However, before resuming our account of
developments in the British American world, some brief observations
on the outcome of the American Revolution and the earliest stages of
state-building in the United States will outline the general
characteristics of the first independent political system to emerge from
British colonial rule.

American independence involved more than simply the repudiation
of imperial rule; it also transformed the very bases of American
political life. Both during and after the conflict with Britain, the
growing influence of popular elements considerably accentuated the
participatory and democratic character of American politics. Between
1776 and 1778, the new states all acquired written constitutions
which, because they were framed by men imbued with ideas about
power taken from the English Whig tradition, brought radical
alterations in the structure of government and distribution of power.
The constitutions of the state governments created to replace British
authority all sought to dilute the power of the executive, despoiling
governors of their powers and making them subject to elections.
While the power of the magistracy was thus reduced, the legislature
was placed at the heart of government, embodying the doctrine of

popular sovereignty and the principle that all political office should be subject to elections. To complete the revolution in government, powers were separated and the social basis of politics broadened by extending the franchise. In some states, the power of established elites was eroded as the large contingents of urban artisans and small farmers who were active in revolutionary resistance to Britain asserted themselves as never before. Independence therefore meant more than simply transferring power from imperial government into the hands of oligarchies of the wealthy and privileged. Now political institutions often became more genuinely representative of, and responsive to, popular needs and aspirations.

The extent of democratization varied between states. Property requirements for voting were generally lowered and in some states were abolished completely, while established procedures of government were overhauled or overthrown. Pennsylvania, the epicentre of radical politics, initially adopted a very distinctive state constitution that swept away the governorship and upper house of the assembly in favour of a directly elected executive council and a unicameral legislature that was open to the public. Institutional change in other states was less striking, but there was a general tendency to diminish the power of the executive in reaction against the institution of the royal governorship of colonial times. With the temporary exceptions of Pennsylvania and Georgia, the new state constitutions followed British traditions and colonial precedents by establishing bicameral legislatures with upper and lower houses, but they also innovated in important respects. Representatives in both houses were chosen by the voters, the period of office-holding in the lower house tended to be limited, and representation was redistributed so as to give more weight to the more recently settled western areas. In most states, members of the legislature controlled appointments to the judiciary; state constitutions also defined the rights of the citizen clearly, guaranteeing freedom of speech and assembly, freedom of religion, the right to bear arms, and so on.[32]

Such institutional reforms did not guarantee immediate political stability. Amidst the economic difficulties of the postwar period, greater participation in politics often brought fierce contests for power. Indeed, the economic distress and rising taxation which resulted from the eight-year struggle with Britain led to violent agrarian unrest in 1785–6. In Massachusetts, there was open rebellion in 1786–7, when western farmers led by Daniel Shays reacted against taxes imposed by the state government by taking over county courts to prevent their enforcement. 'The political pendulum', it seemed, 'was swinging back:

the British rulers had perverted their power; now the people were perverting their liberty'.[33]

Popular politicization and the efflorescence of radical politics did not, however, lead to large-scale violence or prolonged instability. If the elites often had temporarily to give ground to radicals, they gradually reasserted their influence. From the political storms of the Revolution, a stable and united state emerged in 1787-8. Then, the new states accepted a federal constitution that invested Congress with overarching authority, and placed executive leadership in an American president.

At first, it seemed that the legacy of political practices under British rule would hinder the unification of an independent American state. Before the Revolution, the colonies had enjoyed considerable autonomy, exercised through governments that connected with London more than with their neighbours, and which jealously defended their separate identities. After 1765, opposition to Britain had encouraged them to suppress their differences in coalition against metropolitan government, but the adoption of the Articles of Confederation in 1777 had created only a very loose framework for unity. Under the Articles, the Continental Congress had authority to act in matters of foreign policy, but in other respects it fell far short of being a national government. It could not, for example, raise taxes, regulate commerce or create its own army, but had to rely on individual states to provide both money and military manpower. Nor could the Congress transform itself into a more effective instrument of central authority: all the states, whatever their size, had a vote in important matters, and amendment of the Articles of Confederation required unanimity. The weakness of central authority was not accidental. It stemmed from the deep suspicion of strong, centralized and potentially tyrannical authority which had informed the movement against Britain, from the mutual suspicions of colonies which had long been distinctive corporate entities, from the absence of a clear national consciousness, and from a political experience which, supported by current political theories, suggested that liberty was best preserved by small republics under local control. Moreover, after independence, the difficulties of achieving unity were further exacerbated by the fact that the Articles of Confederation applied only to the old colonies, and did not include the western territories ceded by the peace treaty with Britain.

Thus, after the war, the United States still faced an unresolved problem. Were they to continue as a loose confederation of separate sovereign states, or were they to fuse into one national polity? Initially, state governments showed little interest in accepting any authority beyond their own, and centrifugal forces seemed set to prevail. There were, however, countervailing, long-term conditions that disposed Americans to conjure unity from diversity. These were the tendencies towards social and cultural convergence apparent in the colonies before independence, their sense, cultivated in the struggle with Britain, of a common interest in protecting their rights, their fears about the fragility of government, and their experience, under British rule, of multi-tiered, multi-focal government.[34] Added to these pre-conditions for unity were the immediate need to decide on the ordered distribution and government of western lands, the increasingly urgent requirement for a common economic and fiscal policy to guide the United States out of postwar economic dislocation, and the determination of sectors in the elite to assert their political vision. All these factors led the states into fresh political experimentation. In 1787, delegates from twelve states attended a Constitutional Convention in Philadelphia, and after intensive debate agreed that central government should be strengthened by the creation of a new constitution. The result was the Federal Constitution of 1787, which brought into existence a national government that shared sovereignty with the states.[35]

The national government took a form which drew on British traditions in two major respects. First, 'like the empire, the American federal system did not concentrate authority in a single government but distributed it at different levels', thereby projecting into the new republic the principles of a system similar to that which colonials had experienced under British rule.[36] Second, it drew on Britain's 'mixed constitution' by balancing a legislature, an executive and an independent judiciary. The legislature was made of two parts: a House of Representatives, chosen by the voters of the states in proportion to their population, and a Senate in which each state would have an equal number of representatives. The new Congress was invested with the crucial powers which the Confederation Congress had lacked: namely, the right to levy taxes in, and to regulate commerce for all the states of the Union. Executive power was embodied in the president, who was chosen by indirect election and endowed with powers, exercised in conjunction with the Senate, to conduct foreign policy, to veto acts of Congress, and to appoint public officials.

Making a constitution was one step towards the new form of government; the more difficult stage was to have it ratified by a sufficient number of states, in the face of majority opposition from those who feared that federal government would become too powerful. This was, however, accomplished after an intense political campaign. The adherents of federalism triumphed by taking control of the various ratifying conventions in the separate states, and, by June 1788, they had secured the required majority for ratification. Thus, the colonies which had converted themselves into the independent United States of America also became a national federation, uniting both the states and their peoples under a common sovereignty, a sovereignty located in the people. The problem of reconciling central and local authority that had divided the colonies from Britain, and which had threatened to separate them after independence, was now to be resolved within the context of a single federal state.

In one respect, the new republic was deeply flawed. The institution of slavery, a contradiction of the principles of freedom which Americans had espoused in their constitution, remained untouched, leaving most blacks in the same conditions of servitude that they had endured under colonial rule. Indeed, after the Revolution had proclaimed all men to be free and equal before the law, white Americans increasingly sought to justify slavery by intensifying racist denigration of blacks as a lesser breed.[37] The principles espoused by the American revolutionaries did nonetheless promote ideas of freedom which, in the decades that followed, were to encourage the anti-slavery movement in both the United States and in the residual British empire. For whites, meanwhile, the stabilization of the new state marked the beginnings of a new era, in which the United States recovered from the trauma of war and revolution and, during the early nineteenth century, entered a period of rapid expansion which fulfilled the hopes of its progenitors.

NOTES

1 R. Douglas Francis, Richard Jones and Donald B. Smith, *Origins: Canadian History to Confederation* (Toronto, 1988) pp. 173–6.

2 For a discussion of colonial taxes, see Edwin J. Perkins, *The Economy of Colonial America* (New York, 1980) pp. 123–44; for the figures cited, see p. 125.

3 Gary M. Walton & James F. Shepherd, *The Economic Rise of Early America* (Cambridge, 1979) p. 163. It should be noted that these and the preceding figures for British tax payments must be treated with some scepticism because, although the British were undoubtedly the most highly taxed nation in Europe, there were 'literally hundreds of taxes of every kind and their incidence is extremely difficult to determine empirically.' See Patrick K. O'Brien, 'Political preconditions for the

Industrial Revolution', in Patrick K. O'Brien and Roland Quinault (eds) *The Industrial Revolution and British Society* (Cambridge, 1993) p. 145.

4 Pauline Maier, *From Resistance to Revolution: Colonial Radicals and the Development of American Opposition to Britain, 1765–1776* (London, 1973) pp. 51–112; on the 'Sons of Liberty', see pp. 85–9.

5 On the British 'friends of America', and their efforts at conciliation, see John Derry, *English Politics and the American Revolution* (London, 1976) pp. 129–73.

6 Quoted by Gordon S. Wood, *The Creation of the American Republic, 1776–1787* (New York and London, 1972 edition) p. 132.

7 This account of developments in British policy after the Seven Years War and of colonial responses to them is based on Ian R. Christie, *Crisis of Empire: Great Britain and the American Colonies, 1754–1783* (London, 1974 edition) especially pp. 39–101.

8 For a review of these positions, see Robert W. Tucker and David C. Hendrickson, *The Fall of the First British Empire: Origins of the War of American Independence* (Baltimore, Md, and London, 1982) pp. 187–99.

9 Quoted in Ian R. Christie and Benjamin W. Labaree, *Empire or Independence, 1760–1776* (London, 1976) p. 212.

10 For a full discussion of the constitutional debates which took place between 1765 and 1776, see Jack P. Greene, *Peripheries and Center: Constitutional Development in the Extended Polities of the British Empire and the United States, 1607–1688* (Athens, Ga, 1986) Chapters 5–6; quotations from pp. 87, 93.

11 Bernard Bailyn, *The Ideological Origins of the American Revolution* (Cambridge, Mass., 1967) p. ix.

12 On the sources of American eighteenth-century political thought and the theory of power drawn from it, see Bailyn, *Ideological Origins*, pp. 22–93; also Wood, *Creation of the American Republic*, pp. 3–45.

13 Quoted by Bailyn, *Ideological Origins*, p. 101.

14 Greene, *Peripheries and Center*, pp. 144–50.

15 Bailyn, *Ideological Origins*, p. vi.

16 For an early review of this historiography, see Jack P. Greene, 'The social origins of the American Revolution: an evaluation and an interpretation', *Political Science Quarterly* (1973) **88**: 1–22.

17 A collection of essays representing this approach is found in Alfred F. Young (ed) *The American Revolution: Explorations in the History of American Radicalism* (DeKalb, Ill., 1976).

18 For a review of rural disturbances in the later eighteenth century, see Edward C. Countryman, *The American Revolution* (New York, 1985), pp. 79–87.

19 Gary B. Nash, 'Social change and the growth of pre-revolutionary urban radicalism', in Young (ed), *American Revolution*, p. 18.

20 For a full statement of this position, see Gary B. Nash, *The Urban Crucible: Social Change, Political Consciousness, and the Origins of the American Revolution* (Cambridge, Mass., 1979) Chapters 7–13.

21 Greene, *Pursuits of Happiness*, p. 187.

22 Ibid., p. 195.

23 Gordon S. Wood, *The Radicalism of the American Revolution* (New York, 1992) especially pp. 11–168.

24   On the religious and political impact of the Great Awakening, see
      Patricia V. Bonomi, *Under the Cope of Heaven: Religion, Politics and Society
      in Colonial America* (Oxford and New York, 1986), pp. 131–186. For a
      striking study of the meaning of Radical evangelism in Virginia, where it
      had a strong impact, see Rhys Isaacs, *The Transformation of Virginia,
      1740–1790* (New York, 1988 edition) especially pp. 161–77; also, on the
      Great Awakening in Connecticut, see Richard Bushman, *From Puritan to
      Yankee. Character and the Social Order in Connecticut, 1690 1765*
      (Cambridge, Mass. 1967) pp. 235–88.

25   Quoted by Wood, *Creation of the American Republic*, p. 5.

26   Michael Zuckerman, 'Identity in British America: unease in Eden', in
      Nicholas Canny and Anthony Pagden (eds) *Colonial Identity in the Atlantic
      World, 1500–1800* (Princeton, NJ., 1987) p. 157.

27   Maier, *From Resistance to Revolution*, pp. 161–296.

28   For a succinct statement of the role of the Sons of Liberty, the rise of
      popular committees, and the influence of Tom Paine, see Countryman,
      The American Revolution, pp. 97–124. On Paine's influence and activities,
      see Eric Foner, 'Tom Paine's republic: radical ideology and social
      change', in Young (ed) *The American Revolution*, pp. 189 232.

29   For a full account of the American war for independence, see Piers
      Mackesy, *The War for America, 1775–1783* (London, 1964).

30   Ibid., p. 278.

31   Ibid., pp. 510–51, for the factors which led to Britain's defeat.

32   Wood, *Creation of the American Republic*, pp. 127–256.

33   Ibid , p 403

34   On conditions making for separation, and those which favoured
      federation, see Greene, *Peripheries and Center*, pp. 157–74.

35   Wood, *Creation of the American Republic*, especially pp. 471–518, for an
      excellent account of the debate over the Federal Constitution and the
      ideas that informed it. A superb survey of the social and political
      aftermath of independence is given in Wood, *The Radicalism of the
      American Revolution*, pp. 229 369.

36   Greene, *Peripheries and Center*, p. 205.

37   Duncan J. MacLeod, ''Toward caste', in Ira Berlin and Ronald Hoffman
      (eds) *Slavery and Freedom in the Age of the American Revolution* (Urbana and
      Chicago, Ill., 1983) pp. 217–36.

CHAPTER TEN

Realignments of Empire

The separation of the thirteen North American colonies from Britain in 1783 was long regarded as the terminal turning point in the history of the British empire based on colonies in the Americas. For historians of the imperial school, the American Revolution not only delivered a death blow to the first empire, but also initiated a long hiatus in British imperialism; at the turn of the century, it was thought, Britain was distracted by international war and domestic social and political tensions, and, amidst these diversions, was unable to recuperate its imperialist energies and begin to build a second empire based on new regions and new principles until the 1830s and 1840s.

This is, however, a view that no longer commands much support. It was first revised by Vincent Harlow, who argued that, while the American Revolution did indeed mark the collapse of the old colonial system, there was no sharp break between the first and second empires. According to Harlow, the American empire was already losing its importance to Britain and giving way to the building of another, second empire some 30 years before the political crisis caused by the American Revolution. British victory in the Seven Years War, Harlow argued, had given Britain a commanding position in both North America and India and an ascendancy over the routes of world trade; then, after 1763, the combination of supremacy at sea and industrial development at home had induced a 'swing to the east' that was based in a quest for markets and materials to support metropolitan industry and which consequently diminished the importance of territorial poss-ession and formal imperial rule. Thus, when Britain was coming to terms with its rebellious American colonies in 1782, Lord Shelburne glossed over the implications of their loss with the remark that 'we prefer trade to dominion'; for Harlow, this clearly reflected the emergence of a new kind of imperialism, concerned with trade rather than territory, and was nothing less than 'an enunciation of the general principles on which the second empire was based'.[1]

It is doubtful, however, that British colonialism in the Americas was so immediately weakened by the American Revolution, or that the 'shift to the east' proposed by Harlow reflected a decline in the importance of Britain's colonial system and economic links in the Atlantic world. It is true that a new age of discovery, involving systematic exploration of the Pacific Ocean by British naval officers, was in motion at this time, strengthening prospects for an empire of trade in the east. This had started in the 1760s, when Byron's occupation of West Falkland reflected a growing British interest in obtaining strategic bases for penetrating the Pacific, and, though the Falkland garrison was temporarily abandoned in 1771, exploration of the Pacific continued with Captain James Cook's famous voyages between 1768 and 1780, and with George Vancouver's reconnaisance of the northeastern Pacific coast of North America in the 1790s.[2] However, the penchant for Pacific exploration and the search for new routes and regions for trade certainly did not induce Britain to abandon sovereignty over its remaining colonies in the Americas, or to relax its mercantilist policies for exploiting colonial resources; nor, indeed, did it assuage the British appetite for further territorial acquisition. In fact, during the great French wars which opened in 1796 and finally concluded nearly two decades later, Britain was to continue expanding its formal empire. In the Americas, Britain seized new territory in the Caribbean and strengthened its political hold on Canada, while also pressing claims for territory on the north-western coast of North America; at the same time, Britain hardened its formal authority over territories in the east, where the heartlands of a second British empire were taking shape in India. Thus, although Britain had undoubtedly suffered a tremendous blow to its pride and prestige from the loss of the thirteen North American colonies in 1783, it continued to be an imperial power with ambitions and capacity for further expansion.

AFTER THE AMERICAN REVOLUTION: BRITAIN AND THE UNITED STATES

The excision of the thirteen North American colonies from the Anglo-American empire was not the economic catastrophe which many contemporaries feared. In terms of mercantilist thinking, the separation of the United States threatened to have devastating economic effects, since it cost Britain political control over the growing markets, rich agricultural resources, and large mercantile fleet of her erstwhile colonies. But in practice the removal of the United States from the orbit of the colonial commercial system did not deprive Britain of access of their markets and resources. As the United States recuperated from the economic dislocations of war and merged under a federal government that was capable of managing an ordered foreign and commercial policy, the ex-colonies not only resumed their trade with Britain, but did so on a growing scale. In 1781–1785, U.S. trade with Britain was worth £1.8 million; little more than a decade later, its value had trebled, to £7.4 million. Thus, though political relations had been completely recast by the American Revolution, the underlying economic relationship with the mother country continued to flourish and mature.

This relationship had of course changed in some important respects. No longer part of the British empire, the United States were excluded from the system of colonial trade created by the Navigation Acts, and lost the preference which this system gave to colonial producers and traders. This immediately entailed a loss of income from the patterns of trade and shipping which had previously linked the North American colonies to their counterparts in the British Caribbean. American ships were now treated as foreign, and therefore excluded from use in British trade, even by British owners. The recession which this brought to the American shipbuilding industry was exacerbated by the contraction of traditional trades with the West Indies. Although they were not completely cut off from commerce with the British West Indies, the United States lost the very valuable markets that the islands had always provided for their fish and meat. These reverses were short-lived, however. After 1793, the international economic situation changed dramatically, when the leading European powers entered into a long period of warfare, centred first on revolutionary, then Napoleonic France. The ensuing demand for US exports and shipping services brought a boom which restored the ex-colonial economies, allowing them to escape from their post-independence difficulties and to establish export markets outside the British empire.[3]

Renewal of commercial and economic growth in the United States was partly based, then, on a change in patterns of trade, as the ex-colonies increasingly adapted to trading outside the British system. But Britain did not suffer the loss of its North American markets from this realignment of United States' exports. Most American exports still went to Britain, and the United States continued to take most of their imports from the old mother country. This enduring economic tie was prone to break down: in 1812–14, the United States went to war with Britain in protest against the damage done by American trade by British naval interference with neutral shipping. But the war did not permanently damage the underlying trends in British trade with the ex-colonies, where Britain continued to find a very valuable, fast-growing market for its manufactures. The fears that independence would wreck British trade with North America therefore proved unjustified. The United States continued to be by far the largest single market for British goods in the Americas as a whole; and it became clear that, in this case at least, trade could be sustained without dominion.[4]

For all the humiliation brought by the partial disintegration of the American empire, it did little to hinder Britain's continuing progress towards becoming the greatest commercial, colonial and trading nation in the world. Behind this advance lay a series of rapid and cumulative changes in economic structure and technology, bringing to Britain what historians call the 'Industrial Revolution'. Controversy remains concerning the causes of the take-off into industrial, mass manu-facturing. Some historians argue that it was driven mainly by the growth of British overseas trade, while others emphasize the importance of developments within Britain's society and economy. Beyond dispute, however, is the fact that Britain's growing economic strength enabled successive governments not only to retain existing colonial possessions and to sustain imperial pretensions, but also to fight a final, massive struggle against France and Spain, in wars that reduced their empires to ruins.

The resurgence of major inter-power warfare started in 1793 when, as the repercussions of the French Revolution convulsed Europe, Britain re-engaged in its epic conflict with France. Between 1793 and 1795, Spain was also at war with revolutionary France, but soon reverted to its old alliance with France against Britain. From 1796, Spain joined with France against Britain in a wartime partnership that lasted until 1808, when Napoleon seized the Spanish throne; then Britain and France remained the two great contenders for primacy until Napoleon was finally defeated in 1814, and the contest was finally decided in Britain's favour. Let us now turn to examine the reverberations of this conflict in the American colonial world, beginning with the reorganization and realignments that took place in the Anglo-American empire after the American Revolution.

287

IMPERIAL REALIGNMENTS IN NORTH AMERICA

Geopolitically the result of American independence was to refocus Britain's American empire on two areas: the established colonies in the Caribbean, and the lands which had been taken from the French in North America. The configuration of Caribbean colonialism was basically unchanged; we shall return to consider its subsequent development later in this chapter. In British North America, however, the Treaty of Versailles brought striking changes, as the loss of the thirteen seaboard colonies shifted the locus of British sovereignty northwards and towards the continental interior.

The first consequence of the Versailles Treaty of 1783 was, of course, to redefine British North America by redrawing political boundaries. Before the American Revolution, the regions taken from the French had attracted relatively little attention from British governments and few British immigrants; now they became the core of a new British North America, focused around the old French settlements on the Lower St Lawrence River, in the Great Lakes region, and in the maritime provinces north of New England. In its negotiations with the United States, Britain probably ceded more of its territory than was necessary, mainly from ignorance of the geography of the interior. Although British diplomats resisted pressure to cede the whole of Canada, they accepted a border which gave to the United States the huge, potentially rich territories south of the Great Lakes, thereby relinquishing a region which, thanks to the efforts of French settlers and soldiers, had been an integral part of Canada. Thus they betrayed the Indians whose territories they had guaranteed by treaty at the time of the Proclamation Act of 1763, and unhinged the fur-trading economy which French Canadians had created over the previous century. On the other hand, Britain did hold on to the vast, still largely unexplored regions north and west of the Great Lakes, together with the St Lawrence region and the coastal areas of Nova Scotia, Newfoundland and Labrador, all of which provided the foundations for a new colonial development in the decades after the American Revolution.

The other effect of the American Revolution was to transform the human geography of British North America. For the fracture of the empire involved more than simply a redefinition of political boundaries. It also brought into existence a British colonial society in the regions that had been taken from the French in 1763, as communities torn apart by civil strife during the American Revolution generated a flow of refugees in these previously neglected lands. After

1783, the French settlers who had been the first founding people of European colonial society in Canada were joined by another mass of founding immigrants: the loyalists who left the newly independent United States in order to continue their lives under British rule.

The cause of independence had not attracted unanimous support from the populations of the thirteen colonies, and many thousands of people who remained loyal to the crown left the rebel colonies both during and after the Revolution. The emigrant loyalists were a heterogeneous lot, for there was no single, simple pattern to loyalism during the Revolution. To some extent, loyalism correlated with the distribution of those whose livelihood depended most heavily on imperial authority and ties with Britain. Government officials and soldiers, Anglican clergy, agents of British trading companies and merchants who relied on British trade, for example, were the obvious categories among such people. Loyalism also had some correlation with ethnic and religious affiliation. Highland and Lowland Scots generally supported the crown in its battle with American patriots, though for different reasons, and loyalist refugees also included Indians and blacks, some of whom were still slaves. Curiously, allegiance to the Anglican church did not correspond with loyalty to Britain: the Virginia gentry were the most striking example of Anglicans who were vociferously opposed to Britain. Quakers and other pietist sects, on the other hand, often found it difficult to reconcile their pacifism with a situation of political polarization and conflict; some were consequently persuaded that their best future was to leave. Nor did the racial composition of colonies determine their attitudes to Britain. In Georgia and South Carolina, fear that black slave rebellion might follow from any disturbance to the colonial order persuaded some whites that British rule was best, but the majority of whites in colonies like Virginia and Maryland, which also had large slave populations, made the opposite choice.[5] For the present purposes, however, precise specification of the spatial distribution of loyalism is less important than the fact that large numbers of loyalists emigrated from the emerging United States to settle elsewhere, with consequences that affected the character of the remaining body of empire.

Between 80,000 and 100,000 loyalists are thought to have left the United States during and after the American Revolution. Of these, only a small proportion (around 7,000) returned to the mother country.[6] Most went to British colonies, mainly in the northern regions still under British control. At one time, it seemed that East Florida would become a larger and more active British colony, outside of the United States, for during the war it had attracted many thousands of loyalist refugees from the south. However, their hopes for remaining under British sovereignty were betrayed at the Treaty of Versailles, when the metropolitan government decided to return Florida to Spain rather than relinquish its hold on Gibraltar. Many loyalists in Florida were thus forced to move southwards to the British West Indies, mainly to Jamaica and the Bahamas, which between them absorbed between 14,000 and 17,000 loyalist émigrés. However, by far the greater part of the loyalist exodus from the United States went north, to Nova Scotia and Canada, where they formed the nucleus of an emergent British Canadian population. In this sense, 'the American Revolution produced not one country but two: a nation and a non-nation'.[7]

The loyalist migrations transformed and reconstituted two main regions in North America: the maritime province of Nova Scotia, which had been taken from the French in 1713, and Canada, which France had relinquished to Britain in 1763. Of these, Nova Scotia felt the first, and initially strongest impact of the movement of refugees. In 1783 alone, 32,000 migrants were carried there by the fleets which evacuated loyalists from New York, and British officials hastily set up new townships and distributed land to accommodate them. Given the sparse population of the region before the Revolution, there was no lack of land to allocate; as the population grew, the British government subdivided Nova Scotia into several colonies by making Cape Breton Island a separate unit, and establishing New Brunswick. Together with Newfoundland and Prince Edward Island, these became the maritime provinces of the new British North America.[8]

The interior of Canada also felt the impact of migration from the United States, as migrants moved northwards into the frontier lands of the old province of Quebec. This migration was smaller in scale and differed in social composition from that which converged on Nova Scotia, though in the long term it was to prove no less important. Most of the migrants were small farmers from the backcountry of New York, Pennsylvania and New England, who had abandoned their smallholdings in the rebel colonies to restart their life on another frontier. At first, the Governor-General of Canada planned to move them to the coasts and islands of the Gulf of St Lawrence, in order to keep them apart from the established areas of French settlement. But the influx was sufficiently large to persuade him of the need to establish new settlements along the western shores of the St Lawrence River and on the northern banks of Lake Ontario and Lake Erie. Thus a new region of colonization was laid down in the interior, west of the lands peopled by the French in the Lower St Lawrence.

As this immigrant population grew to around 20,000 by 1790, the British colonial government also accepted the need to recognize Quebec as a distinctive region, with its own institutions of government. Accordingly, the Constitutional (Canada) Act of 1791 created Upper and Lower Canada, dividing the old province of Quebec into two parts along the line of the Ottawa River. This was basically a division between a French and a British Canada, distinguishing the new loyalist settlements of the Upper St Lawrence and Great Lakes region from the older French settlements which stretched along the Lower St Lawrence. The division was not perfect – French and English peoples were found on both sides of the divide – but it did reflect the cultural dualism that was to become a central feature of Canadian society, with French Quebec separated from an English Upper Canada by language, religion and law.[9]

Meanwhile, penetration of the vast lands of the interior was beginning, through the explorations and activities of fur traders. By virtue of a charter first granted in 1670, the Hudson's Bay Company still controlled the trade of the entire north-west, while the North West Company, operating out of Montreal, carried the search for furs far to the west, where lone adventurers arriving by land hardened the claims which naval expeditions made for Britain on the northern Pacific coasts. The development of the Canadian west still lay in the future, however; the core of post-revolutionary British North America remained in the North Atlantic coasts and islands, and in the two Canadas of the St Lawrence–Great Lakes axis.

Despite the rapid influx of new settlers, these regions all remained backward and poorly developed compared to the neighbouring United States, and hopes that the St Lawrence River would immediately become the trunkline of a resurgent British empire in North America were too optimistic. However, in spite of the raw quality of much of its society and economy, Canada's regions did assume definite, stable forms in the closing years of the eighteenth century, as population continued to grow and solid networks of production and trade took shape.

Lower Canada changed little, retaining its seigneurial system of landownership and its Catholicism; sheltered from commerce, its old French character was preserved intact beneath the veneer of British institutions. In Upper Canada and the Maritime Provinces, the pace of change was quicker. Upper Canada was an agrarian frontier, where the availibility of good, cheap land continued to attract migrants from the United States and the British Isles into an economy of subsistence agriculture. The Maritime Provinces, on the other hand, were able to

291

develop a more commercial agriculture, tuned to external markets in the British West Indies. This development was severely limited however; fertile land was scarce, and the northern and middle regions of the United States were still able to produce foodstuffs much more cheaply and efficiently. In the end, it was the products of the forests rather than the land which stimulated growth in the region. For, like the United States, Canada derived a sudden economic stimulus from the wars of the European powers. Britain's conflict with France created a new and important market for timber when, between 1809 and 1812, Parliament raised duties on the import of foreign wood and thereby gave preference to colonial suppliers. Wood now replaced furs as the Canadian staple export, generating a trade which became 'virtually the sole support of New Brunswick, the great resource of the Canadas, the origin of traffic, population and plenty for all British North America.'[10]

Economic transformation and political consolidation in British North America advanced during the war between Britain and the United States in 1812–14. Precipitated by American anger at British interference with neutral shipping, the war was fought on two fronts, both of which affected Canada. The first was a maritime campaign, fought in the Atlantic and on the seaboard of the United States, where American privateers harried British shipping and the Royal Navy hunted down the privateers. The resulting disruption of US trade favoured Newfoundland's fisheries, while New England's trading losses generally benefited the Maritime Provinces. Exports of foodstuffs to the British West Indies increased rapidly, as did direct trade with the Mediterranean, while the boom in timber exports to Britain continued, accompanied by the growth of a shipbuilding industry in Nova Scotia and New Brunswick.[11]

The other front was on land, where the Americans aimed at conquering Canada by invasion. However, after some early successes in the land campaign, the United States failed to press its military advantage against overstretched British forces, and when Napoleon was defeated in Europe in 1814, Britain was able to strike back, recapturing much of the territory which it had previously lost. Indeed, in 1814 Britain had an opportunity to redraw the boundaries with the United States which it had accepted at the Treaty of Versailles in 1783, by retaking territories in the interior previously ceded to the Americans. In the event, British governments were too preoccupied with affairs in Europe to give much attention to Canada, and the chance was lost. Hence, the shape of British North America was confirmed at the Treaty of Ghent in 1814, and the United States retained its dominance in the centre of the continent. Nonetheless, British North America had survived and managed to stay apart from the United States, sustaining its separate identity and ensuring that Britain would continue to exercise a strong influence in North America throughout the nineteenth century.

REPERCUSSIONS OF REVOLUTION IN THE CARIBBEAN

While the colonial world of North America was split asunder by the American Revolution, the other heartland of British colonialism in the Americas, set in the Caribbean archipelago, remained intact. The persistence of colonial rule in the West Indies is not difficult to explain. Since the early eighteenth century, British islands in the Caribbean had become ever more dependent on a growing commerce in sugar and increasingly reliant on British markets for their crops.[12] Between 1750 and 1775, growth was particularly rapid; although the expanding sugar trade did not always shelter the debt-ridden planter class from economic difficulties, it tightened bonds to the mother country and further hardened the system of racial hierarchy and black subordination fostered by slavery.

This system was, however, vulnerable to threats from within. Throughout the eighteenth century, the plantation regime remained extremely harsh, and the violence of the slaveowners also engendered resistance from slaves, which made the planters fearful of social indiscipline and conscious of the threat of insurrection. After the 1760s, large-scale rebellion became much less common, but the threat of slave rebellion continued to be a nightmare for the planters, since on all the islands small white minorities inevitably felt insecure amidst huge majorities of black slaves and restless groups of free people of colour.

White apprehension about insubordination within their societies was compounded by fear of military assault from without. Vulnerable to attack by sea and dependent on external supplies of food, clothing and slave labour, the West Indian planters were acutely conscious of the threat posed by the French, who routinely attacked the British islands in time of war; their fortunes, indeed their very survival, depended on naval and military protection provided by the parent power. In these circumstances, the governing elites in the British Caribbean did not doubt that their interests were best served by clinging to colonial rule. The point was made plainly and succinctly by the Speaker of the Barbados Assembly who, responding to North

American taunts of timidity in the face of British 'tyranny', observed that Barbados 'could not so much as exist without the constant protection and support of some superior state'.[13] The Jamaica Assembly also guaranteed its loyalty on similar grounds, stating that 'from the small number of white inhabitants and its peculiar situation, from the encumbrance of more than 20,000 slaves, it cannot be supposed that we intend . . . resistance to Great Britain.'[14] Thus, while colonial assemblies supported the principles espoused by the North American rebels, and declared their rights to control their internal affairs, they refused to join the rebellion of the mainland colonies.[15]

Loyalty to the British crown did not allow the West Indies to escape the consequences of North American disloyalty. Conflict between Britain and the thirteen colonies meant that the islands suffered the loss of both North American markets for their exports of sugar and its derivatives, and North American supplies of basic foodstuffs. The two leading Caribbean colonies were consequently subjected to considerable economic distress during the American War of Independence, worsened by the effects of severe hurricanes in 1780. In Barbados, the slave population fell from 68,000 to 57,000 between 1773 and 1783, as many died from starvation and malnutrition. Jamaica was less severely affected, since it managed to produce more of its own food than the other islands, and took supplies from North American regions which remained under British control during the war. Its economy was nonetheless hit by rising food prices, higher taxes, and the increased costs of trade during wartime. Moreover, after France came into the war in 1778, followed by Spain in 1779, economic disturbance was accompanied by military setbacks, as many British islands fell to the superior naval and military forces of Britain's enemies. Dominica, Grenada, St Kitts, Montserrat and Nevis were all taken by the French; it was only Admiral Rodney's victory over the French Caribbean fleet at the end of the war that prevented a full-scale assault on Jamaica and finally halted the French offensive. In the ensuing Treaty of Versailles, the islands were all returned, and British sovereignty in the Caribbean was restored to its prewar state.[16]

The recovery of Caribbean territories temporarily lost to the French did not immediately restore the British West Indian economies, as they had to adjust to the derangement of the Anglo–American empire caused by the secession of the mainland colonies. Indeed, according to Lowell Ragatz, the American Revolution marked a turning point in the history of the West Indies, in that it hastened the decline of economies that were, he alleged, 'tottering from structural weakness'.[17]

After enduring the pains of war, the islands had to confront the rigours of a peace in which trade in essential foodstuffs was complicated by the secession of the United States. Despite its great influence in London, the West India lobby was unable to persuade Parliament to restore trade with the ex-colonies to its prewar footing. Aware that to do so would wreck the chances of developing the agricultural and fishing resources of the loyalist settlements in Canada, Parliament accepted a new commercial policy which sought to balance the interests of its remaining colonies in North America with those of the West Indies. Thus, it recognized that the West Indies should continue to export sugar and other staples to the United States, and be permitted to import vital supplies of timber, livestock, grain, flour and bread from the United States. This did not, however, restore the traditional patterns of trade between North America and the West Indies. The United States were now treated as a foreign country that was not eligible for the privileges of trading inside the colonial commercial system. All trade between the West Indies and the United States had accordingly to be carried on British ships; to protect the Canadian colonies, all imports of fish and meat from the United States were prohibited. So, after enduring the disturbances of war, the West Indian planters complained that the revised trade regulations prevented their recovery in peacetime.

In fact, for all the difficulties that were inflicted on West Indian planters by the effects of the American Revolution (and worsened by hurricanes and crop failures during the 1780s), the dislocation of empire did not bring a permanent contraction of the British Caribbean economy. Sugar exports to Britain quickly recovered their vitality in the decade after 1783, as did imports from the mother country; although supplies of provisions from the United States declined from pre-revolutionary levels, they were supplemented by supplies from the farmers and fishermen of Canada.[18] Moreover, during the 1790s, West Indian planters benefited from the crisis of their greatest rival, when the French colony of St Domingue was swept by a revolutionary upheaval, in which its plantations were devastated by slave insurrection and war.

Revolution in St Domingue began in 1789, when the great planters of the colony seized upon the difficulties of the *ancien régime* in France to try to obtain greater economic and political autonomy for themselves. This tactic backfired badly. As France plunged deeper into revolutionary turmoil, the whole context of politics in St Domingue was altered: conflict and mobilization spread to other social groups in the colony, extending first to the poorer whites and mulattos, then to the black slaves. In 1791, slave rebellion transformed political protest into race war and revolution. Over the next decade, St Domingue was racked by internal violence of an unprecedented scale and ferocity, exacerbated after 1793 by the intervention of British and Spanish expeditions seeking to embarrass France. By 1801, the colony had become virtually independent, under the leadership of that 'gilded African', Toussaint L'Ouverture; in 1804, formal independence was proclaimed by Dessalines, an ex-slave who made himself Emperor of Haiti, which later became the first black republic in history.[19]

For the planter classes in the Caribbean, this upheaval presented a terrifying spectacle of black insurrection but, horrifying though it seemed in social terms, economically it was a blessing in disguise. The fall of St Domingue eliminated a major competitor of the British planters and, as the British navy asserted its naval supremacy in the Atlantic, gave the West Indies a strong advantage in international sugar markets. Indeed, the decades of Anglo-French wars in 1793–1802 and 1803–15 ushered in a period of prosperity for the West Indies. Prices of sugar, coffee and cotton all rose to record levels, and West Indian trade was of considerable importance in enabling Britain to sustain its economic development in wartime. Cotton from the Caribbean was a vital raw material for the growing textile industries in Britain, the sugar trade helped Britain to beat Napoleon's efforts to cut off trade with European markets, and during the war the West Indies were a vital market for British exports.[20] In this sense, it is not unreasonable to assert that, in the great struggle with France, 'the British Isles were saved by the British Empire'.[21]

When war ended, Britain added to its American possessions some notable territorial gains in the Caribbean region. France ceded St Lucia and Tobago, Spain yielded Trinidad, and Britain purchased the Dutch South American colonies of Demerera, Essequibo and Dutch Berbice. The addition of these territories, with their potential for plantation agriculture using slave labour, reaffirmed the character that British America had taken after the American Revolution, as an empire based on slavery. But, while Britain extended its influence in the Caribbean region, important changes affecting the future character of its colonial system were already underway. Not only had Britain entrenched itself more firmly in India, thereby widening new frontiers for imperialism, but the anti-slavery campaign that had started in Britain during the 1780s also struck its first blow against the old colonial system in the West Indies, when, in 1807, it persuaded Parliament to outlaw the slave trade.

Abolishing the slave trade did not necessarily threaten slavery itself.

Indeed, some advocated ending the trade in order to prevent the spread of slave insurrections and black republicanism from the French to the British West Indies, and thus to conserve slavery in the Anglo-American empire. Others also thought that termination of the trade would strengthen rather than weaken West Indian planter interests, insofar as it would encourage natural reproduction among blacks and create conditions in which 'the structure of West Indian society will more and more resemble that of the compact, firm, and respectable communities which compose the North American states.'[22] In fact, the abolition of the slave trade in 1807 was followed by a lull in anti-slavery activity in Britain, before it revived in the 1820s. Then, drawing support from the movement for reform in Britain's domestic political system, the abolitionists finally achieved their objective, with the passage of the Abolition of Slavery Bill through the House of Commons in 1833. Thus, half a century after Britain acknowledged the independence of most of its subjects in North America, the power which had derived so much profit from Caribbean plantations emancipated the slaves in its remaining colonies and thereby marginalized the West Indian colonies which had so long been at the core of the Anglo-American empire.

THE ATTACK ON SLAVERY

The reasons for this fundamental change have been the subject of energetic controversy among historians, much of it focused on Eric Williams' seminal work, *Capitalism and Slavery*. In this work, Williams argued that Britain abolished colonial slavery because it had outlived its economic utility. According to Williams, slavery was a form of labour which, having been bred in a mercantilist system, withered when the forces of industrial capitalism turned against commercial monopoly in favour of free trade. Drawing on Ragatz's portrait of decline in the plantation economies following the American Revolution, Williams argued that the movement towards abolishing the slave trade and slavery succeeded for two major reasons. On the one hand, he affirmed that the economic decline of the West Indies which had started in the late eighteenth century was exacerbated by world overproduction of sugar during the first decade of the nineteenth century; as sugar became widely available from other sources, the importance of the West Indies to Britain and the potency of their political support was concomitantly reduced. On the other hand, he

297

saw a connection between abolitionism and the rise of a British capitalist bourgeoisie which, born of metropolitan industrialization, favoured wage labour and free trade. 'The capitalists', said Williams, 'had first encouraged West Indian slavery and then helped to destroy it.'[23]

This interpretation has been the touchstone for an intense debate which has left little of Williams's thesis intact. As regards the abolition of the slave trade in 1807, his critics have shown that the island economies did not suffer the decline which Williams identified, and that the correlation between West Indian decline and the end of the slave trade is therefore untenable. Indeed, Seymour Drescher has demonstrated that the slave-based Caribbean economies continued to grow and to make a very significant contribution to British commerce for several decades after the American Revolution. The abolitionists, Drescher argues, confronted a vital and dynamic system, 'not a wasted machine which the British government could phase out like a bank-rupt venture, accumulating moral capital in return'.[24] The abolition of the slave trade in 1808 thus went against the grain in an empire that continued to have a strong stake in slavery in its own dominions and other lands.

Williams's contention that new manufacturing interests were instrumental in ending the trade has also proved vulnerable. Roger Anstey's investigation of the passage of legislation through the House of Commons in 1806–7 shows that abolition of the slave trade cannot be depicted as the work of an organized or coherent group that represented the interests which Williams depicted as the driving force against the West Indian interest. It was, rather, the result of clever political manoeuvring by abolitionists who 'conceived the tactic of so using a particular, fortuitous, conjunction in Britain's politico-economic position, brought about by war, as to present the abolition of up to two-thirds of the British slave trade as an elementary dictate of the national interest in time of war.' In short, abolition of the trade was not a victory for economic interests disguised as altruism; it was the achievement of humanitarian groups who cloaked their altruistic concerns with hard-headed appeals to the national interest, based on evidence that the trade seemed to be serving Britain's enemies better than Britain itself.[25] The importance which Anstey attributed to the peculiar political circumstances that prevailed in 1807 has recently been restated, albeit in broader terms, by Robin Blackburn. For Blackburn, the reactionary ruling oligarchy in Britain acquiesced in abolition in 1807 because it had reached a crucial moment in the war with France. At a time when there was 'a palpable danger of war-weariness, middle-class pacifism, and even explosive social discontent', abolition of the slave trade was a reform that allowed government to rally patriotic support for war, while deflecting radical political challenges and evading more problematic issues of political reform at home.[26]

The idea that Britain's abolition of slave trading and slavery was governed simply by metropolitan economic interests which stood to gain from their destruction has also come under attack from David Brion Davis, who firmly rejects Williams's dramatic reduction of anti-slavery ideology and agitation to class interests. First, Davis points out that anti-slavery sentiment 'emerged from a convergence of complex religious, intellectual and literary trends – trends which are by no means reducible to the economic interests of particular classes, but which must be understood as part of a larger transformation of attitudes towards labour, property and individual responsibility.'[27] Davis does, however, see subtle linkages between the advance of the anti-slavery movement and social changes in Britain, and allows that the evolution of anti-slavery opinion 'reflected the ideological needs of various groups and classes' in British society.[28] For, while he insists that abolitionists were untainted by hidden economic motives, Davis acknowledges that anti-slavery contributed to sustaining the hegemony of Britain's governing elites by allowing them to define and restrict the terms of political debate to areas where their legitimacy and power was not seriously questioned. In appropriating the cause of anti-slavery, the governing classes were able to make a public commitment to moral standards which 'helped legitimate both the existing system of class power and the emerging concept of free labour as an impersonal, marketable commodity' by assuring anxious Britons, caught up in the turmoil of rapid social change, that there were limits to the exploitation of labour.[29]

Davis's work has prompted a further intriguing debate about the ideology of abolitionism and its links with middle-class reformism in Britain, and, on a broader front, about the relationship of the new humanitarian sensibility to the spread of a market model of society.[30] This focus on the ideological context of anti-slavery in metropolitan society should not, however, distract from the fact that British abolitionism was not the sole force behind slave emancipation. For, as Blackburn affirms, the abolition of slavery in 1833 involved more than just changes in political attitudes among British elites and middle classes; it stemmed from a conjunction of forces which included ongoing structural change in the empire, a new assertiveness among people of colour and slaves in colonial societies, and class struggle in Britain.

Structural change in the empire was reflected in the decline of the West Indies after the defeat of Napoleon, when wartime boom was revealed as an Indian summer.[31] After 1815, sugar prices fell sharply; although Britain now dominated the world's sugar plantation regions to a greater extent than ever before, the Abolition Act of 1807 restricted the growth of British slave plantations, and the British share of world sugar exports declined steadily over the next half-century.[32] Meanwhile, Britain's overseas trade was undergoing a general reorientation, and the islands' weight within the British empire diminished markedly. In 1804–6, 21 per cent of British domestic exports had gone to the West Indian colonies; by 1824–6, the level had fallen to only 11 per cent. Meanwhile, British exports to Asia, Latin America and the United States expanded during the opening decades of the nineteenth century, and after 1815 British importers looked more to the United States for their cotton, while also beginning to take small quantities of sugar from Cuba and Brazil. All this made British government less likely to pay a high economic and political cost for defending slavery in the West Indies, and, as their prosperity waned, made planters more ready to consider slave emancipation in return for compensation.

Commercial reorientation and related pressures for free trade do not, however, wholly explain abolition, since there were still powerful interests which defended slavery and were capable of fighting a long rearguard action to sustain it. Slavery was not, in any case, in any way incompatible with British capitalism: it survived in the 'Cotton Kingdom' of the United States and in Brazil and Cuba, all of which attracted British commerce and capital. For these reasons, Blackburn rightly draws our attention to two other major forces undermining slavery. One was the greater assertiveness of free coloureds and slaves. Between 1810 and 1830, the free coloured population in the islands had doubled; in Jamaica, at least, free coloureds helped destabilize the slave regime by expressing a growing demand for civic equality. Slave rebellion also became increasingly threatening, with major rebellions in Demerara in 1823 and in Jamaica in 1831. Meanwhile, in Britain itself, anti-slavery activity was interwoven with pressures for reforming Parliament and disturbances arising from economic dislocation and social distress, and, as an issue which had an appeal that crossed class lines, the campaign for abolition interacted with demands for general reform of the British political system. 'Ultimately', Blackburn concludes, 'colonial slavery was menaced not by a specific, capitalist interest but rather by the social struggles which capitalism had unleashed, in both colony and metropolis.'[33]

Thus the erosion of West Indian trade after 1815, political restiveness among free coloureds and rebellious slaves, combined with a metropolitan movement against slavery, eventually combined to undermine the power of the West Indian planter class. Its fate was finally sealed by the emancipation of slaves in 1833, and its decline accelerated the introduction of free trade in sugar between 1846 and 1854. By the middle of the nineteenth century, the British Caribbean had definitely lost its position as a great redoubt of empire. Although the new colonies of Trinidad and Guiana were to rebuild their plantation economies using immigrant labour from the east, the old island colonies were to pass into relative obscurity during the very years when Britain was reaching towards its zenith as a world economic power.

BRITAIN AND THE FALL OF THE EURO-AMERICAN EMPIRES

While the importance to Britain of its own American colonies visibly diminished during the opening decades of the nineteenth century, that loss was compensated by remarkable growth of British economic influence in other parts of the world, not least in the Americas themselves. Not only did Britain succeed in all but obliterating French colonialism; it was also to benefit from the effects of the cycle of Atlantic wars and revolutions that stretched from 1796 to 1815, which brought the collapse of the other Euro-American empires and left Britain as the leading economic power in the western hemisphere. How did this come about?

In 1783, Britain's loss of its principal North American colonies was a source of considerable satisfaction to the governments of France and Spain, the other leading colonial powers in the western hemisphere, since it deprived Britain of valuable territories and markets and seemed to stem the advance of their most formidable competitor. Moreover, during the years immediately after the Treaty of Versailles, both France and Spain strengthened their hold on the resources of their American colonies. France had of course lost its territory in North America, but its Caribbean colonies continued to provide an extremely valuable commerce, particularly St Domingue, which became renowned as the richest colony in the world. Spain, meanwhile, benefited from the sweeping reorganization of its colonial commercial system introduced by the *Reglamento de comercio libre* of 1778. Between

1783 and 1796, the volume and value of its transatlantic trade grew rapidly, recovering for Spain colonial markets and resources which had previously haemorrhaged into the hands of British smugglers. At the same time, political restructuring within the Spanish American colonies tightened the metropolitan hold on colonial government and increased the yield of American taxpayers to the Spanish treasuries. This had not been achieved without some disruption of political order: there were major regional insurrections in New Granada in 1781 and Peru in 1780–2. But for all the immediate threat that they posed to Spanish government, these rebellions did not become independence movements of the North American kind, and were successfully contained by a mixture of conciliation and violence. Thus, before the start of the French Revolution, the colonial systems of both Spain and France were in a healthy condition, and seemed more capable of withstanding British commercial encroachments and military assaults than they had at previous moments in the eighteenth century.

The apparent vigour of Spanish and French colonialism in the wake of the American Revolution and the setback suffered by Britain were both short-lived. In 1789, France began its plunge into revolution; as the reverberations of the French Revolution spread through Europe during the 1790s, hostilities between the colonial powers were renewed in warfare of unparalleled scale and duration. Over the course of this conflict, it became clear that the loss of North American colonies had not damaged British economic and maritime strength; indeed, during the conflict British influence in the Americas was to grow and spread, while that of the other Euro-American colonial powers was to diminish and eventually disintegrate. This reversal of fortunes was bound up with the interaction of two broad developments in Europe. The first was the swift recovery of British transatlantic trade immediately after the American War of Independence and the continuing, rapid development of the agricultural and manufacturing bases of the British economy. The second development was the collapse of the *ancien régime* in France and the turmoil that it engendered among the nations of Europe.

Although the American War of Independence had toppled one of the pillars of the Anglo-American empire, it is now obvious that Britain was much less weakened by the outcome of the war than was France. Indeed, the defeat of Britain proved to be a pyrrhic victory for France. Support of the North American rebels had imposed enormous strains on French government finances; as the failure to reform national finances interacted with domestic political grievances and social discontents, this led directly to a political crisis which triggered revolution in France and led to a succession of wars that changed the political map of both Europe and the Americas.

The first impact of the French Revolution in the Americas was focused on French colonial territory, where the response of St Domingue to political crisis in metropolitan France engulfed the colony in rebellion, war and revolution. By the early 1800s, France had lost its most valuable overseas possession. The secondary effects of the French Revolution and the European wars that it generated were more oblique, but no less destructive. They were felt by the Iberian colonial powers which, as they were drawn into the Anglo–French conflict, were subjected to pressures that were first to corrode, and later to collapse their authority over their American colonies, to the long-term economic advantage of Britain.

Of the Iberian empires, Spain was the first to suffer the consequences of war. From 1796 until 1808, Spain was allied to France in virtually continuous conflict with Britain; throughout this period, British ability to isolate Spain from its colonial economics slowly undermined the integrity of the Spanish imperial economy while greatly enlarging Britain's economic influence in Spanish America. British merchants had of course been trying to penetrate Spanish American markets throughout the eighteenth century, using the ports of its Caribbean colonies as entrepôts for an illegal commerce with the neighbouring Spanish islands and mainlands. To promote this traffic, the Free Port Act of 1766 had opened certain Caribbean colonial harbours to foreign shipping, partly with a view to encouraging illegal trade with Spanish Americans. Moreover, in times of war, Britain always used its naval superiority to disrupt Spanish Atlantic commerce and promote West Indian smuggling. It was, however, after the declaration of war against Spain in 1796 that British economic influence in Spanish America grew most rapidly, turning smuggling into a regular commerce which was of very considerable value to Britain, especially when Napoleon's blockade of Europe against British imports after 1805 created an urgent need for new markets.[34] Indeed, Britain's merchants were so successful in extending their economic influence in Spanish America that British governments were reluctant to undertake military actions that might disturb it.

Some politicians in Britain favoured taking the Spanish colonies by conquest, but their arguments carried little weight in government. Trinidad was taken from Spain in 1797 and an unauthorized invasion of the River Plate in 1806–7 briefly captured Buenos Aires, but these expeditions were not part of any coherent strategy, nor did they encourage British governments to nurture ambitions for capturing

Spain's empire. In fact, the expedition to Buenos Aires clearly demonstrated the dangers of a policy of direct conquest, because, far from rallying to Britain as an alternative metropolis, the local creoles fought for the Spanish crown and repulsed the invaders.[35]

Informed by this experience, British ministers contemplated a different policy, aimed at extending British influence in Spanish America by supporting creole revolutionaries in efforts to subvert Spanish authority from within. But they did little to advance this aim before 1808, when events in Europe demanded a complete change of direction in policy towards Spanish America. When Napoleon seized the Spanish throne in May 1808, Spain was transformed from an enemy into an ally, and Britain consequently became committed to the restoration and stabilization of the Spanish state which it had previously been intent on defeating. However, this reversal of alliances certainly did not stem the continuing spread of British influence in Spanish America. On the contrary, Napoleon's intervention in Spain produced conditions that were extremely propitious for the spread of British economic and political influence in Spanish America, since it created a crisis in the Spanish colonies which led, after 1810, towards their independence.

At the beginning of Napoleon's Spanish adventure, Britain was fearful that the installation of a French government in Madrid would fulfil its long-standing fears of French hegemony in Spanish America. In 1808, the British cabinet accordingly organized an expeditionary force for dispatch to Spanish America, to ensure that Spain's colonies were not taken over by France. In the event, the fleet assembled at Cork in 1808 was redirected to the peninsula, to give aid to Spanish forces fighting Napoleon's army, and Britain undertook no further military intervention in Spanish America. This did not preclude continuing economic penetration, however. While Spain was reluctant to allow Britain access to its colonies and failed to reach a formal agreement with its new ally concerning relations with Spanish America, the disintegration of the colonial regime after 1810 ensured that British merchants became paramount, and that Britain would eventually encourage the emergence of independent states where it could exercise an unfettered economic dominance.[36] In 1824, after Spain had failed in its last attempts to reconquer its American colonies from creole rebels, the British foreign minister decided to recognize several independent states in Spanish America, thereby sealing the fate of the Spanish empire and preparing the way for British economic hegemony. Announcing that Britain intended to establish treaties of commerce with three of the new republics which had achieved their independence from Spain, Canning asserted that 'Spanish America is free; and if we do not mismanage our affairs sadly, she is English'.[37]

The extension of British influence in Latin America was further advanced by the part Britain played in the politics and economy of the Portuguese empire after 1807. Thoughout the eighteenth century, Portugal had been an ally and increasingly important trading partner for Britain. Through trade with Lisbon, British merchants not only took large quantities of Portuguese port wines, but also imported growing amounts of gold, cotton, rice, indigo and cacao from Brazil. By remaining neutral during the Anglo-French wars that started in 1793, Portugal managed to sustain this position until Napoleon, intent on implementing his continental blockade, called on Portugal to close its ports to British trade. Napoleon's ultimatum forced the Portuguese monarchy into an extremely difficult situation. If Portugal concurred with French demands, it stood to lose Brazil to the British; if not, it faced the loss of Portugal to a French invasion. The decision of Portugal's crown was consistent with its previous policy of depending on the Brazilian economy and the supremacy of Britain at sea. In 1807, the centre of imperial government was transferred from Portugal to Brazil, when, escorted by British warships, the King and his entire court left Lisbon for Rio de Janeiro.

This extraordinary event saved Portuguese sovereignty in Brazil, but at the cost of accepting virtual British control of the colony's commerce. Portugal's old colonial system, which had long denied the British direct access to Brazil, was dismantled by a treaty of 1810 which gave British merchants the right to reside in the colony, freedom to engage in wholesale and retail trade, and low tariffs on their imports. Henceforth, Portuguese merchants were increasingly replaced by British importers and shippers; by 1820, Brazil was taking over £2 million worth of British goods, which was double the value of British exports to Spanish America and only a third less than those taken by the United States. In short, 'the 1810 treaty wedded Brazil's economy to British industry'.[38]

By the 1820s, then, the wreck of the Iberian powers had enabled Britain gradually to engross the commerce of their American colonies and, when Brazil and the Spanish American territories became independent in the early 1820s, to achieve a goal to which her merchants and manufacturers had long aspired; namely, to convert Latin America into a vast emporium for British goods. Thus, although Britain retained colonies in Canada, the Caribbean, and on the margins of Central and Southern America in Honduras and the Guianas, the conservation of territorial dominion was matched by the start of a new stage in Britain's relationship with the Americas. Sustained by free trade and forceful diplomacy, this was attuned to Britain's emergence as the world's leading industrial and maritime power and, in the long term, was to make the independent American states, both north and south, more important to Britain's economy than were its own remaining American colonies.[39]

BRITISH AMERICA AFTER 1815: THE TRANSITION FROM THE FIRST TO THE SECOND BRITISH EMPIRE

What, finally, was the direction taken by Britain's American colonies after the end of the French wars in 1815? Clearly, there was no sudden detachment from British imperial control. Unlike the other European colonial powers, which saw a rapid unravelling of their American empires, Britain had not only preserved the colonial territories that it had held at the start of the wars, but also extended its sovereignty over new areas through territorial seizures and appropriations. However, if victory over France and Spain and the collapse of their empires was sweet revenge for the loss of the thirteen continental colonies in 1783, the importance of the British American colonies was nonetheless to diminish soon after 1815.

The decline of the Anglo-American system did not reflect a general British retreat from imperialism, or a shift towards an 'imperialism of free trade' driven by industrial and commercial interests, as has sometimes been supposed. On the contrary. As C.A. Bayly has shown, in the early nineteenth century British colonialism embarked on its greatest forward surge since the creation of the first American colonies of settlement in the early seventeenth century, in a movement that owed much of its power and momentum to the expansion of state power and state-sponsored nationalism during the French wars.[40] Under a ruling class which felt threatened by the military and ideological challenge of French republicanism abroad and feared social upheaval at home, the British state entered into a great new phase of expansion, 'set in motion and powered by the ferocious reaction of the state and its military apparatus to external challenge and internal revolt.'[41] While unable to exert significant military force in Continental Europe, Britain built up its maritime power and, in the struggle with republican France, deployed it to secure control in the Mediterranean, Southern Africa and India. In India, to take the major case, the financial and military power of the East India Company and the quest for territorial revenues, already implanted in the later eighteenth century, were more important forces for imperialist expansion than the pressures of free trade. There, British statesmen sought to build a sphere of power which could counteract that of France in Europe. As they did so, the trend was toward the construction of colonial despotisms 'characterized by a form of aristocratic military government supporting a viceregal autocracy, by a well-developed imperial style which emphasised hierarchy and racial subordination, and by the patronage of indigenous landed elites.'[42] According to Bayly, these new 'proconsular despotisms' matched the conservative regime in Britain, where landed wealth still dominated the state and held political and cultural sway over mercantile and manufacturing interests. The trend towards a viceregal style of colonial government was not, then, merely a remnant from the past or a 'despotic appendage to a liberal, free-trading industrial state waiting breathlessly for domestic and colonial reform'; it was, rather, the natural extension of a revivified British conservatism.[43]

The second empire which emerged during and after the French wars and embodied this conservatism included the colonial territories of the Americas, and like the newer territories they also felt the heavy hand of a revitalized British imperialism. Until the 1840s, Britain continued to play a central role in directing its American colonies in the Caribbean and Canada, all of which were subjected to closer political control from metropolitan governments that were determined to impose their will on British overseas dominions.

In the Caribbean, the territories taken from the French, Spanish and Dutch were brought under direct government of a kind quite different from the government of the old representative system; there was no intention to allow these new colonies the political rights which had hindered the management of the old colonies. In the old colonies, it was more difficult to impose such centralized control. The planters insisted on their rights, and recalcitrant assemblies were able to frustrate the efforts of the Colonial Office to secure the amelioration of slave conditions that had been envisaged when the slave trade was abolished in 1807.[44] However, as we have already noted when discussing the movement against slavery, the growth of the free coloured population and the restiveness of slaves imposed pressures which, when combined with metropolitan demands, eventually wore down the power of the planters in the old colonies and forced them to accept London's commitment to slave emancipation in 1833.

Canada was also subjected to firmer central control, as Britain sought to mobilize its resources and took steps to pre-empt any insubordination of the kind that had detached the thirteen continental colonies from the empire. Indeed, the reaction of the British ruling elites against the threat of republicanism and radicalism coloured a colonial policy which aimed to make the Canadas 'a North American bulwark against the presumptious levelling tendencies of the age'.45 The Constitutional Act of 1791 created a strong executive, set aside huge reserves of land for crown and clergy, and put in place British governors who tried to ensure that only trusted men were placed in positions of power.

The imposition of more autocratic models of government did not, of course, preclude a decline in the economic importance of the American colonies. As British commerce increasingly shifted towards other regions overseas, so the American colonies were relegated to a relatively minor position in the emerging second empire. This was most obvious in Britain's Caribbean colonies, once the core of imperial commerce. After 1815, the Caribbean colonies became much less important to Britain; their economies were undercut by the scissor action of falling sugar prices and the rising production costs precipitated by abolition of the slave trade in 1807, and greatly accentuated by slave emancipation in 1833. When the novelist Anthony Trollope visited Jamaica in 1859, he described this erstwhile 'land of wealth, rivalling the East in its means of riches,' as 'a spot on the earth almost more poverty-striken than any other'.[46] Not all the sugar economies fared so badly: Barbados was better able to sustain its plantations than was Jamaica because land shortages prevented blacks from becoming independent, self-sufficient peasant farmers, while British Guiana managed to attract immigrant indentured labourers. Generally, however, Britain's plantation colonies were a decaying relic of the old colonial system and, though they were preserved as British sovereign territories, their declining planter elites enjoyed little sympathy or support from central government. Indeed, the relegation of once opulent planter elites to the sidelines of a new empire was starkly revealed when sugar duties were equalized in the mid-nineteenth century, thereby ending the preferential duty which had afforded West Indian sugar planters some protection from their East Indian and Cuban competitors, and bringing their ruin.[47]

Canada fared better after the French wars. Indeed, unlike the Caribbean colonies, it became a vigorous part of the emerging second British empire. In the half-century after 1815, more than a million British immigrants arrived in Canada and, although many moved on to the United States, Canada's population grew sevenfold (to about three and a half million) over that period. So, having previously been formed mainly by settlers who came from the United States after American independence, Canada became more solidly British, as it was peopled by Scottish, English and Irish settlers in search of cheap land to farm. These migrants left a mother country that was very different from that of the seventeenth-century English settlers. They came from a more powerful and wealthy parent power, many carried with them a strong sense of British nationalism, and they moved into lands where they had little or no contact with native peoples. Rather than slowly opening a frontier of settlement based in self-sufficient farming, they came in a single great inrush and, attuned to a market economy, quickly developed the production of timber and wheat for export to Britain. Canada's strong economic ties with Britain were not a guarantee of its political stability, however. Bad grain harvests and depression in the timber trade in 1836–7 triggered rebellions against British authority in Upper and Lower Canada in 1837, and, though duly suppressed by the British army, these insurrections compelled Britain to rethink its policies for governing Canada. Britain was forced first to unify the two Canadas in 1840, then to concede the principle of responsible (devolved) government in the succeeding decade. Thus, after a prolonged experiment with authoritarian government, the loyalty of British North America was preserved by political concessions until, in 1867, the British North America Act conceded full self-government to the Confederation of Canadian provinces, which had blended into a single federal polity – the Dominion of Canada – under British sovereignty.[48]

Thus, by the mid-nineteenth century, the old colonial system in the Americas was finally dismantled in the last of three phases of realignment that had started after the American Revolution. During the decade after the Revolution, the remaining colonies had passed through a process of major readjustment, as Canada absorbed loyalist refugees and the West Indies were forced to adapt to the loss of trade with the newly-formed United States. Then, during and after the French wars, British America entered a phase of expansion: the sugar colonies benefited from the dislocation of French colonial commerce, Britain enlarged its territories in the tropics, and Canadian settlement was consolidated by the beginnings in the 1790s of fresh immigration from Britain. Finally, during the years after the French wars, the American colonies became part of a second British empire, as Britain found in other regions of the world the chance to build the kind of empire based on the exploitation of subaltern native peoples which sixteenth-century Englishmen, influenced by Spain's example, had envisaged but failed to create in the Americas. In the new map of imperial dominion, which was reinforced by the emergence of new colonies of white settlement in Australia and southern Africa, Britain's American colonies occupied a much smaller space than they had. Indeed, when Britain moved to free trade in the mid-nineteenth century, the American colonies which had been the foundations of Britain's first empire were to be relegated to a low rank in the global order of British imperial and economic power.

NOTES

1   Vincent T. Harlow, *The Founding of the Second British Empire, 1763–1793: Volume I, Discovery and Revolution* (London, 1952). Quotations from p. 6.

2   For a brief review of Pacific voyages, see J. H. Parry, *Trade and Dominion: The European Overseas Empires in the Eighteenth Century* (London, 1971) pp. 244–56. For more detail, see Harlow, *The Second British Empire*, vol. 1, pp. 12–61; vol. 2, pp. 419–81. On British and Spanish disputes on the Pacific coasts of Canada, see Warren L. Cook, *Flood Tide of Empire: Spain and the Pacific Northwest, 1543–1819* (New Haven, Conn. and London, 1973), especially Chapters 4–7.

3   Douglass C. North and Robert Paul Thomas, *The Growth of the American Economy to 1860* (New York, 1968) pp. 175–8.

4   Gary M. Walton and James F. Shepherd, *The Economic Rise of Early America* (Cambridge, 1979) pp. 178–200.

5   For a succinct discussion of the main features of loyalism and its regional distribution, see D.W. Meinig, *The Shaping of America: A Geographical Perspective on Five Hundred Years of History; Volume I: Atlantic America, 1492–1800* (New Haven, Conn., and London, 1986) pp. 311–23.

6   Mary Beth Norton, *The British-Americans: The Loyalist Exiles in England, 1774–1789* (London, 1974) pp. 8–9.

7   David Bell, 'The Loyalist tradition in Canada', *Journal of Canadian Studies*, (1970) **5/2**: 22–33; quotation from p. 22.

8   W.S. MacNutt, *The Atlantic Provinces: The Emergence of a Colonial Society, 1712–1857* (Toronto, 1965) pp. 76–128.

9   The following account of developments in late eighteenth and early nineteenth-century Canada is based on Donald G. Creighton, *Dominion of the North: A History of Canada* (London, 1958 edition) pp. 165–223.

10 Ibid., p. 193.

11 MacNutt, *The Atlantic Provinces*, pp. 129–54.

12 Watts, *The West Indies: Patterns of Development, Culture and Environmental Change since 1492* (Cambridge, 1987) pp. 275–7.

13 Quoted by J.P. Greene, 'Changing identity in the British Caribbean: Barbados as a case study', in Nicholas Canny & Anthony Pagden (eds) *Colonial Identity in the Atlantic World, 1500–1800* (Princeton, NJ, 1987) p. 261.

14 George Metcalf, *Royal Government and Political Conflict in Jamaica, 1729–1783* (London, 1965) p. 188.

15 For a detailed review of West Indian responses to imperial reform and

the North American rebellion, see Selwyn H.H. Carrington, *The British West Indies during the American Revolution* (Dordrecht, 1988) pp. 128–61.

16 J H. Parry, Philip Sherlock and Anthony Maingot, *A Short History of the West Indies* (London, 1989) pp. 107–21.

17 Lowell J. Ragatz, *The Fall of the Planter Class in the British Caribbean, 1763–1863* (New York, 1928) p. 206.

18 Seymour Drescher, *Econocide: British Slavery in the Era of Abolition* (Pittsburgh, Pa, 1977) pp. 39–44, 55–64; John J. McCusker, 'Growth, stagnation or decline? The economy of the British West Indies, 1763–1790' in Ronald Hoffman, John J. McCusker, Russell R. Menard and Peter J. Albert, *The Economy of Early America: The Revolutionary Period, 1763–1790* (Charlottesville, Va, 1988) pp. 275–302.

19 The classic account of the Haitian revolution is C.L.R James, *The Black Jacobins: Toussaint L'Ouverture and the San Domingo Revolution* (New York, 1962 edition). British involvement in St Domingue's revolutionary wars is traced in David Geggus, *Slavery, War and Revolution: The British Occupation of Saint Domingue, 1793–8* (Oxford, 1982).

20 Drescher, *Econocide*, pp. 65–91.

21 J. Holland Rose, 'The struggle with Napoleon, 1803–1815', in J. Holland Rose, A. P. Newton and E.A. Benians (eds) *The Cambridge History of the British Empire*, vol. II (Cambridge, 1940) p. 113.

22 Quoted by Robin Blackburn, *The Overthrow of Colonial Slavery, 1776–1848* (London, 1988) p. 301.

23 For the core of Eric Williams's arguments, see *Capitalism and Slavery* (London, 1969 edition) pp. 108–77; quotation from p. 169.

24 Drescher, *Econocide*, p. 165

25 Roger Anstey, 'A reinterpretation of the abolition of the British slave trade, 1806–1807', *English Historical Review* (1972) **87**: 304–32; quotation from pp. 330–1. For a more detailed account of the anti-slave trade campaign, see Anstey, *The Atlantic Slave Trade and British Abolition*, pp. 239–390.

26 Blackburn, *The Overthrow of Colonial Slavery*, pp. 295–316; quotation from p. 313.

27 David Brion Davis, *The Problem of Slavery in the Age of Revolution, 1770–1823* (Ithaca, NY, 1975) p. 82.

28 Ibid., p. 42.

29 For a full exposition of Davis's arguments, on which this very synoptic account is based, see ibid., pp. 343–468. For an encapsulation and clarification of his argument, see D.B. Davis, 'Reflections on abolitionism and ideological hegemony,' *American Historical Review* (1987) **92**: 797–812; quotation from p 808

30 Thomas Haskell, 'Capitalism and the origins of the humanitarian sensibility, Part I', *American Historical Review* (1985) **90**: 339–61. For responses to Haskell's arguments, see 'AHR Forum', *American Historical Review* (1987) **92**: 797–878.

31 West Indian economic performance in the late eighteenth and early nineteenth century is reviewed in J.R. Ward, *British West Indian Slavery, 1750–1834: The Process of Amelioration* (Oxford, 1988) pp. 34–60.

32 David Eltis, *Economic Growth and the Ending of the Transatlantic Slave Trade* (New York and Oxford, 1987) pp. 5–11.

33 Blackburn, *The Overthrow of Colonial Slavery*, pp. 421–68; quotation from p. 444.

34 Francis Armytage, *The Free Port System in the British West Indies* (London, 1953); Dorothy B. Goebel, 'British trade to the Spanish colonies, 1798–1823', *American Historical Review* (1938) **43**: 288–320.

35 John Lynch, 'British Policy and Spanish America, 1793–1808', *Journal of Latin American Studies* (1969) **1**: 1–30.

36 C.K. Webster (ed) *Britain and the Independence of Latin America, 1812–1830: Select Documents from the Foreign Office Archives*, 2 vols (London, 1938) vol. I, pp. 9–26.

37 Timothy Anna, *Spain and the Loss of America* (Lincoln, Nebr. and London, 1983) p. 288.

38 James Lang, *Portuguese Brazil: The King's Plantation* (New York and London, 1979) p. 200.

39 On Britain's economic influence in post-independence Latin America, see Rory Miller, *Britain and Latin America in the Nineteenth and Twentieth Centuries* (London, 1992) especially pp. 48–95.

40 C.A. Bayly, *Imperial Meridian: The British Empire and the World, 1780–1830* (London, 1989); also P.J. Cain and A.G. Hopkins, *British Imperialism: Innovation and Expansion, 1688–1914* (London and New York, 1993) pp. 96–104.

41 Bayly, *Imperial Meridian*, p. 102.

42 Ibid., pp. 8–9.

43 Ibid., pp. 193–216; quotation from p. 194.

44 D.J. Murray, *The West Indies and the Development of Colonial Government, 1801–1834* (Oxford, 1965), passim.

45 Kenneth McNaught, *The Pelican History of Canada* (Harmondsworth, 1969) p. 62.

46 Anthony Trollope, *The West Indies and the Spanish Main* (London, 2nd edition, 1860) p. 101.

47 Parry, Sherlock and Maingot (eds) *Short History of the West Indies*, pp. 163–177.

48 For a general survey of the main developments of this period, see R. Douglas Francis, Richard Jones and Donald B. Smith, *Origins: Canadian History to Confederation* (Toronto, 1988) pp. 190–2, 214–70. For the remarks on immigration, I am indebted to Professor Philip Buckner for access to his unpublished paper, 'Patterns of colonization in the Americas: Canada', given at the Anglo-American Conference of Historians, 1992.

Epilogue

In some ways, the colonial empire which the English built in the Americas had differed little in its origins and basic structures from those of its European rivals. For, aside from obvious differences in the timing and location of their development, the European American empires shared some fundamental similarities. All originated in the explorations and activities of small groups of individuals in search of trade, plunder and land, rather than in the initiatives of governments or ventures sponsored by the state. Similarly, although the English empire is frequently regarded as unusually diverse in character, each of the European empires drew on a spectrum of different interests and created within itself a wide range of distinctive colonial economies and societies. Another shared feature of European colonialism was its destructive ecological impact. To a greater or lesser extent, all the empires had catastrophic consequences for the native peoples whose lands they occupied or exploited; similarly, all became involved, in one way or another, in the inhuman commerce in slaves, which carried millions of Africans into lives of slavery. Finally, all were essentially maritime empires, dependent on communications by sea both to build and to sustain the links between the parent powers and their colonial possessions, and dependent on naval power to defend themselves against their competitors.

Beyond these broad similarities, the empires created by Europeans in the New World had their own singular and special features. These were most apparent in the character of their economies and societies. Some of these differences stemmed from the geographical variety of American environment, but the character of the parent power and the nature of its interaction with native peoples also moulded the social and economic development of their dominions in the New World.

313

The Spanish and Portuguese entered the Americas from the medieval Catholic world of southern Europe, with its traditions of crusades against Islam, and, in the Spanish case, created their colonies by conquering native peoples. The Dutch, French and English colonies, on the other hand, were the progeny of very different political and social environments, formed in a world of emerging nation-states and aggressive commercial capitalism. For the French and Dutch, colonies were primarily commercial outposts, with few pretensions to conquest or colonization. The English, like the Spanish, were more interested in settlement, but accomplished it in a very different manner. In Meso-America and South America, the Spaniards conquered native kingdoms and created societies that superimposed European on indigenous ways; in North America, the English simply pushed native peoples aside and created extensions of the homeland rather than areas of conquest.

In the English case, colonies had developed from several distinctive forces. A fundamental impulse was that of commercial capitalism, which stimulated the formation of export economies in the American South and the Caribbean, and eventually fostered the development of slave-based plantation economies. Another, quite different force was generated by religious heterodoxy in England. This led to the foundation of the Puritan society of New England, and later under-pinned the development of Quaker Pennsylvania. Political conflict in England had also played a part in forming and shaping Anglo-American society, primarily in the Chesapeake region, where refugee royalists had given the society of Virginia its own peculiar tone and character. Founded on these diverse bases, the heterogeneity of Anglo-America was further amplified during the eighteenth century by the inflow of streams of foreigners who were either assimilated into Anglophone society or, in the case of black slave immigrants, sub-ordinated to it. Diversity was, moreover, underpinned by regional economic differences. Of these, the greatest was that which divided the Caribbean colonies from those of North America. All the English colonies began as colonies of white settlement, but when the islands turned to sugar production, they became slave societies that had more in common with neighbouring foreign islands than with the Anglo-American colonies of the North American mainland. The division was not clearly drawn: the adoption of slavery in the American South, particularly in South Carolina, meant that part of the continental mainland shaded into the slave/plantation complex of the Caribbean. All the British colonies were, moreover, cultural domains of England, and later the whole British Isles; they were hybrid extensions of the mother country which drew on her language, social values and political institutions. In the end, however, there was a deep divide between the British colonies of North America and those of the Caribbean. While the North American mainland provinces had enormous scope for growth and expansion and had enough in common with each other to mount a concerted and successful rebellion against Britain, the island colonies were highly specialized economies and unstable societies that depended heavily on the metropolitan power. Thus, while settlement in North America led towards autonomous economic growth and political independence, in the Caribbean it produced economic dependence and political subservience.

In the early 1820s, the great age of European colonialism in the Americas finally came to an end, more than three centuries after Spain had planted its first settlements in the New World. For both the colonizing powers and their colonies, very different futures now began. Once the greatest of the imperial powers, and the donor of an enduring legacy of language and culture in the Americas, in economic terms Spain had ultimately derived little long-term reward from its overseas dominions; on losing its continental empire, Spain fell further back into the ranks of the minor European powers. Portugal also suffered from the loss of Brazil. Following a partly successful attempt to harness Brazilian resources to metropolitan advantage during the later eighteenth century, after 1822 Portugal saw independent Brazil become an economic satellite of Great Britain, leaving only ties of language and culture to unite the Luso-Brazilian world. Both Iberian powers relinquished their hold on empire reluctantly, recognizing that it foreshadowed economic decline and political relegation.

Britain, on the other hand, weathered the first major crisis in its American empire, when the thirteen continental colonies achieved their independence in 1783, and continued to pursue active imperialist policies in both the Americas and other regions of the world. During and after the great struggle with Revolutionary and Napoleonic France, Britain strengthened its authority in the remaining territories of the American empire, established new colonies in Australia and southern Africa, and extended a more autocratic model of empire in the east. Until the end of the French wars in 1815, British statesmen also sought to sustain colonial protectionism, with policies designed to exploit the colonies as protected markets for British goods; emphasis on empire and protectionism ceded only gradually to new approaches and policies in the years before 1850.

There was, then, no sudden, clear break in the history of British colonialism in the Americas at 1815; the remaining American colonies of the first empire were becoming part of a second empire during and after the French wars. However, the end of the French wars did mark a decline in the stature of Britain's American colonies. During the wars and in their aftermath, the Anglo-American colonies were overshadowed by new developments, as Britain put in place the building blocks of a new empire in India, while also extending its economic influence over areas such as Latin America which lay outside its formal control. Then, from 1850, the importance of the American colonies was further diminished. By this time, Britain had created a chain of strategic bases that linked it to a world economy, and had set up a global infrastructure which gave British maritime power unfettered scope for expansion and command over an empire that was larger and more important than the first. The mercantilist economic policies that had long emphasized the need for colonies to provide resources and markets gave way to the theory of free trade; Britain abandoned restrictions on its commerce, including controls over colonial trade, and loosened its political grip on colonies of white settlement. Thus the old colonial system in the Americas was destroyed. In the era of free trade, Britain went on to become an economic power of truly global reach, with another, greater empire in India, Australasia and Africa.

Bibliography

The following is a highly selective bibliography, which reflects the works upon which this book draws, and generally indicates books rather than articles. Where possible I have tried to represent recent themes in the historiography, in works that reflect areas of debate and contention, and which themselves offer guides to the huge underlying bibliography found in specialized monographs and scholarly journals. Reference to academic journals has been kept to a minimum; however, two such journals deserve special mention for a rich array of articles on colonial America: these are the *William and Mary Quarterly* and the *American Historical Review*.

For bibliographical guidance to the history of the colonial United States, see Frank Freidel (ed) *The Harvard Guide to American History*, 2 vols (Cambridge, Mass., 1974), and David L. Ammermann and Philip D. Morgan, *Books about Early America: 2001 Titles* (Williamsburg, Pa., 1989).

GENERAL

Charles M. Andrews, *The Colonial Period of American History*, 4 vols (New Haven, Conn., and London, 1964 edition), a work first published in 1934–8, is the major examplar of the 'Imperial School' of American historiography, and in its first three volumes presents a richly informative narrative of the founding of mainland and colonial colonies. J. Holland Rose, A.P. Newton and E.A. Benians (eds) *The Cambridge History of the British Empire*, vols 1–2 (Cambridge, 1929 and 1940) give a more Anglocentric view, but are rich in information;

Vincent Harlow, *The Founding of the Second British Empire, 1763–1793* (Oxford, 1952) argues that the first empire began to lose its importance in 1763. An extraordinarily full political narrative of the development of England's empire, set in the context of British history, is Angus Calder's long, dense but lucid book, *Revolutionary Empire: The Rise of the English-Speaking Empires from the Fifteenth Century to the 1780s* (London, 1981). An invaluable account of English colonization seen from a geographical, spatial perspective is the work of D.W. Meinig, *The Shaping of America: A Geographical Perspective on Five Hundred Years of History; Volume I: Atlantic America, 1492–1800* (New Haven, Conn., and London, 1986), a book that is enhanced by splendid maps and illustrations. The evolution of British naval power throughout the colonial period is covered by Paul M. Kennedy, *The Rise and Fall of British Naval Mastery* (London, 1976).

Excellent essays on themes in British colonial history covered in this book are found in Jack P. Greene and J.R. Pole (eds) *Colonial British America: Essays in the New History of the Early Modern Era* (Baltimore, Md, and London, 1984) and in Bernard Bailyn and Philip D. Morgan (eds) *Strangers within the Realm: Cultural Margins of the First British Empire* (Chapel Hill, NC, and London, 1991). An important work that places the development of colonial North America within the wider context of British America, including the Caribbean, and proposes a model for understanding their development, is Jack P. Greene, *Pursuits of Happiness: The Social Development of the Early Modern British Colonies and the Formation of American Culture* (Chapel Hill, NC, and London, 1988).

On the colonial United States, there are several good general introductions. A superbly compressed synthesis that deploys a mass of information on most aspects of US history before the American Revolution in a clear chronological framework is R.C. Simmons, *The American Colonies from Settlement to Independence* (London, 1976). An introduction to central themes in the social and economic history of colonial North America is found in James A. Henretta and Gregory H. Nobles, *Evolution and Revolution: American Society, 1600–1820* (Lexington, Mass., and Toronto, 1987). A fuller treatment, also designed for students, is Richard Middleton's *Colonial America: A History, 1607–1760* (Cambridge, Mass., and Oxford, 1992), an up-to-date introductory text on colonial North America that reflects historiographical developments of recent years.

The British Caribbean is less well served in terms of general works that cover the whole period of Britain's first empire. J.H. Parry, Philip Sherlock and Anthony Maingot, *A Short History of the West Indies*

(London, 1989 edition) is a useful introductory survey, while Franklin W. Knight, *The Caribbean: The Genesis of a Fragmented Nationalism* (New York, 1978) places the English Caribbean in the context of European colonies in the Caribbean as a whole.

Comparisons of the Anglo-American empire with the colonial empires of other European states can be pursued by reading J.H. Parry, *The Spanish Seaborne Empire* (London, 1966) and C.R. Boxer, *The Portuguese Seaborne Empire* (London, 1969) and *The Dutch Seaborne Empire* (London, 1965). Explicit comparisons of colonialism in Euro-America are given by K.G. Davies, *The North Atlantic World in the Seventeenth Century* (Minneapolis, Minn., and London, 1974) and Max Savelle, *Empires to Nations: Expansion in America, 1713–1824* (Minneapolis, Minn., and London, 1974).

1 ENGLISH EXPLORATIONS IN THE ATLANTIC

For a general review of European exploration, see J.H. Parry, *The Age of Reconnaissance: Discovery, Exploration and Settlement, 1450–1650* (London, 1963); on the interactions of Spanish, Portuguese and Italian maritime activities in the period before the European discovery of America, see Felipe Fernández-Armesto, *Before Columbus: Exploration and Colonisation from the Mediterranean to the Atlantic, 1229–1492* (London, 1987).

The best accounts of English voyages during the late fifteenth and the sixteenth centuries are the following: David B. Quinn, *England and the Discovery of America, 1481–1620* (London, 1974); Kenneth R. Andrews, *Trade, Plunder and Settlement: Maritime Enterprise and the Genesis of the British Empire, 1480–1630* (Cambridge, 1984) is a key book for the period. The same author provides the most complete study of English (and French) privateering in the Caribbean in this period in his book *The Spanish Caribbean: Trade and Plunder, 1530–1630* (London, 1978). K.R. Andrews, N.P. Canny and P.E.H. Hair (eds) *Westward Enterprise: English Activities in Ireland, the Atlantic and America, 1480–1650* (Liverpool, 1978) has valuable essays on aspects of English expansion. Useful general accounts of English society and politics in the period of expansion are A.L. Rowse, *The Expansion of Elizabethan England* (London, 1973 edition) and John Guy, *Tudor England* (Oxford, 1990). An account of Anglo-Spanish relations seen from the Spanish side is given by John Lynch, *Spain under the Habsburgs*, 2 vols (Oxford, 1965) vol. 1.

Documentation of the major voyages, maritime and colonizing enterprises of the period are found in the following: James A. Williamson, *The Cabot Voyages and Bristol Discovery under Henry VII*, Hakluyt Society, 2nd series, vol. 120 (Cambridge, 1962); David B. Quinn, *The Voyages and Colonising Enterprises of Sir Humphrey Gilbert*, 2 vols Hakluyt Society, 2nd series, vols 83–84 (London, 1940); D.B. Quinn, *The Roanoke Voyages, 1584–1590: Documents to Illustrate the English Voyages to North America under the Patent granted to Sir Walter Raleigh in 1584*, 2 vols, Hakluyt Society, 2nd series, vols 104–5 (London, 1955); V.T. Harlow (ed) *The Discoverie of the large and bewtiful Empire of Guiana, by Sir Walter Ralegh* (London, 1928). On Hakluyt, see George B. Parks, *Richard Hakluyt and the English Voyages* (New York, 1961); for a sample of his writings, see Richard Hakluyt, *Voyages and Discoveries* (Harmondsworth, 1972); for the 'Discourse of western planting', see E.G.R Taylor (ed) *Original Writings and Correspondence of the two Richard Hakluyts*, 2 vols, Hakluyt Society, 2nd series, vols 76–7 (London, 1935) vol. 2.

The lives and activities of Drake and Raleigh are examined in K.R. Andrews, *Drake's Voyages: A Reassessment of their Place in Elizabethan Maritime Expansion* (London, 1967); Norman Lloyd Williams, *Sir Walter Raleigh* (Harmondsworth, 1965); David B. Quinn, *Raleigh and the British Empire* (London, 1947).

2 FIRST COLONIES

For a detailed exposition of economic conditions in England during these years, see Barry Supple, *Commercial Crisis and Change in England, 1600–1642* (Cambridge, 1959). Overseas commercial ventures and those involved are analysed in T.K. Rabb, *Enterprise and Empire: Merchant and Gentry Investment in the Expansion of England, 1575–1630* (Cambridge, Mass., 1967), and Robert Brenner, *Merchants and Revolution: Commercial Change, Political Conflict, and London's Overseas Traders, 1550–1653* (Cambridge, 1993).

Original accounts of the explorations and voyages of the early seventeenth century are collected in D.B. Quinn and A.M. Quinn (eds) *The English New England Voyages, 1602–1608*, Hakluyt Society, 2nd series, 161 (London, 1983).

On early Virginia, Wesley Frank Craven, *The Southern Colonies in the Seventeenth Century, 1607–1689* (Baton Rouge, La, 1970 edition) is an excellent introduction, while Craven's *Dissolution of the Virginia*

Company: The Failure of a Colonial Experiment (New York, 1932) offers a detailed account of the company's demise. The key modern work is Edmund S. Morgan, *American Slavery, American Freedom: The Ordeal of Colonial Virginia* (New York, 1975). For a primary source, see John Smith, 'Description of Virginia and proceedings of the colonie', in Lyon G. Tyler (ed) *Narratives of Early Virginia* (New York, 1907). Recent research questions the view that society in Virginia and the Chesapeake as a whole was as fragile and incoherent as historians have previously supposed. A good example of such work is James R. Perry, *The Formation of Society on Virginia's Eastern Shore, 1615–1655* (Chapel Hill, NC, and London, 1990). For full reviews of the recent literature, see Thad W. Tate, 'The seventeenth-century Chesapeake and its modern historians', in Thad W. Tate and David L. Ammermann (eds) *The Chesapeake in the Seventeenth Century: Essays in Anglo-American Society* (Chapel Hill, NC, 1979); also Jack P. Greene, *Pursuits of Happiness: The Social Development of Early Modern British Colonies and the Formation of American Culture* (Chapel Hill, NC, and London, 1988).

On the early years of the Plymouth settlement, George D. Langdon, *Pilgrim Colony: A History of New Plymouth, 1620–1691* (New Haven, Conn., 1966) is a key work. For the principal primary source, see William T. Davis, *Bradford's History of the Plymouth Plantation, 1606–1648* (New York, 1964 edition) Book 2. An analysis of the social order in Plymouth is given by John Demos, *A Little Commonwealth: Family Life in Plymouth Colony* (New York, 1970). The character of the Puritan leadership in Massachusetts and the colony's foundations are described by Edmund S. Morgan, *The Puritan Dilemma: The Story of John Winthrop* (Boston, Mass., and Toronto, 1958), and by D.B. Rutman, *Winthrop's Boston: Portrait of a Puritan Town, 1639–1649* (Chapel Hill, NC, 1965). Greene, *Pursuits of Happiness*, provides a comprehensive and up-to-date review of the bibliography on early New England.

For the background to early English colonization in the Caribbean, see Joyce Lorimer, 'The English contraband tobacco trade in Trinidad and Guiana, 1560–1617', in Andrews, Canny and Hair (eds) *Westward Enterprise*, and Joyce Lorimer (ed) *English and Irish Settlement on the River Amazon, 1550–1646*, Hakluyt Society, 2nd series, vol. 171 (London, 1989). European expansion is described generally in A.P. Newton, *The European Nations in the West Indies, 1493–1688* (London, 1966 edition).

An outline of the directions of Spanish expansion in North America during the early seventeenth century is given by Carl Sauer, *Seventeenth Century North America* (Berkeley, Calif., 1980).

3 MIGRANTS AND SETTLERS

David Hackett Fischer, *Albion's Seed: Four British Folkways in America* (New York, 1989) is essential reading on the migrations from Britain to North America and on the societies and cultures formed from these movements.

On the origins and early use of indentured labour, see Abbot E. Smith, *Colonists in Bondage: White Servitude and Convict Labour in America, 1607–1776* (Gloucester, Mass., 1965 edition); David Galenson, *White Servitude in Colonial America: An Economic Analysis* (Cambridge, 1981). Hilary McD. Beckles, *White Servitude and Black Slavery in Barbados, 1627–1715* (Knoxville, Tenn., 1989) is an interesting account of white servitude in Barbados.

The standard work on the 'great migration' is Carl Bridenbaugh, *Vexed and Troubled Englishmen, 1590–1642* (New York, 1967). A good general essay is Mildred Campbell, 'Social origins of some early Americans', in James Morton Smith (ed) *Seventeenth Century America: Essays in Colonial History* (New York, 1972 edition). For comparative material on settlers in early Spanish America, see James Lockhart, *Spanish Peru, 1532–1560* (Madison, Wis., 1968). Social types involved in emigration from France, Holland and England are compared by K.G. Davies, *The North Atlantic World in the Seventeenth Century* (Minneapolis, Minn., and London, 1974). For a comparison of migrants to New England and the British Caribbean, see Richard S. Dunn, 'Experiments holy and unholy, 1630–31', in Andrews, Canny and Hair (eds) *Westward Enterprise*.

An insight into the ideas of the Puritan leadership of the Massachusetts colony is John Winthrop, 'A modell of Christian charity' (1630), in Edmund S. Morgan, *The Founding of Massachusetts: Historians and the Sources* (New York, 1964). The relevant chapters in Fischer, *Albion's Seed*, examine the social and cultural character of the Massachusetts migration. For detailed studies of New England towns, see Kenneth A. Lockridge, *A New England Town, The First Hundred Years: Dedham, Massachussetts, 1636–1736* (New York, 1970); Philip J. Greven, *Four Generations: Population, Land and Family in Colonial Andover, Massachusetts* (Ithaca, NY, and London, 1970). On other areas in the New England region, see Bruce H. Mann, *Neighbours and Strangers: Law and Community in Early Connecticut* (Chapel Hill, NC, 1987) and Sydney V. James, *Colonial Rhode Island: A History* (New York, 1975).

On the foundation and early years of Maryland, see Wesley Frank Craven, *The Southern Colonies in the Seventeenth Century*, and Gloria L.

Main, *Tobacco Colony: Life in Early Maryland, 1650–1720* (Princeton, NJ, 1982). The settlement of the Lesser Antilles and their early society are described by Carl Bridenbaugh and Roberta Bridenbaugh, *No Peace Beyond the Line: The English in the Caribbean, 1624–1690* (New York, 1972).

The history of Indian–white relations in the English Caribbean is sparse. there is some information in K.G. Davies, *The North Atlantic World in the Seventeenth Century* and more detail in Philip B. Boucher, *Cannibal Encounters: Europeans and Island Caribs, 1492–1763* (Baltimore, Md, 1992). White attitudes towards and relations with Indians in North America have been extensively analysed. Key works on North America are Francis Jennings, *The Invasion of America: Indians, Colonialism and the Cant of Conquest* (Chapel Hill, NC, 1975), Neal Salisbury, *Manitou and Providence: Indians, Europeans, and the Making of New England* (New York, 1983), Paul Axtell, *The European and the Indian: Essays in the Ethnohistory of Colonial North America* (New York, 1982 edition) and H.C. Porter, *The Inconstant Savage: England and the North American Indian* (London, 1979). William Cronon, *Changes in the Land: Indians, Colonists, and the Ecology of New England* (New York, 1983) shows how Englishmen misunderstood Indian society and economy. The impact of whites on the land and native peoples of another region is given by Timothy Silver, *A New Face on the Countryside: Indians, Colonists, and Slaves in South Atlantic Forests, 1500–1800* (Cambridge, 1990).

4 THE EXPANSION OF EMPIRE

On the repercussions of the English Civil War in North America, see R.C. Simmons, *The American Colonies*; on the West Indies in this period, see A.P. Thornton, *West India Policy under the Restoration* (Oxford, 1956). Stephen Saunders Webb, *The Governors General: The English Army and the Definition of Empire, 1659–1681* (Chapel Hill, NC, 1979), traces changes in English colonial policy after the Civil War in greater detail.

The development of the English commercial policy is described in G.L. Beer, *The Origins of the British Colonial System* (New York, 1928) and L. Harper, *The English Navigation Laws* (New York, 1939); Robert Brenner, *Merchants and Revolution*, has a superb account of the influences shaping policy after the Civil War. The main elements in the debate over the meaning of mercantilism can be found in D.C. Coleman, *Revisions in Mercantilism* (London, 1969). Joyce O. Appleby,

Economic Thought and Ideology in Seventeenth Century England (Princeton, NJ, 1978) offers an illuminating exposition of the character and concerns of contemporary economic thinkers.

Two studies that place the Navigation Laws in the context of competition with the Dutch and relate mercantilist policies to developments in England's economy and commerce in the later seventeenth century are Charles Wilson, *England's Apprenticeship, 1603–1763* (London, 1965) and C.G.A. Clay, *Economic Expansion and Social Change: England, 1500–1700*, vol. 2 (Cambridge, 1984). For the development of Dutch economic power, see Jonathan I. Israel, *Dutch Primacy in World Trade, 1585–1740* (Oxford, 1989). J.R. Jones, *Britain and the World (1649–1815)* (London, 1980) has a useful summary of England's policy towards the Dutch.

For a standard work on the buccaneers, see C.H. Haring, *The Buccaneers in West Indies in the Seventeenth Century* (Hamden, Conn., 1966 edition). Peter Earle, *The Sack of Panama* (New York, 1981) also examines the history of the buccaneers and is particularly good on the exploits of Henry Morgan. Vivid narrative sketches of English pirates are found in Clinton V. Black, *Pirates of the West Indies* (Cambridge, 1989).

On English alliances with Indians in war against France, see Francis Jennings, *The Ambiguous Iroquois Empire* (New York and London, 1984). An introduction to French policy towards America in this period is provided by William J. Eccles, *France in America* (New York, 1972)

5 ENGLISH COLONIES IN THE CARIBBEAN

An essential work on the development of the West Indies, focusing on Barbados, is Richard S. Dunn, *Sugar and Slaves: The Rise of the Planter Class in the English West Indies, 1624–1713* (London, 1973). Gary A. Puckrein, *Little England: Plantation Society and Anglo-Barbadian Politics, 1627–1700* (New York and London, 1984) is a useful supplement, as is Beckles, *White Servitude and Black Slavery in Barbados*. Vincent T. Harlow, *A History of Barbados, 1625–1685* (Oxford, 1926, repr. New York, 1969) is the standard history of the island's first years; a more recent general review of the island's colonial history can be found in Hilary McD. Beckles, *A History of Barbados: From Amerindian Settlement to the Nation-State* (Cambridge, 1990). The development of slave society in Jamaica is examined by Orlando Patterson, *The Sociology of Slavery* (London, 1967).

A basic source for the economic history of the English Caribbean is Richard B. Sheridan, *Sugar and Slavery: An Economic History of the British West Indies, 1623–1775* (Barbados, 1974). For a close examination of the islands' economies, see David Watts, *The West Indies: Patterns of Development, Culture and Environmental Change since 1492* (Cambridge, 1987).

The outstanding work on the Atlantic slave trade for the whole period of New World slavery is Philip D. Curtin, *The Atlantic Slave Trade: A Census* (Madison, Wis., 1969). On the development of the English slave trade, see K.R. Davies, *The Royal African Company* (London, 1957).

For information on the treatment of slaves in the English Caribbean during the eighteenth century, see Michael Craton, *Sinews of Empire: A Short History of British Slavery* (London, 1974) pp. 155–237. For Jamaica, see Orlando Patterson, *The Sociology of Slavery*; for the Leeward Islands, see Elsa V. Goveia, *Slave Society in the British Leeward Islands at the End of the Eighteenth Century* (New Haven, Conn., and London, 1965). An illuminating analysis of Jamaican colonial society is Edward Brathwaite, *The Development of Creole Society in Jamaica, 1770–1820* (Oxford, 1971).

There is a growing body of work on black rebellion and resistance in the eighteenth century. The best general account is Michael Craton, *Testing the Chains: Resistance to Slavery in the British Caribbean* (Ithaca, NY, and London, 1982). Good monographs on slave resistance on the various islands of the British Caribbean are Mavis C. Campbell, *The Maroons of Jamaica, 1655–1796: A History of Resistance, Collaboration and Betrayal* (Granby, Mass., 1988); Hilary McD. Beckles, *Black Rebellion in Barbados: The Struggle Against Slavery, 1622–1838* (Bridgetown, Barbados, 1984); Patterson, *The Sociology of Slavery*; and Goveia, *Slave Society in the British Leeward Islands* offer further material.

6 THE NORTH AMERICAN COLONIES

A comparison of European colonies in seventeenth-century North America is given in Meinig, *The Shaping of America*, and Davies, *The North Atlantic World*. Comparison with the French territories in Canada is facilitated by Marcel Trudel, *The Beginnings of New France* (Toronto, 1973). Meinig, *Shaping of America*, Greene, *Pursuits of Happiness*, and James Henretta, *The Evolution of American Society, 1700–1815: An Interdisciplinary Analysis* (Lexington, Mass., Toronto and

London, 1973) define American regions, and trace salient trends in their economic and social development. The character of the societies formed from British migrations to North America after 1640 is brilliantly evoked in Fischer, *Albion's Seed*.

The studies of Dedham and Andover by Lockridge, *A New England Town*, and Greven, *Four Generations*, trace the development of closed corporate communities into more complex and stratified provincial towns. Richard Bushman, *From Puritan to Yankee: Character and the Social Order in Connecticut, 1690–1765* (Cambridge, Mass., 1967) also portrays a Puritan community that became more open and hetero-geneous during the seventeenth century, while Michael Zuckerman, *Peaceable Kingdoms: New England Towns in the Eighteenth Century* (New York, 1970) stresses the continuities and stability in rural New England towns during the late colonial period. Stephen Innes, *Labor in a New Land: Economy and Society in Seventeenth-Century Springfield* (Princeton, NJ, 1983) contests the view of New England communities as closed corporate societies and offers another, distinctive view of New England social development.

On the Chesapeake region, Morgan, *American Slavery, American Freedom*, remains a major study of Virginia. Tate and Ammerman (eds) *The Chesapeake in the Seventeenth Century*, Aubrey C. Land, Lois Green Carr and Edward C. Papenfuse (eds) *Law, Society and Politics in Early Maryland* (Baltimore Md, and London, 1977), and Lois Green Carr, Philip D. Morgan and Jean B. Russo (eds) *Colonial Chesapeake Society* (Chapel Hill, NC, 1988) are all major collections of essays that reflect the new and flourishing social history of the region.

For material on the development of slavery in the South, Peter Wood, *Black Majority: Negroes in South Carolina from 1670 through the Stono Rebellion* (New York, 1974) is a key work; so, too, is Allan Kulikoff, *Tobacco and Slaves: The Development of Southern Cultures in the Chesapeake, 1680–1800* (Chapel Hill, NC, and London, 1986).

A classic work on white attitudes towards and treatment of slaves is Winthrop D. Jordan, *White over Black: American Attitudes towards the Negro, 1550–1812* (Chapel Hill, NC, 1968). David Brion Davis, *The Problem of Slavery in Western Culture* (Ithaca, NY, 1966) is the essential study of European responses and attitudes to slavery, and of the rise of anti-slavery thought. An excellent interpretative study of slave resistance and rebellion is Eugene D. Genovese, *From Rebellion to Revolution: Afro-American Revolts in the Making of the Modern World* (Baton Rouge, La, and London, 1979).

For a general discussion of the characteristics of North American society, see Ralph Davis, *The Rise of the Atlantic Economies* (London,

1973); a much more detailed and complex picture of the regional elements and general trends within North American society, seen within the context of Anglo-America as a whole, is given by Greene, *Pursuits of Happiness*. For a full review of the demographic and economic trends in colonial British America, which also provides a large and up-to-date bibliography, see John J. McCusker and Russell R. Menard, *The Economy of British America, 1607–1789* (Chapel Hill, NC, and London, 1985). A valuable interpretative essay on colonial society in North America, with a copious bibliographical guide to its regional components, is given in Chapter 1 of Gary B. Nash, *Race, Class and Politics: Essays on American Colonial and Revolutionary Society* (Urbana and Chicago, Ill., 1986), a book that also contains some of Nash's important articles on aspects of colonial North American history.

7 GOVERNMENT AND POLITICS

Leonard W. Labaree, *Royal Government in America: A Study of the British Colonial System before 1783* (New York, 1958) remains the basic account of the system of English government and administration in colonial North America. Part One of Jack P. Greene, *Peripheries and Center: Constitutional Development in the Extended Polities of the British Empire and the United States, 1607–1688* (Athens, Ga, 1986) supplies a sharp, extended analysis of the salient trends in the development of colonial government within the imperial context before the mid-eighteenth century, and is the political companion volume to his *Pursuits of Happiness*.

Robert M. Bliss, *Revolution and Empire: English Politics and the American Colonies in the Seventeenth Century* (Manchester, 1990) is a very useful source on the development of colonial government during the seventeenth century, and gives more attention than most to government before the Civil War. For an interpretation that traces the shift towards imperial centralization from the experience of the English Civil War, see Stephen Saunders Webb, *The Governors General: The English Army and the Definition of Empire, 1659–1681* (Chapel Hill, NC, 1979); Webb pursues his interpretation further in his *1676: The End of American Independence* (New York, 1984). For the English political context in the half-century after the Restoration, see Geoffrey Holmes, *The Making of a Great Power: Late Stuart and Early Georgian England, 1660–1722* (London, 1993).

A full institutional study of the Board of Trade and its activities is given by Oliver M. Dickerson, *American Colonial Government, 1696–1765* (New York, 1962). A useful review of the historiography of colonial politics is given in John M. Murrin's essay, 'Political development', in Greene and Pole (eds) *Colonial British America*. For the Anglican church in North America, and other aspects of the colonial religious experience, Patricia U. Bonomi, *Under the Cope of Heaven: Religion, Politics and Society in Colonial America* (Oxford and New York, 1986) is an excellent guide.

For a full account of Bacon's rebellion, see Wilcomb E. Washburn, *The Governor and the Rebel: The Story of Bacon's Rebellion and its Leader* (Chapel Hill, NC, 1957); also Morgan, *American Slavery, American Freedom*, and Stephen Saunders Webb, *1676: The End of American Independence*. Bernard Bailyn, 'Politics and social structure in Virginia', in J.M. Smith (ed) *Seventeenth Century America*, is a seminal essay on the development and character of political life in late-seventeenth-century Virginia.

The character of participation in politics is analysed by Michael Zuckerman, 'The social context of democracy in Massachusetts', in Stanley N. Katz (ed) *Colonial America: Essays in Politics and Social Development* (Boston, Mass., and Toronto, 2nd edition, 1976) and, more generally, by J.R. Pole, 'Historians and the problem of early American democracy', *American Historical Review* (1962) **LXVII**: 626–46; Jackson Turner Main, 'Government by the people: the American Revolution and the democratization of the legislatures', in Jack P. Greene (ed) *The Reinterpretation of the American Revolution, 1763–1789* (New York, 1968).

On the development of politics in North America after the Glorious Revolution, see Jack P. Greene, *The Quest for Power: The Lower Houses of Assembly in the Southern Royal Colonies, 1689–1776* (Chapel Hill, NC, 1963); Alison G. Olson, *Anglo-American Politics, 1660–1775* (Oxford, 1978); Michael G. Hall, *Edward Randolph and the American Colonies, 1676–1703* (Chapel Hill, NC, 1964); Philip S. Haffenden, *New England in the English Nation, 1689–1713* (Oxford, 1974) and Richard R. Johnson, *Adjustment to Empire: The New England Colonies, 1675–1715* (Leicester, 1981). K.G. Davies, 'The revolutions in America', in Robert Beddard (ed) *The Revolutions of 1688* (Oxford, 1988) is a succinct introduction to the repercussions of the Glorious Revolution in the Anglo-American colonies, while David S. Lovejoy, *The Glorious Revolution in America* (New York, 1972) gives a more extended treatment of its effects in North America. A useful, detailed monograph on early-eighteenth-century administration in relation to

English politics is James Henretta, *'Salutary Neglect':* *Colonial Administration under the Duke of Newcastle* (Princeton, NJ, 1972).

For a general treatment of English administrative policy towards the Caribbean colonies, see G.H. Guttridge, *The Colonial Policy of William III in America and the West Indies* (London, 1966). Accounts of the distribution and use of power on different islands are found in the following: for Barbados, see Dunn, *Sugar and Slaves*, and Puckrein, *Little England: Plantation Society and Anglo-Barbadian Politics*; on government and politics in the Leeward Islands, see C.S.S. Higham, *The Development of the Leeward Islands under the Restoration, 1660–1688* (Cambridge, 1921) and Goveia, *Slave Society in the British Leeward Islands*; on Jamaica, see George Metcalf, *Royal Government and Political Conflict in Jamaica, 1729–1783* (London, 1965) and Brathwaite, *Creole Society in Jamaica*.

8 WAR, TRADE AND EMPIRE

The best general introductions to the development of the European empires in the eighteenth century are J.H. Parry, *Trade and Dominion: The European Oversea Empires in the Eighteenth Century* (London, 1971) and Ralph Davis, *The Rise of the Atlantic Economies* (London, 1973). Peggy K. Liss, *Atlantic Empires: The Network of Trade and Revolution, 1713–1826* (Baltimore, Md, and London, 1983) examines the interactions of commercial, political and ideological developments in the British and Iberian empires.

The bases of Britain's development as a leading power are sharply defined by John Brewer, *The Sinews of Power: War, Money and the English State, 1688–1783* (London, 1989); this book offers a masterly analysis of the interplay between policy, war, and the course of British economic development during the eighteenth century, especially in Chapters 5–7. Most useful on British foreign policy and relations between the powers is J.R. Jones, *Britain and the World (1649–1815)*. Robin Blackburn, *The Overthrow of Colonial Slavery, 1776–1848* (London, 1988) has an astute opening chapter on Hanoverian Britain and its relationship with the colonies, while Linda Colley, *Britons: Forging the Nation 1707–1837* (New Haven, Conn., and London, 1992) has a stimulating and enlightening account of changes in British eighteenth-century politics and political culture.

The growth of English colonial trade can be traced in two seminal articles by Ralph Davis: 'English foreign trade, 1600–1700', *Economic*

History Review, 2nd series (1954) **7**: 150–66, and 'English foreign trade, 1700–1774', *Economic History Review*, 2nd series (1962) **15**: 285–303. These findings are brought together in Ralph Davis, *A Commercial Revolution: English Overseas Trade in the Seventeenth and Eighteenth Centuries*, Historial Association Pamphlets, General Series, no. 64 (London, 1967). Walter Minchinton (ed) *The Growth of English Overseas Trade in the Seventeenth and Eighteenth Centuries* (London, 1969) has valuable essays on several aspects of British trade. Elizabeth B. Schumpeter, *English Overseas Trade Statistics 1697–1808* (Oxford, 1960) compiles figures for British foreign trade in the eighteenth century. A fundamental general source that embraces statistical material found in the previous works is B.R. Mitchell, *British Historical Statistics* (Cambridge, 1988).

There are two basic introductory sources for the economic history of North America in the eighteenth century. A lucid general survey is Gary M. Walton and James F. Shepherd, *The Economic Rise of Early America* (Cambridge, 1979). McCusker and Menard, *Economy of British America*, provides a wealth of information on trends in demography, commerce and production and a massive bibliography on these subjects. Douglass C. North and Robert Paul Thomas, *The Growth of the American Economy to 1860* (New York, 1968) has an interesting compilation of contemporary documents.

The best introduction to the development of the West Indian economies during the eighteenth century is still Sheridan, *Sugar and Slavery*, while Richard Pares, *War and Trade in the West Indies, 1739–1763* (London, 1963) remains the standard work on British military and diplomatic policy and its impact on the Caribbean during the first eighteenth-century war in the region. The opening chapters of Selwyn H.H. Carrington, *The British West Indies during the American Revolution* (Dordrecht, 1988) offer a good summary on the condition of the West Indian economies in the period before the American Revolution, drawing on Eric Williams, *Capitalism and Slavery* (London, 1964 edition).

Williams's *Capitalism and Slavery*, is a seminal work which has been the touchstone for a complex debate concerning the links between the slave trade, slavery and the development of the British economy, and the reasons for the abolition of slavery. Criticisms of connections made by Williams between slavery and British industrialization by economic historians include Stanley L. Engerman, 'The slave trade and British capital formation in the eighteenth century: a comment on the Williams thesis', *Business History Review* (1972) **46**: 430–43, and J.R. Ward, 'The profitability of sugar planting in the British West Indies,

1650–1834', *Economic History Review*, 2nd series (1978) **31**: 197–213. For reassessment and rehabilitation of the Williams thesis, see the essays by Barbara L. Solow, Joseph E. Inikori, and David Richardson in Barbara L. Solow and Stanley L. Engerman (eds) *British Capitalism and Caribbean Slavery: The Legacy of Eric Williams* (Cambridge, 1987).

Discussion of the role of colonial trade in promoting British industrialization involves the larger problem of ascertaining the contribution made by overseas trade, as opposed to domestic markets, in stimulating production and technological innovation in the late eighteenth century, a controversial issue that lies beyond the scope of this book. For a view of the problem, see R.P. Thomas, 'Overseas trade and empire, 1700–1860', in Roderick Floud and Donald McCloskey (eds) *The Economic History of Britain since 1700: Volume I, 1700–1860* (Cambridge, 1981). A recent survey of eighteenth-century English economic history that also discusses this problem, and provides a superbly compressed account of domestic production and overseas trade, is John Rule, *The Vital Century: England's Developing Economy, 1714–1815* (London, 1992). Pat Hudson, *The Industrial Revolution* (London, 1992) accords more importance to overseas trade in stimulating British economic growth. For a broad, polemical appraisal of the contribution of colonial trade to western European economic development as a whole, see Patrick O'Brien, 'European economic development: the contribution of the periphery', *Economic History Review*, 2nd series (1982) **35**: 1–18.

Philip D. Curtin, *The Atlantic Slave Trade*, is the major source on developments in the scale and pace of the slave trade to the Americas, while Bernard Bailyn, *Voyagers to the West: Emigration from Britain to America on the Eve of the American Revolution* (London, 1987) provides a detailed analysis of European immigration into North America. A vivid profile of North American society in the mid- eighteenth century is Richard Hofstadter, *America at 1750: A Social Portrait* (London, 1972); there is no equivalent for the West Indies in this period. Greene, *Pursuits of Happiness*, Chapter 8, gives a major interpretative synthesis of trends in the social and economic development of the British colonies in 1720–80.

9 CRISIS OF EMPIRE

The historiography of the American Revolution is enormous; fortunately, there are a number of general studies that provide excellent introductions to its origins and effects. On the breakdown of British relations with the North American colonies, a good starting point is Ian R. Christie, *Crisis of Empire: Great Britain and the American Colonies, 1754–1783* (London, 1974 edition) or at greater length, Ian R. Christie and Benjamin W. Labaree, *Empire or Independence, 1760–1776* (London, 1976). Greene, *Peripheries and Center*, Part Two, shows how the question of reconciling the need for central power with the liberty and autonomy of the colonies stood at the heart of the disputes between Britain and the colonies between 1764 and 1776. Works that focus more on the rebellion within the colonies and trace the course of the Revolution are J.R. Pole, *Foundations of American Independence, 1763–1815* (Indianapolis, Ind., and New York, 1972) and, with a stronger emphasis on social conflict and popular elements in the Revolution, Edward C. Countryman, *The American Revolution* (New York, 1985). Colin Bonwick, *The American Revolution* (London, 1991) incorporates recent historiography in an admirably lucid and balanced synthesis of the causes and consequences of the Revolution. These books all have substantial bibliographical essays on the historiography of the Revolution which provide extensive further reading.

Several compilations of essays also deserve mention. Jack P. Greene (ed), *The Reinterpretation of the American Revolution, 1763–1789* (New York, 1968), Stephen G. Kurtz and James H. Hutson (eds) *Essays on the American Revolution* (Chapel Hill, NC, 1973), and Alfred F. Young (ed), *The American Revolution: Explorations in the History of American Radicalism* (DeKalb, Ill., 1976), all reflect important developments in the historiography of the Revolution since the mid-1960s.

A brilliant recent contribution, which draws together and re-examines many of the themes raised by the huge historiography on the Revolution in a striking synthesis, is Gordon S. Wood, *The Radicalism of the American Revolution* (New York, 1992).

Two key works examine the political thought that underpinned the movement towards revolution: Bernard Bailyn, *The Ideological Origins of the American Revolution* (Cambridge, Mass., 1967) and J.G.A. Pocock, *The Machiavellian Moment: Florentine Political Thought and the Atlantic Republican Tradition* (Princeton, NJ, 1975).

For a full account of military and diplomatic aspects of the war of independence, see Piers Mackesy, *The War for America, 1775–1783* (London, 1964); Christopher Hibbert, *Loyalists and Redcoats: The War for America, 1770–1781* (London, 1990) provides a brief and readable narrative of the events of the war. Gordon S. Wood, *The Creation of the American Republic, 1776–1787* (New York and London, 1972 edition) pursues political developments in the rebel colonies from the Declaration of Independence to the Federal Constitution.

10 REALIGNMENTS OF EMPIRE

There are several good studies of the loyalists, including W. Nelson, *The American Tory* (Oxford, 1961), Wallace Brown, *The Good Americans: The Loyalists in the American Revolution* (New York, 1969), R. Calhoon, *The Loyalists in Revolutionary America, 1760–1781* (New York, 1973) and Christopher Moore, *The Loyalists: Revolution, Exile, Settlement* (Toronto, 1984). More detail on the loyalist diaspora can be found in Mary Beth Norton, *The British-Americans: The Loyalist Exiles in England, 1774–1789* (London, 1974) and, relating to Canada, in Wallace Brown and Hereward Senior, *Victorious in Defeat: The Loyalists in Canada* (Toronto, 1984) and David Bell, 'The loyalist tradition in Canada', *Journal of Canadian Studies* (1970) **5**: 22–33.

On British North America after the Revolution, see Donald G. Creighton, *Dominion of the North: A History of Canada* (London, 1958 edition). Essential regional studies of Canadian development for this period are Gerald M. Craig, *Upper Canada: The Formative Years, 1784–1841* (Toronto, 1963); Fernand Ouellet, *Lower Canada, 1791–1840: Social Change and Nationalism* (Toronto, 1979); Allan Greer, *Peasant, Lord, and Merchant: Rural Society in Three Quebec Parishes, 1740–1840* (Toronto, 1985); W.S. MacNutt, *The Atlantic Provinces: The Emergence of a Colonial Society, 1712–1857* (Toronto, 1965).

On politics in the West Indies during the American Revolution, see George Metcalf, *Royal Government and Political Conflict in Jamaica*, and Brathwaite, *Creole Society in Jamaica*, both of which are cited above. An interesting essay on the evolution of identity in Barbados is J.P. Greene, 'Changing identity in the British Caribbean: Barbados as a case study', in Nicholas Canny and Anthony Pagden (eds) *Colonial Identity in the Atlantic World, 1500–1800* (Princeton, NJ, 1987).

West Indian economic performance in the late eighteenth and early nineteenth centuries is closely analysed in Seymour Drescher, *Econocide: British Slavery in the Era of Abolition* (Pittsburgh, Pa, 1977) and further reviewed in J.R. Ward, *British West Indian Slavery, 1750–1834: The Process of Amelioration* (Oxford, 1988). John J. McCusker, 'Growth, stagnation or decline? The economy of the British West Indies, 1763–1790', examines the repercussions of the

American Revolution on the Caribbean economies, in Ronald Hoffman, John J. McCusker, Russell R. Menard and Peter J. Albert *The Economy of Early America: The Revolutionary Period, 1763–1790* (Charlottesville, Va, 1988).

The key works on the abolition of the slave trade and slavery in British America are Eric Williams, *Capitalism and Slavery*, Roger Anstey, *The Atlantic Slave Trade and British Abolition, 1760–1810* (London, 1975), Seymour Drescher, *Econocide*, David Eltis, *Economic Growth and the Ending of the Transatlantic Slave Trade* (New York and Oxford, 1987) and the chapters relating to Britain in David Brion Davis, *The Problem of Slavery in the Age of Revolution, 1770–1823* (Ithaca, NY, 1975). An excellent, integrated general analysis of the abolition of the slave trade and the movement towards emancipation in the Americas as a whole is given by Robin Blackburn, *The Overthrow of Colonial Slavery, 1776–1848* (London, 1988).

On the development of British trade with the Spanish colonies during the eighteenth century, see Geoffrey Walker, *Spanish Politics and Imperial Trade, 1700–1789* (London, 1979); Francis Armytage, *The Free Port System in the British West Indies* (London, 1953); Dorothy B. Goebel, 'British trade to the Spanish colonies, 1798–1823', *American Historical Review* (1938) **43**: 288–320. A clear view of British official attitudes towards Spanish America before independence is given by John Lynch, 'British policy and Spanish America, 1793–1808', *Journal of Latin American Studies* (1969) **1**: 1–30. British involvement in independence can be traced in C.K. Webster (ed) *Britain and the Independence of Latin America, 1812–1830: Select Documents from the Foreign Office Archives*, 2 vols (London, 1938). The British position in relation to Spain and efforts to arbitrate between Spain and its colonies are described by Timothy Anna, *Spain and the Loss of America*, (Lincoln, Nebr., and London, 1983). Britain's relations with Portugal and Brazil, seen in the context of Brazilian development during the late colonial period, are briefly observed in James Lang, *Portuguese Brazil: The King's Plantation* (New York and London, 1979).

The reorientation of British colonial policy during the late eighteenth and early nineteenth centuries is analysed by Judith Blow Williams, *British Commercial Policy and Trade Expansion, 1750–1850* (Oxford, 1972) and, more recently and effectively, by C.A. Bayly, *Imperial Meridian: The British Empire and the World, 1780–1830* (London and New York, 1989), and P.J. Cain and A.G. Hopkins, *British Imperialism: Innovation and Expansion 1688–1914* (London and New York, 1993).

Maps

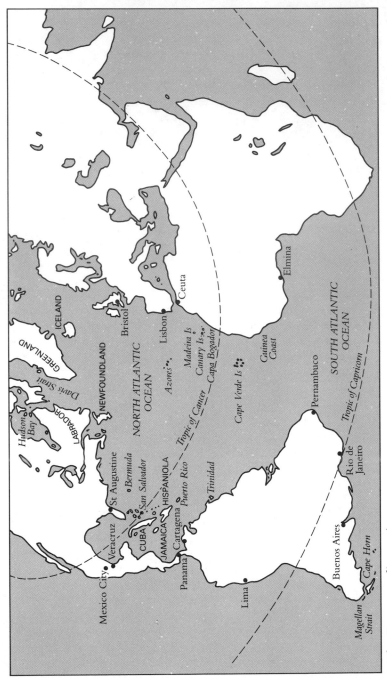

1 The European discoveries

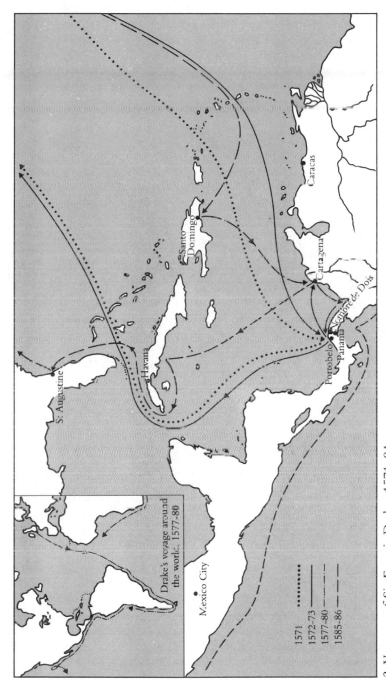

Maps

2 Voyages of Sir Francis Drake, 1571–94
After: Cathryn L. Lombardi and John V. Lombardi, *Latin American History: A Teaching Atlas* (Madison, Wis., 1993).

337

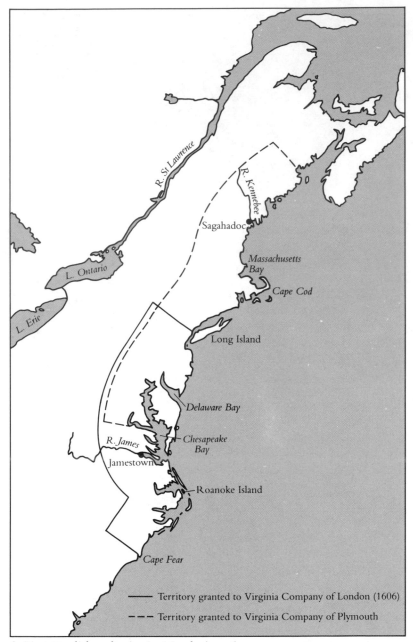

3 First English colonies in North America
After : Martin Gilbert, *American History Atlas* (Wiedenfeld and Nicholson, London, 1968).

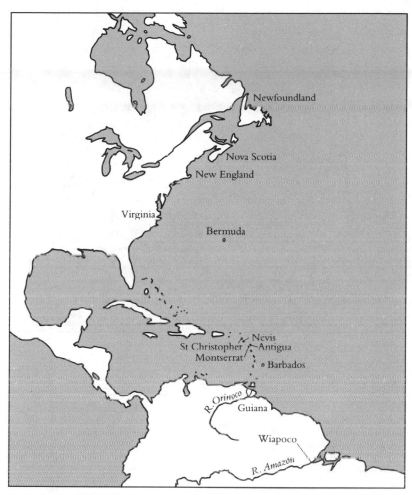

4 Early English colonies in the Caribbean

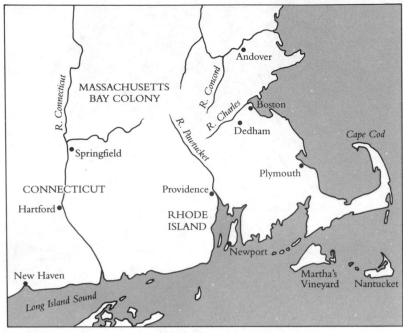

5 First settlements in New England
After: Martin Gilbert, *American History Atlas* (Wiedenfeld and Nicholson, London, 1968).

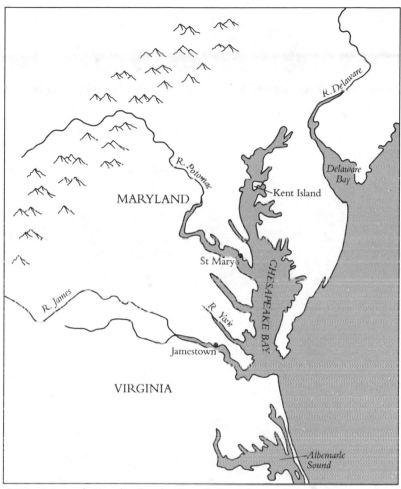

6 Virginia and Maryland colonies of the Chesapeake region

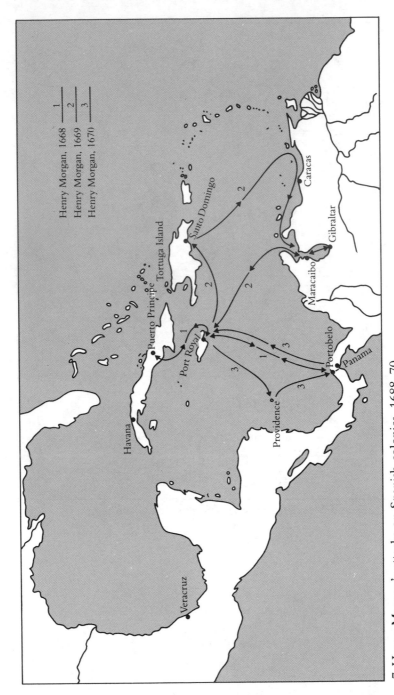

7 Henry Morgan's attacks on Spanish colonies, 1688–70
After: Cathryn L. Lombardi and John V. Lombardi, *Latin American History: A Teaching Atlas* (Madison, Wis. 1993).

8 English colonies in North America, 1660–1732

After: Martin Gilbert, *American History Atlas* (Wiedenfeld and Nicholson, London, 1968).

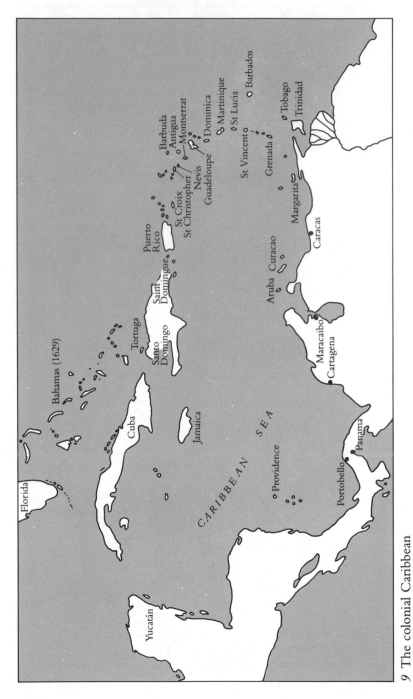

9 The colonial Caribbean

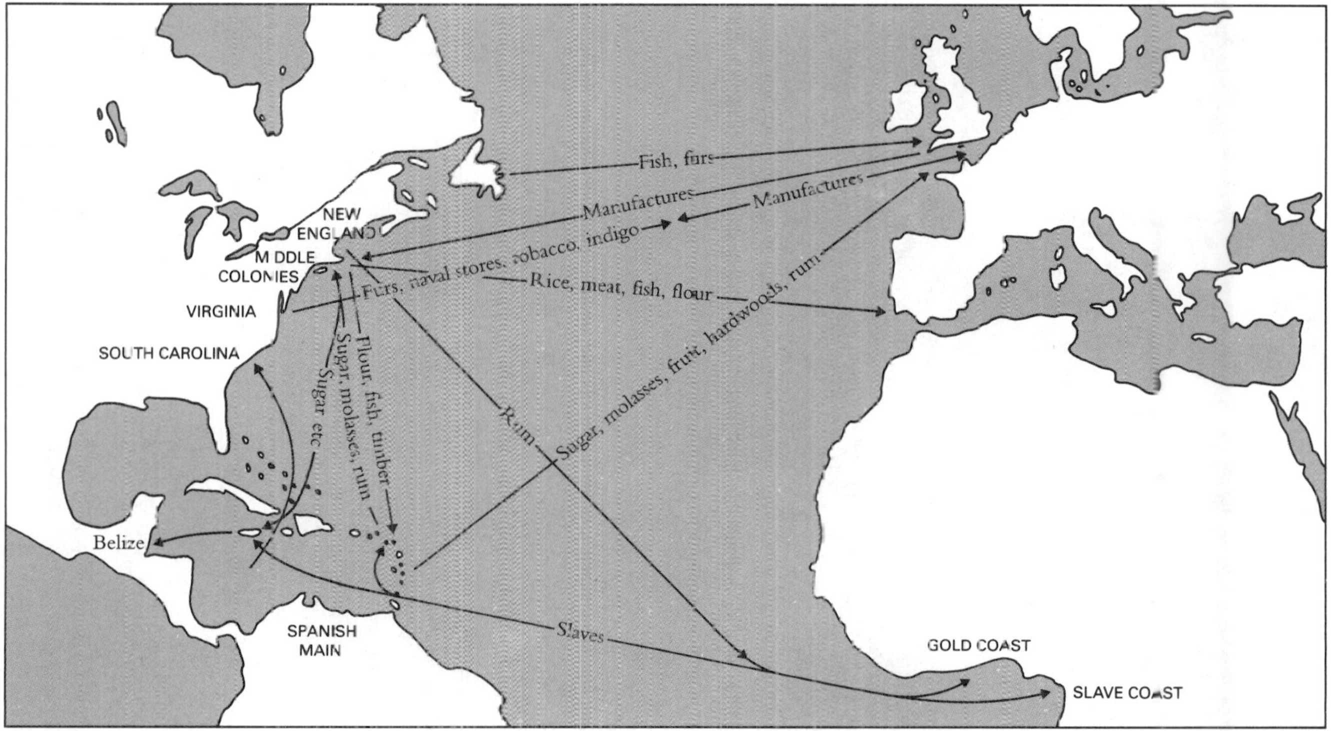
NEW ENGLAND
MIDDLE COLONIES
VIRGINIA
SOUTH CAROLINA
Belize
SPANISH MAIN
GOLD COAST
SLAVE COAST
Fish, furs
Manufactures
Manufactures
Furs, naval stores, tobacco, indigo
Rice, meat, fish, flour
Sugar, molasses, fruit, hardwoods, rum
Rum
Slaves
Flour, fish, timber
Sugar, molasses, rum
Sugar etc

10 English colonial commerce
After: Martin Gilbert, *American History Atlas* (Wiedenfeld and Nicholson, London, 1968).

Index

The British in The Americas 1480–1815